Food
and Beverage
Control

Prentice-Hall Series in Foodservice Management

Food and Beverage Control

Douglas C. Keister, Ph. D.

*Director, School of Hotel
and Restaurant Management
University of Denver
Denver, Colorado*

Prentice-Hall, Inc., Englewood Cliffs, New Jersey 07632

Library of Congress Cataloging in Publication Data

Keister, Douglas Carlyle.
    Food and beverage control.

    (Prentice-Hall series in foodservice management)
    Bibliography: p.
    Includes index.
    1. Food service—Cost control.   I.   Title.
TX911.3.C65K46   658.1′552   76–21295
ISBN 0–13–323022–8

© 1977 by Prentice-Hall, Inc., Englewood Cliffs, N.J. 07632

Printed in the United States of America

10   9   8   7

Prentice-Hall International Inc., *London*
Prentice-Hall of Australia Pty. Ltd., *Sydney*
Prentice-Hall of Canada, Ltd., *Toronto*
Prentice-Hall of India Privated Limited, *New Delhi*
Prentice-Hall of Japan, Inc., *Tokyo*
Prentice-Hall of Southeast Asia Pte. Ltd., *Singapore*
Whitehall Books Limited, *Wellington, New Zealand*

This book is dedicated to my wife, Billie

Contents

Preface

This book is intended for those currently involved with the operation of a food and/or beverage department or those who plan to be involved in the future. This is a management book of techniques of food and beverage operation using control and control information to do a better job of managing.

The purpose of this book is to explain procedures for controlling all your costs. You will need records. Records will give you the information you must have in order to make sensible decisions to control and improve your total food and beverage unit. Throughout this book we will discuss these records and procedures, and the forms, charts, graphs, and so on which you use when you gather and record information. These information-gathering forms and methods are your tools, nothing more. So is the information itself. No amount of information is of any value to you unless you know how to take—and take—managerial action. In this book, we will try to tell you how to do that.

The information contained in this book can be used directly, or with slight modification, by food and/or beverage managers anywhere.

I wish to thank Cary Baker, Editor, for his advice and encouragement in the preparation of this book. Very special thanks go to my wife Billie for editorial work throughout the preparation of the manuscript. To all former students who listened to the lectures that were the basis for this book, I extend my sincere appreciation.

DOUGLAS   C. KEISTER

Food
and Beverage
Control

1

The Food and Beverage Service Industry

Objectives

This chapter gives an overview of the industry. After you have read this chapter, you should have an appreciation of:

1. The size of the industry.
2. The different types of establishments that make up the industry.
3. The need for control in the industry.

The food and beverage service industry consists of every establishment that sells food and beverage to people outside their own homes. On a global scale it is a multibillion-dollar enterprise which employes millions of people and is of vital worldwide economic importance.

Most statistics classify food and beverage service as the fifth largest industry in the United States. In this country it includes approximately 300,000 food and beverage service establishments and employs more than 2½ million people.

Statistics indicate that in the past, Americans ate one out of every four meals away from home. It is predicted that in the future they will eat one out of every three meals away from home—maybe even more. The food service industry will sell them these meals.

In the mid 1970's the American food and beverage service industry's total sales was estimated at more than 50 billion dollars. That's more than twice what it was in the early 1960's. Some of this increase is due to inflation and increased population, but much of it is solid growth. The industry has expanded dramatically in the United States and in other nations during this century and in the past few decades in particular. It flourishes today and its future looks bright. There are reasons why the business of food and beverage service has grown in the past and will probably continue to do so in the years ahead.

GROWTH OF THE INDUSTRY

Since the beginnings of humankind, some people have eaten some of their meals away from home. Cave men and women probably wandered off sometimes away from their caves to munch fruit under or in a tree, maybe just for a pleasing change of scenery. They surely "ate out" when they were off on food-gathering (shopping) excursions and hunting (business) trips. Perhaps our reasons for eating out have not changed much at that.

More formal places for dining away from home—inns and taverns—were really the start of the food, beverage, and lodging service industry. They probably came into being when trade and commerce began. In 500 B.C. there were hostelries in Athens where local people and visiting tradespeople could buy lavish food and drink. Ancient Rome had restaurants. England's ale-houses served meats and ales in the twelfth century. In 1800 there were at least 600 restaurants in Paris.[1] But until quite recently, "eating out" was done by a comparatively small percentage of a population. Today in America drive-ins have sold billions of hamburgers to millions of people in a decade. "Eating out" and the food service industry in general are in a process of worldwide growth.

Now, more than ever before, a much higher proportionate percentage

---

[1] *Encyclopaedia Britannica* (1967), 19, 233-235.

of the population eats out, and they eat out oftener, particularly in the United States.

Why Do People Eat Out?

Today many people cannot eat three meals a day at home, as most could 100 years ago. They commute to their jobs and are too far away to return home for meals. This is especially true at lunchtime, but it also includes the doughnuts-and-coffee breakfasts at work and the dinners in town for those working late. When society was mainly rural and agricultural, people usually worked near their homes and simply went home to eat. But many people have migrated from rural to urban areas. Many now work in cities and live in the suburbs. This increases the need for food service operations close to where people work.

The structure of society has changed in other ways. Some men and women marry later in life and are single working people for a long period. There are many widows, widowers, and divorced people who live alone. They all are apt to go out to eat now and then. A high percentage of women have full-time or part-time jobs. They don't have time for extensive cooking. Working men and women generally have higher incomes than ever before, and whole families go out for dinner oftener. Children are apt to have a say in where the family will eat, and this factor, too, has its own influence on the food service industry.

The automobile and mass transportation have made it feasible to travel to restaurants. Jets have made world travel convenient, and travel in general has shown an enormous increase. People travel for business purposes or for vacation enjoyment, and this obviously adds to instances of eating away from home.

Frozen foods and instant dinners available at supermarkets have also played a part in the growth of the food service industry. So has the Women's Liberation Movement. Society no longer demands that women be trained to cook. People may rely heavily on frozen quick dinners at home. Many enjoy going out for special meals or to enjoy foods prepared by chefs. The frozen dinners they can now heat and serve at home are apt to introduce people to foods that are new and different to them.

The increase in travel, the increase in mobility, and the fact that people are now much more apt to move frequently have all combined to make diners more adventurous in their tastes in food and drink.

Fast and easy transportation, leisure time, travel, women with careers—all of these plus other factors contribute to the total status of the food service industry. The percentage of the population that eats out is increasing. And these percentages will probably continue to increase in the future. Because the food and beverage service industry is growing and expanding, opportunities for employment at all levels in this industry should increase.

TYPES OF FOOD SERVICE ESTABLISHMENTS

There are many kinds of food service operations. They include:

1. Service restaurants.
2. Self-service restaurants (cafeterias).
3. Coffee shops.
4. Drive-in restaurants.
5. Hotel food services.
6. Private club food services.
7. Hospital food services.
8. College dormitory food services.
9. Airline food services.
10. Industrial food services in factories and office buildings.
11. Private catering.
12. Banquet hall facilities.
13. Federal institution food services.
14. Public and private school food services.

This does not mention them all. The list could go on.

Food service operations require many personnel doing many types of work—cooks, waiters, waitresses, buspersons, supervisors, hostesses and hosts, dishwashers, saladmakers, and so on, including managers. The food service industry is huge, employs millions and grosses billions. That's an overview of the entire field.

If you are a food service operation manager reading this, you may be wondering why your own establishment isn't effortlessly earning a fortune since your industry is a flourishing one. No business operation effortlessly earns a fortune, of course, but this is particularly true of a food and beverage service operation. The industry is prosperous, but for individual operations the food service business is full of risks. The industry in general flourishes, but for the individual people who work in the industry and for each food and beverage establishment, success is a hard-won achievement. It takes effort, knowledge, good management, good location, and sound control systems (among other things) for a food and beverage operation to succeed.

The two major reasons why restaurants fail are:

1. Lack of management skills.
2. Lack of good accounting records.

There are estimates that 80 percent of all restaurants change owner-ship on an average of once every five years. Some of these make money and are sold at a profit. But many fail. Money is lost and new owners take over or the building is converted to uses other than a food service operation.

The food service industry is a high-risk business. It is possible to earn high profits. It is also possible to lose a lot of money. Because of the risk, banks do not readily lend money for restaurant ventures, no matter *what* the state of an economy is. The individual in this industry who knows manage-ment and understands the accounting and recordkeeping involved—including the application of control techniques—has a chance of succeeding.

Successful food service management is difficult. Investing in a food service establishment is extremely risky. Competition is fierce. Many go under. Management that survives and goes on to real success is management that makes every possible effort to really control the overall operation of its food service establishment. As economies change from prosperity to inflation to re-cession to depression and back again into varying degrees and stages of these, sound management and sound controls become all the more important.

This book was written mainly for owners, managers, assistant man-agers, supervisors, students, and anyone interested in entering or learning about the food and beverage service industry. In the following chapters we will present, discuss, and try to clarify specific techniques you can and should understand and use. Adapt and tailor them yourself to fit the specific needs of your own operation.

Food service operations come in great varieties. They differ in size, location, clientele, foods offered, reasons for existing, types and number of employees, market, amounts of money invested, and so on. Despite all the dif-ferences, they all do have many routines, basic objectives, structures and systems, and problems in common. They are all food service operations and they all need fundamental management controls. There are management pro-cedures, techniques, and tools that can be of sound service to all, and we will discuss them in this book. If you want to succeed in the field of food service management, it is absolutely essential for you to understand and correctly use the principles and procedures of food and beverage control.

If you, the manager of a food and beverage service operation, do not exert control over your operation, something else or someone else will. That is an ominous fact about food service management (or the management of most businesses, for that matter). If you do not act and maintain specific standards, your operation will have standards anyway, but almost surely not the stand-ards you want. Your operation will be controlled—by your cook, or your cashier, or your customers, or blind luck, or a lot of other factors you don't want in control and may not even know exist. If you are not in control, other people or things surely will be. The purpose of this book is to help you, the manager, see to it that you—not your cook, not luck, not your competitors—do these managerial jobs of maintaining your standards and controlling your procedures. And do them well.

REVIEW AND DISCUSSION QUESTIONS

1. List the reasons why people eat out.
2. What are the different types of food service operations?
3. Why do food services fail?
4. How is the food service industry changing and growing? Why?
5. Should all restaurant managers know the same basic information? Why?

2

Organization for Management

Objectives

This chapter describes the functions of management. After you have read this chapter, you should:

1. Know what managers and supervisors do.
2. Know how businesses can be organized.
3. Know some of the principles of management.

The better organized your establishment is, the more efficiently it can run. Sometimes, though, efficiency is pursued relentlessly and thoughtlessly by business operations. Don't be so totally dedicated to instant efficiency that you neglect to make plans for long-range efficiency. There have been food service managers who have achieved high menu prices, low food cost, low labor cost and no customers! Their establishments may have efficient organization on paper but could scarcely be called efficient or well-organized in reality or in the long run.

The eternal business quest for sound management and *real* efficiency has to be tempered by common sense. Keep your long-range goal as well as your intermediate objectives well in mind. A truly efficient operation has the means to achieve its objectives and its long-term goal. Well-organized management anticipates many problems and works out some valid solutions for them in advance.

There are some fundamental management concepts you can apply to your food service operation. Adapt them yourself to fit your specific needs.

GOAL, OBJECTIVES, AND MEANS

Goal

A food service operation usually has one main goal—long-term profit. (Exceptions to this would be nonprofit operations, such as food services in hospitals and schools, whose goal usually is to break even.) Owners decide on the goal.

Objectives

Owners decide objectives. Objectives are decisions you make, steps you plan to take, characteristics and qualities you try to achieve while you are in the process of working to attain your goal. Objectives are things you do to get your goal accomplished. Examples of objectives would be: type of food service (hamburger drive-in, steak house); standard of cleanliness; type and quality of food; quality of service; type of atmosphere and decor; whether or not to serve liquor; type of market the operation will try to attract; and type of location that will be sought for the operation.

Means

The manager decides on the means, based on the owners' wishes. "Means" are steps you take to get your objectives accomplished. Examples would include: how you organize your establishment; number of people you hire; skill levels of employees; purveyors you select to supply your food; and your methods of recordkeeping. Generally, means can be defined as the total work that a manager does to see that the owners' objectives are achieved and the goal of profit is attained.

WHAT DOES A MANAGER DO?

The manager of a food service operation is responsible for the overall, day-to-day functioning of the operation. The work of a manager involves long-term planning, short-term planning (forecasting), organizing, directing and coordinating, hiring, and training. The manager is responsible for controls. What the manager does in each of these areas will have a direct effect on the overall success of any individual food service unit.

Planning

Planning your business means plotting a course of how you intend to get to where you want to go. It means looking ahead a few days, a few weeks, six months, a year, maybe more. It means making short-term plans (forecasting) and long-term plans. In long-range planning, you consider where you want your business to be one, two, five years or more from now. Plot courses of action to get there. Unless yours is an operation that is supposed to just about break even (like most hospital cafeterias and university dormitory food services, for example), your main goal is to try to make profit now and in the future.

You make basic decisions if options are in your hands. Owners decide on the type of food service operation and the market the operation will try to attract. Managers decide what prices to charge and what the food, labor, and overhead cost per cents should be. Managers decide on the number of employees and what skill levels employees should have.

You will probably have to work toward many intermediate objectives en route toward the ultimate goal, which is getting profits and getting them consistently. There are many intermediate objectives and there is one main goal you want to achieve. You plan a course of action accordingly and follow it, altering your means and objectives when and if you need to.

Forecasting

Forecasting means short-range—plans for a short period of time. Forecasting is an important technique you should use to strengthen your chance of achieving your larger, long-range, long-time plans.

A short-range plan, for example, could be where you forecast your business for tomorrow or for next week. You make a plan, a prediction, for a small period of time. From your forecast you figure how much food you will need for next week, for example, and how many employees you will need, and so on. Forecasting means you do some detailed planning and figuring ahead of time.

You take time to think about next week. You figure out everything you can about what will probably happen to your business operation next week. You do ahead of time anything you possibly can to make sure next week is a success. You use every scrap of valid information you have plus a calculated guess. You look at your records of the business your operation did last week and last month. You check your records of your business for the same week a year ago. (This implies that you make detailed records and retain them for future reference. You do, and we will discuss these records throughout this book.) You cannot, unfortunately, use magic to help you forecast. You do use your written records.

You keep track of conventions due in town, big football games coming up, bad weather predicted. In short, you find out everything you can about anything that could possibly affect your volume next week. Then you put your ideas and estimates into action. You buy food, decide how much of it to cook, and schedule employees for next week based on your forecast for next week.

Aim at trying to achieve correct short-term predictions. When you start making predictions, you will probably make plenty of mistakes. But you will get more accurate with time and experience. The better you do at making accurate forecasts and thus achieving a short-term objective, the easier it will be for you to achieve your long-term goal of profit.

Organizing

This should be done with objectives in mind. Organizing is where you devise the means you use to achieve objectives. Do this by figuring out the types of employee positions you need to fill, how many employees you need, and what work each employee should do. Analyze and list the positions you need to fill.

Another part of organizing is deciding how you will group individuals together. In other words, decide what departments you will have, who will be in charge of each, what work each department should accomplish, and so on.

Directing and Coordinating

These two are closely related. Managers direct people and supervise the work they do. Managers also coordinate departments and general divisions of work so work routines are set and accomplished. Managers must know how to establish and coordinate work routines so department heads and their employees can do their jobs well. Handling people and understanding their problems and differences is a major part of management.

Coordinating means fitting activities together, considering the timing of who does what—and when—and arranging patterns of action in which people can best carry out the work you want them to do. The work of preparing food, for example, must be coordinated with the work of serving food so individual employees can work with the best results. You coordinate each branch and type of working activity with other activities for total functioning which is as smooth, on-time, and as frictionless as you can get it.

Another main function of management should be to give clear directions and make sure they are followed. Employees who follow directions should be thanked, complimented, encouraged, and rewarded. Employees who don't should be reinstructed in precisely what the directions are, precisely how they should carry out the directions correctly, and checked to make sure they do. Some people can only perform well if they have very close supervision and someone constantly telling them what to do. You want employees who do best when you explain to them the job you want them to do, leave them alone to do it, and they go ahead on their own and do it right and they keep on doing it right.

Hiring

You can make your work in directing and coordinating simpler if you exercise care when you hire employees. Many managers insist that only experienced personnel be hired. Others are willing to hire less experienced people and train them. Probably the best method is a combination of both. Some jobs do call for experienced people. For other jobs, many managers feel it is better to hire inexperienced individuals. They would rather train them in the procedures they want followed and not take a chance on having to correct bad habits experienced workers may have acquired on previous jobs.

Obviously you should try to hire the type of individual who seems suited for the position you have in mind. Figure out exactly what qualifications a person must have in order to do a specific job. It is usually best to find a person who fits the job instead of changing the job requirements to fit a person. Some people will find a particular job too easy and will be bored with it. Others would find the same job nerve-racking and too hard. Bored employees leave soon, and so do employees who are not capable of handling their jobs and thus become frustrated and unhappy. Gauge people's interests and abilities as well as you can when you hire them.

Establish procedures for hiring employees. Decide where to seek them —through newspapers, employment agencies, friends of your present employees. Decide what kind of personnel forms you might need, who will conduct interviews, what criteria you will use to select new employees, and so on.

In the food service industry, dependability is frequently a much more important factor for hiring and retaining employees than the level of skill the individual possesses. The individual hired should fit the needs of your establishment *and* be reliable.

Many firms have found that handicapped individuals are especially loyal and dependable workers. Many restaurants have had a great deal of success in retaining mentally retarded individuals—perhaps as dishwashers or whatever their own capabilities indicate. In general, they are consistently on the job and take pride in performing their work well. You should definitely consider hiring handicapped workers—including people with other kinds of handicaps, not just the retarded.

Training

Training is a vital part of this entire process of directing people and activities. You will have to spend a lot of time training your employees, or assign some competent employee or employees to do the job of training. Training is too often delegated to a subordinate who was never trained. A great deal depends on how well training is done originally and on how good and how long-lasting the follow-up supervision is.

Thorough training is extremely important. It can actually affect whether your operation flourishes or folds. It is up to managers to train immediate subordinates and to see to it that they, in turn, train those under them. The success or failure of the chain of training rests solely on the shoulders of the manager.

Control

Control is a management tool. It should be helpful to all and frightening to none. The word "control" should definitely *not* mean tyrannical, unfair, or authoritarian management tactics. There are employees who regard "management" and "control" at their own jobs in this light. Some of them are, unfortunately, justified.

Control should mean methods you use to keep the operation functioning smoothly and profitably for all concerned. Managerial control, as the term is used in this book, means sensible safeguards that management sets up to help the food operation succeed.

Control consists mainly of three things. When you exert management control in your food service operation, you perform the following:

1. *Measure.* You measure what's been done, what's taken place in a period of time.
2. *Evaluate.* You evaluate how well or how badly things have gone, comparing the situations and events with your operation's standard or norm.
3. *Act.* You take action based on your measurement and your evaluation.

Control is really your (management's) action based on your measurement and your evaluation. Managers often check situations and then decide not to act. They conclude that the situations don't require their action or intervention. The fact that they have investigated and *then* decided not to act is an action in itself. Control means managers investigate situations, they understand events, and then they decide they will act or they will not act. Either way, they are exercising control. (Control will be discussed further in Chapter 3.)

SUPERVISORS

All the things we have just been discussing are management activities. Management activities appropriate to each managerial position should be performed at all management levels, from the top executive position to the least authoritative supervisory job. And they should be performed in accordance with overall organizational plans which come from the top administrative level.

Supervisors are part of management. They have their own appropriate duties and responsibilities in some of the management functions. Supervisors should follow the overall plans of the total operation and help make them work.

Supervisors should make both long-term and short-term plans. They should organize and coordinate the jobs in their own departments. They should direct and train all employees who report to them (unless someone else is assigned to do the training) and do follow-up checking on employee performance.

Supervisors should coordinate the work of their own department with the work of other departments. They should gather information about their own departments, compare the results with their departments' standards which have been set by management, and take action where they can to improve and tighten all activities in their departments.

In short, supervisors perform all the broad management activities we have talked about in terms of their own jobs, departments, and responsibilities. And they must have authority to do all this and enforce their decisions.

NEW EMPLOYEES

New employees starting to work in a food service operation may wonder how their own jobs relate to the overall activities of others. If they do not really understand where and why their work fits into the operation as a whole, they may shrug off their own work and perform haphazardly simply because they may conclude their own jobs are not important. It is your job (management's job) to show and convince new employees that they are needed and necessary and that if their work did not have to be done you'd eliminate the job. You would not have hired them if they weren't needed and if their job didn't have to be done (provided, of course, you know what *you're* doing). It's your job to show them how and why they are important to the operation.

The easiest way to begin to teach new employees their jobs is to give them written job descriptions of the work they are to perform. A job description should list the tools employees will work with and the duties they are expected to complete. Written job descriptions simplify training and help speed the adjustment of new individuals. Job descriptions are very helpful for both employer and new employee during the orientation process, when you are trying to acquaint new people with their own work and with the overall working routines of the establishment. But don't just leave it at handing them a dittoed sheet of instructions. Make sure they know who to go to for help and answers. And make sure help really is forthcoming for them whenever they need it.

You decide what employees you need and what jobs need to be done. You determine this when you devise your organization structure.

ORGANIZATION STRUCTURE

Organization structure means the hierarchy of planned relationships between individuals and between departments. An organization chart is just a chart showing the organization structure. There are lots of ways in which businesses can be organized.

Traditionally, the food service industry has been organized departmentally. Departmental organization means that individuals who perform similar work are grouped together in a department. To a certain extent, departmental organization means organizing employees according to their physical location in the establishment. For example, kitchen employees in one department, dining room employees in another department, and so on. This can break down further—cooks in one subdepartment in the kitchen, dishwashers in another subdepartment in the kitchen, etc.

Organization Charts

Shown below are three sample organization charts for three sizes of food and beverage operations. Chart 2-1 illustrates a small operation, Chart 2-2 a medium size, and Chart 2-3 a large operation.

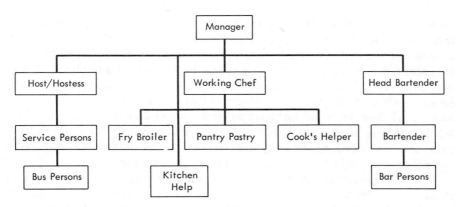

Chart 2-1 Organization chart for small food and beverage operation: 10-15 kitchen employees, 20-30 dining room employees.

Probably no food service establishment will have a chart exactly like any of the three shown. These charts are set up to give you ideas. You can follow them fairly closely where they apply or change them a good deal to suit your own operation. Every operation's chart is apt to be unique and a bit different from any other. The bigger your food service operation is, the more you

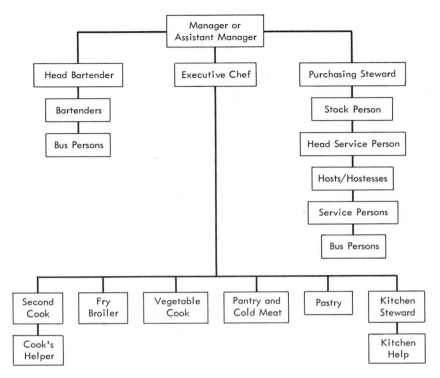

Chart 2-2 Organization chart for medium-size food and beverage operation: 20–30 kitchen employees, 50–75 dining room employees, 5–15 beverage employees.

will probably need to set up more departments and go in for more specialization.

In a small food operation, employees will probably have to be able to perform many different jobs. They will do some tasks well and some tasks not so well. But they will probably have to know how to do a lot of different jobs. In larger establishments, employees are more apt to be specialists. They may know a bit (or even nothing) about the other tasks in the establishment, but they will have to know quite a bit about their own specialty. They will probably perform fewer jobs. They may just do one job—or maybe even just one small part of one job. They may take little or no part in other work in the operation.

There are two important points here:

1. In a bigger organization you need more specialization than in a smaller one.
2. In a bigger organization there is need for more detailed measurement and control than in a smaller one.

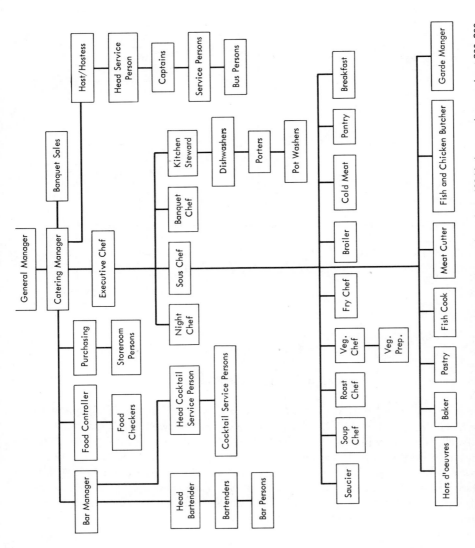

Chart 2-3 Organization chart for large food and beverage operation: about 100 kitchen employees, about 200–300 dining room employees, about 25–75 beverage employees.

When an organization is large, there will be greater need for you to gather information from each area because of the sheer amount of activity going on. You make decisions and take action based on this information. Know and follow the principles of good management when you do.

PRINCIPLES OF MANAGEMENT

1. Every business should have a primary goal. Usually it is long-term profit. Every person in the organization should know the long-term goal and try to help achieve it.

2. Each employee should have only one supervisor, should know precisely who that supervisor is, and should be required to follow instructions *only* from his or her own supervisor.

3. There is a limit to the number of employees a supervisor can supervise. This number varies with the complexities of the job and with the ability of the supervisor. Usually, the more complex the job, the fewer employees one person can effectively supervise.

4. No one can completely delegate responsibility. Work can be delegated, but the immediate superiors at each level still retain responsibility for individuals who work directly under them.

5. Supervisors should not be held responsible for the work in their departments unless they have enough authority to enforce what they say and do.

6. The organization must be flexible. It must be able to adapt readily to change and adjust for the future.

7. The organization should take planned steps to provide for its continued existence and survival.

These ideas cover some of the main principles discussed in most general management books. A lot of managers in the food and beverage industry violate some or all of them. The above list is not complete. There are other principles of management. You can't violate many of them for very long and stay in business.

Examine your own management ideas and your own food and beverage operation closely. Do you have a plausible goal and objectives and means of attaining them? Are they clear? Do your employees know them and understand them? Are there too many "bosses" in your operation? Do owners come in and give employees directions that conflict with manager's or supervisor's directions? Do your employees know precisely which person's directions they are really supposed to follow? Is there a clear line of authority from top to bottom in your operation and from bottom to top? Do you ask your supervisors to be responsible for areas and activities that involve more people and work than they can supervise effectively? Did you ever know a manager who made a flat statement to a supervisor such as: "*You're* responsible for supervising those waiters!'' (Or whatever the task.) ''Go do it!'' If the supervisor goes ahead and tries to solve problems and changes the waiters' procedures, does the manager then bawl him or her out and make another flat statement: ''*You* can't do that! You don't have the *authority* to do that!'' Does the shoe fit? Know the principles of management and use them—with a large dose of common sense.

Another thing you have to do is stay flexible and adjust with the times. There is a danger that your operation could eventually be forced out of business and/or you could be forced out of a management job if you are completely incapable of changing when change is necessary. ''If my restaurant is exactly the same this year as it was last year, I've taken a step backward because other food service operations have moved forward.'' That's a smart food service manager's attitude. Good management includes knowing and correctly applying sound principles of management—and keeping up with the times.

MANAGEMENT ETHICS

As a manager, you are supposed to direct the work of your employees. In the food service industry, you usually direct employees who handle food, beverages, and money. Your own actions and activities must be above reproach. You need a code of good ethics, and you need to follow it in your dealings with your employees and purveyors and customers.

Employees

Dishonest employees may walk out of a food service establishment with a few hamburgers in their pockets without paying for them. They are stealing. Dishonest managers may load their cars with steaks from the establishment, take them home, and eat them without paying for them. They are stealing. (There is one exception to this. Some managers have a prearranged subsistence agreement with the owner. If such an agreement does exist, all employees should know about it and know that it is a legitimate owner-manager arrangement.)

Employees and managers who steal may feel that the food service owes them the food, beverage or money, consider that they are underpaid and some extras are due them, and may even feel consciously or unconsciously self-righteous about taking whatever they take.

You cannot ask or expect your employees to be honest if you are not. You set the example of honesty personally. You will have a slim chance of controlling theft if you're not honest yourself. Your employees will know if you are honest or dishonest. That is a fact that's as old as the food and beverage service business.

Purveyors

You have to be honest and ethical in your dealings with your purveyors, too. Buy from purveyors who supply you with the highest quality of merchandise and service for the price you pay. Some managers buy from the purveyor who pays them the biggest amount of money in personal kickback for choosing them. These managers set an example of dishonesty for their employees, who will, as we said, know what they are doing.

The above examples touch on just a few areas of personal management ethics. Ethical (or unethical) behavior is all-inclusive and comes into play in multitudes of management activities. Your own personal morals and ethics come through loud and clear in your every word and action. If you want to control theft at all job levels, the first essential step is for you to set a personal example of absolute honesty yourself. You may still get employees who steal from you, no matter how pristine you are. But don't let that stop you from being scrupulous. Get a better theft detection and control program going.

Managers and middle management personnel usually have more opportunity to steal from an establishment and they can usually do it on a bigger scale than employees in lower positions. If managers are dishonest, they will fool no one. If they steal or cheat, their employees will not only know about it, they may be tempted to join them. If employees are sure managers are scrupulously honest with them and with the food operation, they may be tempted to join them in that, too.

It is economically profitable in the long run (and, of course, right in any run) to be honest, fair, and ethical in the true sense of those terms.

In this chapter we have discussed various factors you should consider as a manager. Have a goal and objectives and have the means to achieve them. As a manager, you should perform organizing functions for your business so it runs smoothly and operates efficiently. Apply general management knowledge to the specific problems of your food service operation. While you are performing these management functions and activities, your own business activities must be honest and above reproach.

REVIEW AND DISCUSSION QUESTIONS

1. What are the functions of a manager?
2. Why are the principles of management important to managers?
3. Why must a manager's ethics be above reproach?
4. Managers decry the lack of trained employees. Those who speak the loud-

est seldom train employees. How should managers solve the problem of lack of trained employees? How should they train?

5. Draw organization charts for small, medium, and large food service operations.

6. What is your philosophy of management?

3

Fundamentals of Control

Objectives

This chapter discusses the basic aspects of control. After you have read this chapter, you should:

1. Know the cycle of control.
2. Know the major areas of cost, and their relationship to the sales dollar.
3. Know the basic requirements for any control system.

There are some procedures you will have to follow and some things you will have to do if you expect to control your costs. You will have to gather information (or have it gathered for you), study it, and act on it. You will have to follow good management procedures when you buy, prepare, and sell foods. "Food cost control" means that you stick to your own predetermined standards while you exercise restraints or direction over the price you pay to buy, prepare, and sell food.

PREDETERMINED STANDARDS

"Predetermined standards" is a key phrase in control. "Pre," of course, means "before," and in this case it means that you decide what you should do before you start to do it. Applied to the food selling business, the phrase predetermined standards means that you set total and detailed standards of operations before you buy, cook, and sell food. Sounds simple. But it isn't.

It's up to you to decide what you want in the way of goods, preparation, and service. Do not leave it to your employees to develop their own standards. If you leave matters of standards entirely in the hands of employees, it is a pretty sure bet your employees' ideas about food service standards will not precisely match yours. If they do, your job and your employees' jobs are interchangeable and you're not "managing" a thing.

You are the one who is supposed to plan and control your food service operation. Show your employees how to make effective contributions to the general plan you've created. Your ideas will change, and so will your theories about predetermined standards. You will learn what is possible and what isn't. Employees will offer ideas and information to you. If you're smart you will listen and use what is valid. But it is up to you to initiate control programs and stick to your predetermined standards, making changes when necessary. If you do not, you are not managing and you're not succeeding in using control systems so that they work for you.

Later in this book we will discuss in detail how you exercise restraint and direction when you buy food (Chapter 14), prepare food (Chapter 17), and sell food (Chapter 19).

YOUR MARKET

Each food operation caters to a specific market. Standards vary for different markets. When owners have all the information they can possibly get about the market they want to attract, it is then up to you, the manager, to set standards appropriate for this selected market before you buy, prepare and sell the food.

There are many different kinds of markets. Markets range through all stages from very low price to very high price. Food service establishments try to attract different markets and they also purchase goods of different qual-

ities. The goods you purchase should be appropriate for—and in demand by—
your own particular market. And you should buy goods that are appropriate
for the specific kinds of uses you will make of them.

Some owners decide they want a very high quality, luxury operation.
They want only fresh meats, fresh fruits, fresh vegetables—absolutely top
quality of everything to be served. They want all service personnel in formal
attire. They want a plush atmosphere. They want an exclusive operation and
they want to attract a high economic market. They will expect their manager
to see to it that service personnel consistently give fine and meticulously correct service to guests. This is one type of market and one set of standards.
Other owners opt for the middle ground—good food, pleasant service, and
moderate prices. Some owners may decide they want a food service establishment that buys second and third-grade foods, purposely maintains an informal type of service, and caters to and goes after a low-price, high-volume
market. Markets vary and standards do, too, according to the market that is
sought.

Types of standards vary with different operations and different
markets catered to. Have standards of food, preparation, and service that are
appropriate for your own market and suitable for the kind of operation you
run.

COST CONTROL PROCEDURES

The purpose of this book is to explain procedures for controlling all your
costs. You will need records. We will discuss these in the following chapters.
Records give you the information you must have in order to make sensible
decisions to control and improve your total food service unit. We will discuss
these records and procedures throughout the rest of this book and talk about
forms, charts, graphs, and so on which you use when you gather and record
information.

These information-gathering forms and methods are your tools, nothing more. So is the information itself. No amount of information is of any
value to you at all unless you take—and know how to take—managerial
action. In this book we will try to tell you how to do that.

Cycle of Food Control

The following is a quick rundown of the main areas where you apply
controls. In later chapters we will discuss them in detail. Briefly, the cycle of
food control consists of the following major steps:

Operations Analysis

You make an overall general analysis of everything you are doing in
your total food service operation. What are your sales? What is your current

food cost? What steps are you taking to control food cost? Go into specific areas for detailed information. Establish procedures in every area listed below.

Menu

Consider your menu. It is your most important sales tool. It lists everything you will sell. You "pre-cost" your menu. This means that before you put any item and its price on your menu, you figure out just what it costs you to prepare and serve that item. Then you decide on the appropriate selling price and put the item and its price on your menu.

Purchasing

You have to purchase the food you will need to have in order to prepare and sell the items on your menu. Purchasing must have controls.

Receiving

As you receive the food you have purchased, some goes into your storeroom and some goes directly into the production area. You need controls when you receive the food you have bought.

Storeroom

You need control procedures to check food in and out of your storeroom. You need a storeroom control system to keep records and to prevent theft.

Food Production

Establish procedures. You need standardized recipes to prepare the food listed on your menu, to make sure your costs and portion sizes are being maintained in line with what you pre-costed, and to make sure that your predetermined standards are being met.

Service

Decide what kind of service you want to offer. Train your employees to provide it.

Selling and Control of Cash

Establish controlled selling procedures. Controls for collecting payment from guests and handling cash are very important.

Sales Analysis

Examine how well various items on your menu have sold. Did you sell the items you wanted to? Or did guests buy something else instead? Should you keep your menu as it is or change some items?

Start Again

After you have considered all these factors and studied all the information you have gathered, go back again to step number one—operations analysis. Did you get the food cost you wanted? Did things go as you wanted or not? Why? Start the whole process of operations analysis from the beginning again. Do the same entire routine for each meal period, each day, each week, continuously. The cycle of food control is a circle with no beginning or end.[1]

Step in Any Control System

How do you control any cost? Among other things, you do the following:

1. You try to know what is going on in your operation. Everywhere. All the time. You find out.
2. You carefully examine, weigh, and ponder information, figures, results, facts, reports, and statistics. How extensive all of this material and data will be will depend on your own nature, knowledge, and experience. It will also depend on what kind of operation you manage—a three-employee ice-cream shop, a five-employee hamburger drive-in, a 50-employee luxury restaurant, a hotel food service with 300 food and beverage employees, and so on.
3. You keep detailed records (or have a well-trained, reliable employee or staff do it for you) of everything you actually need to know. You collect pertinent facts and information about your establishment. You don't collect any information you won't actually use.
4. You do not put all this information in a folder and forget it.
5. You study and analyze the information and compare it with your past records.
6. Then you take appropriate action if needed. Without management action there is no control.
7. You do all of these things continuously.

Management Action

"Management action" means you decide to take either positive action or passive action. Then you do one or the other.

Positive Action

(Yes you do take action. This is a conscious decision on your part based

[1] Douglas C. Keister, *How To Increase Profits With Portion Control.* National Restaurant Association. Chicago, 1966.

on information you have.) "Positive action" is when you examine information and on the basis of this information you decide to do something—revamp purchasing procedures, change your receiving controls, get a different purveyor. Because of the information you have, you decide to do something.

Passive Action

(No you do not take action. This, too, is a conscious decision on your part based on information you have.) "Passive action" is when you examine information and on the basis of this information you decide to do nothing. You decide that action by you is not called for, at least not right now—you leave your purchasing procedures alone, you do not change your receiving controls, you will keep the same purveyor for now, and so on. Because of the information you have, you decide to do nothing. You have looked at information and made a conscious decision. You have elected not to do anything to change something at the present time. You are on top of things. There is control. This is a far cry from doing nothing because you don't know what is going on. Or because you don't have information. Or because you don't look at information even if you have it.

In your food service operation you should continuously be taking either positive action or passive action. Constantly. Know what's going on. Act or don't act, but in either case base it on knowledge, not obliviousness. Obliviousness is not sound management, although it is unfortunately not an uncommon managerial condition.

Sometimes you will have a terrible time deciding what you should do about a situation. Sometimes you will lack the experience or knowledge to know how to figure out what's the right move to make. Some situations *are* confusing. You will probably encounter some problems that you do not have the power to solve.

Sometimes you will make bad decisions. Even after you have checked figures and data and looked at all the information you can get and weighed alternatives as well as you can, you will still do some things wrong. The purpose of this book is to try to help you know how to find answers and how to make more right decisions and fewer wrong ones. That's what good control and good business are all about.

Management's Role

Cost control systems come in a great variety of assorted sizes, types, and degrees of complexity. Fortunately, however, the fundamentals of cost control—the reasons you have them, the basic way they work, and the help they can give you—can be applied to any kind of food service operation, in any country, now and in the future.

There can and will be great variation and flexibility in details when you apply cost controls to your own needs, but the rules of cost control hold true. Large operations will probably need more detailed information than small ones, but both will need the same *kinds* of information.

In a larger operation, management is generally farther removed from where employees' work is actually being performed. If you are the manager of a large operation, you cannot usually observe for yourself everything that goes on, so you will probably need to gather more information to help you make decisions and set up controls. This is a difference in quantity only. All cost control programs—whether extremely extensive and detailed or very brief and involving only a handful of employees—will be the same except for length. You use a control program—any program from very extensive to very small-scale—to get yourself the same types of facts to prepare you to act.

Effective control systems start at the top of a business with top management personnel and influence all employees at all levels in the organization. Responsibilities and expected performances of each individual employee must be decided upon by management and clearly defined to each employee. Decisions that are not clearly explained to the staff and then followed up with supervision and instruction are useless. No control program can function well unless you as manager take an active role in initiating the courses of action and in giving clear directions to others. Then you check on a continuing basis to see that the policies you as manager have decided on are really being carried out.

MAJOR AREAS OF COST

There are four major areas of cost for a food service operation:

1. Food.
2. Labor.
3. Profit.
4. Overhead (all other expenses that are not food cost, labor cost, or profit cost).

Profit as Alternative Cost

Profit is sometimes called "alternative cost." The profit you get from investing your time (and money, if you're an owner) in a food service operation should be equal to or greater than the profit you would get from investing your time and/or money in a different, "alternative" (and probably less risky) business or investment. In other words, money put into a food service operation and time spent administering it could have been invested elsewhere (in a clothing store, hardware store, grocery store—anything). People who put time and money in any of these alternative businesses instead of the food service business certainly do expect a return. It is true of the food service business, too. If you invest money in food service, of course you expect a return.

Profit as a Real Cost

According to the traditional accounting viewpoint, profit is not called (or treated as) a cost of doing business. From an economic viewpoint, however, profit most definitely is a cost of doing business. In the food service business, you must consider profit as a cost and treat it just like any other cost—just like overhead, labor, food. Treat profit exactly like you treat these. Allot money beforehand to pay for profit exactly as you allot money beforehand to pay for overhead, labor, or food. (Chapter 5 gives details on how you do profit planning.)

Profit

Most people go into business primarily to make a profit, although many simultaneously achieve personal fulfillment and make a contribution to society. The reason—in fact the *only* reason—for having cost control systems is to help you make profits and avoid loss. If you cannot construct cost control systems through which you can achieve this, you are not likely to succeed in the food and beverage industry.

Cost control can help you maintain your present level of profit, if you are satisfied with it. If you are not satisfied, cost control can probably help you increase your profits. If you are now losing money, a good cost control system can generally help you make a profit unless you face events that are beyond any managerial remedy. Some things may be beyond your power or the power of cost controls to remedy—overall deterioration of the chain for which you work, unstoppable new competition, an unforeseen highway rearrangement that takes traffic flow away from your location, and the like.

THREE PARTS OF CONTROL

1. You learn by gathering information. Gather and compile all the information and facts you can that will help you make decisions. You put these into records and reports, or you have someone do it for you. You do not put these in your desk and forget them. You study them. If they are of no use to you, you quit gathering them.

2. You measure. Analyze the facts you obtain and compare them against standards. Maybe you use an industrywide standard. Or your company's standard. Or the standard of your own unit's past performance. Maybe you will use all of these plus other standards in your comparisons and measurements.

3. You act. Take action (positive or passive action, discussed earlier in this chapter). You act because of the information you have gotten and studied and because of the measurements you have made.

PROFIT VERSUS BREAKEVEN

There are food services for which making a profit is not a goal. Examples of this might be hospital cafeterias, college dormitory food services, in-plant restaurants owned and operated by manufacturing plants. Most of these types of food operations are, however, expected to break even. They may not have to show profit, but usually they do not want to lose money.

Food service units either operate at a profit or at a loss. No one breaks even to the penny. There is an extremely thin dividing line between slight profit, breakeven, and slight loss—in fact, the difference between profit and loss is one cent. You could theoretically make as little as a one cent profit, you could break even, or you could have a loss as microscopic as one cent. It is not realistic to expect food services to operate so closely that they wind up *precisely* at breakeven.

Almost all operations (with the possible exception of well-to-do clubs which could assess members for losses) which are expected to operate at close to breakeven do want to avoid loss, so it is sensible for them to plan as if they did have to make some profit. If they do get a profit it will probably be small, and the money is usually put back into the operation to improve the food service for the clientele.

The concept of nonprofit business is a method of financial organization. Under tax law, establishments can be organized on a nonprofit basis. Thus they don't pay income tax. But most food service operations that are hypothetically expected to break even should really plan for a little profit. This will help them achieve close to breakeven or small profit and avoid loss. If you manage an operation where breakeven is expected, plan for a small profit. If you plan for exact breakeven, you can very easily wind up with a loss.

A WORD ABOUT DATA PROCESSING

In business today there is a lot of interest in the use of data processing. Most of the procedures discussed in this book are basic and not complicated. You can do most of your information-gathering and recordkeeping with simple forms and a pencil. But the fundamental theories involved also apply to more complex or computerized systems.

Before you embark on a computerized data processing system, you've got to know exactly what information you are trying to accumulate, why you want it, and how to use it after you get it. In general, you will be going after the same information and answers whether you use computerized data processing or very simple hand methods.

Some advantages of computer data processing over hand systems are:

1. You can get more information.

2. You can get it quicker.

3. You can usually get more accurate facts.

In developing a computer data processing system for you, data programmers would analyze your current manual system of data gathering. They would offer suggestions and ideas for additions or changes if you or they feel that some adjustments in your system would help you. If what you are doing manually is working for you, they would write you a computer program based mainly on your current systems and needs. Many mechanized data programs just computerize the programs you have been doing by hand.

Computerized programs can be excellent and real work-savers. Look into the idea if you feel it could help you. There is one potential danger in computerized programs, however. They can make it so easy and fast for you to get information that you may be tempted to ask for much more information than you need or can use. Managers can fall into this pattern. The result can be confusion, waste of time, and ineffectiveness of the cost systems. People in the computer business have a pertinent saying—"Garbage in, garbage out."

You have to collect and record information about your food operation. Throughout this book we will be discussing this information, how you get it and how you use it. Whatever data-gathering methods you use—from the simplest handwritten forms you make up yourself to the biggest, most sophisticated computer information-collecting techniques—make sure the system is doing its work as a valid tool for you and that you are using it effectively. Figure out precisely what information your data-compiling methods should help you get. Gather facts with your objectives clearly in mind. Make sure your data-collecting methods really work for you and make it easier for you to control your own food service operation. If they don't, there is no reason to have them, and you're wasting time and money on them. If they do, your work in food service management should be more efficient and profitable.

BASIC REQUIREMENTS FOR COST CONTROL SYSTEMS

Some of the fundamental necessities for a cost control system are discussed below. They are not listed in order of importance—they are all important. What is really important is how you put them all together so the combined procedures work well for you.

Adequate Information

You need "adequate" information. "Adequate" means whatever amount *you* need—enough information so *you* can make good, successful decisions. If you manage a large operation or food service unit, you will probably need to have much more information gathered for you so you can make sound decisions than would the manager of a smaller unit.

The following list is certainly not complete, but it will give you an idea of the types of things about which you may want to collect information:

1. Sales for each day.
2. Items purchased.
3. Items received (categorized or not categorized).
4. Items requisitioned and issued from storeroom.
5. Number of guests (per hour, per meal, per day—whatever you need to know).
6. Number of employees on duty (by hours, meal periods, days, weeks).
7. Average check.
8. Amount of food prepared.
9. Amount of food sold (by items or totals).
10. Opening and closing storeroom inventories.

A completely adequate amount of information for one manager in one establishment might be a very inadequate amount of information for another manager in a different establishment. Or you may be the manager of a relatively small food operation but find that you want a lot of detailed information—as much as some larger establishments want. It's up to you. Get enough so you can make good decisions. Don't get more than you need or will use.

Prompt Information

The second basic requirement is to get information promptly. "Promptly" is another vague word. This, too, is up to you to decide. "Prompt" should be soon enough so you can take appropriate action—so you can do something quickly to reduce costs if they are too high for the current period, for example.

Timing will vary with your type of operation. Remote resorts may put figures together weekly, and for them this may very well be plenty prompt. Maybe their purchasing, deliveries, room rentals, and the like are all predicated on a weekly basis. Even if managers of places like these wanted to change their procedures, perhaps they could not do much (except make plans) to really initiate action and change things for a week anyway.

In sharp contrast to this, the managers of many large, urban hotels can tell you at 11 a.m. what their food cost was for the breakfast they served from 7 to 10:30 that morning. A large hotel, located in a metropolitan center and serving vast numbers of people, will probably want to be able to take action that very same day that will affect the food cost of the breakfast they will serve the next morning. They may have deliveries, meal plans, and the like set up on a fast daily schedule. When they call for prompt information, they may mean 10 minutes or 30 minutes, not seven days like the resort manager.

"Prompt" means fast enough so you can take the quickest action possible to correct situations or activities if you need to.

Brief Reports

Information or reports you get and use should be as brief as possible, but not so brief they don't tell you what you should know. Reports normally should not take more than two pages, and many may be much shorter— perhaps just several lines on one page. You will have many other demands on your time. If you need lots of lengthy forms filled in with facts and figures, get a trained employee (or a staff of employees, depending again on your own situation) to gather the information and summarize it for you. If some figures come in too high or you have any questions about any reports, then you check further into detailed sheets to get more background so you can take action in those particular areas.

It is not generally necessary for you to get total, detailed information routinely day after day if the information is long and could be successfully boiled down by someone else to save you time. This works only if vital information is not being left out of the summaries you get. You are the one who decides what is vital.

A lot of food service operations collect stacks of information about their inner workings. But no one does a useful thing with all this hard-come-by information. Don't make the mistake of thinking you have a good control system just because you have a lot of information gathered. Many managers ask their employees to gather information and they do it. But the information never gets to the manager. Employees gather lots of information, record it, and file it. Make sure the information reaches you—or that a valid summary of it does.

You have to:

1. *Get* information.
2. *Study* it.
3. *Comprehend* what it tells you.
4. *Act* on it (positive or passive action).

If you don't do all four of these, you have no control whatsoever.

Some food service operations collect a lot of information about their establishments and really put it to good use. Some go into great detail—even to the point of finding out the precise number of guests served per hour, which waitress or waiter served them, what they ate, how long they stayed at the table, and so on. But it is worth it to them if they use this information to change the menu, schedule employees, control payroll costs, make guest reservations based on table turnover, and so on.

It costs you time and money to compile facts about your operation. Some waste the time and money spent on this, some don't. If you use your findings to make sound changes in the number of employees and wisely adjust the amount of your payroll cost, for example, the information is worth getting. You are acting from knowledge and are using a control system. If you discover you do not need to make any use at all of the information you gather, don't gather it.

Noninterference in the Conduct of Business

Cost control should not interfere with the conduct of business. Don't let your studies of your operation or the steps you need to go through to gather information and set up your cost control systems interrupt your business. You will need to make detailed studies and observations of various cost areas and departments to start or revamp control systems and maintain them. Do these things when it's a convenient time for everyone. Don't interfere with mealtime food production. Check to see if your directions are being followed and make your tests and ask your questions without disrupting actual production.

No matter who is doing and/or watching tests, for example (you, your cooks, a hired food controller—whoever), choose convenient times. Inform everyone that tests or discussions will take place. Observation, checkups, and investigations that you or your staff need to make in devising, checking, or improving any control systems should not interfere with actual business operations. Surprise spot checks are fine if they do not throw production into a turmoil.

Managers have to gather information. You have to make sure employees are told what portion sizes they should use. You have to have yield tests conducted, do costing of portions, and teach employees how to use and control correct portion sizes. (Chapter 11 discusses pre-control and pre-costing the menu.) Do watch and listen and see what is going on at noon. Do come in unexpectedly just to observe. You can—and occasionally should—watch what is happening in your operation during your peak business periods. But do not interrupt production at noon to get into a yield test or a cost test or to work out details of any cost control system. Talk about it when you and your employees have time.

Gather information intelligently. Don't saunter unexpectedly into the kitchen at the height of the lunchtime rush and launch a discussion with, for example, your sandwichmakers. "How many ounces of beef did you put in that sandwich? How many sandwiches will you get from that roast?" Managers do behave this way. It does not endear them to their kitchen staffs. If the sandwichmakers, for example, have to try to give you detailed information while they are also killing themselves trying to make 40 sandwiches in three minutes, they are not apt to be very cooperative. In fact, they are apt to be quite the opposite—and with good reason.

Avoid Waste

Your cost control systems should help you avoid waste wherever it can occur. This includes wasted food, wasted time—*any* waste in the entire operation.

A very small amount of waste is virtually unavoidable in the food service industry. For small-scale examples, you will always have to throw away the outside leaves of lettuce, unless your purveyor does it for you. And you will always have to trim excess fat from meat, unless your purveyor does that, too. That is unavoidable waste. Avoidable waste, on the other hand, is waste, big and small, that you *can* cut out or reduce, and that can add up to cost you real money if you do not control it. This means waste caused by poor planning and bad organization which results in allowing a lot of food to spoil. Or preparing much too much food, which is then thrown out. It also means wasted motions and steps by employees, which could be avoided if you change what can be changed in the kitchen, dining room, storeroom, receiving dock, or any area. Physical structures and arrangements will vary from unit to unit, and you will probably be forced to set up work routines in accordance with some unchangeable confines of your building. But you can probably do a lot to decrease wasted steps and wasted motions by employees if you are careful to arrange whatever objects and activities you can to make work easier and more efficient.

Some examples of avoiding waste include:

1. Plan food production to avoid overproduction of food.
2. Develop alternative uses for food items if you do overproduce.
3. Check portion sizes and food coming back from the dining room. Are your portion sizes too large?
4. Schedule employees for times they are actually needed so they do not just stand around.
5. Use wheels, inclined planes, or the like to save time moving goods.
6. Turn out lights, broilers, and all equipment when not needed.
7. Wherever possible, make changes in structure or equipment location to increase efficiency in production, service, and storage (for example, set up coffee and cups at stations in dining room; put plates on shelves or carts where they are easier to reach).

These are possible examples. It is up to you to perceive all kinds of waste in your own operation and take steps to correct situations where waste is occurring.

Some waste is trivial, some is extremely expensive. If you check into this you can probably come up with many economies, small and large, that can help you reduce costs by cutting waste in all areas of food, overhead, and labor. Reduced waste can mean reduced costs and more profit.

Your Cost Control Systems Should Pay for Themselves

It will probably be hard for you to figure out exactly what your total control program is costing you in dollars, but you can make pretty good estimates. There will be individual employees in different areas in your operation involved in keeping control systems functioning usefully. You can compute the direct cost of the papers and forms you use and the cost of direct payroll if you have full-time or part-time personnel who work on nothing but cost control. But there will still be other employees involved in cost control. Some of their duties will be to provide information and follow procedures to assure the success of the cost systems and the total food operation.

You should be able to figure out fairly closely what your control systems cost. They should be saving you money. Cost control systems should pay for themselves in terms of dollars. Your cost control systems should save you all the money the systems themselves cost plus more. If they don't, they're not working right. They should be made to work right. You should have more money with them than without them.

Good cost control systems are composed of many things. They should not be just "recordkeeping." They should be integral parts of total management philosophy, practice, and procedure. Good cost control systems can help you achieve and maintain the level of profit you want. Good controls can be the difference between success and failure.

REVIEW AND DISCUSSION QUESTIONS

1. What is food control?
2. What is the cycle of food control?
3. How does positive action differ from passive action?
4. Why is profit considered a cost?
5. Distinguish when you would apply the cycle of control and when you might want to concentrate on a single facet of the cycle.
6. Why must control start with the manager?
7. How could you apply the basic requirements of a food control system to a specific food service operation?
8. What are the steps in a control system?

4

Economics of the Food and Beverage Industry

Objectives

This chapter shows how economic theory can be applied to the food and beverage industry. After you have read this chapter, you should:

1. Know how the economic theory of supply and demand can affect your business.
2. Know ways to identify your market.
3. Know why you should not engage only in price competition.

HOW IMPORTANT IS PRICE?

Many food service operators firmly believe that their customers know a lot about comparative dining costs and are very price conscious. They are determined to set prices *solely* on what they think customers want to pay. They go to extremely low prices trying to attract customers. Others set out on purpose to charge high prices, expecting to get away with it with no counteractions from their competition. It is foolish to go to either extreme in pricing.

Customers are not as overwhelmingly interested in price as many food service managers believe. They are interested in what they get for their money, but they are influenced by other factors, too.

When food service customers have decided they will go out to eat, they usually decide ahead of time what type of meal they will have. They decide on a general price category. Customers know about comparative prices *between different categories* of eating establishments—hamburger drive-ins versus coffee shops versus steak houses versus luxury restaurants, and the like. But most customers are not very well informed about comparative prices of meals *within one category* of eating establishment—one hamburger drive-in versus another hamburger drive-in, one coffee shop versus another coffee shop, and so on. And to most individuals, price difference *within one general category* of eating establishment is not as significant as the four factors placed ahead of price in the following list of factors which do affect people's decisions on where they'll go to eat:

1. Good food well prepared.
2. Good service.
3. Pleasant surroundings.
4. Clean surroundings.
5. Price.

This list paraphrases and consolidates the results of a research survey by the J. Walter Thompson Company, conducted for Standard Brands, Inc., in 1958.[1] In this author's opinion, the findings of the study are still true today.

The cost of eating out is the number one factor that stops people from eating out. But after people *have* decided to eat out and *have* decided what general category and general price range of establishment they want to go to, *then* price is not the number one reason they choose one restaurant over another in the same general category.

For example, if people have decided they will go out to eat and they want pizza, price is not the number one reason they will select one pizza place

[1]*Consumer Panel Report On Dining Out Habits And Attitudes.* J. Walter Thompson Consumer Panel. Standard Brands, Inc. and The National Restaurant Association, 1958.

out of several they could probably go to. If they've decided they want steak and champagne, price is not the number one reason they select one luxury restaurant out of several they could probably go to. According to the J. Walter Thompson survey, price is number five on the list. This should have a bearing on your price-setting decisions.

Location is omitted from the above list. It's a factor which affects different kinds of operations in different ways. If guests are selecting a hamburger drive-in, they're apt to go to the closest one although they may really prefer one that is farther away. If they want to go to a luxury restaurant, though, they may be willing to travel to get to a particular restaurant, bypassing several closer, comparable restaurants in order to get to the one they really want. Location (accessibility, convenience, distance) has less impact on the luxury operation's market and pricing than it does in the case of other categories of food service operations. (We will discuss this in more detail later in this chapter.)

Pricing and Word-of-Mouth Advertising

Word-of-mouth advertising is the most powerful advertising any food service can have. It is just as potent whether people say good things to each other about your establishment or grumble bad things.

If people like a steak restaurant (or a pancake establishment, or a Greek specialty restaurant, or whatever), they are apt to tell their friends. Sooner or later these friends will probably decide to go to a steak restaurant (pancake establishment, Greek specialty restaurant, or whatever) and they'll probably go to the specific one their friends recommended—even if it costs more than another restaurant in the same general category of eating establishments.

If this restaurant—the one the friends recommended, and the one with the higher price—does give these people good food, good service, and pleasant, clean surroundings, and if the restaurant really has made the total dinner an enjoyable occasion for them, then they are apt to be glad friends told them about the place and consider the money well spent. They will probably recommend the place to *their* friends. Here you have a step in the cycle of good word-of-mouth advertising, which is very pleasant and very important to the restaurant involved.

Although this restaurant charged more than others in the same general category, many guests seem to feel, "I don't mind paying more if I really get what I pay for." Guests do expect quality to be commensurate with the price they pay. If they get it, they're apt to be satisfied. If they don't, they won't like it a bit. They probably won't go back and they may tell their friends *not* to try the restaurant. Grumbling, derogatory word-of-mouth advertising can get started, and no restaurant wants that.

To you as a food service manager, what all of this means is that it costs you more to maintain high quality. You should charge a reasonably higher price to cover your costs. Even though you are charging a higher price, the price can still be reasonable for the food, service, atmosphere—for everything you're selling. If your food service operation gains a reputation through word-of-mouth advertising as a superior place to eat, it may be all right for you to charge reasonably higher prices in consideration of this fact.

DEMAND

Every night there's an X number of people who will go out to eat in any community. It is up to each individual food service operation in a community to try to attract as many of this X number of people as it can. In some communities there are just a few restaurants, in some towns there are dozens, in some cities hundreds. Theoretically, the people going out for dinner in a community could select any of its restaurants (although really they are limited by distance and by how much money they can afford to spend).

This total X number of people who will eat out in a community on one night constitutes the total potential clientele for all the restaurants in that community for that night. In economic terms, this X number of people constitutes the "demand for the industry" in that community that night.

The people from this X group who select a specific food service operation on that specific night are called, in economic terms, the "demand for a given firm." It is up to you as an individual food service operator to attract enough of them so you get a profit.

YOUR PRODUCT—SERVICE

What's the product of a food service operation? The product is "service." A lot of food service operators think they sell just food. They don't. They sell a total service package including a lot of factors:

1. Food that is cooked and served to guests.
2. A type of service (elegant or informal, cheerful or grouchy, and so on).
3. Decor.
4. Location (convenient for a certain market).
5. Maybe music.
6. A standard of cleanliness.
7. A total product in exchange for a price (which is supposed to give the operation a profit in dollars and be a reasonable buy for guests).
8. A specific type of place (to relax and forget worries, conduct an interview or business deal, get hot food served very fast, etc.).
9. Charm, welcome, warmth (or lack thereof).

Food service operations sell a lot more than just food. All of the above come under the general heading of "service." Some operations offer a good product. Some don't.

Competition

The food service business is, of course, a competitive business—extremely so, in fact. But it is not "pure" competition as an economist would define the term. "Pure" competition means that the suppliers of a product can not influence the price of the product, and this is not true in the food service business. The suppliers (the food service operators) *can* influence the price of their product. They can increase it or decrease it. Different types of food service operations can buy exactly the same size, quality, and type of steak—even from the same purveyor—and charge their guests different prices for the steak. If restaurants were engaged in pure competition, this would not happen. All would charge exactly the same price. They do not because there are variations in the ways each operation cooks and serves its steaks and the steaks are served in different restaurants with different atmospheres. This is why their costs are different and the prices they charge can be different. This is why food service businesses are not in pure competition with each other.

Differentiated Product

Food service operations sell a "differentiated product." The term means two operations can start out with practically identical food items but when the items reach the customer they are different. One food service broils steaks on a gas broiler. Another uses a charcoal broiler. The two steaks are very much alike when they reach the food service operations, but they are prepared and served differently and they are served in different establishments. They are differentiated products. And it is not just the difference in cooking. It is a combination of differences—in the establishments, types of service, atmosphere, decor, market attracted, location—that result in a differentiated product. (The exception would be chain or franchise restaurants—expecially fast-foods operations. These sell virtually identical food, cooked and served the same way. Each restaurant in a chain or franchise may have practically identical decor, employee uniforms, architecture, and so on. Probably the only actual difference from one to another is location. Restaurants within one chain probably do not offer a product that is differentiated from the products of the other restaurants inside their own chain. Their product is differentiated from products of nonchain, nonfranchise operations [the independent operations] and differentiated from products of other chains and other franchises.)

A differentiated product could be a steak sold by a restaurant that turns its lights low, installs red plush chairs and expensive paintings, employs a maitre d'hotel, and charges a high price for the steak because the steak is beautifully presented in elegant surroundings. This restaurant would charge more for its steak than another operation would charge for a nearly identical steak prepared and served in a large, brightly lit and bustling restaurant catering to the fast-service, family trade market. The two steaks we're talking about can be the same size and quality steak and can cost both food service operations the same money per pound from a purveyor. The luxury restaurant gets more money per steak from a few people. The fast-service restaurant gets less money per steak from a lot of people. They sell the steaks to different markets. The steaks they sell are a "differentiated product." The "service" they sell (the steak, the atmosphere, the service, location and so on) is a differentiated product, too.

Monopolistic Competition

"Monopolistic competition" is a term peculiar to economics. Monopolistic competition is not really a monopoly and it is not pure competition.

For an example of monopolistic competition, let's say there are several steak houses in your community. Each of them sells the same general kind of steak but each uses different selling devices. One emphasizes luxury furnishings, dim lights, wines, and so on. Another emphasizes fast service and low price. Another emphasizes its "sizzling charcoal-broiled steak." In economic terms, they are engaged in monopolistic competition. Each restaurant (the economist calls each a supplier) sells a differentiated product—a product that's slightly different from that of its competitors and does not have an exact substitute. These restaurants can charge various prices for similar steaks because the total product package they offer along with the steak is different.

Monopolistic competition does not mean price competition. It's not when you compete to see who can charge the lowest price for the differentiated product. Monopolistic competition means you compete with other restaurants to see if you can convince customers that your "differentiated-product" service is more attractive than your competitors' differentiated-product service. Monopolistic competition means that the supplier (the food service operator) is selling a differentiated product.

Another factor in monopolistic competition is that the guests do not know the exact price charged by each restaurant within the same general category of type of establishment and the same geographical area. They may have an idea of approximately what these restaurants charge, but they are not so price-conscious that they call each establishment to get the precise price and then choose a place solely because its price is lowest.

Oligopoly

Chart 4-1 shows a circle drawn around a metropolitan area. Inside this metropolitan area, let us say there are several hundred restaurants. Area A

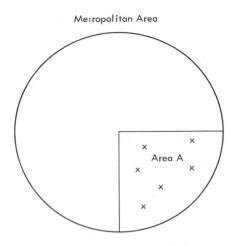

Metropolitan Area

Metropolitan Area: Entire community. Contains several hundred
food service operations.
Area A: Contains total of 50 food service operations.

6 "x's" in Area A: Similar food service operations. These 6
form an oligopoly.

Chart 4-1 Illustration of an oligopoly in a metropolitan area.

is one section of the community. Inside Area A, let's say there are 50 food service establishments. The six x's are six similar restaurants. They are the same
type of eating place. Let us call them six hamburger establishments and the
only six hamburger establishments in the Area A section of town. These six
restaurants are owned by different companies but they are quite similar—all
are hamburger establishments selling shakes, fries, and hamburgers for comparable prices. These six are infinitely more in competition with each other
than they are with the other 44 restaurants in Area A or with other similar
hamburger establishments located off away from Area A somewhere else in
the metropolitan area.

   If one of these six hamburger establishments tries to lure customers by
lowering prices, the other five can take action to retrieve customers. They can
lower their prices, too. Each of the six hamburger establishments in Area A
has to worry primarily about the prices charged by the other five hamburger
establishments in Area A. Each can influence the pricing of the other five restaurants to a certain extent. This does not mean that all six restaurants will
charge exactly the same price. It means that no one of them can get extremely
far out of line from the other five—unless it makes extreme changes in the type
of operation it is. Unless, in other words, it quits being a "similar hamburger
establishment" and starts being a very different type of food operation. Then
it joins a different oligopoly.

If one of the six cuts its prices, customers will eventually learn about it and may go to it *if* they like the place and its food and if it meets the four criteria that are (for the same general type of food operation) more important to them than price. People like a bargain if they feel it's a true one. The other five restaurants can lower their own prices to counter the maverick restaurant's price reduction. This situation is an agreeable one to the uncaring, hungry customer who is glad to pay less for comparable quality. This situation is also potentially deadly to all six hamburger establishments in Area A.

Economists call the six hamburger establishments an oligopoly. It means a few firms are engaged in very similar business and are trying to attract the same market. Actions any one of them takes will affect others in its own oligopoly. All can be affected by what is going on in their own oligopoly. What this means to you as a manager is that you cannot charge prices which are extremely different from others in your own oligopoly. You need to know what they are charging and keep your prices reasonably comparable to theirs.

Economists classify business neatly into competition, monopolies, oligopolies, monopolistic competition, and so on. But they overlap. Your food service operation can engage in monopolistic competition and be in an oligopoly situation at the same time. Nearly all food service operations are in monopolistic competition and oligopoly situations and sell a differentiated product.

All this ties together and means you cannot charge extremely different prices from the rest of your own oligopoly. Others in your oligopoly can react and counter you if you try extreme pricing. Because of this, most food service operations (like most other business firms engaged in monopolistic competition) do not and should not *stress* price. Instead, you should stress your differentiated product. You emphasize anything you uniquely can offer the guest—any way in which your operation differs from, or tries to make itself more attractive than, the others which are part of your own oligopoly.

THE MARKET

As a food service manager, you should be very much aware of what market your own food service operation or firm should be trying to cater to and attract. Know where your guests come from and how and why they decide to come to your establishment. If you know, you can direct your advertising and the emphasis of your total food service toward the people who make up your own specific potential market. You will not have to resort to advertising with a scattered, "shotgun" approach which may or may not reach your own real market. The prices you will charge—expensive, moderate, or low—will affect and help define what your market is. And the market you try to attract will have a bearing on what you should charge.

There are different kinds of markets. Most food service operations appeal primarily to one general market, depending on their prices, service, location, and what kind of food they sell.

Some food service customers indulge in a luxurious meal at an expensive restaurant only for a very special occasion, and they will travel to get it. This means there is generally a much broader geographical market (and an oligopoly that covers a bigger geographical area) for a luxury unit than for a low-cost establishment, whose customers may choose it mainly for convenience. People going out to celebrate a birthday or anniversary, for example, may drive 20 or 30 miles or more to have dinner in an elegant restaurant they really like. When those same people want to go out for hamburgers, they will probably head for the hamburger restaurant that is closest. They may like hamburger restaurant A better, but it is five miles from home, and hamburger restaurant B (comparable to A) is just three blocks away. So they go to B. The product is not so differentiated a product that they will drive five miles to get it. And they're mainly after a hamburger, not a special celebration.

If you are the manager of a luxury food service operation, the kind that serves elegant dinners that people will go out of their way for and travel to get to for a special occasion, you should be aware that your market is very apt to have a much broader geographical span than a typical fast-food service establishment. Know what your own market is and cater to it, whatever type of food establishment you have (luxury, fast-food, and so on). If most of your guests live within a few miles of your restaurant, you ought to know that. What your own market is or can be influences your pricing, your advertising, and your total approach to running a food service operation. If you know your market, it should help you decide how to advertise—by billboard, by radio (rock or classical), by citywide newspapers or local newsletters, and so on.

Find out what your market is. There are ways. During the past several years, industry research has shown that the average fast-food operation has its major market within a three-mile radius of the establishment. For example, a restaurant manager checked into this to find out for himself. He made a simple survey of his restaurant's market by having a contest. His guests had a chance to win a free fresh strawberry pie if they filled in a contest application form presented to all customers when they received their orders of food. The contest ran for one week. Twelve pies were given away. The response was good, so apparently most guests felt it was worth their while to take time to fill in the contest form.

The service personnel filled in what food the customers ordered and the time of day or night. Customers filled in their names, addresses, and ages. The blanks were filled in *only* by guests actually being served food at the restaurant, so it was a valid survey of the people who patronized the place.

Through the survey the operator was able to plot the geographical market area his guests came from. He learned that over 70 percent of his customers lived within three miles of his restaurant. He was also able to analyze his clientele by age bracket. He found out what time of day customers in different age groups were most likely to come to his establishment and what food they ordered.

For a total cost of $50 for the 12 pies and a lot of printed forms, he was able to get a fairly accurate determination of the major market for his own firm. This information helped him to:

1. Direct his advertising more effectively toward the specific market appropriate for him. He put ads in a local suburban paper aimed at his close-in market. He also advertised in the local high school paper because he found that teenagers were a considerable part of his market. He supported student activities at the high school.
2. The information helped him offer items most apt to appeal to his market.
3. The information helped him become aware of the fact that at different times of the day his restaurant was patronized by different specific age groups. Armed with this knowledge, he did a better job of catering to the wishes of these various groups of customers during the hours they came in.

You need to know about your market. The possibility of making a survey like this one, or any variation of it appropriate for your own operation, is something to keep in mind. It is a way to check the market you are now getting. It could also give you ideas for changes and improvements in your operation, and perhaps ideas for going after additional markets you had not thought of.

Supply and Demand

The meaning of the economic terms "supply" and "demand" are obvious, but ways in which the concepts involved in these two words can affect your operation may not be. When you offer products for sale to a market, you are a supplier for that market. People who come to you to get the product you sell constitute the demand for your product.

As a food service manager, you are a supplier of food service. You decide, based on many factors, what prices you will charge. The guests who eat at your food service operation make up the demand for what you supply.

In the following discussions, we will consider the relationships between the price of a product and the quantity of it that will be demanded. In general, the lower the price, the higher the demand.

Demand Curve

An easy way to picture a "demand curve" is to think of a group of Americans surveyed to find out how many have eaten a 100-dollar dinner (very small number), a 50-dollar dinner (a few), a 10-dollar dinner (quite a few more), and a 50-cent hamburger (probably virtually 100 percent of them have). On a graph, connect the points representing the number of people who have eaten a 100-dollar dinner, a 50-dollar dinner, a 10-dollar dinner and a 50-cent

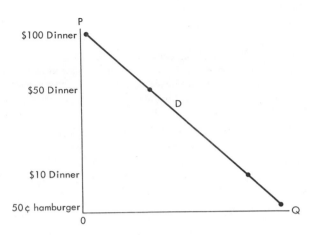

P: Price
D: Demand Curve
Q: Quantity of people who ate a meal for price indicated.

Chart 4-2 Construction of demand curve.

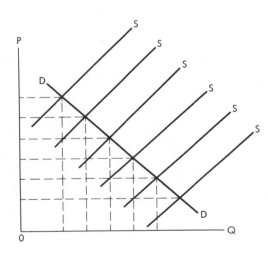

P: Price
D: Demand Curve
Q: Quantity (number of meals sold)
S: Supply Curves

Chart 4-3 Many different supply curves on the same demand curve.

hamburger and you've constructed a demand curve. That's what Chart 4-2 illustrates.

Chart 4-3 shows a demand curve with different food establishments supplying at different price points on the same demand curve. Different types of food operations supply at different price levels. At very high prices, there will probably be a small quantity demanded (very high prices, very few customers). At very low prices, there will probably be a large quantity demanded (very low prices, many customers). If you multiply the price charged for the item by the quantity demanded, you get the total revenue of sales for an establishment.

As a food service operator, you want to get all the revenue you can. Try to set prices that will appeal to the maximum number of individual customers for your type of business. This should increase the quantity demanded and maximize the revenue.

Types of Demand Curves

The following discussion concerns demand curves in terms of price elasticity (what happens when prices go up or down). The theory of demand curves can be applied in the food service industry. Later in this chapter we will discuss how these theories do apply to you.

1. Elastic Demand Curve (Chart 4-4).

Chart 4-4 shows a perfectly elastic demand curve. According to this chart (which is theoretical), an unlimited quantity of a product can be sold at price P_1. Nothing can be sold above P_1 because people can buy all they want

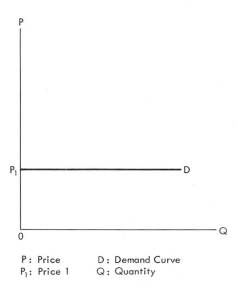

P : Price   D : Demand Curve
P_1 : Price 1   Q : Quantity

Chart 4-4 Elastic demand curve.

of the commodity at price P_1. It would be foolish to sell below P_1 since the buyer is willing to pay price P_1. The individual supplier can have no effect whatever on price.

A fairly good example of an industry with an elastic demand curve is the wheat market. Theoretically, one farmer can sell unlimited quantities at price P_1. Another farmer can sell unlimited quantities at the same price P_1. No one farmer alone can affect the price. But if all farmers join together and produce more wheat, this would increase the supply of wheat and cause P_1 to go down—cause the demand curve to fall. Or if all farmers join together and produce less wheat, this would decrease the supply of wheat and cause P_1 to go up—cause the demand curve to rise. But it would take the combined action of all farmers to cause the demand curve to move up or down. One individual farmer (or just a few farmers) cannot change the demand curve. There is a steady demand for wheat. Wheat is produced by thousands of farmers. No one farmer alone can affect the market. There are substitutes for wheat (rice, rye, barley, corn, etc).

2. Inelastic Demand Curve (Chart 4-5).

Chart 4-5 illustrates a perfectly inelastic demand curve. According to this chart (which is theoretical), any price can be charged for a certain item up to the point where quantity Q_1 has been consumed. It is an important item and consumers really want it. They are willing to pay nearly any price for it. But once they have satisfied their need for it and have enough to suit them, they don't want any more of the item now.

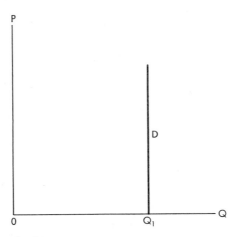

P: Price
D: Demand Curve
Q: Quantity
Q_1: Quantity 1

Chart 4-5 Inelastic demand curve.

A fairly good example of this type of item would be salt. People will pay what they must to get the quantity of salt they want—say, one pound. When they have bought their pound of salt and have it in the cupboard at home, they won't buy more until they're running low again. They will only buy one pound of salt at a time. They will buy more salt later, when the first pound is nearly used up, but for now they have plenty of salt and will not buy more. There is no good substitute for salt.

Neither of these two examples (wheat for elastic demand curve, salt for inelastic demand curve) is perfectly accurate. There are no "perfectly elastic" or "perfectly inelastic" demand curves except in theory.

3. Unit Elasticity Demand Curve (Chart 4-6).

Chart 4-6 illustrates a unit elasticity demand curve. The line that forms the 45-degree angle between the price axis and the quantity axis is the demand curve. A food service that sells at P_1, Q_1 would have the same total revenue (price times quantity) as a food service that sells at P_2, Q_2. Movement along this demand curve will not change total revenue. But it will change the price and the quantity consumed. As the price rises, quantity declines. As the price declines, quantity rises.

4. Combined Demand Curves (Chart 4-7).

Chart 4-7 shows all three demand curves—elastic, inelastic, and unit elasticity—on one graph. The area between the elastic demand curve EDC and

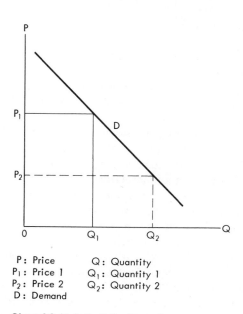

P: Price   Q: Quantity
P_1: Price 1 Q_1: Quantity 1
P_2: Price 2 Q_2: Quantity 2
D: Demand

Chart 4-6 Unit elasticity demand curve.

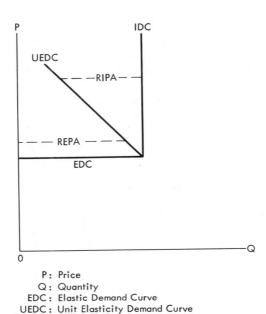

P: Price
Q: Quantity
EDC: Elastic Demand Curve
UEDC: Unit Elasticity Demand Curve
IDC: Inelastic Demand Curve
REPA: Relatively Elastic Price Area
RIPA: Relatively Inelastic Price Area

Chart 4-7 Combined demand curves showing elastic demand, unit demand, inelastic demand, relatively elastic area, and relatively inelastic area.

the unit elasticity demand curve UEDC is an area of relative price elasticity— relatively elastic price area REPA. The area between the unit elastic demand curve UEDC and the inelastic demand curve IDC is an area of relative price inelasticity—relatively inelastic price area RIPA.

If you are a student of food service, by now you're probably thinking (among other things), "When I'm a manager, how will I *know* the shape of my operation's demand curve and what am I supposed to do about it if I *do* know?" If you are already in the industry, maybe you're thinking, "I *don't* know the shape of my operation's demand curve and so what?" You don't have to know it. You should, however, understand the characteristics of a relatively elastic demand curve and a relatively inelastic demand curve. If your demand curve is relatively elastic (extremely rare for any food service operation) and you lower your prices, your number of guests should increase more than enough to offset the decrease in price. Your total revenue should increase. But if you have a relatively inelastic demand curve (and virtually all food service operations do have a relatively inelastic demand curve) and you lower your prices, your number of guests should increase but not enough to offset the decrease in price and your total revenue would decrease. This is a reason why you should not, as a general rule, lower your prices in an effort to attract more guests.

5. Relatively Elastic Demand Curve Showing Price Rise (Chart 4-8).

Chart 4-8 illustrates a relatively elastic demand curve showing price rise. The chart shows that you raise prices from P_1 to P_2. Quantity demanded decreases from Q_1 to Q_2. Area Q_1, Q_2, X, Y is bigger than area X, P_1, P_2, Z. Total revenue has decreased.

If you raise prices and your total revenue declines, or if you lower prices and your total revenue increases, then you have a relatively elastic demand curve. This means your customers are responding to price alone. They are informed about prices and are reacting to them. If your operation has a relatively elastic demand curve, price is the number one attraction. Price is more important to your guests than anything else. This would be extremely rare for any food service operation.

6. Relatively Inelastic Demand Curve Showing Price Rise (Chart 4-9).

Chart 4-9 illustrates a relatively inelastic demand curve showing price rise. You raise prices from P_1 to P_2. Your quantity declines from Q_1 to Q_2.

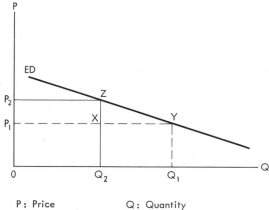

P: Price   Q: Quantity
P_1: Price 1 Q_1: Quantity 1
P_2: Price 2 Q_2: Quantity 2
ED: Elastic Demand

Price rose from P_1 to P_2

Quantity demanded fell from Q_1 to Q_2

Total quantity demanded fell from P_1, Y, Q_1, 0 to P_2, Z, Q_2, 0

The area represented by Q_1, Q_2, X, Y is greater than the area represented by X, P_1, P_2, Z

Total revenue has decreased

Chart 4-8 Relatively elastic demand curve showing price rise.

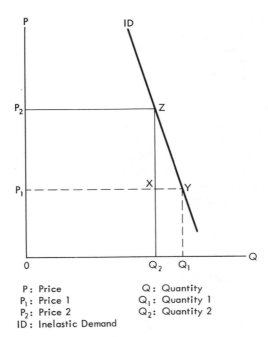

P : Price   Q : Quantity
P_1 : Price 1 Q_1 : Quantity 1
P_2 : Price 2 Q_2 : Quantity 2
ID : Inelastic Demand

Price rose from P_1 to P_2

Quantity demanded fell from Q_1 to Q_2

The area represnted by Q_1, Q_2, X, Y is smaller than the area
represented by X, P_1, P_2, Z

Total revenue has increased

Chart 4-9 Relatively inelastic demand curve showing price rise.

Area Q_1, Q_2, X, Y is smaller than X, P_1, P_2, Z. Your total revenue has increased. If your restaurant has a demand curve that is relatively inelastic and you raise prices, total quantity demanded should be reduced but total revenue should increase. If you lower prices, quantity demanded should increase but total revenue should decrease.

Restaurants have demonstrated this is true in recent years. They made reasonable increases in prices. Demand fell temporarily, if at all. But for many establishments, demand increased again not very long after prices were raised. This indicates that these food service establishments operate with relatively inelastic demand curves.

Purveyors' Demand Curve (example of relatively elastic demand curve)

It will probably make demand curves easier to understand if we take a minute here to examine relatively elastic demand curves. Purveyors have a *rel-*

atively elastic demand curve. Purveryors' customers are food service operations. Food service operations have a *relatively inelastic* demand curve.

There are two reasons why purveyors do have a relatively elastic demand curve:

1. Most food service operators (purveyors' customers) *are* very well-informed
   about prices.
2. Most food service operators *are* price-conscious.

Purveyors' customers (food service managers—you) are supposed to
be very price-conscious and knowledgeable about comparative prices. Food
service operators' customers (your customers), on the other hand, are not
usually very aware of comparative prices for similar items. They are not apt to
make extensive comparative studies of costs concerning what they are buying.
You (food service operation managers) are. That is why there is a difference
in demand curves. When food service operators buy food from purveyors,
there is a relatively elastic demand curve. When guests buy food from food
service operators, there is a relatively inelastic demand curve.

If all other things are equal, food service operators will buy from purveyors who offer them the product they want at the lowest price. Friendship,
degrees of service, convenience, reliability, honesty of purveyors, and other
factors can all affect the buyer-seller, operator-purveyor relationship. Thus
"all other things" are seldom equal. If they were equal, the demand curve
would have the characteristics of nearly perfect elasticity instead of relative
elasticity.

Most food service operators occasionally run into a situation where
purveyors call and say they've got too much of some item on hand and would
be willing to sell the item at a price below normal. Many food service operators
might take advantage of this lower price and go ahead and order some extra.
It's this type of thing that tends to make the purveyors' demand curve more
elastic. Food operators know normal prices and know if they're getting a bargain. They check with other purveyors, they're cost-conscious, and they take
pains to buy the best ingredients at the lowest possible price. (At least you're
supposed to do all this.) Your food service customers are not this meticulously
concerned with comparative prices and values. (At least the vast majority of
them aren't.)

Your purveyors' demand curve tends to be relatively elastic. Yours
is relatively inelastic.

What Demand Curves Mean To You

All of this discussion of economics and demand curves is meant to
convince you that you should not drastically lower your prices in an attempt
to attract customers unless you're positive your own customers:

1. Are very much aware of prices and know what prices are.
2. Consider price more important than any other factor.

If both of these situations are true in your case, your restaurant has a relatively elastic demand curve, which is very rare for a food service operation.

It's much more likely that your food service operation has a relatively inelastic demand curve and you should *not* drastically cut prices to attract customers.

The shape of your own operation's demand curve isn't the fact that's essential to you, although the more you know and understand about all these factors the better. What's vital for you to know and understand is *what* happens to your operation when you raise or lower your prices, and *why* it happens.

When a food service operation raises prices, it's usually a very small increase. For example, a steak house may raise its price for a steak from $5.00 to $5.50—a 10-percent increase in price. A hamburger establishment may raise the price of a hamburger from 20 cents to 25 cents—a 25-percent increase from its previous price. If both these restaurants had a relatively elastic demand curve, the steak house should have more than a 10-percent decline in the number of steaks sold, and the hamburger operation should have more than a 25-percent decline in the number of hamburgers sold. But it doesn't happen—because their demand curves are relatively inelastic.

Restaurants do make reasonable price increases. As their costs increase, they pass the increase on to their customers. (If the economy declines, they may have to reduce prices accordingly.) But many food operations don't experience a decline in quantities sold and this means they have inelastic demand curves. The price rise more than offsets any temporary decline in business, and their total revenue increases.

During inflationary periods, restaurants raise prices because of rising costs and inflation. But they don't generally lose so much business that their total revenue declines. In fact, just the opposite is true in many cases. Some restaurants serve fewer guests than they did before, but their total revenue increases. Most restaurants increase prices during inflation and, for a variety of reasons, serve more guests than previously. Total revenue may increase because people usually don't respond to price alone.

HOW THE ECONOMICS OF THE
FOOD AND BEVERAGE INDUSTRY AFFECTS YOU

There are managers of food service operations (although they are not managers for long, usually) who figure as follows: "I'll build up my food business by *really* lowering my prices. I'll take customers away from all my competitors. Then, after I get plenty of customers coming to my place, I'll raise prices.

I'll wind up with all the business I can handle and then I'll get my prices up there so I make a lot of money." It doesn't work.

The idea sounds great and a lot of food service operators do fall for it. But the premise is false. Guests are not really accurately informed about actual, specific prices within a general type of category of eating establishment. They rarely call a restaurant or ask anyone precisely how prices compare between eating establishments in the same general category. They are influenced by a restaurant's reputation in the community. They are definitely influenced by friends who say, "Yeah, go there. It's great. Costs a little more, but it's worth it," or, "Naw. Terrible. Slow. Cold steak."

Guests are not very conscious of price differences between comparable, competing restaurants unless these restaurants charge prices which are really quite different from each other. They don't care what restaurants are in direct competition with each other. If competing restaurants' prices are comparable and not very different from each other, they don't think *primarily* of price. They don't generally know or care whether you charge 11 cents more or less for your hamburgers at your hamburger restaurant than your competitors do, or $2 more or less for your steak at your luxurious steak house than your competitors do. If they've decided to go out to eat hamburgers and you have a hamburger restaurant they could go to, they are interested in the following factors in pretty much the following order:

1. How good your food is.
2. How good your service is.
3. How pleasant the surroundings are at your restaurant.
4. How clean your restaurant is.
5. Your price.

If they've decided to go out and eat steak, and you have a steak restaurant they could go to, they'll follow the same pattern, putting price, consciously or unconsciously, down in the line of the qualities they're looking for.

This reemphasizes the point that customers are interested in other factors besides price. Don't try to attract customers with price *alone*.

Don't engage in price competition. As a food service operator, you almost surely work in a situation of monopolistic competition. You almost surely sell a differentiated product. You're also pretty sure to function in an oligopoly. All of this applies unless you're in a very small, isolated town, or in some unusual situation where there just isn't any competition.

The above factors make price competition foolish if you do it past a reasonable degree. Others in your oligopoly can react to your prices if you get them very far out of line from theirs. If your prices get *way* too high, guests won't ignore it forever. They will eventually quit coming to your establishment and go to the other establishments in your oligopoly. If you set your prices *way* too low, the other operators in your oligopoly will not ignore it. If you don't cut quality to save yourself money, you will almost surely lower your profit and maybe take losses when you cut prices to extremes. If you do cut portion size and/or quality, you will probably only be able to cut prices to extremes if you offer a poor product and *that* will probably drive guests away, thus cutting your profit.

Others in your oligopoly will react to your actions, particularly if you *cut* your prices. They can react quietly by just watching you lose money. Or, if you're taking away their customers with your low prices, they can be forced to lower their prices to match yours. Then total revenue and profits for all food service establishments in your oligopoly will decline. Then you all will have lost. A price war is easy to start and hard to stop.

What *should* you do? Charge a *reasonable* price that's not too far out of line from your competitors' prices. You will have to decide what the term "reasonable" means in your own situation, and it is not always easy. There is no exact set of rules and no formula to help you. It will help you, however, to know who your competitors are, what prices they charge, and what they offer customers in return for the prices they charge. Charge prices that are *reasonable* for your guests and allow you to make a *reasonable* profit.

This chapter has concerned the economics of the food service industry. We have talked about prices in relation to quantity demanded. Food service owners decide what kind of food service operation they will have. They determine what type of establishment they will operate (hamburger restaurant, chicken house, steak house, luxury establishment with gourmet food). Prices should be appropriate for the type of establishment. Owners decide to supply food service at a particular point on a demand curve. Managers set actual prices. (Pricing procedures are discussed in Chapter 12.)

Knowledge of demand curves and general economics is simply another tool you use as a manager. The shape of your operation's demand curve in and of itself is not the vital thing. What counts is what happens to your food service operation's business when you raise or lower your prices. Setting the proper relationship between price and quantity can help you get the most total revenue and profits. If you know about relative elasticity and relative inelasticity, you should be able to predict what will happen when you raise or lower prices. This should help you make these adjustments sensibly. You should be able to predict whether your total revenue will increase or decrease if you raise or lower prices. Don't get your prices way too high or way too low.

In the next chapter we'll look at profit planning and investigate how you work in a planned way to get the most profits you can out of your total revenue. In Chapter 12 on menu pricing, we'll get into the details and mechanics of what you do when you sit down to decide what actual dollar and cents prices you'll print on your menu.

REVIEW AND DISCUSSION QUESTIONS

1. In what ways does a restaurant belong to an oligopoly and also engage in monopolistic competition at the same time?

2. What do restaurants offer for sale?

3. Explain the difference between relatively elastic demand and relatively inelastic demand.

4. Why is a purveyor's demand curve usually different from a restaurant's demand curve?

5. Why shouldn't restaurants plan to lower prices to attract more guests, try to get more guests coming to them, and then raise prices?

6. How can knowledge of economics help you when you price your menus?

5

Profit Planning

Objectives

This chapter discusses profit planning. After you have read this chapter, you should be able to:

1. Determine how much profit you want in dollars based on the owner's investment, and how much minimum profit you want as part of the sales dollar.

2. Determine how much money you can spend for overhead and labor cost.

3. Compute the maximum dollars you can spend for food cost and still obtain the profits you want.

In Chapter 1 we said that one of the main reasons why food service operations fail is the fact that managers do not understand accounting records. You, as a manager, should understand basic accounting. Accounting is a vital tool of management.

ACCOUNTING RECORDS

In the food and beverage industry, you use accounting records mainly to:

1. Keep track of assets, liabilities, and capital accounts. (Capital means owner's investment in the business—the same thing as owner's equity.) These three are called "balance sheet accounts."
2. Keep track of income and expense accounts. These two are called "profit and loss accounts."

Balance Sheet (Chart 5-1)

A balance sheet is a statement of the financial condition of a business at a specific instant in time. The balance sheet is dated the last day of a month or the last day of a year. Our sample balance sheet (Chart 5-1) is dated De-

Chart 5-1 Restaurant balance sheet December 31, 19_____

ASSETS		
CURRENT ASSETS		
Cash	$20,000	
Accounts Receivable	13,000	
Inventories	11,000	
Prepaid Expenses	6,000	
Total Current Assets		$50,000
FIXED ASSETS		
Land	$20,000	
Building	90,000	
Furniture and Fixtures	40,000	
Total Fixed Assets		150,000
Total Assets		$200,000
LIABILITIES AND CAPITAL		
CURRENT LIABILITIES		
Accounts Payable	$20,000	
Taxes Payable	4,000	
Accrued Expenses	16,000	
Total Current Liabilities		$40,000
First Mortgage		60,000
CAPITAL		
Capital	$75,000	
Retained Earnings	25,000	
Total Capital		100,000
Total Liabilities and Capital		$200,000

cember 31, 19_____, which means this statement reflects the balances in the assets, liabilities, and capital accounts as of the close of business on December 31, 19_____.

Profit and Loss Statement (Chart 5-2)

The profit and loss statement shows income and expenses of a business over a period of time. A profit and loss statement would be headed "For the month ending (date) " or "For the year ending (date) ." Our sample profit and loss statement (Chart 5-2) is headed "For the year ending December 31, 19_____," which means this statement shows all sales and expenses during the year 19_____ through the close of business on December 31, 19_____.

Chart 5-2 Restaurant statement of profit and loss for the year ending December 31, 19_____

Food Sales	$400,000	100.00%
Cost of Food Sold	176,000	44.00
Gross Profit	$224,000	56.00%
Controllable Expenses		
Payroll (labor)	$124,000	31.00%
*Payroll Taxes and Employee Benefits	10,000	2.50
*Direct Operating Expenses	17,000	4.25
*Advertising and Promotion	5,000	1.25
*Utilities	6,500	1.63
*Administrative and General	12,000	3.00
*Repairs and Maintenance	4,500	1.12
Total Controllable Expenses	$179,000	44.75%
Profit Before Occupation Costs	$45,000	11.25%
*Occupation Costs	11,000	2.75
Profit Before Depreciation	$34,000	8.50%
*Depreciation	7,500	1.87
Profit Before Income Tax	$26,500	6.62%
*Income Tax	6,500	1.63
Net Profit to Retained Earnings	$20,000	5.00%

*These are overhead.

Occupation costs includes real estate taxes, interest, and insurance.

Total desired profit:	$20,000	5%
Total labor:	124,000	31
Total overhead:	80,000	20
Total food:	176,000	44
Total:	$400,000	100%

Your profit and loss statement will tell you which one of the three following situations your operation is in:

1. Your sales are greater than your expenses. You have a profit.
2. Your sales and your expenses are close to equal. You are close to break-even.
3. Your expenses are greater than your sales. You have a loss.

The object of this chapter is to tell you how to plan for and get a profit.

Uniform Systems of Accounts

In the food, beverage, and lodging industry there are four very important books:

1. *Uniform System of Accounts For Restaurants.* [1]
2. *Uniform System of Accounts For Hotels.* [2]
3. *Uniform System of Accounts and Expense Dictionary For Motels—Motor Hotels, Small Hotels.* [3]
4. *Uniform System of Accounts For Clubs.* [4]

These four books tell you how to classify accounts for recordkeeping purposes for the various types of operations indicated. If you are in a corresponding type of food and beverage operation, study the Uniform System of Accounts that applies to your own unit. If you happen to be in a food operation not included in the Uniform System of Accounts just listed (hospital food service, for example), your food department will probably have its own system. You might suggest that your unit use the *Uniform System of Accounts For Restaurants* for your food service department if it seems feasible.

When you have learned how to use one of the Uniform System of Accounts books, you will know how to classify and set up the books for your firm. Make your books conform to the appropriate system. (There is infor-

[1]*Uniform System of Accounts For Restaurants,* 4th ed. rev. National Restaurant Association. Chicago, 1968.

[2]*Uniform System of Accounts For Hotels,* 6th ed. rev. Hotel Association of New York City, Inc. New York, 1963.

[3]*Uniform System of Accounts and Expense Dictionary For Motels—Motor Hotels, Small Hotels.* American Hotel and Motel Association. New York, 1963.

[4]*Uniform System of Accounts For Clubs,* 2nd ed. rev. Club Managers Association of America. Washington, D.C., 1967.

mation about understanding and using the systems in *How To Use The Uniform System of Accounts For Hotels and Restaurants.*[5])

As a food and beverage operations manager, you should not have to learn how to use a lot of different accounting systems. You should learn how to use the appropriate Uniform System of Accounts well and make your own unit's books conform. If you do, you can easily compare how you are doing with industry averages (which you can get through your Trade Association). It will also make it easier for you to move from one food and beverage operation to another. Set up the books wherever you are working and make them conform to the appropriate Uniform System. You will not have to learn a new way of keeping books. If you shift from one type of operation to another (from a motel to a club, for example), get out the Uniform System that now applies to you, learn it, and use it.

PLAN FOR A PROFIT

Chart 5-1 (p. 59) is a balance sheet. Chart 5-2 (p. 60) is a profit and loss statement. (These two sample charts use the same figures as the profit planning discussion in this chapter.) You need to understand these two types of financial statements so you can do profit planning. Do not just subtract expenses from sales to find out what your profit *was*. Instead, subtract *ahead of time* from *expected* sales the amount of profit you want to get so you know what's the maximum amount of money you *will* be able to spend for expenses and still get your profit. That's what profit planning is.

It is correct to use the following traditional accounting formula when you write up your monthly profit and loss statement: SALES minus ALL EXPENSES equals PROFIT.

For profit planning, however, use the following profit planning formula: ESTIMATED SALES minus DESIRED PROFIT equals MAXIMUM AMOUNT YOU CAN SPEND FOR EXPENSES.

Don't just hope that profit will be there when you receive you profit and loss statement. Don't wait until a period of time has ended to find out if you have a profit. Plan ahead of time—*before* you go after profit and *while* you're going after it. Use the profit planning formula stated above (ESTIMATED SALES minus DESIRED PROFIT equals MAXIMUM AMOUNT YOU CAN SPEND FOR EXPENSES) and make it work as you go.

Procedures for Profit Planning

The next table shows a procedure in both dollars and percents for profit planning. Deduct profit first. What is left is the maximum you can

[5]Douglas C. Keister, *How To Use The Uniform System of Accounts For Hotels and Restaurants.* National Restaurant Association. Chicago, 1971.

spend for labor cost, overhead cost, and food cost. Then deduct labor and overhead. What is left is the maximum you can spend for food. Deduct labor and overhead before food because labor and overhead are relatively fixed. Food cost is the only *truly* variable cost that is supposed to vary in relation to sales.

	$	%
ESTIMATED SALES	$400,000	100%
minus DESIRED PROFIT	20,000	5%
equals MAXIMUM AMOUNT YOU CAN SPEND FOR LABOR, OVERHEAD, AND FOOD	$380,000	95%
minus LABOR	124,000	31%
equals MAXIMUM AMOUNT YOU CAN SPEND FOR OVERHEAD AND FOOD	$256,000	64%
minus OVERHEAD	80,000	20%
equals MAXIMUM AMOUNT YOU CAN SPEND FOR FOOD	$176,000	44%

Say your total investment (net worth) is $100,000 and you want to earn a 20 percent rate of return on this total investment. You arrive at the profit dollars you want by doing the following:

1. $100,000 total investment multiplied by 20% desired rate of return equals $20,000 desired return on investment in dollars.
2. $20,000 desired return in dollars divided by $400,000 estimated sales equals 5%. This 5 percent is your minimum profit percent of the sales dollar.

In the rest of this chapter we will discuss and explain how and why you do the above procedure. For purposes of this discussion, let us say you are the sole owner of a food service establishment. Consider the amount of money you have invested in your business. ("Amount invested" means only the owner's equity and retained earnings, not the total assets of the business.)

Steps in Profit Planning

There are eight steps in profit planning. They are:

1. Total investment.
2. Desired return on investment.
3. Estimate your sales for next year.
4. Calculate profit percent.
5. Labor.
6. Overhead.
7. Food.
8. Labor, overhead, and food costs.

Total Investment

First, examine your balance sheet. It is important to separate your investment (total capital) from total liabilities. Your investment is composed of your original investment plus your retained earnings. "Retained earnings" means any profits you have put back into your business. The amount of your total investment will have a direct bearing on the amount of profit you should expect. The more you invest, the more profit in dollars you should get.

Desired Return on Investment

You know what your total investment is in dollars. Now decide what return in profit dollars you want. Most owners say, "All I can get." This is forthright but not very informative. You may be satisfied with a percentage return of 10, 15, 20, or 25. Say you have a total investment of $100,000, composed of $75,000 original investment and $25,000 retained earnings. A 10 percent annual return would be $10,000 a year profit; a 15 percent return would be a $15,000 profit; a 20 percent return would be $20,000 a year profit, and so on. We are just talking about return on investment now, not return on sales dollar.

You arrive at a feasible amount for return on investment by considering these factors:

1. Returns on money.
   What return would you get if you had put your money into insured savings accounts or insured certificates of deposit instead of into a food service operation? You would get the current rate of bank interest (5, 6, 7, 8 percent—depending on the current money market). You would also get no work, no worry, and no danger of losing any of your money.

2. Risk.
   The riskier a business is, the higher the rate of return from that business should be. People who invest their money in the food service business (or any other business) should get a higher return than they would if they had put their money into savings accounts or bank certificates. The food service industry is a *very* high risk business, so investors should expect an even higher return than they would from some other types of businesses. Many people who invest in food service operations are very disappointed with their profits. In fact, many go broke. High risk in any investment heightens the expectation of and hopes for large profit. It also increases the possibilities of failure. Risk is an important factor. In the food service business, risk is very high.

3. Entrepreneurship.
   This means you assume the ownership and risks of a business operation. You have taken your knowledge of the food service business (if you have any), you have sought out and hired individuals who (you hope) know their special functions in a food service operation, and you have placed these individuals in an operation that you hope will be attractive enough to draw clientele into the establishment. You are performing a service for the community by providing a food service operation. For this service you are justified in expecting a return.

4. Combination of return, risk, and entrepreneurship.

Suppose you have put $100,000 of your own money into your food service operation. As we said above, you could have invested your $100,000 in certificates of deposit, which would pay you perhaps 5 to 7 percent interest a year, and you would get $5,000 to $7,000 return each year for your investment with no work or risk whatever. If you invest in a food service operation instead, you cannot be blamed for wanting something like a 5½ percent return on money, *plus* a 10 percent return for risk, *plus* a 4½ percent return for service, for a total of a 20 percent return on your total investment. A 20 percent return is higher than return would be for lower risk ventures. Because of the greater risk involved, you should always get a higher return in this industry. You are providing a food service unit for your community and you are risking your money. You could lose your entire $100,000. Many have lost much larger amounts of money than that in the food service business.

It is easier to evaluate return than it is to evaluate risk and entrepreneurship. How do you put a value on risk and entrepreneurship? As a general guideline, 12 to 20 percent is considered a reasonable total return for your money in the food service industry. This will vary with the money market. Ask your local restaurant and/or hotel association, or check current trade publications for more information on this. Perhaps you will also have access to special studies prepared by national accounting firms for their clients. Consider the risk you take in investing your money in the food service business. What chance do you really have of succeeding? How much do you know about the food service business, its problems and intricacies? Some who invest have no food industry background whatsoever. Some of these people do well, some don't. Even if you do have knowledge of the industry it is no guarantee that you will be successful. A food service operation is virtually always a high-risk venture.

Unfortunately, there is no definite, perfectly accurate guideline for deciding what return you should get and for setting values on risk and entrepreneurship. Most food service owners want and try for a total return on investment (for risk, entrepreneurship, and interest return) of more than 15 percent.

5. Payback period.

Another way of looking at return on investment is: how long does it take you to recover your original investment? Many in the industry believe that if food service owners recover their original investment in five years or less, they have a good food service operation. The number of years it takes to recover the original investment is called the "payback period." If the payback period is five years, there would be an average return of 20 percent per year; 100 percent divided by five years would equal a 20 percent return on investment per year.

6. Actual rate of return on investment.

To compute the rate of return you actually do receive, you do the following:

NET PROFIT divided by TOTAL INVESTMENT equals RATE OF RETURN ON INVESTMENT.

If you are satisfied with your current return, then use your current return figure as your profit figure when you do profit planning for the future. If you are not satisfied with your current level of return, use a higher rate of return figure in your profit planning for the future.

7. Desired return in dollars.
Based on all the preceding information, decide on your desired rate of return. Multiply it by your total investment. For example, we've said you've put $100,000 as your total investment in your operation, so you'd say: TOTAL INVESTMENT $100,000 multiplied by your DESIRED RATE OF RETURN 20% equals your DESIRED RETURN IN DOLLARS $20,000.
You have invested $100,000 and you want at least $20,000 as your profit every year. (NET PROFIT equals TOTAL INVESTMENT multiplied by RATE OF RETURN.)

Estimate Your Sales for Next Year

The third step in profit planning is to estimate your sales for next year. Look at your past records. Examine past and recent trends in your sales. Consider the economy, local changes, competition, local city's growth patterns, and the like. Analyze next year from every angle you can think of. For example, if your food service operation did $379,000 in annual sales last year, and if you have some new promotion ideas for increasing sales, maybe you will feel safe and justified in estimating next year's sales at $400,000.

The key is—settle on a *realistic* figure of what you honestly do expect next year's sales volume will be.

Calculate Profit Percent

Use your desired return in dollars you calculated above in step 7, *"Desired return in dollars."* Divide this return in dollars figure by your estimated sales figure. This gives you the figure for the minimum profit percent you want per sales dollar.

In our example above, you want a $20,000 return on investment in dollars. This means you want $20,000 *minimum* profit each year—$20,000 desired minimum profit return in dollars divided by estimated sales of $400,000 means a minimum of 5 percent profit of the sales dollar. In this situation, sales is 100 percent and minimum profit is 5 percent. You can spend 95 percent of each sales dollar—no more—for food, labor, and overhead combined. Individual percentages for food, labor, and overhead can go up and down and vary in relation to each other, but do not let the *total* of these three exceed 95 percent or you're cutting into your profit.

Labor

To make an estimate of what you expect your labor cost will be in the future, the first thing you do is find out how much you spent for labor costs in previous years. Decide whether you think this amount is apt to increase or decrease or stay about the same. Think ahead. Presumably you will intend to try to reduce payroll through increased efficiency. But maybe you are also contemplating raises for your employees, which could overcome reductions for more efficiency and result in an increase in your payroll costs anyway.

Suppose last year your payroll was $120,000. You hope and expect to increase efficiencies and thus reduce your payroll by $2,000 ($120,000 minus $2,000 equals $118,000). But you also plan raises for your employees, which will increase your payroll by $6,000 ($118,000 plus $6,000 equals $124,000). So you estimate total labor cost for next year will be $124,000.

You started with $400,000 estimated sales. Subtract $20,000 for profit. This leaves $380,000 maximum available for all other expenses—labor, overhead, and food. Now subtract $124,000 labor from the $380,000. This leaves $256,000—the maximum amount you can spend for overhead and food.

Estimated labor cost is 31 percent—$124,000 ESTIMATED LABOR COST divided by $400,000 ESTIMATED SALES equals 31% ESTIMATED LABOR COST.

Overhead

The sixth step in profit planning is to estimate the dollars you will spend for overhead. Examine your books from previous years. You will probably find that overhead was a fairly constant percent of sales. If it was not and if it has been increasing, examine the areas where it has increased. Find out why overhead has increased and figure out ways you can lower it if you possibly can. Make a realistic evaluation of each item in overhead expense. Decide whether you think each is apt to increase, decrease, or stay about the same. Consider cost of utilities. Is your rent stable? Taxes going up? Cost of cleaning supplies increasing? Can you cut the cost of cleaning supplies by changing brands or training employees how to use them more economically? Look realistically at all overhead costs. Examine details. Cut where you can and realize that some costs will go up. Examine all factors as well and as thoroughly as you can.

Now you have analyzed all items in the overhead category and you have estimated a total dollar amount for overhead. Subtract this dollar amount estimate for overhead from the amount available for overhead and food. This gives you the amount you can spend for food. If, for example, you decide you will probably spend about $80,000 for overhead, then subtract the $80,000 from the $256,000 available for overhead and food. This leaves $176,000, which is the maximum amount you can spend for food.

Estimated overhead cost is 20 percent—$80,000 ESTIMATED OVERHEAD COST divided by $400,000 ESTIMATED SALES equals 20% ESTIMATED OVERHEAD COST.

Food

We just concluded in the preceding step that the most you can spend for food is $176,000. Estimated food cost is 44 percent—$176,000 ESTIMATED FOOD COST divided by $400,000 ESTIMATED SALES equals 44% ESTIMATED FOOD COST.

If any expense—food, labor, or overhead—goes over your estimated percentage, then you must reduce something else somewhere in food or labor or overhead so you do not go over 95 percent for the three of them combined. That untouchable 5 percent is your profit.

Labor, Overhead and Food Costs

Now use labor, overhead, and food cost per cents as guidlines to help see to it as you go along, day by day, that you will get that minimum 5 percent profit percent you're after.

Percentage Analysis

"Tradition" has at times taught the food service industry to put too much emphasis on percentages and not enough on actual dollars. "Percentage analysis" is also called "common size analysis." It means you have reduced a business to a common size—in other words, sales equals 100 percent.

Percentage analysis can help you analyze your business. In the food service business, percentage analysis means:

1. Sales is 100 percent.
2. Every other item is expressed as a percent of sales.
3. Sales is the denominator.
4. Expenses is the numerator.

Percentages are helpful guidelines in achieving dollars of profit. For most people, it seems to be simpler to compare increases or decreases in percentages from one period to another than it is to compare increases or decreases in dollars from one period to another.

Your costs are going to fluctuate during the year (or whatever time period your profit planning is being applied to). If labor cost is 30 percent, food cost is 45 percent, and overhead cost is 20 percent (95 percent total), you're okay. If labor is 32 percent, food is 44 percent, and overhead is 19 percent (95 percent total), you're okay. If one cost increase is offset by another cost decrease within the 95 percent total of costs, okay. Individual costs will vary. But keep track of the total combined cost. You've set 5 percent as your profit goal. So, if your total combined food, labor, and overhead costs go over 95 percent, you're going into that 5 percent which is your only hope for profit. Act fast. Put cost reduction policies into effect. Make reasonable increases in prices. Do both. Take action. Do something to help you make sure that by the end of the year (or whatever time period you're working on) you will get that 5 percent minimum profit percent you started out to get. You can't wait until the end of the time period to take corrective action. That's too late.

If your operation is running soundly, if your standards are where you want them, if your volume is where you want it, if your costs are currently below the levels computed and your profits are higher than you had planned (perhaps 7, 8, or 9 percent profit instead of the 5 percent profit you had planned according to our example), it does not mean you have to increase costs and lower your profit goal. It means you are getting more profit than you had set as your minimum profit goal. Great! In our example, 5 percent is the *minimum* profit you want. If more comes in, fine. The purpose of profit planning is to find out what your minimum profit should be and help you get that amount or more.

Owner's Salary

So far we have not discussed a salary for the owner. If you are an owner of a food service operation that is set up as a corporation and you also work as manager, you will pay yourself a salary. Deduct your salary along with the rest of the labor expenses. If you are an owner and also work as manager and *don't* pay yourself a salary (and you won't pay yourself a salary *if* your operation is set up as a partnership or a proprietorship because of tax law), then you should add to your return on investment the amount you would have to pay someone else to work as manager.

PROFIT PLANNING IS A GUIDE

Profit planning is another tool you use to give you a better chance of actually making profits. It has proved very effective for many who have used it correctly. It is not magic and it won't guarantee that you will get the return you want. But if you use profit planning, you will have a much better chance. It is certainly a better approach than no approach, or a play-it-by-ear approach, or an approach in which management reacts thoughtlessly to ups and downs without a logical, complete plan. If you do use profit planning, you will know what cash and what percent amount of your sales dollar you can safely spend for expenses and still get profit.

Don't just wait to look at figures when you get them in a profit and loss statement at the end of a period of time. When you see a profit and loss statement, the statement is history. So is your profit or loss. Keep analyzing all your costs. Constantly. Take positive and corrective action, if you need to, *before* you see your profit and loss statement.

It is vital that you know as you go along whether you are earning a profit or not. If it looks to you like your sales won't cover expenses and give you profits, then try increasing your advertising to raise your sales. Or make safe and reasonable price increases. Or decrease your costs without seriously damaging quality. Do all three. Do *everything* you can.

Profit planning, like any other management control technique, is just words if you don't act when you should. Plan in advance. Try your best to foresee what will happen. Do everything you can ahead of time to get the profits you want. That's what profit planning is. If you give yourself time to learn how to do it and if you use it right, it can serve you very well.

REVIEW AND DISCUSSION QUESTIONS

1. What are the steps in profit planning?
2. Why is food cost calculated last?
3. How can owner's salary affect profit?
4. How can you put a money value on risk and entrepreneurship?
5. A restaurant owner has $170,000 in investment and wants an 18 percent return. Estimated sales are $600,000. Estimated payroll cost is $180,000. Estimated overhead cost is $116,000.

   a. What should be the minimum profit in dollars? (Answer: $30,600.) Show how you arrive at the answer.

   b. What should be the maximum food cost in dollars and percent? (Answer: $273,400 and 45.57%.) Show how you arrive at the answer.

6

Breakeven Analysis

Objectives

This chapter tells you how to compute a breakeven point. After you have read this chapter, you should:

1. Be able to calculate your own breakeven point.
2. Know the relationship of fixed and variable costs to the sales dollar.
3. Know why breakeven analysis can be a useful tool.

Chapter 6

Breakeven analysis can be another useful tool for you. Your breakeven analysis tells you the point in dollar sales where your sales have exactly covered your expenses but you have earned no profit—the point at which you "break even." At breakeven point, your sales income exactly equals your combined total costs for food, labor, and overhead. There is no profit and no loss.

The formula for breakeven point is:

SALES equals LABOR COST plus OVERHEAD COST plus FOOD COST.

This chapter explains the steps in breakeven point calculation. We will also discuss the factors that affect the breakeven point.

Normally, you figure your breakeven point once a year based on your lowest possible costs. If conditions change dramatically—if your sales decline to a new low, for example—by all means do compute a new breakeven point.

To compute your breakeven point, you have to consider labor cost, overhead cost, and food cost. To do the breakeven formula, assume your labor and overhead are fixed costs and food is your only variable cost.

FIXED AND VARIABLE COSTS

Costs are fixed or variable in relation to what your sales are. Your breakeven point can go up or down if your costs go up or down. If the figures you use when you compute your breakeven point change, your breakeven point will change accordingly. Any changes up or down in your costs make your breakeven point move up or down, too. For example, if you hire another employee, it increases your labor cost and raises your breakeven point. If you switch to a meat purveyor who will sell you the same quality meats at lower cost, it decreases your food cost and decreases your breakeven point.

Costs are fixed or variable in actual fact, not just theory, in relation to what your sales are. An example of variable labor payroll would be where you anticipate greater volume and add more personnel to take care of it. In this situation, predicted labor costs have varied in proportion to predicted sales. The same thing is true in terms of overhead. If you use more napkins or linen because of increased sales, it's a variable cost. You expect to use more of these items as sales increase.

Heat and light are examples of costs that do vary, but that do not vary because of sales. They are, however, called fixed costs for the purposes of making a breakeven analysis. You turn up the heat if a room is cold. The expense for gas has increased. But it has not varied because of sales. It has varied because of the weather. If it is cold outside, you heat the room. If the room is dark, you turn on the lights. Heat and light vary because it is cold or dark, not because of sales and the number of people in the room, although we should note that you may want to turn the heat up or down or hike up or lower the air-conditioner setting depending on the size of the crowd in a room. For purposes of making a breakeven analysis, however, you have to assume that overhead and labor are fixed and only food is variable.

A fixed cost does not change because sales go up or down. A fixed cost is not affected by your volume. For example, your rent doesn't change, your depreciation doesn't change, your interest payments don't change, no matter what your sales are. These bills are due no matter what kind of volume you are getting. They are not affected by sales.

If your business is operating, you will automatically have certain minimum expenses. You have to have employees. You have to have heat, light, and supplies whether you get customers or not. At a minimum anticipated level of sales, you have to anticipate minimum expenses for payroll and overhead. For this minimum anticipated level of business, payroll and overhead are fixed costs.

Say you estimate $4,000 to $5,000 business next week. Based on this estimate, you schedule 10 employees for next week. Payroll will be Z amount of dollars next week. But if you estimate $3,000 to $4,000 worth of business next week instead of $4,000 to $5,000, you schedule 8 employees for next week and expect a payroll of Y amount of dollars instead. Predicted payroll is fixed for the predicted amount of business. When you have made your estimate and have done your scheduling for next week, your payroll is fixed for that estimate.

ANALYZE AND ESTIMATE YOUR LABOR, OVERHEAD, AND FOOD COSTS

In the following example of how to make estimates of costs to use in your breakeven analysis, we will assume that you estimate your operation will do $4,000 to $5,000 sales next week. We will suppose that your sales have never gone below $3,000 a week nor over $6,000 a week. You will assume that this $3,000 to $6,000 level of business will continue next week. Based on this, you anticipate certain expenses for next week. In the example below, you anticipate that your sales for next week will be between $4,000 and $5,000. You don't expect to hit minimum $3,000 or maximum $6,000 next week.

The following approach to breakeven analysis is simple. You have to examine and make estimates of three costs:

1. Labor.
2. Overhead (all costs besides labor and food).
3. Food.

Food services usually operate on a weekly cycle. Most managers schedule employees on a weekly basis, purchase on a weekly basis, etc. For most operators, it is more realistic to annually calculate a weekly breakeven point.

Labor Cost

For breakeven analysis, labor is called fixed. For your estimated

$4,000 to $5,000 business next week and your employee schedule for next week, it *is* fixed.

Make an estimate of what you think your sales will be for next week. We'll say you estimate your sales will be between $4,000 and $5,000 next week. You'll have to have a certain number of employees to handle the work involved in doing the $4,000 to $5,000 level of business you predict for next week. Make a list of all the employees you will need next week—manager, department heads (such as chef, hostess), waiters, dishwashers, and others— the *minimum* number of personnel you'll need to take care of this estimated $4,000 to $5,000 business. Consider both full-time and part-time employees. Figure only the hours people will actually work—hours you will actually pay for. Add up what it will cost you for employees for next week. This is your estimate for next week's total labor cost. This is the minimum payroll you'll pay for the minimum number of employees you'll need if you are to satisfactorily conduct this $4,000 to $5,000 worth of business you've predicted.

Schedule the minimum number of employees to take care of this estimated volume of business. In terms of this estimated $4,000 to $5,000 volume of business, your payroll is a fixed cost. If you estimate a sales volume higher than $4,000 to $5,000, you will plan more employees, more wages, and a higher payroll cost. If you estimate a lower sales volume, you will plan for fewer employees and lower wages. But for this $4,000 to $5,000 estimated volume of business, your payroll is fixed. It's fixed by your prediction only.

Overhead Cost

For breakeven analysis, overhead costs are called fixed because for your estimate they *are* fixed.

For overhead, get a yearly figure and then divide it by 52 to get a weekly estimate. Use the weekly figure for next week. It's best to estimate a yearly overhead figure and then divide by 52 to get a weekly figure. Overhead expenses vary in such a way that the manager has only limited control over them. Air conditioning will increase during summer, heating costs will go up in winter, and so on. Overhead costs can vary from one time of year to another. Contrast this with labor, which the manager can control to some extent by scheduling.

Your overhead estimate cannot be exact from week to week because you use costs that have been averaged out for the whole year. Your average weekly estimated overhead costs will always fluctuate from actual weekly figures. During some weeks, costs will go higher than your average figure. During other weeks they'll be lower. But this procedure should give you a fairly good indication of your average weekly overhead expenses.

Overhead includes all expenses that are not food cost or labor cost. Overhead includes direct operating expenses such as utilities, repairs, and maintenance; cost of cleaning supplies; paper and linen costs, and more—any and all of your direct operating costs excluding labor costs or food costs.

Overhead also includes all of your capital expenses, such as depreciation, rent, taxes, interest, and general insurance.

Analyze each overhead expense carefully to see if any of them can be cut down through efficiency, economy, or other means. Or if some may increase. Then add up a year's overhead costs. The total figure you get is your estimated overhead cost for next year. Make your year's estimate as realistic as you can. Divide this figure by 52. The figure you get is your average estimated overhead cost per week, and you use this figure as your weekly amount for overhead when you do breakeven analysis.

In order to do your breakeven analysis, you do call overhead a fixed cost. It's fixed by your estimate only.

Food Cost

The only cost that is really variable is food cost—this is the only cost that does vary with sales.

Food cost is usually stated as a percentage of sales: FOOD COST divided by FOOD SALES multiplied by 100 to convert to a percentage equals FOOD COST PERCENT PER DOLLAR SALE.

As your sales increase, the dollar amount you spend to buy food will increase. But the proportionate relationship of food cost to sales should stay constant. Your food cost in dollars will change. Your food cost percent should not change.

FORMULA FOR BREAKEVEN POINT CALCULATION

The formula for breakeven point is:
SALES equals PAYROLL COST plus OVERHEAD COST plus FOOD COST EXPRESSED AS A PERCENT OF SALES.

At breakeven point, your sales equal your payroll cost plus your overhead cost plus your food cost.

When you do a breakeven analysis, you do not know your sales in dollars or food cost in dollars yet, but you can put your estimates for the other figures into the formula. For example, say your estimated payroll cost is $1,500 for next week based on your $4,000 to $5,000 anticipated level of sales. And the figure you've come up with (taken from your year's overhead total) for average weekly overhead cost is $1,000. For our example, let's say you want a 40 percent food cost percent. You can fill in some of the formula:

SALES (don't know sales figure yet) equals LABOR COST $1,500 plus OVERHEAD COST $1,000 plus FOOD COST PERCENT OF SALES DOLLAR 40%.

You want a 40 percent food cost percent. Sales is 100 percent. Move the food cost percent of sales dollar (40 percent) from one side of the formula to the other. You get:

SALES 100% minus DESIRED FOOD COST PERCENT OF SALES DOLLAR 40% equals LABOR COST $1,500 plus OVERHEAD COST $1,000.

Then you can say:

60% OF SALES equals LABOR COST $1,500 plus OVERHEAD COST $1,000.

Then you can do the following:

SALES equals $2,500 divided by 60%

and:

SALES equals $4,166.66.

Now you know your breakeven point. It's $4,166.66. That is the breakeven point in the example we have been using.

Then you can go on:

BREAKEVEN POINT $4,166.66 minus $2,500 (OVERHEAD $1,000 plus LABOR $1,500) equals FOOD COST $1,666.66.

There's another way to find your food cost. Do the following:

BREAKEVEN POINT $4,166.66 multiplied by DESIRED FOOD COST PERCENT 40% equals FOOD COST $1,666.66.

Do both of these formulas directly above to see if you made a mistake. You should get the same answer from both formulas.

Now you've got your food cost in dollars as a proportion of sales. So now you can write your breakeven formula as follows:

SALES $4,166.66 equals LABOR $1,500 plus OVERHEAD $1,000 plus FOOD COST $1,666.66.

Sales is equal to total of labor, overhead, and food costs.

This is the breakeven point.

At this point you have exactly covered your costs. But you haven't got any profit.

The above example shows the steps you do to compute your breakeven point.

The above breakeven formula can be useful to you. It is a tool you can use to analyze your business and it can help you. Breakeven analysis can tell you when you start to earn profit based on your estimate of sales in dollars. In the case of our example, your breakeven analysis would tell you that if your sales next week start to decline toward $4,166.66 (breakeven point), you have to watch costs and reduce them wherever possible—more than normal. It tells you to make *every* effort to promote sales—more than normal. Many firms that make good use of their knowledge of their breakeven point and stay right on top of things will increase their advertising budget the minute their sales start to decline toward the breakeven point.

Use common sense in your reactions to sales ups and downs. If sales start to slip, don't go overboard and fly into a frenzy of unplanned moves. Don't rush into hysterical activity. But don't ignore it if your breakeven analysis does warn you that you should act. Move logically and thoughtfully if breakeven analysis indicates you should. Most businesses are cyclical. You will have high periods and low periods of sales. If you know your breakeven point, you know what volume of business you need to have in order to cover costs and not lose money.

There's an old saying in the food service business: "Volume of sales can cover a multitude of sins." The "sins" include poor management and poor planning. Don't count on volume to take care of you.

Through proper planning, you should be able to compute your breakeven point and find the dollar amount of sales revenue needed to exactly equal your expenses. When your sales start to exceed your costs, you will begin to get profit. Know what volume you must have in order to cover your costs.

Be realistic and sensible in using your breakeven point information. In the example discussed in this chapter, breakeven point was calculated to the exact penny. But we used an average breakeven point based on some average costs and assumptions pertinent to that particular example only. If *your* sales get down *around* your breakeven point level, you know you're not earning a profit and you should get going to improve the situation. That is the important thing to remember.

Chart 6-1 shows our example of breakeven analysis in chart form. Costs are plotted on the vertical axis and sales are plotted on the horizontal axis. The sales line shows increase in cost and revenue proportionately. Because the cost scale and the sales scale increase at exactly the same proportionate rate on our graph, this line is drawn at a 45-degree angle to the vertex of the graph. Overhead and payroll are shown as straight lines to cost because these are fixed costs. The food cost line varies. It is proportionate with sales and it's the only *truly* variable cost. After the food cost line intersects the sales line, costs do not exceed sales.

When sales are higher than costs, a business gets a profit. That is the *only* time a business gets a profit.

As we said at the beginning of this chapter, knowing what your breakeven point is and how you should react as business gets below, at, or above breakeven can be a very useful tool for a food service manager. It helps you pinpoint the dollar sales level at which profits are earned. If you're getting down toward your breakeven point, try to reduce total costs so a smaller sales volume will cover costs. Reduce food cost percent. Reduce labor and overhead costs. Then you can earn profit at a lower volume of sales. You will have a lower breakeven point. But don't reduce your costs so much that you impair your service or quality. It is a good idea to reduce costs *and* step up your sales promotion program to help you increase sales during slow periods when you

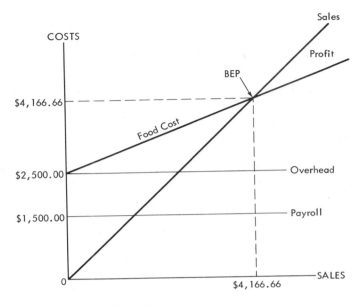

BEP : Breakeven Point

Chart 6-1 Breakeven Chart

are heading down toward your breakeven point. If your costs have changed, compute a new breakeven point so you know where you stand.

Knowing what breakeven point means and how to figure out your own is important. Breakeven point tells you when your costs are exactly equal to your income. If your sales are heading down toward your breakeven point, you're apt to be in trouble. Act to reverse the decline. If you are *at* your breakeven point or below it, you do indeed have troubles and must make an all-out effort to change your predicament and get above your breakeven point.

If your breakeven analysis tells you you are at or near your breakeven point, reduce all the costs you can, except probably advertising cost. If costs are absolutely as low as you can get them and you're at breakeven point, any further reduction of costs might cut quality of your total operation and hurt future business. Then you can still try to increase sales through planned advertising, extra promotion, and better service to guests. You could, for example, advertise on radio or in newspapers, bring in some entertainment on what you expect to be an extra slow night (if you can afford it and if this is appropriate for your operation). Analyze your own market again, more thoroughly, and aim promotion and advertising more accurately at it if you can. See if you can expand your market, and consider adding another type of market to what you already have.

Breakeven analysis is another tool that can help you. Like any of the other tools and controls we've talked about or will discuss in the rest of this book, it's absolutely a waste of time if you don't *act* and act correctly if any of your tools or systems tell you it's time for you to act.

REVIEW AND DISCUSSION QUESTIONS

1. When you are calculating your breakeven point, why do you consider labor cost a fixed cost?

2. Why is food cost the only *truly* variable cost?

3. What are the steps in breakeven point calculation?

4. How can knowledge of breakeven point make you a better manager?

5. A restaurant manager has estimated sales for next week at $6,750. The manager has scheduled employees at a cost of $1,725. Average overhead is $1,150 and desired food cost is 38%.

   a. What is the breakeven point in dollars? (Answer: $4,637.) Show how you arrive at the answer.

   b. What is the food cost in dollars at the breakeven point? (Answer: $1,762.) Show how you arrive at the answer.

   c. If sales are $6,750, what should the profit be? (Answer: $1,310.) (Don't forget to multiply your sales by your desired food cost percent to get your food cost in dollars.) Show how you arrive at the answer.

7

Payroll Cost Control

Objectives

This chapter discusses things you can and cannot do to control payroll costs. After you have read this chapter, you should be aware of:

1. The importance of scheduling, and other factors that affect your payroll cost.
2. Steps that you can take to control your payroll cost.
3. Methods and procedures for doing payroll analysis and payroll budgeting.

For a lot of food and beverage operations today, the biggest problem is payroll cost and trying to control it. For many, it's a bigger problem than food control or beverage control. Many operations that do successfully control food and beverage costs experience extreme difficulty controlling payroll costs.

Wages have risen continuously since the late 1930s. For many establishments, payroll cost is higher than material cost. Large hotels, for instance, can have food cost near 30 percent, but their food and beverage payroll cost may top 40 percent.

PAYROLL COST PERCENT FORMULA

Use the following formula to calculate your payroll cost percent:
COST OF LABOR divided by TOTAL SALES multiplied by 100 to convert to a percentage equals LABOR COST PERCENT OF SALES DOLLAR.

This formula gives you historical information. It tells you what your payroll cost was for the past month or week (or whatever accounting period you used it for). The information comes too late to help you control payroll costs for the payroll period it has covered. Use the formula to get information about your labor cost percents for your historical records. These records inform you of what *has* happened so you can act from your knowledge of your past experience to control what *will* happen to your labor cost percent in the future.

TIME-SAVING AND LABOR-SAVING DEVICES

"Time-saving" and "labor-saving" devices can cut payroll cost under certain conditions, or they can actually wind up raising your costs if you're not careful. Make sure you are saving money by using them, not losing money. If you use time-saving and labor-saving devices, you may be paying less, the same, or more than you would pay for payroll without them. You should know what costs are involved in these devices and whether you are saving money, losing money or breaking even if you are using them. If you use these items, appliances, and devices thinking they'll save payroll cost, find out if they really do or not. You might decide to use them anyway, even if they do increase payroll costs, but you should be fully aware of all the cost facts before you decide.

Examples of time-saving and labor-saving devices include:

1. Conveyors for moving goods to and from dining room.
2. Vertical and horizontal cutters, slicers, dicers, shredders, and the like to replace knife work by hand.
3. Liquid dispensers, which can speed up beverage service and save handling

time. Many of these can also measure the exact amounts of beverage you want if they can be set to do the work of portioning.

4. Electric mixers, blenders, beaters, and such to replace the work of blending ingredients by hand.

5. Electronic ovens, which can reduce food cooking, reconstituting, and handling time.

6. Food items that reach you pre-portioned and/or fully cooked—ready to heat and serve. These can include entrees of all types—roasts, steaks, stews, chicken, fish—plus items such as frozen French fries, instant mashed potatoes, soup base, biscuit mix, canned puddings, ready-to-use sauces, instant whipped toppings, and so on.

Most of the above items and devices are used in the kitchen area. Guests don't see them. Guests are very interested in the quality of food they get from you, but they're not concerned about whether your operation made all the food items "from scratch" or bought them fully or partly pre-prepared or used time-saving equipment to prepare them—just so they taste good.

Offer good quality food and good service in pleasant surroundings. If you can streamline your operation and reduce payroll cost enough or do enough extra volume to pay for time-saving and labor-saving devices without lowering the quality of food, service or atmosphere below your standard, then you can use time-saving and labor-saving devices.

Substitute Pre-Prepared Items for Labor

Some operations do well serving all sorts of special foods which they do make from scratch. It depends on what is appropriate for an operation, its market, and its prices.

You may be able to cut payroll costs by buying and using pre-prepared items instead of having your own labor prepare them from scratch. For example, it is less expensive for most food service operations to buy bread and pastries from purveyors instead of making their own. Purveyors are geared to serve many food service operations. Wholesalers and purveyors can probably produce and sell baked goods to you in the quantities you need for less cost to you than it would cost you to bake your own goods in your own operation. The same idea usually holds true for cutting your own meat. Many operations would save money buying pre-portioned meats.

In the future, the food service industry will probably use more pre-packaged (or at least pre-cut) meats as well as salads, cole slaw, and other items. Many food service operations no longer peel their own potatoes, for example, but buy them already peeled. Where you can pay less for a wholesaler's labor than you would pay in payroll to your own employees, do it *if* quality meets your standards and if total advantages outweigh any disadvantages.

The key, of course, in terms of payroll control versus time- and labor-saving devices is that every time you switch from doing something using your own labor and substitute a pre-prepared item (pre-cut salads, pre-cut steaks, goods already baked, potatoes already peeled, and so on), you *must* also reduce the number of your employees or hours worked. If you don't, you haven't cut payroll. If you don't save money by cutting payroll, then your sales must increase so you serve more guests and achieve greater volume with the same number of employees and the same payroll.

If you buy pre-prepared labor-saving items but don't cut down on your personnel and payroll *or* increase your volume, you can wind up paying more than ever. You can use labor-saving devices or pre-prepared foods successfully and economically only if you can actually reduce the number of employees you have or if you can do more business without adding personnel. Salespeople will tell you, "Buy my product. It will save you labor costs." If you forget to cut payroll simultaneously, or don't get enough increased volume to cover you, then your only correct answer to this sales pitch may be, "Come back next month. I can't afford to save any more money that way this month."

Pre-preparation and labor-saving methods used behind the scenes (not where customers see it) is probably where you can reduce the number of personnel who run the operation. Don't reduce service personnel to the point where you cut the quality of your service. In the kitchen you can probably try to use fewer personnel to handle more work through the use of pre-cut, pre-portioned, and pre-prepared foods.

The number of guests that your kitchen crew can take care of will vary depending on what type of work they have to do. Substitute pre-prepared items where the work has been done for you if you don't lose money doing it. Purveyors can mass-produce items that you would have to prepare in limited quantities. They can probably use their labor more efficiently than you use yours to produce the same goods per employee.

The food service industry has a reputation for low productivity. Other industries have used various phases of pre-preparation of goods to increase productivity. The food service industry should be able to do it, too. There is a shortage of skilled employees in the food service industry. Substitution of pre-prepared entrees instead of food items made from scratch can help offset this shortage of skilled workers if you do it on a careful, selective basis.

If you use pre-prepared foods, you should analyze what food products are available. You can probably find a product at a price you can afford that will satisfy your standards and help you cut payroll.

FACTORS WHICH AFFECT PAYROLL COST

A number of factors will affect your payroll cost. They include:

1. Type of business.

2. Volume of business.
3. Peak periods.
4. Physical facilities.

Type of Business

A service restaurant with tables and/or booths will need more service personnel than a fast-food operation. A cafeteria is different from either and will have different needs concerning the number of personnel it uses. Type of business and type of service affect the skill level needed by employees. This in turn affects the number of employees needed, which in turn affects payroll costs.

Volume of Business

Usually the more volume you have, the more personnel you need. As we discussed in Chapter 6 on breakeven analysis, a minimum staff is necessary to keep the operation functioning. If volume drops very low, you still may *have* to keep a certain minimum number of personnel on your payroll even though your volume doesn't justify it. This is particularly true if you have a hard time replacing employees when you have temporarily laid some off. You also have the problem of guaranteeing full-time work for the personnel you must keep.

Volume of sales has a very strong effect on payroll cost. During periods of high volume, payroll costs will usually get smaller in percentage terms (although not necessarily in dollars) because the same employees should do more work than they do during periods of slower business.

Peak Periods

1. Time of day. You will probably have certain times of the day when you are busier than you are at other times. Volume usually does vary with the time of day. Many food service establishments today serve more customers at lunch, although they may generate more dollar volume at dinner. They have to have personnel on duty to take care of guests whenever guests are there.

2. Days. You will probably get peak periods in terms of different days of the week. Many food and beverage operations do more business on Friday and Saturday nights, for example, than they do during the rest of the nights of the week combined. This certainly has a bearing on payroll costs.

3. Weekly. Employees are usually scheduled a week at a time. Persons making out the week's schedule estimate business for each day for the coming week, realizing that business will vary from day to day. Weekly projections and schedules affect the weekly payroll cost. Weeks are then combined into months to find the monthly cost, but payroll scheduling is usually looked at on a weekly instead of a monthly basis. When you analyze weekly and monthly payroll, however, you look at past records to see if employees were scheduled properly.

4. Seasonal. A lot of businesses experience seasonal fluctuation. Some food service operations located in cities encounter reduced business during summer months, when their regular guests may engage in outdoor leisure activities instead of going out for dinner or may leave town for vacations. For summer resorts, on the other hand, summer is the peak business period. For winter resorts, of course, the peak is winter. Both summer and winter resorts will probably have very sharp changes between their peak periods and their off-seasons. Resort operations usually face extreme problems in terms of seasonal peak periods.

   Seasonal resorts that try to stay open year-round usually have great difficulty. Some resorts have large summer business and/or large winter business, but fall and spring can wipe out their profits because volume is so low. And they still may have to keep key employees on the payroll year-round just to stay open even during their slowest periods.

5. Banquets. There is another possible peak factor. Banquets may mean much higher volume for you. You may have to bring in extra employees to take care of the work involved in serving a banquet. This can throw quite a strain on your entire food service unit, particularly if you don't serve many banquets. Payroll can skyrocket. Your payroll cost in actual dollars may increase, but payroll cost as a percent of sales may decrease due to the increased volume of sales. For example, let us say your sales usually run about $10,000 a week and your payroll is usually $3,000 (30 percent). When you serve a banquet, your sales can go up to $13,000 for the week and your payroll can go up to $3,500 (down to 27.77 percent).

   When you serve banquets, don't allow the quality of your service to go down—particularly for non-banquet guests.

Physical Facilities

Facilities and layout can have a very definite effect on payroll costs. For example, if your storage areas and kitchen are badly organized, it can cost you money for extra payroll. If it's a long walk from your kitchen to your dining room, it can cost you extra money in payroll. If your facilities prevent efficient work, you are probably paying for wasted time and motion. Poorly laid-out facilities can result in confusion, waste, and increased payroll cost.

Normally, a manager cannot make changes in the physical layout of the operation's facilities without getting special approval from the owners. Sometimes correcting and improving physical facilities can entail a lot of money, and many owners will not spend it.

On the other hand, placing hot plates and coffee pots at strategic locations in the dining room can cost relatively little and can save a lot of time for your service personnel. Moving the storage area for clean dishes in the kitchen so the dishes are closer to the food may be an inexpensive way to help speed up service and reduce wasted motion and effort.

As a manager you may want to recommend to your employer that more complex, extensive changes should be made to achieve top efficiency. Your recommendations may or may not be approved. Nevertheless, you should always examine and analyze your present facilities and layout. Figure out if, where, and how you *could* make minor changes in areas within your own jurisdiction which will promote greater efficiency, save time, and allow more guests to be served better with no increase in payroll costs.

PAYROLL COST IS HARDER TO CONTROL THAN FOOD COST

Payroll cost is much harder to control than food or beverage cost. You pay for food, prepare it, and offer it for sale. If you don't cook food and sell it today, you can cook and sell it tomorrow. If you have cooked it today and do not sell it today, there is still a chance that you can rework it into another dish and sell it tomorrow. But payroll cost is different. You pay your labor and there are no variations or alternatives available to help you. If labor is not used effectively today, you pay for it anyway. It is wasted and no cost recovery is ever possible. Payroll money spent on employees who just stand around is gone forever. You cannot store up labor you pay for like you can store food you pay for. If labor payroll is wasted, it is irretrievable.

Your employees may work harder on certain days than they do on others. Say, for example, Friday's business is three times bigger than Tuesday's. Does this mean all your employees worked three times harder on Friday than they did on Tuesday? Probably not.

On slow days, extra work should be done to prepare for busy days. Slow business days are the times when employees should do work they cannot do at all or cannot do thoroughly on very busy days. On very busy days, employees can usually just manage to take care of guests with no time for other work for which they're responsible.

SCHEDULING

There *is* something you can do to control payroll costs—develop sound procedures for scheduling employees. Schedule your employees so they will be on hand when you need them and won't be there when you don't need them. Scheduling is *the* major tool you can use to control payroll costs.

You have to use your forecasts of expected business in order to come up with good scheduling plans. If you make up one basic schedule for employees and use it unchanged week after week, you will probably get high payroll costs. Change and adapt schedules as you go. Business fluctuates from day to day and week to week, and you have to make allowance for this when you schedule your employees. You have to know some fundamental facts about your own operation. You have to be able to forecast how busy you will probably be during different days, weeks, and months. You have to become adept at anticipating your future business on an hourly, daily, weekly, and seasonal basis. Schedule accordingly. If your forecast is too high, you will schedule too many employees and pay too much payroll. If you forecast too low, you will schedule too few employees, and the quality of service and total product can go down.

There will be times when you will need only a minimum crew on hand and other times when you will need a maximum crew. Sometimes you will be able to schedule almost perfectly and you will need almost precisely the number of personnel you scheduled. There will be other times when you will make wrong predictions and overschedule or underschedule. If you over-schedule, your payroll cost will be too high. You will pay employees to stand idly around or to do small jobs they *could* squeeze in another time when they really should be there. If you underschedule, you will not have enough em-ployees on hand to serve your guests adequately.

Review and adjust your employee work schedules constantly. Try to schedule employees so they will be there only when you need them.

You will also have to leave some leeway in your scheduling to accom-modate your employees' wishes. Be ready to shuffle and rearrange work schedules depending on when your employees are available. All employees have individual problems and outside obligations. When you have come up with good, accurate schedules based on sound predictions of business, that's only half the battle. The rest consists of arranging all kinds of individual accommodations so employees and schedules are compatible.

OTHER STEPS YOU CAN TAKE TO HELP CONTROL PAYROLL COST

Scheduling is your major tool for controlling payroll. There are other methods and ideas you can use, too. They include:

1. Spanner shift.
2. Schedule employees to arrive when they're needed.
3. Report to work in uniform.
4. Part-time employees.
5. Have employees on call.
6. Use of overtime.
7. Send employees home early.

Spanner Shift

Many operations schedule employees on a shift basis. Some employees work 7 a.m. to 3 p.m., others 3 p.m. to 11 p.m., and so on. It may work best for you if you don't schedule everyone to arrive and depart in the same one or two shifts. Say you have two basic shifts—7 a.m. to 3 p.m. and 3 p.m. to 11 p.m. It might be good to have some individuals scheduled to arrive and depart intermittently during the day, not with either basic shift. For example, you could schedule some people to work a noon to 8 p.m. shift. This would be called a "spanner shift"—it spans both of your regular shifts. The idea of the spanner shift is to bring individuals in when you need them most. A spanner shift of noon to 8 p.m. means spanner shift employees are there to help during the busy lunch period and during the busiest part of the dinner hour. Spanner shift employees can work two busy meal periods, or any time you need them. Set up spanner shifts to suit your needs.

Schedule Employees to Arrive When They're Needed

When you make up schedules, pay attention to your own operation's time factor of peak work load hours. You will probably schedule your cooks so they get to work first. You'll probably want them there early to get the food started. If your food service opens at 7 a.m., maybe your breakfast cook should arrive at 6 a.m. Service personnel should probably be scheduled to get there at 6:45. They won't serve food until the dining room opens. Maybe you'll schedule the dishwasher to come in at 8 a.m., when the dishes start coming back from the dining room to the kitchen. If you and your cooks can't stand the sight of dirty dishes sitting around, you may want to schedule the dishwasher to arrive earlier. If there is room to stack dirty dishes in the kitchen and you have an ample supply of dishes, it doesn't hurt to have plenty of work for the dishwashers to do when they arrive—as long as your kitchen is always kept sanitary. One reason why many operators schedule dishwashers to get there at 7 instead of later is that they want time to call other dishwashers if the scheduled ones don't get there.

When you make work schedules, it can help you a lot if you know your individual employees pretty well and can judge how dependable they are. Many managers have learned the hard way which employees they can rely on to show up the day after payday and which ones they can't.

Report to Work in Uniform

Most food service operations require employees to wear uniforms. Most provide facilities on the premises for employees to change clothes. Employees should punch in at the time clock or sign in on a time sheet only after they are in uniform and ready to go to work. (This could depend on a union contract.) It is not a good idea to permit employees to come to work, punch in, and then change clothes, which can take them fifteen minutes or more per employee per day. Pay employees for working, not for changing clothes.

Part-Time Employees

For many operations, it is a good idea to schedule part-time employees on a regular basis. This can generally help reduce payroll costs. Part-time employees might be scheduled, for example, for full shifts two days a week. You might schedule others on a regular basis for four hours a day, five days a week, for example, or for whatever hours you need. This could be especially useful to you if you have a busy lunch (or dinner) period and need extra service personnel to cover just your busiest hours.

Maybe you could schedule part-time service personnel for four hours a day, five days a week, perhaps on a schedule of something like 10:30 a.m. to

2:30 p.m. Employees on this schedule could help finish setting up the dining room, take care of a busy lunch period, and then go home at 2:30. Service personnel on a schedule like this will make most of their money from tips, not from wages you pay. A source of part-time service personnel for a schedule like this could be people who want to earn money during the hours when their children are at school.

Another source of part-time employees is students. If you hire students, you have to be prepared to give them flexible scheduling. Generally it is sensible to schedule them for three or four days a week, not more. Students have to have time for studies, and most want time for some social life. They want money, probably enjoy working, and are generally apt to do a good job for you. But they do have other commitments and other demands on their time. They may, for example, need extra days off when they are facing exams. You'll have to expect to make schedules extra flexible for students.

Have Employees on Call

In addition to part-time employees, it's a good safety measure for you to have a list of employees who can work at irregular times and sporadically as you need them. It can help you to have some employees "on call." If a regularly scheduled full-time or part-time employee calls in sick, it's a good idea to have a list of emergency back-up people you can call on at a moment's notice.

These "on call" employees could also be used on an irregular basis for special banquet service, for example. There are people who like to work periodically but can't or won't work regularly for you.

Don't make the mistake of relying on these people too much and too often, unless it turns out to be mutually satisfactory to you and them. The people on your emergency list should be people who will work for you for special parties or help out if someone is sick. But they probably can't or don't want to work on a constant or regular basis. Some for example, will refuse to work more than three days a week. These individuals can be extremely valuable to you if they are available on a planned-ahead or fast-notice basis. They can help correct some of the imperfections of your scheduling.

Some managers have too many emergencies due to lack of foresight and planning and try to convert these "emergency list employees" to full-time personnel although the employees don't want this. Don't do this. If you do, your "emergency" people may refuse to work for you at all because you are calling them too often. This is something you have to work out with each individual on your emergency list of employees "on call."

Use of Overtime

Depending on your own union contract situation, another thing that can help you schedule is to plan overtime sometimes for some employees. Some employees welcome the opportunity to work a few hours overtime for extra money, particularly if it is on a regular, prearranged basis. For example, if you have scheduled employees to work noon to 8 p.m. on Fridays and Saturdays, perhaps you could change the schedules of a few so they always work from noon to 9 p.m. just on Fridays and Saturdays. This will help you take care of increased volume and later dining hours on Friday and Saturday nights.

If you schedule employees so they know ahead of time that they will always work an hour later on Fridays and Saturdays than they do other days, they can adjust their own personal schedules. Usually it will be cheaper for you to pay overtime to a regular employee who will work an hour late till 9 p.m. Fridays and Saturdays than it would be to bring in an extra employee who would have to be scheduled just Fridays and Saturdays 5 p.m. to 9 p.m., for example. It's a pretty sure bet you can't get *anyone* to come in and work just 8 p.m. to 9 p.m. Fridays and Saturdays.

Watch overtime very closely, though. Be sure it is really necessary and doesn't "just happen." Use overtime on a planned and preferably a pre-arranged basis. Sometimes employees will suggest, "It's extra busy tonight, do you want me to stay an extra hour?" This is great. The employees care enough about the business to offer to help. They shouldn't stay automatically, though. They should check with you to authorize the overtime. You will be fortunate if you have some employees who will observe when you do need to have someone stay late, who will offer when you really do need them, and who won't try to stack up a lot of overtime pay for themselves if you *don't* need them.

Send Employees Home Early

Depending on union arrangements, you may be able to plan ahead to send some regular employees home early on slow days. They will get wages just for the hours they are there. This idea seems to work well only for service personnel. Cooks and dishwashers, for example, generally rely more on receiving a definite, fixed income every week than do service personnel. If you go too far in reducing the hours and pay of nonservice employees by sending them home early, they may decide to find jobs elsewhere. It is a little different for service personnel. They generally depend on tips for a large portion of their income. If there is little or no business, they won't lose tips. Many service personnel would probably welcome the opportunity to go home early when business is slow.

It is usually normal policy (although not necessary unless it's in a union contract) for employees to receive a minimum of four hours pay if they report for work. When business is slow, many operators have employees spend the four hours taking care of guests plus doing extra jobs that can't be done when the place is really busy. Try asking your service employees if a couple of them would like to go home early when it isn't busy. You will usually get some volunteers. Those who stay can take care of the remaining business and make some money in tips. Those who leave early may be pleased to have the time off. They must know, however, that you will only pay them for the time they are there and will not pay them for a full normal shift if they go home earlier.

Use discretion in deciding who stays and who leaves early. Try to keep it on a volunteer basis. If no one wants to go home early, don't force them to. If they are scheduled to stay but you force them to go home, they may look for other jobs. If more volunteer to leave early than you feel should, then rotate the privilege on a methodical, organized basis. Don't permit yourself to show favoritism. Ruined morale results from that. Sending employees home early can give you a little help in reducing payroll costs for slow days.

TIPS ARE IMPORTANT

If yours is an operation where the service personnel get part of their earnings and income through tips, it is to your advantage as well as theirs to have tips as high as possible. The better the tips and total income your employees can get, the better it is for your employees and for you. Your employees have a chance for high tips if your guests like the service, food, and atmosphere of your establishment. In order to maintain a good atmosphere, you need to maintain good standards and quality of service. An operation that is financially rewarding for its employees has the right to impose higher and stricter standards on its employees than an operation where combined tips and wages are not as good.

High standards usually mean better volume. Good service personnel are apt to want to work for you if your standards are high. This in turn *keeps* standards high. You get better profits through the presence of better employees and you are less apt to have fluctuation of business. If you are busier, it usually means employees are busy working and you are not wasting payroll on employees who just stand around.

A good, efficient organization usually generates better tips for employees who work harder and help create a good, efficient organization. It's a nice cycle to have going for you.

SET STANDARDS

Set reasonable standards for how you want food prepared and served. Standards are a factor in the success of your business and should be *reasonable* for you and for your employees. Some operations impose stricter standards on employees than others. Some want service that is meticulously and formally correct. Others stress friendliness and informality. If you expect your employees to achieve and maintain the standards you want, you must see that they are compensated for their work. You also have to be sure they are trained to know what standards you want them to maintain and how to do their jobs so they do maintain them.

High standards generally attract high quality service personnel who provide good service. Good service attracts more guests and more repeat-business guests, and this means greater sales and probably fewer peaks and valleys in business—which means employees are being used more effectively and payroll isn't being wasted.

TRAINING

Have clear-cut standards of what you want done in your establishment and how you want it done. Train your employees to do their jobs the way you want them done. Training usually can be handled by the employee's immediate supervisor. The steps in training are:

1. Show the employee.
2. Tell the employee.
3. Show and tell the employee.
4. Let the employee do the task.
5. Correct mistakes.
6. Let the employee do the task again.

Training is not, "Hey, Joe, show this new guy Charlie what to do." Joe may or may not know what Charlie should do—especially if you haven't trained Joe in the first place. And even if Joe *could* teach Charlie, he may not do it. Training means good, thorough instruction on an organized basis with follow-up checking to see that the new employee knows how to do things right, does so, and continues to do so.

JOB DESCRIPTION

As we discussed in Chapter 2, make up and use written job descriptions for each job classification in your establishment. This is a most helpful training tool. Most basic books on personnel cover the details of the procedures for writing job descriptions. Job descriptions can help you control payroll costs. If you write them yourself, it forces you to really analyze what work needs to be done. A written job description is important to employees, too. It helps them learn what is expected of them.

A job description is nothing more than a list of the duties the employee is expected to perform. It may also include descriptions of the work areas and equipment the employee is expected to know how to use and take care of.

Job descriptions decidedly are not something for you to hide in your office. Make them available to your employees. Job descriptions are useful when you are training new employees for any positions—dishwashers, cooks, bartenders, service personnel—anyone.

MORALE

There is a strong relationship between happiness (morale) and productivity. Employees who basically like their jobs and generally enjoy their work usually perform much better than employees who dread their jobs, hate to go to work, and work *only* because of the necessity of earning money.

Most employees would rather be fairly busy, not idle, at their jobs. There are some people who like their jobs and have high morale because they *don't* have to work very hard. But normally this is not the case. The majority of employees like to work and like to feel they have accomplished something by the end of the day. They like to feel pride and satisfaction from a job they do well. Work can be fun. People can have a good time at work in the food service business, even in the midst of a very hectic rush hour.

"Work" does not have to mean gossiping, bickering, dissatisfied individuals arguing with—or even yelling at—each other. But, sadly, these situations do occur as part of the work atmosphere in many food service operations. In the food and beverage industry, "work" can be a group of people working together, serving guests, and having a good time themselves. If you can get an atmosphere like this going in your operation, you will have a much better operation. It's worth a lot of effort from you if you can, through your own leadership, encouragement, and fairness, wind up with a happy crew who work hard. This is good for all concerned (including you, who save money by not wasting payroll on employees who work badly because they hate you, each other, and their jobs).

There are still managers who believe in "motivating" their employees through fear. It seldom works. They would do much better to help their employees achieve pride, enjoyment, and satisfaction in their work. In this day and age, managers who motivate from fear are sure to have considerable employee turnover. They will probably have high labor costs, too. Scared or hostile employees waste time and energy being confused, apprehensive, and unhappy.They do not work as well or as much or as hard as happy ones.

EMPLOYEE TURNOVER

A certain amount of employee turnover has to be expected in the food service business. There are many transient and temporary workers in the industry. People move across the country, change jobs, and so on. Individuals are trained and learn skills, then they may move onward and upward—or they just move away—and go to work for someone else.

A food service operation which has nothing but old-time, many-year employees may grow outdated and stodgy, and perhaps unprofitable as a result. But it is worse to have such tremendous employee turnover that an "old-timer" in the establishment may be one who has been there three months. Too much turnover is usually more costly than stagnation. Neither situation is good.

Some managers follow a false premise. They decide that when an employee leaves, it is economical and they will save on payroll if they don't replace her or him immediately. They purposely wait a few days or more, expecting other employees to take up the slack and do extra work. They think this saves payroll and is a good idea. It may save payroll. But it is probably not a good idea. The overall quality of service in any operation can suffer if work does not get done or is done wrong while other employees try to fill the gap.

It takes time and effort to train employees so they work the way you want them to and do their jobs to suit you. If you constantly have employees coming and going on a large scale, it is almost sure to reduce the efficiency of your total organization. Efficiency and maintenance of standards usually go hand in hand with the turnover rate. If turnover is high, your efficiency and standards are apt to be low. You will probably need more employees to do less work. You will have higher payroll costs.

An obvious way to help reduce employee turnover, besides training employees and making every effort to run a good place where employees like to work, is to give raises to satisfactory employees after they have been there for a specified period of time. Employees are usually worth less to you when they are brand new than they are after they have been with you for, say, 90 days. By the time employees have worked for you for about 90 days, you should have trained them in the basic ways you want jobs performed. Plan for increases on a regular basis for your employees. This will increase your payroll cost per employee, but it should help reduce turnover. It should also mean there will be more work done by fewer employees, and this can have the overall effect of reducing your total payroll cost.

Some food service operations have actually reduced payroll costs by raising wages. They seek above-average individual employees, pay them above-average wages, and expect above-average work. They find that a smaller number of well-qualified, well-paid, hard-working employees can take care of more guests. Even though individual wage rates are higher, total number of employees, and thus total payroll cost, is lower. This idea will not work for all operations—and it is hard to find above-average employees. Some employees will work harder and produce more than others.

Review the job performances of employees currently working for you. Maybe you should give raises to a few selected individuals who work hard. Too often these employees are overlooked until after they're gone. A small raise can provide recognition as well as better income for these people and may prevent them from leaving.

If an excellent employee leaves, it may be necessary to hire more than one individual to replace him or her. It is dangerous to hire new employees at a wage close to what you paid the trained, hard-working individuals who left.

New ones will not be worth that much until they have had some training. It may turn out that they're not worth it *after* they're trained, either. It is up to you to find out if they are or not and pay accordingly.

Gradual and normal employee turnover can cause a change in your labor force. You may end up with a work force not as efficient as you had but still be paying them above-average wages. If you go in for the policy of paying high wages and expecting better work, be sure all employees are worth the high wages.

UNION CONTRACTS

All the factors we've been discussing can be affected by union contracts. Many large food service establishments are organized under collective bargaining and have union contracts. A union contract usually sets rules concerning what you can and cannot do in terms of layoffs, sending employees home early or keeping them late, hiring practices, and so on. If your operation has a union, you should be well informed about what you can and cannot do under the contract. Work cooperatively and sensibly with the shop steward and other union representatives.

Some words of caution—on matters of policy where a contract is not clear to you, check with your employer before you commit yourself to policies and precedents that could prove very expensive for your food service unit in years to come.

According to law, there are rights of management and rights of labor. Both must be recognized with or without a union contract. You must be well aware of these laws. If you have a union contract, know exactly what is in it, and learn the major labor laws of your state. You must obey these laws, live up to contracts, and recognize the rights of others. Recognizing the rights of others and acting fairly can help you gain the respect of your employees. If you know what you expect from your employees and they know what you expect, and if your attitude toward them is consistent, fair, and reasonable, you are apt to have a better work force and thus be in a stronger position to be able to control your labor costs.

PAYROLL ANALYSIS

As we said earlier in this chapter, a key to controlling payroll costs is scheduling. To test the effectiveness of your scheduling practices, you should perform a payroll analysis on a regular basis.

Payroll analysis means computing cost percent on a departmental basis as well as a total payroll basis, and comparing it to a standard. The standard to which you compare your percentage should be your desired departmental and total labor cost percents.

A payroll register is where you list all employees, hours worked, their basic rates of pay, the deductions from pay, and the net cash each employee is to receive. It is the basic record where you record and compute the earnings of each employee.

Set up your payroll register so you can do a payroll analysis. Be sure employees are listed by departments on the register. You can list employees alphabetically or numerically or by date hired. Individuals should be listed on the payroll register so all in the same department are grouped together. It is acceptable to list alphabetically or numerically or by date hired—whatever is easiest, but do separate employees into departments. Break work areas into departments—hot foods, cold foods, sanitation department, service personnel, bartenders—by departments in a logical way suitable for your own operation so you can get departmental payroll cost percents as well as your total payroll cost percent.

The formula you use to find departmental payroll cost percent is:

DEPARTMENTAL PAYROLL COST divided by TOTAL PAYROLL COST multiplied by 100 to convert to a percentage equals DEPARTMENTAL PERCENT COST OF TOTAL PAYROLL EXPENSE.

Say, for example, your service department payroll cost is $200 per week. Your total payroll cost for the entire operation is $1,000 per week. $200 divided by $1,000 multiplied by 100 equals 20 percent service department cost percent of total payroll expense. Do this calculation every time you pay your employees so you can see whether the department's cost percent increases or decreases. Make the calculations for each department and watch each department. This information can serve as a guide for you when you establish schedules for employees based on the maximum dollars you can spend based on anticipated volume of business.

For example, say you anticipate $5,000 sales next week. You want a maximum total payroll cost of 30 percent next week. $5,000 multiplied by 30 percent equals $1,500. $1,500 is the maximum you can spend for payroll next week. $1,500 multiplied by 20 percent equals $300. $300 is the maximum amount you can spend for your service department's payroll next week and still maintain the service department's 20 percent payroll cost you want.

Use your departmental payroll cost percent as a guideline to help you investigate the productivity of each department. Departmental payroll breakdown tells you what percent of your total payroll dollar is consumed by payroll for each department.

Maybe you have high payroll costs in the production department. Maybe you could reduce them if you analyzed the situation and did something about it (used fewer people, used more pre-prepared entrees, and so on). You won't even *know* your production department's payroll cost is too high, however, unless you examine and analyze where your payroll dollar is going. Do it. Then try to find out what you can do to reduce costs if they are out of line.

Every time the payroll is made up and employees are paid (whether it is weekly, every two weeks, twice a month, or whatever), you should do a payroll analysis and calculate departmental payroll as well as a total payroll percentage. This tells you the trend your departmental and total payroll costs are taking for the period of time involved.

You can calculate percentages and use results as guidelines during the month. Don't wait until the end of the month when you get your profit and loss statement. *Then* you will know all about your payroll costs, and if you don't like them it's too late to do a thing about it.

Some establishments even go so far as to maintain daily payroll figures. They figure out their daily payroll cost and use this information when they plan work schedules. If you do this, the benefits you get from it should justify the expense of obtaining this data.

Payroll analysis is strictly historical, but you do use the information you get from payroll analysis when you plan future scheduling and payroll. You cannot change yesterday's payroll cost, but you can try to change tomorrow's payroll cost.

PAYROLL BUDGETING

Most successful operators of food and beverage establishments work with forecasts and budgets. They forecast business for the future (for tomorrow, next week, next month) and then use their forecasts in the following formula:

ESTIMATED SALES (forecast) multiplied by DESIRED PAYROLL PERCENT equals DOLLARS AND CENTS AMOUNT THAT CAN BE SPENT FOR PAYROLL.

They use this dollars and cents figure for payroll as a guideline in establishing work schedules. Some people have trouble converting dollars and cents into a payroll forecast. They find it easier and better for them if they convert the dollars and cents into hours. Do what's easiest for you.

Say, for example, you use the information you got from your payroll analysis and you use your forecast of business and you figure out that your budget for waitresses next week will be $420. The average wage paid to waitresses will be $1.25 per hour (plus meals, uniforms, and so on). Divide $420 by the average wage of $1.25 per hour, and you get 336 hours. You use this figure of 336 hours for scheduling waitresses. Based on your estimate of business, the maximum total number of hours all waitresses can work is 336. If you go over this, your payroll cost will be higher than your budget allows for payroll.

When they do their scheduling, some managers and/or supervisors find it easier to work in terms of hours than in terms of dollars and cents. Do it that way if it's easier.

FRINGE BENEFITS

If you offer fringe benefits, they add to your total payroll cost. But most food service operations do not include fringe benefits when they compute payroll cost percentage. Many industries other than the food service industry figure the cost per hour on an average basis for the fringe benefit package they provide for their employees. It is a good idea for a food service operation to do this, too. Fringe benefits could amount to 30, 40, 60, 80 cents—to over $1 per hour per employee.

Compute for fringe benefits as follows:

TOTAL ANNUAL DOLLAR COST ALL FRINGE BENEFITS PACKAGE PER EMPLOYEE divided by AVERAGE ANNUAL NUMBER OF HOURS WORKED PER EMPLOYEE equals AVERAGE COST PER HOUR FOR FRINGE BENEFITS PER EMPLOYEE.

Fringe benefits normally include:

1. Life insurance.
2. Health and hospitalization insurance.
3. Vacation.
4. Social Security taxes.
5. Worker's compensation insurance.
6. Employees' meals.

A business operation may pay all or part of all or some of the above (and there can be other fringe benefits besides those in the above list). Some food service operations also:

1. Give annual bonuses to employees.
2. Give employees Christmas or birthday gifts or both.
3. Establish profit-sharing plans for employees.
4. Establish plans for employees' retirement.

Any of the above factors that apply to you (plus perhaps some others) do affect your total payroll cost. Fringe benefit factors usually are not included as direct costs in a payroll analysis by most food service operations, but they should be.

Another thing to consider is that every time you add a new employee, you are not just adding the cost of the basic wage. You are also adding the cost of your fringe benefit package. The reverse is true, too. If you dismiss an employee, you save regular payroll cost plus the cost of the fringe benefits for that employee.

Determine what your fringe benefit package costs you per employee and add this to the hourly rates for your employees. This gives you the total cost of payroll including fringe benefits for each employee. And inform your employees about the fringe benefits they are receiving in addition to their regular wages. Fringe benefits which are paid for by management may or may not call for additional contributions by the employee.

Don't make the mistake, as many food service managers do, of overlooking or ignoring fringe benefits when you analyze your payroll. Fringe benefits cost you money and must be included in your payroll analysis and in your payroll cost figures.

COST OF EMPLOYEES' VACATIONS

The cost of your employees' vacations can distort your payroll analysis and the results you get from it. Many establishments send their employees on vacation when business is slow and charge the cost of the vacation to the accounting period during which the employee is gone on vacation. This tends to overstate the cost of payroll for that accounting period by charging the cost of the vacation as a direct expense just to the period when the vacation occurs.

Paid vacations are an expense of doing business. You should spread the cost of all vacations evenly throughout the year. To do this, you do the following:

1. Estimate a yearly total cost for all vacations.
2. Debit a proportional part of total vacation expense to "vacation pay expense" and credit "accrued vacation pay" every time you make up your payroll.

When an employee actually takes a vacation, charge the cost to "accrued vacation pay," not as a direct expense and not to "current expense." For example, we'll use $3,600 as the total annual cost for eligible employees' vacations. Divide the $3,600 by 12 months and you get $300 per month vacation pay cost. During each month, debit $300 to "vacation expense" and credit $300 to "accrued vacation pay." Include it in current payroll costs. When you credit "accrued vacation pay" for $300, the expense becomes a liability. When the vacation is actually taken, debit "accrued vacation pay" and credit "cash" for the actual cost of the vacation. Don't include the cost of the vacation (other than the regular, proportional $300 share for that month) in current payroll costs.

This may seem like a minor item. But your costs for employees' vacations can distort your payroll costs for some accounting periods if you do not do the above. This is especially true since most vacations are taken in the summer during a relatively short span of time. The employee works throughout the year to earn the vacation. Consider vacations a yearly cost, not a limited-period cost.

PAYROLL IS AN INCREASING COST

As we said at the beginning of this chapter, payroll is an increasing cost in dollars and cents—and probably also as a percentage of your sales dollar. Effective control of payroll costs calls for good management and the use of management tools such as:

1. Budgeting.
2. Analyzing payroll costs.
3. Forecasting business.
4. Scheduling employees as carefully and accurately as you can so they are there when you need them and not there when you don't need them.
5. Setting and maintaining standards for employees.
6. Dealing reasonably and fairly with your employees.

Your employees are there to do a job. So are you. Everyone should be working for the improvement of the total food service. This can only be achieved if:

1. All employees know what they are supposed to do.
2. All employees really do carry out their specified duties.
3. Management sees that the operation runs efficiently and profitably.

Payroll cost is a very difficult cost to control. It is much harder to control than food or beverage cost. Unlike food or beverage, labor cost cannot be stored and saved for later use. When you are dealing with foods and beverages, you are dealing with commodities. In the area of labor costs, you are dealing with people and the work they do. You are probably also dealing with minimum wage laws and maybe union contracts. These factors can make things more complicated. Like all your other cost areas, you have to constantly scrutinize and evaluate your payroll costs in an endless effort to keep them as close as possible to where you want them.

REVIEW AND DISCUSSION QUESTIONS

1. What are the factors that affect payroll cost?
2. Why is payroll harder to control than food cost?

3. How can you build flexibility into your employee scheduling?

4. Why are employees' tips important to managers?

5. Why should fringe benefits be considered a part of total payroll cost?

6. How can time-saving and labor-saving devices actually reduce payroll cost?

7. Can the use of pre-prepared food items reduce payroll costs?

8. How can you combine forecasting, budgeting, and employee scheduling to help you control payroll costs?

8

Overhead Cost Control

Objectives

This chapter discusses all costs that are not labor cost, food cost, or profit cost. After you have read this chapter, you should know:

1. What expenses are non-controllable.
2. What expenses are controllable.
3. Why advertising and sales promotion expense is not necessarily a cost that you should reduce when you need to cut costs.

Simply defined, "overhead costs" means all costs not included in food and beverage cost or payroll cost. Overhead covers a wide area of cost. It is divided into two main categories:

1. Non-controllable expenses.
2. Controllable expenses.

NON-CONTROLLABLE EXPENSES

A "non-controllable expense" (also called a "capital expense") is an overhead expense that a hired manager cannot control. The owner or owners may have some degree of control over a non-controllable expense. A manager who does not have any of his or her own money invested in the operation, and is simply hired to manage the operation, does not have any control.

The following six items are non-controllable expenses:

1. Interest.
2. Depreciation.
3. General insurance.
4. Real estate taxes.
5. Rent.
6. Income taxes.

Interest

This means interest owners pay on their mortgage. Interest is an expense of business and it is deductible for income tax purposes. The way in which the owners decide how they will finance their business can affect how much interest they have to pay, so owners are able to exercise some small degree of control over the amount of interest they will pay. The owners—not a hired manager—get a loan to establish their food service business, and they agree to pay interest on the loan. Money is a commodity, so owners can "shop around," compare interest rates of various lenders, and take the lowest rate they can get. To this extent they have a slight degree of control over interest before they borrow money, but not afterward. A low interest rate means correspondingly low interest payments; a high interest rate means correspondingly higher interest payments.

It is up to the owners, not hired managers, whether they borrow funds to start a business and pay interest, or pay cash if they can and thus don't pay interest. Most food service owners do not have enough cash of their own to buy a food service operation outright and are forced to borrow money, get a mortgage, and pay interest. Managers (with no money of their own in the business to make them owners) have no control over or effect in the area of this expense of interest.

The more money the owners borrow, the more interest dollars they will have to pay. If the owners borrow a lot of money and this borrowed money represents a big percentage of the operation's total assets, they will usually have to pay a higher rate of interest. If, for example, a food operation has total assets of $200,000, and $100,000 of this is mortgage, then the mortgage is 50 percent of the assets. We will say, for example, that the owners would pay about 7 percent interest on this mortgage. But if a food service operation has total assets of $150,000, and $100,000 of this is mortgage, then the mortgage is 66 percent of the assets. The interest in this case might be 9 percent instead od 7 percent. Interest might be higher because it is riskier for the lender to lend a higher percent of the total value of a business. Lenders may demand a higher interest rate because they are financing a bigger proportion of the business in the second example than they are in the first example.

After owners have borrowed, they have no control and must pay the interest agreed on. For a hired, salaried, non-owner manager, interest is an overhead expense that is completely non-controllable.

Depreciation

Depreciation means you reduce the value of an asset during the period of the asset's estimated useful life. Depreciation is a continuing overhead expense. It permits the food service operation to recover the cost of assety by reducing income (by an estimated expense) over the useful life of these assets.

Depreciation is the only expense not actually paid in cash. It is deducted from income, but the money, assuming sales were for cash, can be used for increasing other assets, decreasing liabilities (what you owe), or decreasing owners' investment (paying dividends).

Accelerated depreciation means you charge more to depreciation expense during the early years of the asset's life. Accelerated depreciation during the asset's early years means you charge a greater amount to depreciation expense than you would if you used straight line depreciation.

Straight line depreciation means the total cost of the asset divided by the estimated number of years of the asset's useful life. This figure is the amount you charge every year to depreciation expense.

The current accelerated depreciation method permitted by law is the 150 percent declining balance method. The 150 percent declining balance accelerated depreciation method means you charge to depreciation expense 150 percent of what you would charge if it were straight line depreciation. For example, an asset costs $1,000 and has a 10-year estimated useful life. $1,000 divided by 10 years equals $100 per year. This $100 would be charged to depreciation expense every year under straight line depreciation. But if you use 150 percent declining balance, you charge $150 to depreciation expense the first year ($100 multiplied by 150 percent). During the second year, straight line depreciation would still be $100, but 150 percent declining balance would be $141.66 charged to depreciation expense. ($1,000 minus $150 charged during first year equals $850. $850 divided by 9 years remaining life equals $94.44 multiplied by 150 percent equals $141.66.) Note that under the declining balance, the amount you charge to depreciation expense decreases each year.

But under straight line depreciation, you charge the same unchanging amount to depreciation expense every year.

In the past, owners were allowed to use various forms of accelerated depreciation. They could recover the cost of assets faster by accelerated depreciation than they could if they used straight line depreciation.

Owners who use 150 percent declining balance accelerated depreciation can charge more for depreciation expense in the early years than they can if they use straight line depreciation. There are, however, certain types of assets for which you cannot use 150 percent declining balance accelerated depreciation. Ask your lawyer or tax accountant about methods of depreciation you can legally use.

Depreciation expense reduces income. It also reduces the amount of income tax owners pay. In other words, the owners end up with a lower net profit.

If hired managers are evaluated by owners strictly in terms of how much net profit the operation makes, they cannot appear to be doing as good a job of managing if accelerated depreciation is used as they can if straight line depreciation is used. That is because more is charged to depreciation expense, and the result is lower net profit. During the early years of an asset's life, the net profit and income tax will be higher if straight line depreciation is used instead of accelerated depreciation.

When owners use accelerated depreciation, they will have greater cash flow. "Cash flow" means income minus expenses actually paid in cash. In the food service business, most income is cash. Even accounts receivable are eventually turned into cash, usually in 60 days or less.

Depreciation is the only expense you don't actually pay in cash. We just defined "cash flow" as income minus expenses paid in cash. Another definition of "cash flow" is income plus depreciation. Owners have the use of this cash flow generated from business if they make the deduction for depreciation against actual dollars of income. You have to have enough dollars in income so you can deduct your depreciation expense and still have dollars left over. You have earned your depreciation. Then your depreciation contributes to cash flow.

A manager can recommend how to apply cash flow. Cash flow is applied by increasing assets, decreasing liabilities, and decreasing owner's equity. But methods of depreciation are ownership decisions that affect profit and income tax. A hired manager has no control over depreciation decisions, so depreciation is called a non-controllable expense.

General Insurance

General insurance usually covers buildings and contents. It includes insurance against fire, wind, hail, and so on. It is usually a cost borne by the owners of the building. If the owners of a food service operation lease the building from someone else and do not own it themselves, general insurance will be part of their leasing costs directly or indirectly. General insurance is not controllable by a hired manager. The only effect managers might have here is if they can make limited savings by comparing various insurance programs and coverage and find one program which satisfies the operation's needs and is less expensive than other insurance programs. They can recommend the less expensive program to the owner, who makes the decision.

Real Estate Taxes

Real estate taxes are not controllable by the owner *or* the hired manager. They are an expense of owning property. If food service owners don't own the building that houses their food service operation, but just rent it instead, their lease payments will include tax payments. The more valuable the property is, the higher the tax rate will be. The tax rate also depends on the location of the property. If it is in an area with a lot of commercial property, businesses, factories, and such, the rate is apt to be lower than it would be if the property were in an area with more residential properties. Communities need money, and frequently they find it politically expedient to assign heavy taxes to businesses instead of private residents.

Today many leases are written so that the leasee pays the real estate taxes. This has come about because of increases in real estate taxes in recent years. The leasees have always paid real estate taxes directly or indirectly as part of lease cost. Leases written in recent years usually include a provision stating that any increases in real estate taxes will be passed on to the leasee. The manager cannot control the overhead expense of real estate taxes.

Rent

If food service operators don't own the building they are in, they pay rent to whoever does own it. They don't pay depreciation expense or interest for the building because they did not borrow money to buy the building.

Food service owners negotiate rent or leases with whoever owns the building. A common lease today stipulates that the business gives a stated amount of dollars to the owners of the building. In addition to this stated amount, the leasee may agree to pay the cost of insurance and the real estate taxes. This is frequently referred to as a "net lease." Insurance and real estate taxes have been increasing, and from the standpoint of the building's owners—to protect themselves—they have passed these costs on to the business operator. The owners of the building may have asked for minimum fixed payment or a percentage of sales, whichever is greater.

Regardless of how the lease is written, after it has been agreed upon by the food service operator and the owners of the building, then the lease payment or rent is a fixed cost and is non-controllable by the manager.

Income Taxes

Income tax is another cost of doing business that can be affected by whether or not there is interest to be paid on a mortgage. The method of depreciation used will also affect the amount of profit earned and the amount of tax that has to be paid. Managers have no control in these matters.

Evaluating Managers

Because of all the factors mentioned above, owners should not evaluate managers only in terms of *net* profit. Net profit is income minus all expenses. Managers can be evaluated fairly only in terms of how much *operating* profit they can get. Operating profit is income minus all the expenses the manager *can* control. Managers' job performances should not be evaluated on a basis that includes factors they cannot control. And they cannot control the non-controllable, capital expenses we've discussed above.

CONTROLLABLE EXPENSES

A controllable overhead expense is an expense the manager *can* control to some extent. Many expenses technically called "controllable" overhead expenses are not actually very controllable. You should analyze each of the following categories in terms of your own operation and try to make cost reductions wherever possible. All of these expenses can be controlled to some extent, particularly by avoiding waste in every area.

The following are controllable expenses:

1. Heat, light, and power.
2. Paper supplies.
3. Glass, china, and silver.
4. Linen, laundry, and uniforms.
5. Cleaning.
6. Maintenance and equipment repair.
7. Security and protection.
8. Advertising and sales promotion.
9. Internal advertising and promotion.
10. Charity donations.

Heat, Light, and Power

The amount of heat you need in your operation can be affected by building construction and the weather, among other things. Lighting needs vary according to whether it is noon or night, cloudy or sunny. Turn lights out when you don't have to have them on. Watch heating and air-conditioning thermostats constantly. Cut down whenever you can. This can have quite an effect on your yearly electric bill.

The same things apply to kitchen fuel. If the kitchen has two broilers, heat just one if you can get by with one. This can mean a saving in yearly gas bills.

Economize strictly in use of any equipment—broilers, deep fat fryers, ovens, whatever. Turn off any appliance not in use. Many cooks come to work in the morning, light every oven, start up every range, get every piece of equipment in the kitchen going full blast and up to maximum heating capacity, and *then* pick up the menu for the day to find out what they are going to cook. Maybe they will need all that equipment—but maybe they won't.

All employees should help to economize on heat, light, and power overhead expenses. There is information available from your Trade Association on methods of energy conservation.

Paper Supplies

Paper supplies is an overhead expense you can control, and it can add up into a surprisingly costly expense if you don't. One small example of a way to save is to use a roller-type paper towel dispenser in the kitchen and restrooms so the person using it has to punch a button and roll out a single sheet at a time. Don't use a dispenser that dispenses individual folded paper towels. They can easily fall out of the dispenser, or employees can stack them on a shelf where they can be knocked to the floor and wasted. This sounds trivial, but it adds up.

Another small example of paper supplies control is to have employees use clean cloth towels to wipe up spills on counters instead of handfuls of paper napkins or paper towels. This is only a good idea, however, if employees use *clean* cloth towels. No guest likes to sit down at a counter or on a chair that has just been mopped with a greasy towel.

These are very small items. Find every area like this you can, add up all the small economies you can make, and you can save some money.

Paper supplies *can* be a very big cost item, particularly in many fast-foods operations that use paper products in a lot of ways—bags for hamburgers, bags for French fries, paper cups for drinks, sacks for customers to carry the food in, paper trays to carry drinks in, paper napkins. Train employees not to waste these paper supplies.

If you use paper cups or sandwich sacks extensively, there is a simple, effective control technique you might consider to help you control the overhead cost for paper products *plus* keep track of what you sell. It is used by some large, fast-foods operations. For example, they keep exact count of the number of cups they use during each shift. At the end of a shift, they compare the number of cups used with the number of drinks recorded as sold. If there is a discrepancy, they check to find out what happened. They do the same things with the number of French fries bags or hamburger bags used and compare numbers of paper bags used with their records of sales of these items. Every time a paper item is used it should mean a sale. If it doesn't, they find out why. This procedure can be an effective two-way control system—for paper products and food.

Glass, China, and Silver

Most food service establishments use china, glassware, and silver or stainless steel. These items are classified as assets by the business and they are depreciated over their useful life. Some operations do not depreciate these assets, though. Instead, they charge their replacement costs to expense. Do not economize by using glassware, china, or silver that is in bad condition, but do get the longest period of service you can from these items.

Usually you use glasses until they get cracked, chipped, or broken. Occasionally detergents will cause the glaze of glasses to deteriorate to the point where they are no longer perfectly clear. If that happens, throw them away. Replace all glasses that are not in perfect condition. Check glassware periodically and get rid of imperfect glasses.

China is usually used until it cracks, chips, loses its glaze, or breaks. China, like glassware, should be replaced when it is no longer acceptable for service. Someone should periodically inspect china to see if any needs to be discarded.

Cracking, chipping, and breaking of china and glassware are generally caused by mishandling. Sometimes employees can't help it. Sometimes the problem is really caused by the managers' neglect. A lot of food service managers tell their employees again and again, "Watch the breakage! Be more careful with those dishes and glasses! You've got to stop breaking everything!" But these managers may never think to provide glass racks where glasses can be stored safely. They may never examine the kitchen set-up to see if better shelf space, for example, or a different way of handling things is really what is needed. A lot of managers don't do a thing to correct the situation if employees are forced to stack soiled dishes, glasses, cups, and plates all together in deep tubs, where breakage is practically unavoidable.

It is up to you to analyze things and improve situations. Ask your employees to help. Use their valid ideas and suggestions. Provide safe storage for china and glasses when they are not being used. Open shelves where items can be knocked down can increase breakage. Provide proper equipment for storing clean and soiled china and glassware to protect them from breaking. Teach employees to handle china and glassware carefully. If you provide proper equipment and storage space and train employees to handle china and glass correctly, breakage can be reduced. China and glassware can be expensive. If you save more of it and buy less, it can save you quite a bit of money in a year.

Silver, silverplate, or stainless steel knives, forks, and spoons can represent an expensive dollar investment for you. Make every effort to cut down on the loss of silver. When it is lost, it is usually thrown out in the trash (very common) or stolen by guests or employees (much less frequent).

Take steps to avoid having silver accidentally thrown out with the trash. Try setting up special temporary containers for soiled silver in the dining room. The purpose is to separate the silver from dishes and trash. Have special areas for soiled silver after it gets to the dishwashing room. When silver is lost, it generally happens when paper napkins, food scraps, and general trash are all scooped up from a table and tossed into one busbin. It is hard to ignore a plate or cup if you pick it up along with a handful of paper napkins, but it is very easy to grab up silver right with napkins, cigarette wrappers, and other trash on a table and empty it all into a trash bin and never know it. This can be very expensive. Train buspersons to be very cautious about checking closely for silver, which can easily get tangled in with paper trash.

As for theft, you might train your service personnel to count each item and know exactly what is there when a guest sits down and then check the table immediately when the guest leaves. If an employee is positive a guest is taking silverware (or other items), you could consider adding a charge to the guest's bill. If something is missing, you may or may not want to confront a guest. That is up to you. It can be a touchy business and may not be worth a possible scene or offending an innocent guest mistakenly accused of stealing.

Some items are particularly tempting to guests—demitasse spoons, steak knives, special silver items, special glassware, or coffee mugs. Items with a crest, logo, or name of the establishment on them are usually the most tempting to souvenir hunters.

For items that really tempt guests, one thing you could consider doing would be to offer these for sale at the cash register at a reasonable price. Some establishments cover the cost of their breakage by the profit they make from selling their special glasses, Irish coffee mugs, or attractive silver items.

Breakage and some loss of some items is unavoidable. But through foresight, planning, common sense, and training employees, you can do a lot to reduce your overhead costs of replacing china, glass, and silverware.

Linen, Laundry, and Uniforms

Linen and laundry is another overhead cost area where waste can occur. Many food service operations use place mats because they cost less than linen. It is up to you to decide which is better—place mats or linen—in terms of cost and in terms of what is more appropriate for your establishment.

You can buy linens or (in most areas) you can rent them. If you buy your own, you have to arrange for washing them. If you rent them, the company you rent them from will usually take care of that. Linen service varies from one community to another.

You can get tablecloths and napkins made of synthetic fabrics, which don't usually need any ironing. Some food service operations install their own washers and driers. This cuts down on the amount of linen lost and may reduce overall linen costs. It is worth checking into to find out what is the easiest and most economical way for you to take care of linens and laundry. You can get into other problems (labor cost, cost of equipment and operating equipment, problems of machine breakdowns) if you do decide to buy linens and operate your own laundry service, but the idea does offer some possibilities for reducing costs.

Whether you buy or rent linens, wash them yourself, or send them to a laundry, insist that your linen items be used only for the purposes for which they are meant. Use towels or rags, not napkins, to wipe up grease spills. Napkins used for this can get so stained that they can never be used again as napkins. Using any linen items for purposes for which they were never intended can damage them and increase your costs. You may have to pay more if you are renting them. If you have bought them, you will have to remove linens from dining room service yourself if, through incorrect use, they get stained beyond renewal.

Management usually provides employees' uniforms and provides for cleaning them. If you do this, you need a control program to handle it and cut the costs. Employees should have to check in their dirty uniforms before they get clean ones. Don't have open shelves where employees help themselves to clean uniforms. They may knock clean uniforms to the floor looking through the stack for their own uniforms or for the right size.

Have a check-out control for issuing clean uniforms. Employees should be neat and clean when they are serving your guests or working in any other area—food production, for example, where it is vital for good sanitation. Set up a control for issuing clean uniforms, or wastefully excessive costs for cleaning and maintaining uniforms can occur.

Cleaning

Don't waste cleaning supplies. Budget tightly when you buy cleaning materials, supplies, and equipment. Train employees how to use equipment and supplies without waste.

The day and age of a single, all-purpose cleaner is long past. There are cleaners that are best suited for your own type of machines. There are special cleaners made for washing pots and pans. Others are meant just for washing walls; some are especially formulated for scrubbing floors. Today most cleaning compounds are designed for very specific uses. All should come with instructions and directions for use. Evaluate cleaning agents carefully. Choose what is best suited for particular jobs and watch the costs simultaneously. Make sure employees are taught how to use cleaning compounds and what quantities to use so they don't waste them. Many employees feel that if one cup of a cleaner is good, two cups are better. With many cleaning compounds today, that's not true and it's wasteful.

You can have your own employees do your cleaning and supervise them yourself, or (in most areas) you can consider hiring contract cleaning companies.

A problem with doing your own cleaning is lack of skill on the part of employees for particular jobs. Another problem in having your own employees do the cleaning is the cost of having someone supervise and direct the work to make sure cleaning is done the way you want it done.

Many food service operations do their own light cleaning but contract for window washing and heavy cleaning. You could hire a firm to come in periodically to strip and rewax floors. Or contract a company to come in and shampoo carpets on a regular schedule or as needed. You can have your own employees do routine cleaning or you can hire cleaning companies to do this, too. Some cleaning companies will come in every day and vacuum, scrub, wash, sweep—whatever you want.

Most of your cleaning will have to be done at night after your food operation is closed so it will not disrupt business. Figure out whether a cleaning company will do what you want the way you want it or whether you are better off having your own employees do it. If you aren't careful, cleaning may not be done well, and cleaning is very important.

Cleaning equipment is expensive to buy and it has to be kept in good working order. Big cleaning companies can afford to buy their own heavy equipment and keep it in good condition. Maybe you can't.

Weigh the costs and other factors and decide what is best for your own operation. Generally, most food service operations seem to find that it is less expensive and more satisfactory for them in the long run if they buy their own cleaning equipment and have their own employees do the cleaning—except for the extremely heavy and infrequent jobs, which they hire cleaning companies to do.

Maintenance and Equipment Repair

Maintaining and repairing all kinds of equipment is another major area of overhead expense. You could consider hiring a service company to make regular inspections of all your machines and equipment. They will check equipment on a regular periodic basis, repair minor items that need fixing, and make arrangements for major repairs. For many operations, this is a good idea. You can usually work out different types and varieties of equipment service contracts to suit your needs if you decide that you do not want complete service contracts.

If you cannot hire a service company, set up your own equipment maintenance and repair system. Have employees check and clean equipment and repair it as needed. Someone has to inspect, adjust, and fix equipment continuously—*before* machines really break down due to neglect. Keep equipment in good working condition. Don't ignore this.

All machines, appliances, and equipment will eventually need repair. Things may break down just when you need them most. The air conditioner, for example, can quit during a banquet on the hottest day of the year. Essential equipment can break down at the most inconvenient time, and you can be forced to call repair people on an emergency basis and pay them time and a half or double time. And it is exasperating and not efficient to struggle along with machinery that is ailing and not working right. Lots of expensive repair work can be avoided entirely if you have good routine maintenance on a regular schedule.

Maintenance and repair of equipment is a controllable overhead expense. Management can take steps to control it.

Security and Protection

Another overhead expense that is controllable is security and protection.

1. Fire.

   There are various types of fire detection and prevention systems available. Investigate them for possible use in your own operation. You may be required by law to have certain types of fire equipment in addition to simple fire extinguishers. Check your local fire laws.

   Food service operations are prone to fires. They use heat and fire in cooking, and they serve guests who may leave smoldering cigars and cigarettes in ashtrays, on rest room shelves, on the floor. Make sure your employees turn off ovens and broilers and are *extremely* careful about emptying ashtrays—particularly near closing time. This can be a big help in preventing fires in your establishment.

2. Theft.

   Various types of burglar alarm systems are available. Prices range from inexpensive ones, which simply sound an alarm, to very expensive systems, which sound alarms at a private protective agency or a police station. Your decisions about your need for such equipment will probably depend on costs, on the location of your establishment, and on the amount of crime in your immediate area. The location of your food service operation will have a bearing on the type of security you need.

3. Night guards.

   Night guards can save you from disaster if they detect smoldering cigarettes in wastebaskets after you have closed for the night. They can also help protect you against break-ins and theft. The use of guards is expensive, but many establishments have night guards patrolling to check for fires and break-ins. Some food operations use night cleaning crews who are on the premises part of the night anyway to serve the functions of night watchpeople.

4. Closed-circuit television.

   You could use closed-circuit television, which is periodically monitored day and night to watch for break-ins or theft, or stealing by your own employees. Many food service operations do this. These systems can get quite expensive, however. It is a question of how much protection you need and can afford.

5. Inspect packages.

   You might consider having a routine inspection procedure for regular employees carrying parcels in and out of your establishment. Routine inspections will help cut down on the temptation for your own employees to steal things from your food service establishment. This procedure can also help protect innocent employees who bring their own packages into the establishment (from shopping, for instance) and take them home but feel quite uneasy about it, fearing other employees think they are stealing from the establishment. Routine checking of employee parcels and bags will eliminate worry by those who innocently carry packages to and from work. It will also slow down potential thieves. Despite the fact that the vast majority of employees are honest, a planned procedure for inspecting packages employees take in and out is a good idea.

6. Protection agencies.
   Another security measure is the use of "spotters." A spotter is usually someone you hire from a private agency. They check on anything you want them to—from the quality of service your employees give guests to watching for dishonest activities by your employees. Generally the good you might get from using spotters to check on poor service or dishonest employees may be more than offset by the decrease that the practice causes in employee morale. It is usually better for you to do the work of a spotter yourself. Do it subtly. Check your own operation and employees instead of hiring an outsider to do it. Do not encourage a spy system among your own employees.
   If you suspect theft (if you think a cashier is pocketing money, for example, or a bartender is stealing), the use of an outside professional agency may be the only way you can prove employees are guilty (or not).

Advertising and Sales Promotion

Advertising and sales promotion expenses are controllable overhead costs. You spend dollars for advertising to attract guests into your establishment. Sales promotion encourages them to spend more while they are there.

Advertising can be expensive, especially if your ads are not directed toward the group you should be trying to reach. Be sure you know your market and be sure the advertising and promotion media you use aim at and reach your market. If your advertising fails to reach, interest, and influence your own market, you're wasting money.

In general, an average advertising budget for a food service operation is 2 percent of sales. Some spend more, some less. Have a planned program so the advertising dollars you spend really will reach your market, attract guests to your establishment, and encourage them to spend money when they're there.

Food service establishments are not noted for their excellence in advertising. Many fail to analyze their market or develop specific advertising programs that will result in specific response and build their image. Many waste their advertising money.

Advertising and promotion is a controllable overhead expense. It's an area where you should *not* skimp. But be sure you spend your advertising money according to an intelligent, effective plan, or it is wasted.

Usual advertising methods used by food service operations include:

1. Newspapers.
   You might be better off if you placed your newspaper advertising in a local shopping guide that is read by people in your immediate area rather than in a large, citywide newspaper where most of the people reading it will not

travel to your establishment because it is too far from them. If yours is a neighborhood restaurant, this is especially true.

2. Radio.

Some establishments have used radio advertising very effectively. For others the cost of radio advertising is greater than the revenue derived from it. If you do use radio stations, be sure they do reach people in the market you're trying to cater to.

3. Television.

Television is seldom used by the small, independent restaurant because it can cost more in dollars than the revenue it brings in. Television is an excellent media for advertising where many units of a same type with the same parent company are located in the same community. The cost of advertising on television can be shared by all of these units and it can be economically feasible for them to advertise on television because dollars spent do bring in sufficient business to cover the cost of television advertising. Television ads might be feasible for you. Consider it.

4. Billboards and signs.

Billboards are used to call travelers' attention to a restaurant and direct people to it. Signs on the restaurant itself identify the operation and can help attract guests inside. The highway restaurant may have a sign "X Restaurant 10 Miles Ahead, Turn Right, Go 2 Blocks." Federal, state, county, and city regulations can prohibit or restrict the use of signs.

5. Magazines.

National magazines are normally used only by large, national chains or franchise companies because of cost and because they have a nationwide market. It might pay you to consider advertising in a local dining magazine or other local periodical where you can anticipate attracting enough business from the market reached to more than cover the expense of the advertising.

Internal Advertising and Promotion

In addition to your external advertising, give some thought and care to internal promotion. This includes things like giving away matchbooks with the name of your operation printed on them, printing your operation's name on your bar napkins, and so on. Encourage creativity and selling by your employees—this is internal promotion, too. Your internal promotion should be designed to increase your average check, promote the name of your establishment, and encourage repeat business.

Charity Donations

In addition to traditional types of advertising, many food and beverage establishments consider their donations to charities as a tax-deductible form of advertising, promotion, and general public relations. Most businesses, including food service operations, do engage in some types of community activities. This can simultaneously contribute to a business's image in its community. Some food service managers establish a list of organizations they want to help and include contributions in their budgets.

SUMMARY

In this chapter we have discussed overhead expenses—controllable and non-controllable. Non-controllable overhead expenses cannot be controlled by a hired manager. Controllable expenses can be controlled—some more so than others. Owners should judge managers on how effectively they supervise controllable expenses, not the non-controllable ones.

With a systematic approach and attention to detail, you can do much to cut your controllable overhead expenses in terms of dollars and percentages. If you could, for example, cut your overhead by just 2 percent—perhaps down from 20 to 18 percent—you might realize substantial savings. If your food service has annual sales of $500,000, for example, a savings of 2 percent would be $10,000. Usually your savings in reduced overhead for any one area will not be large and dramatic. They will be comparatively small. But savings in many areas can add up to significant total savings. It is foolish not to save wherever you can. Some of your overhead expense is waste. Any time and any place you can save money by stopping waste, do it.

REVIEW AND DISCUSSION QUESTIONS

1. What is the difference between a controllable and a non-controllable expense?
2. Why can't managers control non-controllable expenses?
3. How can managers control the controllable expenses?
4. How could you devise a paper control system for a fast-food operation?
5. Food service operations are prone to fires. What should managers do to prevent fires?
6. Should food service operations do their own cleaning or should they contract it out?
7. How should a manager devise a program of equipment maintenance to prevent breakdown?

9

Food Cost Formulas

Objectives

This chapter discusses various formulas for computing daily, weekly, and monthly food costs in dollars and in percents. After you have read this chapter, you should:

1. Know how to use a simple food cost formula.
2. Know how to use a more complex formula that is more accurate.
3. Know why your daily and weekly food cost formulas will not agree exactly with your monthly profit and loss figures for your food cost.

The main emphasis of this book is on one area of cost control—food. By food we mean all food items plus all non-alcoholic beverage items.

"Food cost" (which usually means the same thing as "cost of food sold") means all the money you spent to prepare the meals you served. Food cost includes *only* food and non-alcoholic beverage items. It does not include anything else—not labor and not overhead and not profit.

"Food cost percent" means the percent of your sales dollar you spent for food.

A food cost formula is a method you use to find your food cost and your food cost percent. You need this information to help you plan and control business.

If your food cost percent is too high, you take immediate steps to correct it. You can do the following:

1. Increase efficiency of operation by applying and tightening all controls (purchasing, receiving, storing, production, cash and sales controls, and so on).
2. Put in a slight price increase—or maybe more for some items. A price increase can be small in money (you raise hamburgers from 20 cents to 25 cents apiece, only a nickel more) but big in percentage (that nickel is a 25 *percent* rise from your hamburger's previous 20 cent price).
3. Charge the same prices but cut your quality so your costs go down. (Try not to do this.)

USE A FOOD COST FORMULA

There are two food cost formulas described in this chapter. Either one will show you how your food cost and food cost percent are going from day to day during the month. Use whichever formula suits you and your food operation best, or modify one of these formulas, or make up your own combination of both formulas to suit your own needs. But *do* use a food cost formula to keep track of your food cost and food cost percent so you can control them *during* the month. You can't control your food cost or your food cost percent if you have no idea what they are. And you certainly can't control a month's food cost or food cost percent when that month has ended. A formula tells you what is happening to your food cost while a month is still in progress, so you can act during that month to control your food cost and change it if you need to.

FOOD COST FORMULA NUMBER 1 (PURCHASES FORMULA) (CHART 9-1)

How to Use Formula 1

This is the easiest food cost formula to use. It can be used by food service units that do not need a more sophisticated system or do not have time

1	2	3	4	5	6	7	8
Date	Day	Today Food Purchases	Today Food Sales	Today Food Cost Percent	To-Date Food Purchases	To-Date Food Sales	To-Date Food Cost Percent
Mar. 1	M	412 93	897 23	46 02	412 93	897 23	46 02
2	T	526 60	926 44	56 84	939 53	1823 67	51 52
3	W	649 03	1138 16	57 02	1588 56	2961 83	53 63
4	Th	526 30	956 41	55 05	2114 94	3918 24	53 98
5	F	1017 96	1528 52	66 60	3132 90	5446 76	57 52
6	S	133 81	1649 38	8 11	3266 71	7096 14	46 04
7	S	—0—	1081 33	—	3266 71	8177 47	39 95
8	M	419 12	905 56	46 18	3685 83	9085 03	40 57
9	T	552 36	953 32	57 94	4238 19	10038 35	42 22
10	W	607 96	1206 15	50 41	4846 15	11244 50	43 10
11	Th	563 59	881 43	63 94	5409 74	12125 93	44 61
12	F	995 91	1604 12	62 08	6405 65	13730 05	46 65
13	S	168 91	1713 68	9 86	6574 56	15443 73	42 57
14	S	—0—	1031 71	—	6574 56	16475 44	39 91
15	M	432 73	924 41	46 81	7007 29	17399 85	40 27
16	T	639 57	938 16	68 17	7646 86	18338 01	41 70
17	W	791 55	1209 24	59 50	8438 41	19547 25	43 17
18	Th	574 09	822 58	69 79	9012 50	20369 83	44 24
19	F	1010 20	1581 62	64 28	10022 70	21951 45	45 66
20	S	109 46	1757 93	6 23	10132 16	23709 38	42 73
21	S	—0—	1002 48	—	10132 16	24711 86	41 00
22	M	420 66	972 43	43 26	10552 82	25684 29	41 09
23	T	640 10	891 18	71 83	11192 92	26575 47	42 12
24	W	782 09	1247 06	62 71	11975 01	27822 53	43 04
25	Th	493 48	871 28	56 66	12468 49	28693 81	43 45
26	F	1141 98	1627 84	70 15	13610 47	30321 65	44 89
27	S	120 49	1698 01	7 10	13730 96	32019 66	42 88
28	S	—0—	1080 08	—	13730 96	33099 74	41 48
29	M	486 76	906 74	53 68	14217 72	34006 48	41 81
30	T	498 66	938 38	53 14	14716 38	34944 86	42 11
31	W	407 09	1262 55	32 24	15123 47	36207 41	41 77
Total for Month		15123 47	36207 41	41 77	15123 47	36207 41	41 77

Chart 9-1   Food Cost Formula Number 1 (Purchases Formula)

or personnel to devote to a more complicated system. Formula Number 1 is not as thorough or accurate as Formula 2 (discussed later in this chapter), but it can be effective and it is certainly better than nothing.

There is only one equation in Formula 1. It is: ALL FOOD PURCHASES divided by FOOD SALES multiplied by 100 to convert to a percentage equals FOOD COST PERCENT PER DOLLAR SALE.

The easiest way to use this formula is to prepare a chart on column paper as shown in Chart 9-1 and do the steps described below. The following comments on each column tell you how to fill it all in, day-by-day and column-by-column, as you go through a month. Check the following comments about each column with Chart 9-1 as you read. This may look complicated, but it really is not. (This is also true of Chart 9-2 discussed later in this chapter.)

1. Column 1: Date.
   Always start a new chart the first of each month, so your Date column starts with 1.

2. Column 2: Day.
   In the Day column, put whatever day the first of the month happens to fall on. (S for Saturday, W for Wednesday, and so on). In our sample Chart 9-1, you are starting on March 1, a Monday.
   COLUMNS 3, 4, AND 5 ARE TODAY FIGURES—JUST DAILY, DAY-BY-DAY—NOT INCREASING, NOT ACCUMULATING AS YOU GO.

3. Column 3: Today Food Purchases.
   To get this figure, you add together all your invoices for all the food you receive each day. In Chart 9-1, on Monday, March 1, your invoices total $412.93.

4. Column 4: Today Food Sales.
   This figure is your total food sales for Monday, March 1. Get this figure from Monday's cash register tape. In our chart the figure is $897.23. Get your closing cash register tape figure every day and put it in this column.

5. Column 5: Today Food Cost Percent.
   To get this figure, divide Column 3 Today Food Purchases by Column 4 Today Food Sales. For example, to get this figure for Monday, March 1, you divide Column 3 Today Food Purchases Date 1 figure $412.93 by Column 4 Today Food Sales Date 1 figure $897.23. You get .4602. Multiply .4602 by 100 to convert to a percentage, and you get 46.02 percent. Monday's food cost percent is 46.02 percent.
   COLUMNS 6, 7, AND 8 ARE TO-DATE FIGURES. THESE COLUMNS DO INCREASE AND DO ACCUMULATE FOR THE MONTH AS YOU GO ALONG.

6. Column 6: To-Date Food Purchases.
   Just for the first day of the month, your Column 6 To-Date Food Purchases figure Date 1 is the same as your Column 3 Today Food Purchases Date 1 figure—$412.93.
   After the first day of the month, you start adding.
   To get your Column 6 To-Date Food Purchases Date 2 figure for Tuesday, March 2, add your Column 3 Today Food Purchases Date 1 (Monday) figure $412.93 and your Column 3 Today Food Purchases Date 2 (Tuesday) figure $526.60. You get $939.53. This $939.53 is your Column 6 To-Date Food Purchases Date 2 (Tuesday) figure.
   To get your Column 6 To-Date Food Purchases Date 3 figure, you add your Column 3 Today Food Purchases Date 3 figure $649.03 and your Column 6 To-Date Food Purchases Date 2 figure $939.53. You get $1,588.56. This $1,588.56 is your Column 6 To-Date Food Purchases Date 3 figure.

Follow this procedure every day the rest of the month.

For Thursday, March 4, your Column 6 To-Date Food Purchases figure is $2,114.94 (the total of Column 3 for Monday, Tuesday, Wednesday, and Thursday).

Keep going this same way until the end of the month.

Your Total for the Month figures at the bottom line of the chart should be identical in Columns 3 and 6.

You spent $15,123.47 for food in March.

7. Column 7: To-Date Food Sales.

Use the same method for Column 7 as you do for Column 6.

Just for the first day of the month, your Column 7 To-Date Food Sales figure is the same as your Column 4 Today Food Sales figure $897.23. After the first day of the month, you start adding.

To get your Column 7 To-Date Food Sales figure for Date 2 (Tuesday), add your Column 4 Today Food Sales Date 1 (Monday) figure $897.23 and your Column 4 Today Food Sales Date 2 (Tuesday) figure $926.44. You get $1,823.67. This $1,823.67 is your Column 7 To-Date Food Sales Date 2 (Tuesday) figure.

To get your Column 7 To-Date Food Sales Date 3 figure (Wednesday), you add your Column 4 Today Food Sales Date 3 figure $1,138.16 and your Column 7 To-Date Food Sales Date 2 figure $1,823.67. You get $2,961.83. This $2,961.83 is your Column 7 To-Date Food Sales Date 3 (Wednesday) figure.

Follow this procedure daily for the rest of the month. Your Column 7 To-Date Food Sales Date 4 (Thursday) figure is $3,918.24—the total of Column 4 for Monday, Tuesday, Wednesday, and Thursday.

Keep going this same way until the end of the month. The Total for Month figures at the bottom line of the chart should be identical in Columns 4 and 7.

Your food sales were $36,207.41 in March.

8. Column 8: To-Date Food Cost Percent.

Just for the first day of the month, your Column 8 To-Date Food Cost Percent Date 1 figure is the same as your Column 5 Today Food Cost Percent Date 1 figure.

After the first day, it gets cumulative. This is the column you watch like a hawk.

To get your Column 8 To-Date Food Cost Percent Date 2 figure, you divide Column 6 To-Date Food Purchases Date 2 figure $939.53 by Column 7 To-Date Food Sales Date 2 figure $1,823.67. You get .5152. Multiply this .5152 by 100 to convert to percent. You get 51.52 percent. Your Column 8 To-Date Food Cost Percent Date 2 figure is 51.52 percent.

To get your Column 8 To-Date Food Cost Percent Date 3 figure, you divide your Column 6 To-Date Food Purchases Date 3 figure $1,588.56 by your Column 7 To-Date Food Sales Date 3 figure $2,961.83. You get .5363. Multiply this .5363 by 100 to convert to percent. You get 53.63 percent. Your Column 8 To-Date Food Cost Percent Date 3 figure is 53.63 percent.

Keep going this same way until the end of the month.

The Total for Month figure at the bottom line of Chart 9-1 for Column 8 To-Date Food Cost Percent is 41.77 percent. The Total for Month at bottom line of Column 5 Today Food Cost Percent is also 41.77 percent. Totals should be identical in Columns 5 and 8.

This 41.77 percent is your food cost percent for March.

The bottom figures in Column 5 Today Food Cost Percent and Column 8 To-Date Food Cost Percent are not totals. You get the bottom figure 41.77 percent in Column 5 by dividing Column 3 Total For Month Today Food Purchases figure $15,123.47 by Column 4 Total For Month Today Food Sales $36,207.41.

You get the Column 8 bottom figure 41.77 percent by just bringing down your last figure for the last day of the month in this column. Column 8 is the result of your cumulative figures for the month. The figures in Columns 6, 7, and 8 for Wednesday, March 31, are the cumulative figures through the last day of the month. These cumulative figures in Columns 6, 7, and 8 for Wednesday, March 31, are the same as Totals for Month figures in Columns 3, 4, and 5.

Advantages in Food Cost Formula Number 1

What are the advantages of using Formula Number 1? What can it tell you?

1. Formula 1 is simple and easy to do.
2. Formula 1 gives you a general indication of the trend your food cost is taking for the month. About 10 days after the beginning of each month is an important time for your food cost control program because that is when cumulative figures begin to mean something concrete to you.

   Look at Chart 9-1, Column 8, Date 10, Wednesday, March 10. Your To-Date Food Cost Percent is 43.10 percent. Let us say you want a food cost percent of 42 percent for the month of March. It is only the 10th of the month, so you have 21 days left in March to reduce your food cost percent for the month. Look at the very bottom line of Column 8—Total for Month. Your cumulative To-Date Food Cost Percent for the month of March winds up at 41.77 percent. This is 1.33 percent lower than the cumulative To-Date Food Cost Percent of 43.10 percent you had on Wednesday, March 10. 1.33 percent may sound like a small percent, but it can represent a lot of dollars. In our example, 1.33 percent multiplied by Column 7 To-Date Sales Total for Month $36,207.41 equals $485.60— quite a few dollars.

   The point is, if you don't like *your* Column 8 figure after the first week or 10 days of a month, do something about it. You know where you stand and you've still got time during the month to take action that will fix your cumulative food cost percent so you *will* like the figure that counts—the figure at the bottom of Column 8 in your chart which is your food cost percent for the month—at the end of the month.

   The first 10 days of every month indicate the trend your food cost is taking for the month. If it is high, reduce your purchases. *Try* to buy less. The

10th day of the month is important when it comes to perishable food, too. By the 10th you should have used up any perishable food you bought on the first of the month. If you haven't, it is probably spoiled. Despite freezing and special spoilage-retarding chemical additives, foods still do spoil. By about the 10th, if you have thrown out perishables you bought the first week, your food cost percent will be high because these foods are not in inventory (they went out in the garbage) and you have no revenue from them.

3. Another advantage of Formula 1 is that after the first 10 days of the month, each daily input of purchases and sales does not drastically change your to-date cost percent, as daily inputs of purchases and sales are apt to do in the first two or three days of the month. As the month progresses, each input of daily food purchases has a smaller impact on your total food purchased figure. Each input into Column 6 To-Date Food Purchases has a smaller impact on Column 6 as the month goes along.

As a month progresses, any one day's accumulated purchases constitutes a smaller percentage of the total purchases for the month. So, as the end of the month gets closer, the food cost figure you get from Formula Number 1 will come closer to your actual food cost.

To illustrate this point, look at Chart 9-1. Look at Column 8 To-Date Food Cost Percent Date 1 (Monday, March 1) figure. The figure is 46.02 percent. For the next day, the Column 8 Date 2 figure (Tuesday, March 2) is 51.52 percent. There is a difference of 5.50 percent between these two figures. Now look at Column 8 To-Date Food Cost Percent Date 24 (Wednesday, March 24) figure. Your cumulative food cost percent so far for March is 43.04 percent. Look at the Column 8 figure for the next day, March 25. The figure is 43.45 percent. There is only .41 percent difference between these two figures.

As you go along in the month, closer to the end of it, your cumulative To-Date Food Cost Percent figure in Column 8 settles into a pattern of figures that vary less from each other day to day and that are closer to what your actual food cost percent for the month is going to be.

After you have kept your chart for the first 10 days of a month, you can begin to see the pattern in your purchasing and sales and food cost percent. It is still early in the month and you have time left to take corrective action if your food cost percent for the first 10 days is too high. If you are over the food cost you want, look in your storeroom. Estimate whether your inventory has increased. If it *looks* to you as if it has increased, you are probably okay. If it *looks* as if it has decreased, you have probably used food from inventory instead of purchasing food and your food cost at the end of the month will probably be higher than Formula 1 indicates. "Looks" seems flimsy. It is—until you develop ability in judging your inventory. This takes a little time but your judgments can eventually become fairly accurate.

You can only control your food cost percent in Formula 1 by effectively purchasing for immediate use. Purchase carefully so you use food without increasing or decreasing your inventory. Some days you will increase your inventory; some days you will take food out and decrease it. But, on the average, inventory should be stable. You want it to be, for example, $2,000 on the first of the month and $2,000 on the 31st of the month. In between, it will fluctuate.

Disadvantages in Food Cost Formula Number 1

Formula Number 1 has some disadvantages, too.

1. Your Column 5 Today Food Cost Percent figure is not apt to be very accurate. Formula 1 is a simple formula. It does not allow for inventory fluctuation from the end of one month to the end of the next month, and therefore Column 5 will only be as accurate as the accuracy with which you manage your inventory. Formula Number 1 assumes that all purchases will be charged and used immediately—but in most establishments that is not really what happens. On some days, you buy more than you use up that day. The excess goes into your inventory. On other days, you use more than you buy that day, so you take food out of inventory. This makes Column 5 higher if you increase your inventory and lower if you decrease your inventory.

To illustrate this, look at Chart 9-1, Column 3 Today Food Purchases for all the Sundays—March 7, 14, 21, and 28. The figure is always zero. No items were counted as purchased on any Sunday because you did not get any deliveries of food on Sundays. But (in our chart) you were open for business on Sundays, so you took food out of inventory and used it on Sundays. In Column 5, all Sundays are zero because you did not buy anything, and you cannot divide a sales figure into zero.

For each Sunday, the Column 6 To-Date Food Purchases figure is the same figure as the figure entered for each Saturday right above it. Purchases are the same on Saturday and Sunday each week. Sales are not, however, You do sell food on Sundays. Sales figures in column 7 To-Date Food Sales are not the same Saturday and Sunday every week.

The fact that you do not receive food on Sunday but you do use food from the storeroom decreases your Column 8 To-Date Food Cost Percent figure for each Sunday. You do use food out of inventory, and this definitely lowers your cumulative To-Date Food Cost Percent for Sundays.

2. Formula Number 1 does not include the cost of feeding employees. Formula Number 2 does. (This factor is the main reason for the difference between the cumulative Column 8 To-Date Food Cost Percent for March in Chart 9-1 for Formula 1 and the cumulative Column 17 To-Date Food Cost Percent for March in Chart 9-2 for Formula 2.)

The Key to Success with Formula 1

The key to making Food Cost Formula Number 1 food cost control system work is inventory management. With experience you should be able to develop some accuracy in judging inventory fluctuations. If your food cost is high for the first 10 days, but you see that you have a lot of food in the storeroom, your accumulated food cost percent should go down later in the month because you should not have to buy much food. The actual physical inventory figure at the end of the month should not be very different from your actual physical inventory figure at the beginning of the month. (The ending inventory figure for one month is the opening inventory figure for the next month.)

One thing you can do to control inventory fluctuation is to try to limit what you buy toward the end of the month. You will have to buy some items at the end of the month. Maybe you will have to buy extra items for a banquet you will serve at the beginning of the following month. You will get the banquet revenue next month. Next month your to-date food cost percent should be lower because you have already bought some of the banquet food and should have fewer banquet purchases next month. This should reduce your food purchases for next month and give you a lower food cost percent next month.

If you get—and keep on getting—a lot of inventory fluctuation from month to month, the Food Cost Formula Number 1 system is not working well for you. Your inventory will fluctuate up or down on a day-to-day basis. But you want your inventory to be very similar in actual dollars and cents from one month end to the next month end. If your closing inventory February 28 was $2,500, for example, then you want your closing inventory on March 31 as close to $2,500 as you can get it. After you have used this system for a while, you will probably be able to eliminate or at least reduce some of the inventory fluctuation. Don't give up on Formula 1 too quickly. It will generally serve you better as you get more adept at making it work for you.

Inventory can and will fluctuate some, but this does not have to have a drastic effect on the to-date cumulative food cost percent you get with Formula 1. Even when your inventory does fluctuate, Formula 1 can still give you an indication of the trend your food cost percent is taking. Say, for example, your food service operation has average monthly sales of $30,000. You spend an average of $12,000 a month for food purchases. You maintain an average food inventory of $2,000. Suppose your inventory varies down $200 or up $200 from this $2,000 figure. Down $200 means a food cost of $11,800 and a food cost percent of 39.33 percent. Stationary at $12,000 means a food cost of $12,000 and a food cost percent of 40 percent. Up $200 means a food cost of $12,200 and a food cost percent of 40.66 percent.

With Formula 1, you calculate your corresponding changes in food cost percent. With $200 inventory fluctuation up or down from average, you have still stayed relatively close—two-thirds of a percent up or down—to the food cost percent for food purchases of $12,000. Your food cost has fluctuated up or down 10 percent. Even with inventory fluctuation, Formula 1 does tell you the trend of your food cost percent.

Food Cost Formula Number 1 is not as accurate as Formula 2, but it is certainly better than nothing and it can give you some helpful information. Nothing is helpful, however, if you don't *act* on information. Take action to correct a food cost that is not what you want it to be.

If you take pains, Formula 1 can work quite accurately. Ideally your to-date food cost percent for the month should be within 1 percent of your actual food cost percent.

If you use Food Cost Formula Number 1, you can help to see to it that you do come close to your actual food cost percent by:

1. Watching your purchases throughout the month and reducing purchases where you can if food cost percent gets too high.
2. Attempting to minimize inventory fluctuations.

Formula 1 can tell you the trend your food cost is taking. It can give you a pretty good indication of what your actual month's food cost will turn out to be before you deduct for employees' meals.

How Food Cost Percent Figure is Obtained for Profit and Loss Statement

Your food cost percent is the figure that is put on your profit and loss statement for the month. It is calculated as follows (only for use with Formula 1):

1. DOLLAR VALUE OF OPENING PHYSICAL FOOD INVENTORY (this figure was your closing total food inventory figure last month) plus TOTAL DOLLAR VALUE OF FOOD PURCHASES FOR THE MONTH (add up all invoices for month or get figure from your general accounting records where you have records of all food purchases for month) equals TOTAL FOOD AVAILABLE.
2. TOTAL FOOD AVAILABLE minus DOLLAR VALUE CLOSING PHYSICAL FOOD INVENTORY and minus DOLLAR VALUE EMPLOYEES' MEALS (if you feed your employees free meals, see Chapter 13 for how you get this figure) equals COST OF FOOD SOLD.
3. COST OF FOOD SOLD divided by TOTAL FOOD SALES FOR MONTH (add every day's closing cash register tapes for month or get from your general accounting record) multiplied by 100 to convert to percentage equals FOOD COST PERCENT FOR MONTH AS IT APPEARS ON YOUR PROFIT AND LOSS STATEMENT.

FOOD COST FORMULA NUMBER 2 (CHART 9-2)

How to Use Formula 2

This formula is more complex than Formula 1. It takes more time, but it is more accurate.

There are five equations in Formula 2. They are:

1. OPENING FOOD STOREROOM INVENTORY plus STOREROOM PURCHASES equals TOTAL FOOD AVAILABLE STOREROOM.
2. TOTAL FOOD AVAILABLE STOREROOM minus FOOD REQUISI-TIONS equals CLOSING FOOD STOREROOM INVENTORY.
(This second equation can also be written: TOTAL FOOD AVAILABLE STOREROOM minus CLOSING FOOD STOREROOM INVENTORY equals FOOD REQUISITIONS.)
3. FOOD REQUISITIONS plus DIRECT PURCHASES plus TRANSFERS TO KITCHEN equals COST OF FOOD USED.
4. COST OF FOOD USED minus EMPLOYEES' MEALS minus TRANS-FERS TO BAR equals COST OF FOOD SOLD.
5. COST OF FOOD SOLD divided by FOOD SALES multiplied by 100 to convert to percentage equals FOOD COST PERCENT PER DOLLAR SALE.

Start a new chart the first day of each month.

The easiest way to use this formula is to prepare a chart on column paper as shown in Chart 9-2 and do the following steps:

1. Column 1: Date.
   You always start a new chart the first of each month, so your Date column always starts with 1.
2. Column 2: Day.
   In the Day column, put whatever day the first of the month happens to fall on. (S if it's Saturday, W if it's Wednesday, and so on). In our sample Chart 9-2, we say you are starting on March 1 and we say it's a Monday. COLUMNS 3 THROUGH 14 ARE TODAY FIGURES—JUST DAILY, DAY-BY-DAY—NOT INCREASING, NOT ACCUMULATING AS YOU GO.
3. Column 3: Opening Food Storeroom Inventory Beginning of Day.
   This figure is the total dollar value amount of all food in your food store-room on the first day of the month—Monday, March 1 in our chart. You get this figure from your closing physical food storeroom inventory for the last day of the preceding month. Or you could take the bottom figure in Column 3 from your February chart if you did not take a physical in-ventory at the end of February.
   In Chart 9-2, on Monday, March 1, your Column 3 Opening Food Store-room Inventory Beginning of Day figure is $1,985.07. Get this figure from your closing physical storeroom inventory you took the last day of last month. On Monday, March 1, you start the day with $1,985.07 worth of food in your storeroom.

1	2	3	4	5	6	7	8	9
Date	Day	Opening Food Storeroom Inventory Beginning of Day	Storeroom Purchases	Total Food Available Storeroom	Food Requisitions	Direct Purchases	Transfers to Kitchen	Cost of Food Used
Mar. 1	M	1985 07	319 67	2304 74	327 15	93 26	2 19	422 60
2	T	1977 59	445 22	2422 81	389 64	81 38	1 58	472 60
3	W	2033 17	586 89	2620 06	421 52	62 14	—0—	483 66
4	Th	2198 54	487 89	2686 43	356 81	38 49	—0—	395 30
5	F	2329 62	912 43	3242 05	533 16	105 53	3 47	642 16
6	S	2708 89	104 15	2813 04	513 92	29 66	1 86	545 44
7	S	2299 12	—0—	2299 12	438 37	—0—	—0—	438 37
8	M	1860 75	337 21	2197 96	338 76	81 91	5 12	425 79
9	T	1859 20	458 49	2317 69	397 29	93 87	59	491 75
10	W	1920 40	533 64	2454 04	406 38	74 32	—0—	480 70
11	Th	2047 66	522 56	2570 22	339 24	41 03	—0—	380 27
12	F	2230 98	883 34	3114 32	587 63	112 57	3 62	703 82
13	S	2526 69	134 78	2661 47	579 94	34 13	74	614 81
14	S	2081 53	—0—	2081 53	426 18	—0—	—0—	426 18
15	M	1655 35	348 17	2003 52	322 37	84 56	2 14	409 07
16	T	1681 15	562 89	2244 04	366 34	76 68	—0—	443 02
17	W	1877 70	709 46	2587 16	445 48	82 09	1 81	529 38
18	Th	2141 68	517 28	2658 96	359 60	56 81	—0—	416 41
19	F	2299 36	911 73	3211 09	594 23	98 47	59	693 29
20	S	2616 86	80 15	2697 01	586 18	29 31	4 62	620 11
21	S	2110 83	—0—	2110 83	404 20	—0—	—0—	404 20
22	M	1706 63	328 78	2035 41	319 61	91 88	—0—	411 49
23	T	1715 80	576 59	2292 39	362 33	63 51	3 22	429 06
24	W	1930 06	687 36	2617 42	424 58	94 73	—0—	519 31
25	Th	2192 84	456 32	2649 16	401 16	37 16	—0—	438 32
26	F	2248 00	1027 66	3275 66	537 43	114 32	4 38	656 13
27	S	2738 23	94 41	2832 64	613 26	26 08	1 17	640 51
28	S	2219 38	—0—	2219 38	415 35	—0—	—0—	415 35
29	M	1804 03	409 32	2213 35	302 11	77 44	1 39	380 94
30	T	1911 24	412 84	2324 08	316 78	85 82	—0—	402 60
31	W	2007 30	332 16	2339 46	477 69	74 93	67	498 29
		1916 77						
Total for Month		1916 77	13181 39	—0—	13249 69	1942 08	39 16	15230 93

Proof of Inventory	
Opening Inventory	1985 07
Storeroom Purchases	13181 39
Total	15166 46
Requisitions	13249 69
Closing Inventory	1916 77

Chart 9-2   Food Cost Formula Number 2

10	11	12	13	14	15	16	17
Employees' Meals	Transfers from Kitchen to Bar	Today Cost of Food Sold	Today Food Sales	Today Food Cost % Per Dollar Sale	To-Date Cost of Food Sold	To-Date Food Sales	To-Date Food Cost % Per Dollar Sale
28 50	6 57	387 53	897 23	43 19	387 53	897 23	43 19
26 00	8 23	438 37	926 44	47 32	825 90	1823 67	45 29
26 25	4 19	453 22	1138 16	39 72	1279 12	2961 83	43 19
25 50	3 28	366 52	956 41	38 32	1645 64	3918 24	42 00
25 00	6 51	610 65	1528 52	39 95	2256 29	5446 76	41 42
29 75	8 13	507 56	1649 38	30 77	2763 85	7096 14	38 95
27 00	–0–	411 37	1081 33	38 04	3175 22	8177 47	38 83
28 50	7 14	390 15	907 56	42 99	3565 37	9085 03	39 24
26 25	6 29	459 21	953 32	48 17	4024 58	10038 35	40 09
26 25	5 25	449 20	1206 15	37 24	4473 78	11244 50	39 79
25 00	3 04	352 23	881 43	39 96	4826 01	12125 93	39 80
27 00	6 73	670 09	1604 12	41 77	5496 10	13730 05	40 03
28 75	9 07	576 99	1713 68	33 67	6073 09	15443 73	39 32
27 00	–0–	399 18	1031 71	38 73	6472 27	16475 44	39 28
28 50	5 98	374 59	924 41	40 52	6846 86	17399 85	39 35
26 00	6 53	410 49	938 16	43 75	7257 35	18338 01	39 58
26 25	4 42	498 71	1209 24	41 24	7756 06	19547 25	39 68
25 00	3 81	387 60	822 58	47 12	8143 66	20369 83	39 98
28 00	9 74	655 55	1581 62	41 45	8799 21	21951 45	40 08
29 75	8 26	582 10	1757 93	33 11	9381 31	23709 38	39 57
27 00	–0–	377 20	1002 48	37 63	9758 51	24711 86	39 49
28 00	6 38	377 11	972 43	38 78	10135 62	25684 29	39 46
26 25	5 79	397 02	891 18	44 55	10532 64	26575 47	39 63
25 50	4 83	488 98	1247 06	39 21	11021 62	27822 53	39 61
25 00	3 18	410 14	871 28	47 07	11431 76	28693 81	39 84
28 50	7 56	620 07	1627 84	38 09	12051 83	30321 65	39 75
29 75	8 35	602 41	1698 01	35 48	12654 24	32019 66	39 52
27 50	–0–	387 85	1080 08	35 91	13042 09	33099 74	39 40
28 00	5 21	347 73	906 74	38 35	13389 82	34006 48	39 37
26 00	6 68	369 92	938 38	39 42	13759 74	34944 86	39 38
25 00	4 88	468 41	1262 55	37 10	14228 15	36207 41	39 30
836 75	166 03	14228 15	36207 41	39 30	14228 15	36207 41	39 30

Proof of Cost	
Opening Inventory	1985 07
Storeroom Purchases	13181 39
Direct Purchases	1942 08
Transfers to Kitchen	39 16
Total	17147 70
Employees' Meals	836 75
Transfer to Bar	166 03
Closing Inventory	1916 77
Cost of Food Sold	14228 15

Chart 9-2 Food Cost Formula Number 2 (continued)

Column 3 always has one figure more than it has days in the month. That is because you are using Column 3 to record both opening and closing inventories for the month.

Your closing inventory figure for Monday, March 1, is your Column 3 Opening Food Inventory Beginning of Day figure for Tuesday, March 2. Closing inventory for Date 1 is $1,977.59 (see a and b below). Put this in Column 3 Date 2 because closing inventory for Date 1 is Opening Food Inventory Beginning of Day for Date 2.

To get Date 2 for Column 3, do the following steps:

a. Add Column 4 Storeroom Purchases Date 1 $319.67 and Column 3 Opening Food Inventory Beginning of Day Date 1 $1,985.07. You get $2,304.74. This $2,304.74 is your Column 5 Total Food Available Storeroom Date 1 figure.

b. Subtract Column 6 Food Requisitions Date 1 $327.15 from Column 5 Total Food Available Storeroom Date 1 $2,304.74. You get $1,977.59. This $1,977.59 is your Column 3 Opening Food Inventory Beginning of Day Date 2 figure.

4. Column 4: Storeroom Purchases.

On Monday, March 1, you received Storeroom Purchases of $319.67 worth of food. You get the figure for Column 4 Storeroom Purchases by adding the dollar value of all food invoices for the food you put in the food storeroom each day. This figure is all food items that will go into the storeroom. When they leave the storeroom, requisitions will be written for the items and they will go into food production. The food should *not* leave the storeroom unless it is requisitioned in writing.

Put as many purchase items into this Column 4 Storeroom Purchases category as you can instead of into the Column 7 Direct Purchases category, which are *not* requisitioned. Storeroom Purchases items are issued only by written requisition, and when you have written requisitions you can get a more accurate food cost with Formula 2.

5. Column 5: Total Food Available Storeroom.

To get this figure for Monday, March 1, you add Column 3 Opening Food Inventory Beginning of Day $1,985.07 and Column 4 Storeroom Purchases figure Monday, March 1, $319.67. You get $2,304.74. This $2,304.74 is your Column 5 Total Food Available Storeroom figure for Monday, March 1.

This figure is the dollar amount of your total inventory plus items you received and put into the storeroom that day. This is the value of food you had to start with Monday morning March 1 plus what you received Monday—the total value of food available to you on Monday, March 1.

6. Column 6: Food Requisitions.

You get this figure by adding up all your food requisition slips for Monday, March 1. For Monday, March 1, the figure on Chart 9-2 is $327.15. Add up all your food requisitions for the day to get your total dollar cost of all food items removed from your storeroom that day.

$327.15 worth of food was removed from your storeroom on Monday, March 1. Requisitions were written for all this food. All this food went to food production in the kitchen.

7. Column 7: Direct Purchases.

In Chart 9-2 for Monday, March 1, the figure is $93.26. On Monday, March 1, you received Direct Purchases of $93.26 worth of food. This food goes right to production. It never goes to the storeroom at all. There are no requisitions.

Examples of these types of items could be bread, milk, ice cream, pies, pastries—items that should be used that day. These items generally have to be called Direct Purchases. They must go right to the kitchen and cannot sit on a shelf in the storeroom. But don't classify any food as Direct Purchases unless you have to—the fewer the better. Put everything that can reasonably go to the storeroom in the Column 4 Storeroom Purchases category instead, so you *do* use requisitions and will have more accurate records for your food cost.

8. Column 8: Transfers to Kitchen.

Transfers to kitchen are items you use in the kitchen in food production. But you do not requisition them from the food storeroom. They are not direct purchases, either. These are items you transfer to your kitchen from another department in your operation, usually the bar. The chef (or anyone you authorize in the kitchen) makes written requisitions for items the kitchen wants from the bar and gives them to the bar in exchange for the items. Whoever makes up this Formula 2 chart gets the information from the bar and puts the dollar amount of transfers to kitchen for the day in this column.

Examples of transfers to kitchen would be beer requisitioned from the bar and used in the kitchen to make welch rarebit; wine requisitioned from the bar and used in the kitchen for cooking, and so on. These are bar beverage items. But they are not beverage items available for bar beverage sale. They are used in the kitchen as ingredients in food. Charge their cost to food cost, not bar or beverage department cost. (And don't forget—if your cook drinks some of this beer or wine, it is part of your food cost for the day.)

9. Column 9: Cost of Food Used.

To get this figure, you add Column 6 Food Requisitions, Column 7 Direct Purchases, and Column 8 Transfers to Kitchen. Put the total in Column 9. It is the total dollar value of food available each day.

In Chart 9-2, Column 9 Date 1 is $422.60. You get this by adding Column 6 Food Requisitions Date 1 $327.15 and Column 7 Direct Purchases Date 1 $93.26 and Column 8 Transfers to Kitchen Date 1 $2.19.

To get Column 9 figure for Date 2, add Column 6 Date 2, Column 7 Date 2, and Column 8 Date 2. Keep doing this the same way the rest of the month.

10. Column 10: Employees' Meals.

You deduct for employees' meals because if you give food to your employees free (or at discount price) it costs you money to feed employees. (There are several different ways you can get this figure, and we will discuss them in Chapter 13.)

In the food service industry, you generally feed the employees who are on duty in the food service department. If food service employees put in an eight-hour shift in a food service operation, they usually get one meal, maybe more. If you buy food that you give free to your employees, it is a cost for you, and you must recognize it and deduct for it from cost of food used. The dollar value for employees' meals for each day is recorded in Column 10.

11. Column 11: Transfers from Kitchen to Bar.

This means items you transfer from the food department to the beverage department. The bar can requisition things like cream, milk, eggs, oranges, lemons, limes, cherries, or olives from the kitchen. They are food items taken from the kitchen, sent to the bar, and used in drinks. Don't charge these to food cost. Charge them to the bar.

Bartenders write requisitions for food items they need and give them to the kitchen personnel—probably cooks, or anyone you designate. Cooks keep these requisitions until you (or whoever is keeping the Formula chart) get them from the cooks, add them up for the day, and put the figure in this column.

Some operations ignore transfers to kitchen and transfers to bar because they don't think there is enough money involved to bother with making the calculations and putting them in the chart. It is up to you to decide if you think it is worthwhile for you or not. You should, however, be aware that food items from the kitchen used in drink preparation cannot be sold as food, and beverage items used in the kitchen cannot be sold as bar items so there will be an effect on bar and kitchen costs if there are transfers. How big the effect will be will depend on how much transferring goes on and how much the items cost.

12. Column 12: Today Cost of Food Sold.

To get this figure, you add Column 10 Employees' Meals Date 1 $28.50 and Column 11 Transfers from Kitchen to Bar Date 1 $6.57. You get $35.07. Subtract this $35.07 from Column 9 Cost of Food Used Date 1 $422.60. You get $387.53. This $387.53 is your Column 12 Today Cost of Food Sold Date 1 figure.

Follow this same procedure through the rest of the month.

Note that there are only two deductions you make from Cost of Food Used to get your Column 12 Today Cost of Food Sold. They are Employees' Meals (Column 10) and Transfers from Kitchen to Bar (Column 11).

You subtract these two costs (if they occur) from Column 9 Cost of Food Used to get dollar value for Column 12 Today Cost of Food Sold. Any mistakes in direct purchases, requisitioning, overproduction, discarded food, and the like should be (and by this method will be) charged into the cost of food sold for the day they happen.

13. Column 13: Today Food Sales.

The Date 1 figure in this column is the total food sales for Monday, March 1. You get this figure from your cash register tape for Monday. In Chart 9-2 you had $897.23 in food sales on Monday, March 1.

Get the closing figure from your cash register tape each day for this column.

14. Column 14: Today Food Cost Percent Per Dollar Sale.

You get this figure by doing the following: Divide Column 12 Today Cost of Food Sold Date 1 $387.53 by Column 13 Today Food Sales Date 1 $897.23. You get .4319. Multiply by 100 to convert to a percentage. You get 43.19 percent. Your Column 14 Today Food Cost Percent Per Dollar Sale for Date 1 is 43.19 percent.

Follow this procedure for the rest of the month.

COLUMNS 15, 16, and 17 ARE TO-DATE FIGURES. THESE COLUMNS DO INCREASE AND DO ACCUMULATE FOR THE MONTH AS YOU GO ALONG.

15. Column 15: To-Date Cost of Food Sold.

For Date 1, Column 15 is the same as Column 12 Today Cost of Food Sold Date 1—$387.53.

To get Column 15 Date 2, add Column 15 To-Date Cost of Food Sold Date 1 $387.53 and Column 12 Today Cost of Food Sold Date 2 $438.37. This gives you Column 15 To-Date Cost of Food Sold Date 2—$825.90. To get Column 15 Date 3, add Column 15 To-Date Cost of Food Sold Date 2 $825.90 and Column 12 Today Cost of Food Sold Date 3 $453.22. This gives you Column 15 To-Date Cost of Food Sold Date 3—$1,279.12.

Follow this procedure the rest of the month.

16. Column 16: To-Date Food Sales.

For Date 1, Column 16 is the same as Column 13 Today Food Sales Date 1—$897.23.

To get Column 16 Date 2, add Column 16 To-Date Food Sales Date 1 $897.23 and Column 13 Today Food Sales Date 2 $926.44. This gives you Column 16 Date 2—$1,823.67.

To get Column 16 Date 3, add Column 16 To-Date Food Sales Date 2 $1,823.67 and Column 13 Today Food Sales Date 3 $1,138.16. This gives you Column 16 Date 3—$2,961.83.

Follow this procedure the rest of the month.

17. Column 17: To-Date Food Cost Percent Per Dollar Sale.

To get this figure, divide Column 15 To-Date Cost of Food Sold Date 1 $387.53 by Column 16 To-Date Food Sales Date 1 $897.23. You get .4319. Multiply by 100 to convert to a percentage. You get 43.19 percent. Your Column 17 To-Date Food Cost Percent Per Dollar Sale for Date 1 is 43.19 percent.

Follow this same procedure for the rest of the month.

Note: When you compute Column 17 To-Date Food Cost Percent, *always* divide Column 15 To-Date Cost of Food Sold by Column 16 To-Date Food Sales. Don't ever try to average your cumulative food cost percents. It will not be accurate.

The figures you put in Column 17 To-Date Food Cost Percent each day are the figures you go through the entire routine to get. Every day, all month, you watch Column 17 like a hawk. You take action if you need to in order to get the daily, and thus ultimately the monthly, food cost percent you want.

"Food cost percent" is just a guide for you. It can be a *very* good tool to use, but it is just a tool. Treat it that way. "Food cost percentage" is just words unless you understand and use the facts the words symbolize. Your *goal* is not "food cost percent." Your *goal* is net profit in dollars. Controlling your food cost percent *as you go* can help you achieve that goal.

Advantages in Food Cost Formula Number 2

What are the advantages of Food Cost Formula 2?

1. Formula Number 2 is more accurate than Formula 1 because Formula 2:
    a. Includes changes in inventory in storeroom.
    b. Includes transfers to and from kitchen and to and from bar.
    c. Deducts for cost of employees' meals.
2. Formula 2 makes it possible for you to calculate what your closing storeroom inventory should be. (Formula 1 does not.)

Disadvantages in Food Cost Formula Number 2

This formula also has disadvantages.

1. Formula 2 is more work than Formula 1 because with Formula 2:
    a. You must write down all requisitions and make extensions on requisitions.
    b. You must write down and make extensions on all transfers from kitchen to bar and from bar to kitchen.
    c. You must compute the cost of feeding all your employees every day. (But you should do this last one anyway.)
2. Formula 2 *does* recognize food storeroom inventory, but it does not consider total inventory because it does not consider goods in process in the kitchen. (Formula 1 does not recognize *any* inventory.)

The Key to Success with Formula 2

The key to having Formula Number 2 work right for you is to keep accurate records. Some food service operations find Food Cost Formula Number 2 unsatisfactory because they fail to do this. Formula 2 will not work well if you can't or won't keep accurate records and make accurate extensions for requisitions. "Extensions" means you multiply the cost of each item by the number or amount of that item. (One pound of butter costs $1, five pounds costs $5—$5 is the extension.) It does take time and effort to see that all items are written on requisitions and that proper price extensions are made on all requisitions.

Many operations also fail to keep track of requisitions to and from the bar and to and from the kitchen. They think that the dollar amounts involved are so small that they are unimportant and that ignoring transfers will not have any significant effect on their cost formula. Other operations do keep track of all requisitions to and from the bar and kitchen. For them, there *is* enough money involved to make it significant. That is a decision you have to make based on the cost of doing the work and on the amounts of money involved. Whatever you decide, do recognize that when beverage items from the bar are used in the kitchen in food preparation, it is a food cost, and when food items from the kitchen are used in the bar, it is a bar cost. Be aware of how much transferring goes on and decide whether you really need to keep records on these transfers or not. If there is enough money involved, it can affect the accuracy of Formula 2.

The same holds true for other situations where there are transfers to and from other departments besides kitchen and bar. Maybe you have more than one kitchen and have transfers between them. Or maybe you have an employee cafeteria and transfer items to it from the main kitchen. In hospitals, there may be special diet kitchens that transfer items back and forth between the main kitchens. It is up to you to decide how detailed your records should be and how closely you need to be able to predict the results. Some food service operations do not keep track of transfers to and from the kitchen, but they do keep track of food requisitioned from the storeroom directly to other departments besides the kitchen. For example, the bar may requisition items directly from the food storeroom. In the chart, the operation would recognize this by an additional column "Requisitions from Storeroom to Bar." This would be used in computing Inventory Storeroom Beginning of Day, but the bar requisitions would not be included when the operation computes today and to-date food cost and food cost percents.

How Food Cost Percent Figure is Obtained for Profit and Loss Statement

At the end of the month the food cost percent you get from Formula 2 should be very close to the food cost percent on your profit and loss statement. To get the food cost percent figure for the profit and loss statement, do the following (for use only with Formula 2):

1. OPENING TOTAL PHYSICAL FOOD INVENTORY IN DOLLARS (this figure is your closing physical inventory figure from the preceding month) plus TOTAL FOOD PURCHASES IN DOLLARS (take Chart 9-2 Column 4 Storeroom Purchases Total for Month figure plus Column 7 Direct Purchases Total for Month figure, or if you don't use the chart, add up all food purchases invoices for month or get from your general accounting records where you record all food purchases) plus TRANSFERS TO KITCHEN (add up all requisitions for items sent from bar to kitchen Column 8 Transfers to Kitchen) equals TOTAL FOOD AVAILABLE IN THE ESTABLISHMENT.

2. TOTAL FOOD AVAILABLE IN THE ESTABLISHMENT minus DOLLAR VALUE FOR TRANSFERS FROM KITCHEN TO BAR

(Column 11 Transfers from Kitchen to Bar, or if you don't use the chart, add requisitions of all items sent from kitchen to bar) minus DOLLAR VALUE EMPLOYEES' MEALS (see Column 10 Employees' Meals, or if you don't use the chart, see Chapter 13 on how to get the figure) and TOTAL CLOSING PHYSICAL FOOD INVENTORY IN DOLLARS (take physical inventory—this figure will be your opening inventory figure next month) equals COST OF FOOD SOLD AS IT SHOULD APPEAR ON YOUR PROFIT AND LOSS STATEMENT. (This cost of food sold figure is the one that appears on your profit and loss statement.)

3. COST OF FOOD SOLD divided by FOOD SALES (Total Column 13 Food Sales or add all closing cash register tapes or get from general accounting records where you have recorded all food sales) multiplied by 100 to convert to percentage equals ACTUAL FOOD COST PERCENT PER DOLLAR SALE.

Differences Between Formula 2 Inventory Figure and Physical Inventory Figure on Profit and Loss Statement

Both opening and closing inventories for physical inventory figures on the profit and loss statement are composed of two parts:

1. Inventory Food in Storeroom.
2. Inventory Food in Process.

Inventory Food in Storeroom

Formula 1 takes no consideration of any inventories at all. Food Cost Formula Number 2 does take opening and closing inventory of storeroom into consideration. But it does not take opening and closing inventory of food in process into consideration. Fluctuation between opening and closing inventory food in process will cause the variation between the Food Cost Formula Number 2 figure and the cost of food sold figure on the profit and loss statement.

At the end of the month, compare the inventory you get from Food Cost Formula Number 2 for the storeroom with the physical inventory figure for the storeroom you get by counting everything in your storeroom.

The formula you use for calculating the dollar value of your food storeroom inventory is:

OPENING FOOD STOREROOM INVENTORY plus FOOD STOREROOM PURCHASES minus FOOD REQUISITIONS should equal CLOSING FOOD STOREROOM INVENTORY.

This helps you compare the results of your month's work and test the accuracy of your procedures for checking food in and out of the storeroom. For example, in Chart 9-2, on Monday, March 1, you had a Column 3 Opening Inventory Beginning of Day figure of $1,985.07. To this you add Column 4 Total Storeroom Purchases Total for the Month figure $13,181.39. This gives you a Food Available Storeroom Total for Month figure of $15,166.46 (this figure is not on Chart 9-2). From this you subtract Column 6 Food Requisitions Total for Month figure $13,249.69. You get Column 3 Opening Food Inventory Beginning of Day bottom figure in Column $1,916.77 (same as "Closing Inventory" figure under "Proof of Inventory" at bottom of chart).

In Chart 9-2, $1,916.77 (bottom figure in Column 3) is your calculated figure for your closing food storeroom inventory. $1,916.77 (or within 1 percent of it) is the figure your actual physical food storeroom inventory and extensions should give you, too.

The first few times you use Formula 2, the physical food storeroom inventory figure you get will probably be less than your calculated inventory value. Why? The explanation is simple. Somebody took items from the storeroom and didn't fill out requisitions. Now the question is—what happened to the items? Did someone use them in food production without handing in a requisition? Were the items stolen? Take action to stop the theft or the lack of requisitioning causing the unaccounted-for disappearance of food from your storeroom.

Some very slight discrepancy between calculated inventory and physical inventory is almost sure to occur due to the necessary rounding off of cents in requisitioning items and valuing inventory. This is a small matter, and there's no way to avoid it. The usual way to round off figures is to round down one cent if the figure is less than one-half cent and round up one cent if it is more than one-half cent. For example, an item that costs $0.124 may appear on a requisition as $0.12 (the 4 is less than 5). An item that costs $0.168 may appear as $0.17 (the 8 is more than 5). The difference between calculated inventory and physical inventory that this causes will be very small—a few cents or a few dollars.

As a guideline, the value of the inventory you get by your calculated method should not vary by more than 1 percent of total dollar value of inventory from the value of the inventory you get when you make physical count and do extensions and multiply the individual items by their own cost. If there is more than a 1 percent variation, Formula Number 2 is not working as well as it should. On a $2,000 inventory, a 1 percent variation would be $20; on a $3,000 inventory, it would be $30, and so on. One percent is not a very large variation, but you should not get more than that.

Inventory Food in Process

The food cost percent you get from Food Cost Formula Number 2 should vary less than 1 percent from the actual food cost percent on your profit and loss statement. As we said, there will be some variation between Formula 2 food cost percent and profit and loss statement food cost percent because Formula 2 does not count food in process in the kitchen and the profit and loss statement does.

There will be some food in the kitchen at the beginning of the month when opening physical inventory is taken, and there will be some food in the kitchen at the end of the month when closing physical inventory is taken. This food is counted in a profit and loss statement but not counted in Formula 2.

There will always be some food in the kitchen in varying stages of production—a half-gallon of mayonnaise, some portions of cold roast beef for sandwiches, a partially used bottle of chicken stock, and so on. Under normal conditions, however, the overall amounts of these items—considering them over a period of time—will probably be relatively constant. When you actually do take your physical inventory, you will have to make estimates concerning the items in this food-in-process category in the kitchen. The half-gallon of mayonnaise is probably a little more or a little less than precisely a half gallon, but you can write down the amount as half a gallon. Maybe you should actually weigh or count some of the more expensive items and compute a fairly accurate value for them.

After you have tried to count, measure, and evaluate everything in the entire kitchen, you just about have to lump remaining odds and ends together and assign them as close a cash value as you can. This is a standard, normal practice and there is nothing wrong with it. These should be calculated estimates. You cannot be totally accurate, but try to be consistent. Your estimates of cash value may be a bit off, but if you are consistently off by about the same amount, it will not really distort your food cost.

When you have counted some of the expensive items in the kitchen and added your "lump sum" for the rest, you have your "food in process in kitchen" figure. Add this total dollar value to your dollar value of storeroom inventory figure. This gives you total dollar value of total food inventory.

SUMMARY

The main difference between the final results you get from Formula 1 and Formula 2 is that Formula 2 includes employees' meals and Formula 1 does not. There is a difference of 2.47 percent between the 41.77 percent (bottom of Column 8, Chart 9-1) monthly food cost percent you get from Formula 1 and the 39.30 percent (bottom of Column 17, Chart 9-2) monthly food cost percent you get from Formula 2. Most of this 2.47 percent difference is because employees' meals is in Formula 2 and not in Formula 1.

In Chart 9-2, the employees' meals cost percent is 2.31 percent. (COST OF EMPLOYEES' MEALS Column 10 Employees' Meals $836.75 divided by MONTHLY FOOD SALES Column 13 Today Food Sales Total for Month $36,207.41 equals COST PERCENT OF EMPLOYEES' MEALS 2.31%.)

If you subtract the 2.31 percent employees' meals cost percent from the 2.47 percent difference between formula figures, the difference is reduced to .16 percent. This shows that the major cost difference between Formulas 1 and 2 is the cost of employees' meals.

You use a food cost formula (either Formula 1 or Formula 2, or your own variations) as a management tool to help you know what direction your food cost is taking for a certain period of time, usually one month. The cumulative results you get from the first 10 days of the month are important indicators to you of what direction—above, below, or on target—your food cost percent is taking that month.

Food cost is a variable cost. It goes up and down with your sales. But as sales and food cost go up or down together, you want your food cost percent to stay the same. This is what you are aiming for. It is worth a lot of time and trouble if you can succeed in getting the month's cumulative food cost percent and the actual end-of-month food cost percent you wanted and tried for right along.

In later chapters we will discuss how to get the information you need to use in whichever food cost formula you use. We will try to pinpoint areas of cost that you must watch on a planned, systematic basis to help you get the food cost you are after. We will also discuss what you should do as you go along to help you see to it that you do achieve the food cost you want.

REVIEW AND DISCUSSION QUESTIONS

1. What is the equation for Food Cost Formula Number 1?
2. What are the equations for Food Cost Formula Number 2?
3. Why are costs during the first 10 days of the month important in Formula 1 Chart 9-1 and Formula 2 Chart 9-2?
4. Explain why Formula Number 2 is more indicative of food cost than is Formula 1.

10

The Menu

Objectives

This chapter discusses the importance of menus to food and beverage operations. After you have read this chapter, you should:

1. Have some ideas about organizing and writing your own menu.
2. Know about the different types of menus.
3. Know the various factors that affect and are interrelated to your menu.

THE MENU AS A SALES TOOL

Your menu is one of your most important sales tools. There are many advertising techniques you can use to attract guests into your food service establishment. Once they are inside, your main sales tool is probably your menu. It lists and describes what you offer for sale. Everything that goes on in your food service operation has a direct or indirect effect on your menu. It's a very important central factor.

Before a food service operation is ever opened to the public in the first place, owners and/or management should have made plans concerning what type of food to offer on the menu. The items you offer for sale directly affect the prices you will charge. The prices you charge directly affect the market you will cater to. This in turn affects the atmosphere of the establishment, the skills your employees will need, and so on. They are all interrelated. The menu is basic to everything else.

Suggestions for Your Menu

You should consider a number of factors in planning your menu to make it your most important sales tool. Some of them are discussed below. (Menu pricing will be discussed in Chapter 12.)

1. Ease of reading.
   The menu should be easy to read. Except for foreign food specialty establishments, the tendency today in the United States is toward English wording. If you do use foreign terminology, consider including a translation and/or explanation with the menu listing. For example, if you list "Filets de Sole Pochés au Vin Blanc" you might add a description: "Filets of Sole Poached in White Wine."

2. Cleanliness.
   The menu should be clean. The use of plastic-coated menus is a good idea for many operations. Plastic coating is relatively inexpensive, and it makes menus durable and easy to wipe clean. When a menu gets worn or permanently soiled, throw it away.

3. Size of menus.
   You can order practically any size menu you want. Menus can be so large that they cover half the table or so small that they are probably only appropriate for use at a counter. Larger menus are more expensive to buy and are usually used in luxurious establishments. Choose a size that will fit the general atmosphere of your establishment. Be sure the size of the menu you decide on gives you enough space to list everything you want to offer for sale.

4. Size of print.
   You may want to use a variety of type sizes—perhaps large type for entrees and smaller type for accompanying items. Your printer can show you the

great varieties of styles and sizes of type that are available. Try to make your menu easy to read but also interesting to look at.

5. Color photographs.
   Color photographs printed on the menu are a good idea for some types of food service operations. Use of color photos substantially increases the cost of the menu, but good pictures can be very appetizing. If you do use color photos, try to be sure that the food you serve looks as good as the pictures.

6. Souvenir menus.
   If you use large, beautiful, or in some way unique menus, some guests may want them for souvenirs. If many guests want to keep them and they are expensive menus, you could consider selling them to guests.
   Some restaurants print miniature copies of their menus. They are usually not printed on expensive paper stock and can be quite inexpensive—especially if you order them in large quantities. You might use miniature menus for sales promotion and give them to guests who want copies of your menu. Some restaurants have miniature menus printed as postcards, which guests can buy (or receive free) and mail to friends.
   These souvenir menu ideas probably apply mostly to expensive, luxury food service operations which develop exotic or unusually interesting menus.

7. Gimmick menus.
   Some food operations use gimmick menus—pumpkin-shaped Halloween menus, turkey-shaped for Thanksgiving, Christmas-tree shaped for Christmas, and so on. These are specialty promotion items. Many operations also develop their own ideas.
   Some use special children's menus. These may convert into hats or masks, have children's games printed on them, or use other features meant to amuse children.
   Other restaurants may use a regular menu layout with humorous terminology. If people get a big enough kick out of a silly menu (and if the food service operation is also a good one), guests may bring friends along to enjoy the amusing menu (and the good food).
   If you are interested in trying the humor menu, make sure it is funny, not a forced try at being funny.

Whale Stuffed with Yacht $433,500.00

Unflamed Cherries Jubilee $5.00

Flaming Cherries Jubilee $37,566.00
(Waiter is a
pyromaniac)

Breast of Boiled Peasant $250.00

The examples will give you the general idea. Your guests' reactions will tell you what they find funny.
Some operations insert outrageous joke items or subtly amusing comments right into their serious menus. Others have copies of silly menus plus sepa-

rate real menus and have the staff trained to present both menus to guests in a planned way—so that all guests see a silly menu for fun but also get a copy of a menu that really tells them what food is available.

How Many Menus?

The number of menus you will need will vary depending on what type of operation you have and what type of menu you use. Luxury restaurants may use elaborate menus that are expensive to print. Coffee shop operations are more apt to use less expensive, plastic-coated menus. Fast-food operations have brought back the simple menu board posted on the wall listing items and prices.

It costs you less per menu when you order large quantities. The major expenses of menus are the design, the artwork, and the printer's set-up work time. The printing and the paper stock used are usually inexpensive compared to the other costs. As a result, you can order 1,000 menus for not a great deal more than you would pay for 500. But if you need only 300, there is no point in ordering 1,000.

You could consider buying paper stock for 1,000 menus. You could have the name of your establishment, standard decorations and front page, and so on printed on each and leave the rest of each menu blank. You might be able to have your printer hold these in storage for you or store them yourself. When your 300 menus have been printed, there will still be 700 pieces of the paper stock, already partially printed, left over. If you want to change your menu item offerings and get new menus, it is a simple, fast matter to have the printer make them up on the paper already there. And you have saved some money by buying paper in quantity and doing some preprinting. Flexibility and ease of reprinting are strong arguments for having fewer menus printed at one time and being prepared to print new ones whenever you should.

Do not be afraid to reprint your menus if you need to adjust for price changes. Many operators refuse to do this and it is usually false economy. Say, for example, because of rising meat prices, you should now sell your steaks for $1 more than the price printed on your menus. Suppose you sell about 200 steaks a week. The revenue you will lose because of the improper pricing of steak on your menu could be $200 a week. Say it costs $150 to reprint menus. In this example, if you reprint menus to adjust the price of just the steak item, you recover the cost of printing the menus plus another $50 for just one week's sales of just the one steak item. You will probably have other items, too, that could use some price adjusting at the same time.

Do adjust menu prices when necessary. If you absolutely cannot afford to reprint all your menus, paste tape over the incorrect prices and write new prices on the tape. Or, if there is no other way, cross out old prices with a marking pen and write in new ones. Don't leave a price on a menu if it is not right. Fix it.

How Guests Read Menus

Chart 10-1 is a very simple diagram of a two-page menu. It shows how most people naturally tend to read a menu. When they open a menu, most people glance first at the right-hand side. They look first at the top area 1 on the chart, then down to area 2. Only after they have looked at sections 1 and 2 will their eyes naturally range up to section 3 and down to 4. Take advantage of this normal reading pattern when you make up your menu.

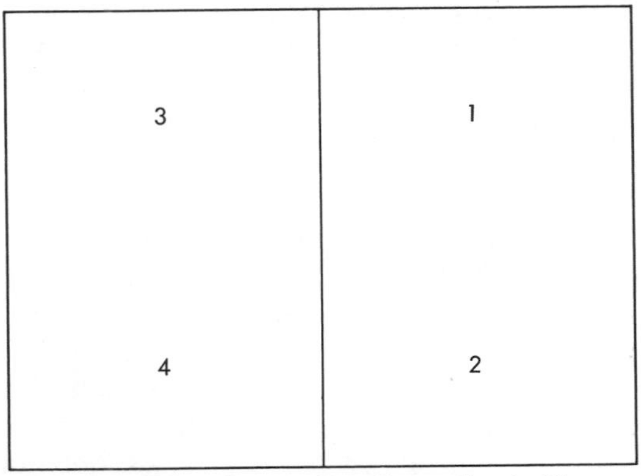

Chart 10-1   Menu Layout How Guests Read a Menu

Consider listing appetizers in section 1 and entrees followed by accompanying items in sections 1 and 2. You might promote wines in section 3 and use section 4 for listing desserts and nonalcoholic beverages. Modify these ideas, or work out your own arrangement. But it is smart to use sections 1 and 2 to list items you particularly want to sell. Specialty items or specialties of the house, which give a good average check and good profit, should be listed in sections 1 and 2. That is where most guests will look first, and you don't want them to miss these. Many people will not read the entire menu.

TYPES OF MENUS

Basic Menus

There are three types of basic menus used in food service operations:

1. Table d'hôte menu.
2. À la carte menu.
3. Combination menu.

Table d' Hote Menu

Table d' hôte means "table of the host." This type of menu originated with innkeepers and is hundreds of years old. When travelers stayed at an inn, they ate with their host, the innkeeper, and they ate whatever foods the inn-keeper happened to be having for dinner. All guests ate the same dinner for the same price.

Today a table d'hôte menu lists complete dinners. Each dinner generally includes appetizer or soup, entree, potato, vegetable, salad, dessert, and coffee. There is usually an asterisk and a note saying, "The price of the entree is the price of the complete dinner." Since accompanying items (or choices of them) are the same for all dinners, the only variable cost is the entree. It costs a food service operation less to buy turkey than steak, so you charge less for a turkey dinner than for a steak dinner.

The table d'hôte menu is not as popular as it used to be. Many guests seem to feel that there is too much food and that it costs too much.

À la Carte Menu

À la carte means that each item is individually priced. Usually the only thing included in the price of the entree is the entree's own garnish (lettuce, parsley, watercress). Each entree, vegetable, salad, dessert, beverage—every item—is listed separately with its own individual price.

Because of individual pricing, an à la carte dinner is more expensive for the guest than a comparable table d'hôte dinner. But the dinners are not usually comparable. From an à la carte menu, guests select only what they want. They don't have to pay for a several-course meal, part of which they may not want. For example, from an à la carte menu, guests may choose clams as an appetizer, a chef's salad, a sirloin strip steak, and coffee. If that is all they choose, that is all they get and all they pay for. They won't get a baked potato included, for example, and they won't pay for it.

À la carte prices may be higher than table d'hôte prices because most of the items are prepared and cooked to order. This can mean a higher labor cost. Also, there may be some waste because of leftovers of items ordered. À la carte menus tend to offer a wider variety of items than do table d'hôte menus. Say, for example, one portion of a vegetable is ordered. The cook opens a can or whatever and prepares one order. But no one orders any more of that vegetable. This means that the food service operation will probably wind up with leftovers in the kitchen. If they can't use them, they have to throw them out. This is just one type of waste problem that can result from an à la carte menu.

The à la carte menu tends to be used in expensive, well-appointed restaurants catering to couples and business people. The table d'hôte menu is more apt to be used in medium-priced restaurants catering to families.

Combination Menu

This is a combination of the table d'hôte and the à la carte menu styles. Certain items are grouped together for a set price (like the table d'hôte menu) and other items are priced individually (like the à la carte menu).

The combination menu became popular in the 1930s with the so-called blue plate special. For one, all-inclusive set price, you received, for example, an entree, a potato, a vegetable, bread and butter, and beverage. No appetizer or dessert was included in the set price. The combination menu reduced cost for the customers because they did not have to buy items they did not want or pay the higher price of ordering each item individually.

In recent years the combination menu has gained in popularity for the following reasons:

1. Changing eating patterns of the public.

   The public no longer wants heavy, complete meals. People are more weight conscious today. During the 1930s the blue plate special became popular because it was all that people could afford and it usually provided a filling meal. Now many nutritionists tell us that many Americans have eaten too well, too much, too often, and not healthfully.

   A lot of Americans are not satisfied with their weight. A few are underweight and want to gain, but most people want to be thinner, and this affects their ideas about eating. Some may splurge and eat a lot when they go out for dinner, but many try to stay with a diet even when they eat out. For whatever reasons, guests today are not usually eating big, complete meals. Many do not want an appetizer or dessert. But they are apt to want and expect larger entrees—bigger steaks, for example. A few years ago an 8 or a 10-ounce strip steak was acceptable to most guests. Today many want a 12 to 14-ounce steak, perhaps with just a salad, possibly a potato, and a beverage. Some operations simply offer a steak and salad combination. Potato and beverage are extra.

   The public's eating patterns can change again, of course. Keep yourself current on what the public does want, because preferences can alter at any time.

2. Increased costs.

   By switching from a table d'hôte menu to a combination menu, food service operations found it possible to raise their prices without seeming to do so. Years ago they could afford to serve a complete steak dinner for $5. As inflation increased, they could no longer do that. But many food service operators felt that they did not want to charge more than $5. So they changed from a table d'hôte to a combination menu by pricing appetizers and desserts à la carte. Perhaps they listed steak, potato, and salad for

$4.95, staying just under the $5 price. They would start juice and soup appetizer prices at about 30 cents extra à la carte price and go up to $1 or more for shrimp cocktail. Desserts probably would start at about 35 cents extra à la carte for a dish of ice cream and go up to 60 cents extra or more for pastries and other items. They probably set beverage prices at 15 cents and up.

In the past, many food operations offered a complete (table d'hôte) meal for $5. Later they offered a combination of steak, potato and salad for $4.95 but anything extra was priced à la carte. If guests chose to add other items to their meals, the bill could go up to $6 or more. Since this trend to combination menus began, more and more establishments have converted to this type of pricing. Even though the combination steak-salad-potato price is generally now much higher than the $5 mentioned, the idea of using combination menus prevails.

3. Combination menu as a means of building total guest check.

Instead of serving just a hamburger, for example, for 60 cents, the food service operation may offer a hamburger plate, which might include hamburger, French fries, and cole slaw all for $1.05. At à la carte prices, the hamburger might sell for 60 cents, the French fries for 30 cents, and the cole slaw for 25 cents, for a total of $1.15. But the combination plate can be sold for $1.05 combination menu price instead of $1.15 à la carte menu price. The amount of cole slaw and French fries served would usually be slightly less than an à la carte portion of either. The average check, however, has increased. It is less expensive for the customer to buy the total hamburger plate package. More people will probably buy the hamburger combination plate because they feel it is worth the $1.05 price and is less expensive than the same items priced à la carte.

Many other combinations of foods have been developed and offered to customers at a combination price (lower than individual item price) in an effort to increase the amount of the average check. An example would be the businessperson's lunch. This may include entree, potato or other vegetable, and salad. Guests can buy this for a lower price than the same food would cost if they ordered the same items separately from an à la carte menu.

The businessperson's lunch has gained in popularity with customers. Guests pay a reasonable price for the food they receive. And it allows operators to prepare larger quantities of fewer items, which they can serve quickly. This can help to increase guest turnover, increase volume, and give operators a better chance for bigger profits.

STANDARDIZED MENUS

Standardized menus can be any of the three types of menus just described. When you set your menu prices, the three types of menus—table d'hôte, à la carte, and combination—are the basis for arranging what you offer for sale.

A standardized menu is exactly what it sounds like—it is standard; it doesn't change. This menu has become very popular in recent years. Put a special amount of effort and thought into the preparation, design, and layout of a standardized menu. It lists on one menu all the items you offer for sale, but you don't change this menu often. You use the same menu day in and day out, over and over again for at least several months without changing the selection of food items offered, although you may have to adjust some prices.

One advantage of the standardized menu is that it helps to control costs. If you don't sell an item today, you can probably sell it tomorrow because it is on the menu both days. You only have to purchase the food for the items on your standardized menu. You do not have to have other items in stock. This reduces your inventory.

The standardized menu has gained considerable popularity as a dinner menu. During the past few years dinner business has declined for many food service operations, particularly for those located in the downtown sections of many cities. Transportation costs, parking problems, and crime have contributed to this situation.

Many people work downtown and eat out for lunch there, but many of them live in the suburbs. If they do decide to eat out at night, they generally go home to the suburbs first and then go to an establishment closer to their homes—one which can be reached easily and offers plenty of parking space. Parking is a major concern to the guest, and many downtown food service operations can't provide it. Dinner business for a downtown operation may have wide fluctuation because suburbanites may come in unexpectedly and unpredictably, or you may get convention business from hotels, more people during the tourist season, and the like.

The standardized menu lists the same foods day after day, usually for different people each night with not much daily repeat business. Most items are cooked to order. This works out well because guests dining out in the evening are more apt to want a leisurely meal and are less apt to mind the extra time it takes to have foods cooked to order. Preparing entrees to order means less waste for the food service operation.

The luncheon menu may also be standardized except for one, two, or maybe three daily specials you can change. The luncheon menu will usually be composed of cooked-to-order items plus a variety of sandwiches. Specials can add variety to the menu. This is especially important where there is much repeat business, which you may have at lunchtime.

The breakfast menu is almost always standardized. It usually offers eggs (prepared in a variety of ways), ham, bacon, sausage, pancake specialties, French toast specialties, hot and cold cereals, and variations or combinations of these. You might have a different "hot cereal of the day," but breakfast menus do not normally change much.

Cyclical Menus

A cyclical menu (like the standardized menu) can be any of the three basic menu types (table d'hôte, à la carte, or combination). "Cyclical menu" means that you use a different menu in one cycle every day for the duration of the cycle. Then you can start the same cycle over again, or you can begin a different cycle (or you can repeat the same cycle several times in a row, then switch to different cycles).

A cycle may be for seven days—a different menu for each day of the week. Then you repeat the same seven menus, starting the cycle again with Monday's menu. The cycle can apply to the whole menu or to only a few daily specials, for which you attach flyers to your standardized menu.

There are 14-day cycles, 28-day cycles, 35-day cycles, or any other cycle you want. Cycles are usually based on sevens, and there is a reason for this. Foods that are appropriate Monday through Friday may not sell well on weekends, and vice versa. Saturday and Sunday have a different effect on the cycle. Saturday may be a day of increased or reduced business for you and can call for different menu offerings. Sundays will almost always call for different types of food items. Use seven days as the basis for cycles.

For a cyclical menu, you put certain items together on your menu for the same day, but you do not put them together again in the same combination in that same cycle. Individual items will be repeated, but not with each other. For example, there may be hamburger steak, calves liver, and breaded pork chops. Each of these can be repeated during a cycle but not in combination with each other. Menu cycles are especially useful for institutional food services where the same clientele are served day after day. You can build variety into the menu and still control your costs.

The concept of a cyclical menu can be used for daily specials. For example, a restaurant may use a standardized menu but offer three or four new specials each day. The daily special could be set up on a rotating cycle for, say for example, 14 days. On the 15th day, the cycle starts over again. This allows for planning and ordering and helps to control costs. But you can still offer variety for customers who come to your food service operation regularly.

Cycles of 28 and 35 days have become popular in institutions (hospitals, university food services, penal institutions). Usually one cycle is repeated three times and then a different cycle is started.

Make adjustments for seasonal changes in eating habits. People usually want heavier foods in cold weather and lighter foods in hot weather. Ideally, you should change cyclical and standardized menus at least twice a year, perhaps in the spring and then again in the fall. Menu items and appropriate price changes could be adjusted at these times.

MENU FACTORS

Guests come to a food service establishment to have needs satisfied. They want food, of course, but they want other things, too. These can vary and may include specifics like relaxing atmosphere, pleasant service personnel, clean and attractive surroundings, or prompt service. These factors affect your menu. The following factors affect it, too:

1. Market.
   As a food service operator, you should know what your own market is and cater to it. (We discussed market and how it affects you in economic terms in Chapter 4.)

2. Changing eating patterns.
   We have mentioned the changing food habits of guests (dieting, demand for bigger steaks, decreased demand for desserts and appetizers). These attitudes may change again. Be aware of current tastes. Consider changes in the types and quantities of foods that guests want when you make up your menu.

3. Regional preferences.
   Be aware of regional food preferences and cater to them. Some foods are very popular in one part of the country (or world) but unpopular or unknown in another. Consider that some regional foods can transfer well and might bear introducing to different geographical areas.

4. Employees' skills.
   You have to evaluate and conform to the skills of your employees—unless you are prepared to train them or hire others with different levels of skills. It is foolish to put an item on your menu if your employees can't prepare it well, or if preparing it is so complicated or difficult that it would disrupt production of other foods. If your employees don't know how to prepare something and it is too much of a problem to train them to prepare it well, don't insist on that item. Adapt and make changes.

5. Physical layout of kitchen.
   The physical layout of your kitchen affects your menu and what kinds of foods you can offer. A well-designed kitchen means fewer wasted motions for employees and simplified production. Food service managers usually have little or nothing to say, however, about originally designing or later changing the layout of the kitchens at their operations. Making big changes in an existing kitchen is a major cost and owners will seldom approve. If you are an owner or an owner/manager, put great forethought into kitchen design before you buy or build a food service operation. Get the help of kitchen design experts if you can. If you are a manager, study the existing physical kitchen layout and plan the work and the menu accordingly. Plan the menu and the work so that your kitchen layout does not make production formidable. Keep it as easy and fast as you can. This will take some serious study and analysis by you of your layout. Observe and arrange objects and work routines so that things are easiest. Be your own efficiency expert if you cannot hire one.

6. Balance the work load.
   Plan your menu so that the work load is sensibly balanced. Don't, for example, put a fruit plate and a shrimp salad plate on a menu as the two daily specials and expect one individual to prepare both if the same person also has to produce all the cold sandwiches. And definitely don't do this to anyone on a hot day! Assign someone to help. Keep the work load fair.

You (and your supervisors) should balance the work load so all departments *and* all individual employees in the kitchen perform a fair share of work.

7. Labor cost.

When you write your menu, keep labor costs as well as food costs constantly in mind. Some items require very little labor, some a great deal. Steak, for example, is usually just taken from a refrigerator, cooked on a grill or broiler, and served. But preparing stew means a lot more time and work for your employees. Specialty items "made from scratch" can give you a wide menu offering but they can also increase the work load so much that you might have to hire extra personnel. This is where convenience or pre-cooked entrees have proved exceptionally useful. Watch your costs closely for these, however. Pre-cooked and/or frozen entrees can be used to give variety to the menu without overtaxing your labor force and usually without increasing production costs or waste if you are careful.

These are some of the factors that affect your menu. Plan a menu taking sensible account of all possible factors.

Separate Menus

Today many food service operations have a separate menu for each meal period—breakfast, lunch, dinner, and supper (very late evening meal). This is generally the recommended procedure.

Each meal period is different. At different times of the day you will serve different foods, and you will probably be catering to different customers eating out for different reasons. For many people in the United States lunch is just a food break. Or it may be more important to them if it gives them a chance to promote a business deal. Lunch is many things to many people.

Dinner is apt to be more special to your guests. People use more care in selecting a place for dinner.

You may be dealing with different markets at different meal periods. So you will probably find different menus appropriate for different meal periods.

Menu Format and Content

Format and content means what foods (and food combinations) you will sell and how you will write them on the menu. You should consider each item you put on your menu with reference to the other items in the same category and in all your other categories. Say, for example, you decide that for lunch you will offer eight entrees, two vegetables, two salads, four desserts. Establish a menu format so that you get enough variety to appeal to many people, not monotony or duplication, which are not appealing to anybody.

Of the eight entrees, you might select one fish, one egg, three extended meat (meat plus other ingredients, such as beef stew, salisbury steak, chili), and three solid meat items. You might decide to offer French fried potatoes and one other potato dish prepared by another method (mashed, boiled, scalloped); one green vegetable and one vegetable of another color; dessert of pie, cake, ice cream and so on. Put things together for balance as you select, classify, and categorize food items on your menu.

Your dinner menu should probably be different from your lunch menu. A luncheon menu may include a standard selection of sandwiches that are the same day after day, with only entrees and their accompaniments changing daily. You will probably want to list more entrees for dinner, especially cooked-to-order entrees that can help you cut waste.

When you have decided what items to offer, and which ones you want to emphasize and sell most of, then it is time to consider the physical written arrangement of the menu. Some food managers like to list the entree with specific vegetable, potato, and salad all together as a unit. Others prefer to list all their entrees and let guests choose the vegetables, potatoes, or salad they want. The first method has the advantage of balancing the entree with its accompanying items. The second method has the advantage of flexibility and gives guests more choice in selecting food.

Varieties of Menus

You should be aware of how many different kinds of menus there are when you decide what suits you. Some food service operations—cafeterias, for example—may have nothing more than a big menu sign board posted on the wall. Some establishments have no written menus whatsoever. Their service persons tell guests what is available. Other establishments may use a mimeographed or dittoed menu, perhaps produced daily. Others have a separate printed menu for each day of the week. Some use a partially standardized menu with an insert to list items that change daily. Still others may list their daily special by the use of a table tent, which is a small, folded card set on the table. Use a menu that helps you to sell foods most effectively and at reasonable cost to you and your customers. Use menus that induce guests to buy.

MASTER MENU INDEX

When you have decided on the type of menu you want and the contents, the next thing to do in the process of making up your menu is to develop a good, complete master menu index. This is a time-consuming undertaking, but when you have a good one in working order, it is an invaluable tool. A master menu index is a listing by separate classification of all the food items you will offer for sale. Just list foods, no prices.

Almost all food service operations should use a master menu index. In most establishments the breakfast menu is set and used day after day. The luncheon menu may vary daily, or at least part of it will. The dinner menu may be standardized or it may vary, depending on the type of establishment. A steak house may have a set menu for dinner. A college dormitory would have a separate menu for each night, and so on. Even those who use a standardized menu will probably want to change it in the future. A master menu index can help virtually every type of food service operation.

Classifications for a Master Menu Index

Here is a suggested list of headings you could use in setting up your master menu index. Adapt and expand the list to suit your own needs.

1. Appetizers.
2. Soups.
3. Entrees.
   a. Meat

      Beef

      Lamb

      Pork

      Veal

      Variety

      Extended (beef stew, salisbury steak)
   b. Fish and Sea Food
   c. Eggs
4. Sauces.
5. Potatoes.
6. Vegetables.
7. Salads and Dressings.
8. Desserts.
9. Beverages (nonalcoholic).

A loose-leaf notebook is probably the best thing to use for your master menu index. Set up the notebook with all the headings you want. Use a separate section for each category and a separate page for each heading or subheading. Then list all the items you might serve. You should probably have two separate master menu indexes—one for lunch and one for dinner. Many of the items will be the same, but it is better to have things listed twice than to forget them or have to shuffle back and forth in one notebook trying to find something.

To illustrate how the master menu index might be set up under "Soups," for example, you might have a list of between 20 and 35 types of soups you may want to serve (depending on your type of operation).

Soups

1. Broth.

    a. Chicken Broth

    b. Beef Bouillon

    c. Scotch Broth

2. Cream.

    a. Cream of Chicken Soup

    b. Cream of Tomato Soup

    c. Cream of Mushroom Soup

3. Chowder.

    a. Corn Chowder

    b. Manhattan Clam Chowder

    c. New England Clam Chowder

You could also list under each type of soup any details of variations you will use in addition to serving it plain—for example, Chicken Broth with Rice, Chicken Noodle Soup, Chicken Egg Drop Soup.

For another example of a heading for your master menu index, you could set up "Potatoes" as follows:

Potatoes

1. French Fried Potatoes.

    a. Julien Potatoes

    b. Shoestring Potatoes

    c. À la Met Potatoes (Matchstick Potatoes)

    d. Long Branch Potatoes

2. Baked Potatoes.

    a. Baked Potato

    b. Baked Potato with Special Sour Cream Dressing

    c. Special Baked Potato with Ham, Onion, and Cheese

When you write your master menu index, use the same words you will use when you actually print the item on the menu. For example, don't just list your vegetables as "peas," "corn," and so on. Write down exactly what you intend to print on your menu—"Buttered Peas with Mushrooms," "Green Peas with Tiny Whole Onions," "Creamed Peas," and so on. Write the entire, exact descriptive phrase just as you want it to appear on your menu. Then just copy it when you write your menus.

The brief sample master menu index list above illustrates only a couple of categories. You need an extremely complete listing (without prices) of every item you know you will offer, plus anything you think you might ever want to offer in the future. Keep adding new ideas. Make revisions. Cross out items that are not successful. Write it all down. It is impossible to remember all potential items.

Put real thought, time, and work into developing your master menu index. A good one will greatly simplify the actual mechanics of menu writing. You won't forget ideas because you write them in constantly. You will have everything at your fingertips. It is efficient and it is a good management menu control tool, which will make it much easier for you to attain variety on your menu. Once you have your master menu index in working order, you will use it from then on. It will save you a great deal of time and energy when you plan and write your menus. This is especially true if your operation uses cyclical menus.

MENU WRITING

In talking about menu format and content, we discussed the types, number, and arrangements of entrees and accompanying items on the menu. We have also discussed a master menu index and making comprehensive lists of food items you might offer for sale. When you actually write your menus, you apply all these ideas and make real use of your master menu index.

To assure good variety, try to plan several days' menus or daily specials simultaneously. Better yet, plan a complete cycle (7, 28, 35 days) all at once if you possibly can.

When you set out to plan and write a menu, the first thing to do is get out your master menu index. Copy the wording you used in the master menu index. List the entrees first. List all the entrees you will offer for several days or for a cycle. Many of these entrees may be the same day after day, but there will probably be some variation. (Put items together on the menu so that you get some range and variation in prices. This will be discussed in detail in Chapter 12.)

When you have listed the entrees, go back to each separate classification and list all appetizers, soups, potatoes, vegetables, salads, and desserts that will best accompany these combinations of entrees. This process will help you achieve balance of your menu items for color combinations, variety, and costs.

Wording

Be careful how you use descriptive words in your master menu index and on your printed menu. How many times have you seen a menu listing "Garden Peas"? Does the phrase mean anything? "Garden" is a silly descriptive word for peas. "Field-Grown Peas" would be more accurate, less picturesque, but just as silly.

Take, too, the menu that promotes "Half-Fried Chicken." These words mean literally that the chicken is a bit raw. It has been fried for only half as much time as it should have been. Customers will know what you *mean*. Some will catch careless wording and laugh. They will hope your cooks cook better than you write. "Fried One-Half Chicken" does the job accurately.

Listing Accompaniments

When people go out to eat, most expect to receive some sort of accompanying dishes. List the accompaniments you are going to serve. Do serve accompaniments and do list them on your menu in appetizing (lavish if you wish) but grammatically correct terms.

Failure to serve adequate sauces, accompaniments and garnishes and to list them on the menu is a major mistake. Many operators make it, though.

Preparing Food

Of course your job doesn't stop when you have written a menu. You cannot just hand the menus to your chef or food production specialist or chief hamburger frier and say, "Here's the menu. Fix the food." You have to tell (and maybe show) your employees how you want the food prepared, what time you want it ready, and how much of it you want. (This is described in detail in Chapter 17.) You should also prepare and use standardized recipes (discussed in Chapter 11).

Overproduction and Underproduction

When you write your menus, you must pay attention to potential problems of overproduction and underproduction. If you prepare too much, leftovers may have to be discarded. If you prepare too little of an item, you can run out of it too soon. Don't be like the manager is implied to be in the old restaurant joke: "A restaurant opens for lunch. One customer comes in, looks at the menu and orders liver. A few minutes later the second customer comes in, looks at the menu, and orders liver. The waitress says, 'Sorry. We're out. Someone just ordered it.' " Not much of a joke. Not much of a manager, either.

Plan for *reasonable* run-out times, particularly for foods that are expensive to prepare. For example, if you anticipate and forecast that you will probably sell 100 orders of Swiss steak for lunch, you might want to *try* to run out of it at about 1:30 although your dining room will stay open until 2:00. You don't want Swiss steak left over because it may be a comparatively expensive entree in relation to others you are offering on that menu. Swiss steak takes time to prepare properly, and there is not much you can do with it profitably if it is left over. Leftover Swiss steak probably won't have a satisfactory alternative use. You might put it into stew or croquettes, but neither of these alternative uses will bring you the price Swiss steak should.

Try to sell all of everything you prepare that is not cooked to order. This may mean you will run out of some items. But try not to run out *too* soon. It is acceptable to run out of one or two items toward the end of the meal period. Most customers understand this *if* it's toward the end of a meal time.

But if an item is listed on your menu for lunch and a guest orders it at noon, he or she may well be irritated if you have "run out."

If you do unexpectedly run out of items early, or if you plan purposely to run out reasonably early in a meal period, you had better know what foods you will have ready to substitute in their places and what prices you will charge for them. Try to have substitutes ready which at least have a fighting chance of pleasing a guest who wanted what you ran out of. If you run out of Swiss steak, for example, you might plan to substitute one of your regular menu items such as cube steak at the same price. Perhaps a cube steak portion costs you a few cents more than a portion of Swiss steak. But you can cook the cube steak to order. And you are substituting one of your regular menu items (used, for example, on a cube steak platter or in a cube steak sandwich), which makes the substitution much easier for you.

Consider problems of overproduction and underproduction for every item you have to cook ahead of time. Foods cooked after a guest has ordered them do not pose these real overproduction and underproduction problems unless they have to be partially altered or partially prepared ahead of time. Then they are also a problem.

Always try to figure out in advance what uses you can make of leftovers. It is impossible to be 100 percent accurate all of the time in your forecasting. All food service operations will have leftovers. If you possibly can, use leftovers so they will produce revenue for the operation. Food service managers who consistently permit leftovers to be thrown away are throwing away money, and maybe their own jobs, too.

Perhaps you can use leftovers in employees' meals, but be very careful about this. Employees' meals must always be of good quality, even if they are relatively inexpensive for the food service operation. If the meals you serve your employees are not good, the psychological—not to mention gastronomical—effects on employees will not be conducive to happy employees. You may intentionally plan for some extra production of a particular menu item, *planning* to use this for employees' meals because it is good quality and low in cost.

BANQUET MENUS

Food service establishments with separate banquet dining rooms should have separate banquet menus. There are two ways to write banquet menus:

1. Group certain classes of items together. The guest who is making banquet reservations can choose from these. For example, you may offer a choice of appetizer, vegetable, potato, salad, chicken or chopped steak, and a sundae for a certain set price. Steak or prime rib would be listed at higher prices than the chicken or chopped steak even though the rest of the accompanying items would be the same. Usually the potatoes and vegetables

offered for banquets will be the ones you are serving in your regular dining room that day.

2. Price each item individually (à la carte) and let the persons doing the booking select the specific items they want.

Booking Banquets

Several typed or printed copies of the complete banquet menu should be made up and available at all times for use by the manager, assistant manager, catering manager, secretary, sales manager—any personnel who book banquet parties and meetings. Your personnel should be ready at all times to give firm price quotes, menu selections, and complete information whenever a guest inquires.

Too often people call food service operations to make arrangements (or just ask about making them) for a banquet and are told to call back because no one is there who can give them the information. You should always have someone available, who does know about banquets and can provide information. If you don't you are almost sure to lose some banquet business.

Along with the banquet menu, you might consider having a notebook made up for your sales personnel to show to potential banquet and business meeting customers. The notebook could have color photos showing your banquet rooms with various seating and table arrangements, different table set-ups, china set-ups, service set-ups, and so on. The notebook should indicate the number of occupants the room can accomodate with different types of room set-ups. Complete menus and prices should be included.

A complete descriptive notebook on your banquets and meetings facilities could be an extremely useful sales tool. You might make up several of these notebooks for interested customers to look at. Have at least one always available on the premises if others are being used elsewhere in attempts to get banquet business. You might also consider having less expensive brochures made up to give or mail to prospective banquet and business meeting customers. The main thing is to be sure that you have complete and valid information ready at *all* times when potential banquet or meetings customers inquire in person or by phone.

Explaining Your Banquet and Meetings Facilities to Customers

Private parties, business and club meetings, and banquets can be a good sales bonus for you above and beyond regular business. Prices you charge and foods you offer should be appropriate for your food service operation. You should probably decide on a minimum number of guests for a banquet or meeting and a minimum dollar amount to be sure that your costs will be covered.

Sometimes a person calling to make banquet reservations will say, "We are all ordering the same thing (the roast beef dinner or the chicken dinner, for example), so will it cost us less per person than it would in your regular dining room?'' It will usually cost them more. The following are examples of some of the factors that can contribute to making it necessary for you to charge more for banquet facilities than you do for your regular dining room service:

1. You have an extra investment in your private dining room and facilities.
2. Your private dining rooms are not used continuously. When they are idle you still pay rent and some utilities for them.
3. You may have to hire extra personnel to take care of service for a private party, banquet, or meeting.
4. Guests can have private dining rooms set up in any way they want.
5. In your private dining room, guests can all sit together, have privacy, make noise, give speeches, and conduct meetings. They cannot do these things in your regular public dining area.

These are just samples of factors that may or may not apply to your own operation. Make a list of factors that do apply to your own operation banquet facilities and make sure that any of your staff who may be asked about banquets know the facts. Don't underprice your banquet facilities. Some food service establishments sell their banquets at their regular menu price but charge rental for the private dining room. Others charge higher prices for the banquet menu plus a room rental charge.

SUMMARY

In this chapter we have gone over some of the factors involved in menu writing and have emphasized the importance of the menu. As we said at the beginning, your menu is a very important sales tool. It is actually more than another cost control tool. It is the foundation around which all other cost control activities revolve. Take pains when you plan, design, organize, and write your menu. It is important.

REVIEW AND DISCUSSION QUESTIONS

1. What are the three basic types of menus?
2. What is the difference between a standardized and a cyclical menu?
3. What factors affect your menu?
4. How can a master menu index help you to write better menus?
5. Why must food service operators consider overproduction and underproduction when they write menus?

11

Pre-Control and Pre-Costing the Menu

Objectives

This chapter discusses ways to control your costs before you put a menu into effect. After you have read this chapter, you should:

1. Know what pre-control is, and know methods of doing pre-costing.
2. Know how to calculate your potential food cost.
3. Know how to use a method of forecasting and know why forecasting is important.

PRE-CONTROL

An important part of any control is to anticipate what will happen and act to influence events before they happen. In the food service industry, you are in the business of purchasing, preparing and selling food—all according to pre-determined standards. Pre-control means that you have established your standards and you follow them concerning food—and concerning all the items and procedures involved in the entire process—*before* you purchase, prepare, and sell food.

The concepts of pre-control and pre-costing can be applied to the menu, to staffing, to purchasing, to portioning, and so on. In the case of staffing, for example, you try (based on your estimated sales) to anticipate the number of people you will need to staff your food service operation *before* you make up employee work schedules. In purchasing, you make the most accurate predictions of how much food you will need next week *before* you call your purveyors and order your food for next week. Apply this idea of figuring and plotting ahead of time to as many of your decisions as you can.

PRE-COSTING THE MENU

When you do menu pre-costing, you do it in dollars and cents, not in percentages. When you pre-cost your menu, you are making estimates based on ideal conditions. Your figures are based on having cooks follow recipes *precisely,* for example. Your figures are based on having your kitchen personnel follow predetermined portion sizes *precisely.* You are assuming you will sell *all* you prepare. The costs you arrive at by pre-costing are the very best costs you could possibly get.

If your ideal costs are too high and you want to lower them, decide whether you wish to use ingredients of lower cost and quality or not. Or you could decide to charge higher menu prices. If your ideal cost is too high in relation to your selling price, you have to do something beforehand (such as using lower cost materials or raising your prices) to assure that you get your desired cost.

Because pre-costing assumes *ideal* conditions, you should add a "tolerance" percent—usually one percent—to your food cost to help bring things closer to a realistic food cost. This realistic ideal cost is called "standard" or "potential" cost. The word "potential" as used in this book means "ideal."

Terms You Should Know

The following terms are used in purchasing. How you purchase your items will have an effect on your cost. Most of these terms apply mainly to meat.

Chapter 11

1. As Purchased—AP.

   As Purchased items are food items that have arrived at your operation direct from your purveyor and have not been altered in any way by your operation. Most foods in this category will need some work or pre-prep before you serve them to guests. Examples are unpeeled potatoes, short loins that need to be cut into steaks, oranges that need to be peeled.

2. Ready to Cook—RTC.

   These are food items that are completely ready to cook. Any needed pre-prep work has been done. Steak has been pre-portioned, ribs are oven-ready. All work that needs to be done before cooking has been done.

3. Ready to Eat—RTE.

   Ready to Eat items are food items that are ready to eat when you receive them. They arrive at your operation already cooked and need no additional cooking. Examples of RTE items would be canned hams, some smoked hams, pre-cooked rib roasts. You do not have to cook them, but you probably have to slice and portion them.

4. Edible Portion—EP.

   This is the amount of food left for actual eating after everything has been done. The food has been cooked, if it needed cooking. Bones and excess fat have been removed. The meat has shrunk due to moisture loss while it cooked. Everything that is left is edible. It may or may not have been portioned, but it is all edible.

Yield Tests (Chart 11-1)

Normally you perform yield tests only on high cost items or lower cost items you use in large quantities. Usually you perform yield tests on food you buy As Purchased and need to convert to Ready to Cook. There is no need for you to do a yield test on items you receive already pre-portioned. You might do them on some foods you receive Ready to Cook.

Yield tests tell you:

1. Yield of pounds, pints, ounces, portions, and so on.

2. Cost per pound, pint, ounce, portion, and so on.

Yield tests are a pre-cost technique because you determine the cost of an item before you serve it. It's a pre-control technique because you know what the item costs you and you can adjust your menu selling price *before* you serve the item.

Many of the items you purchase are not immediately ready to use when they reach your establishment. Many will have to have pre-preparation work done. This will add to the cost of the item because it will cost you something to have your employees trim, peel, or whatever—do some work on the items after you have received them.

Item: _Short Loin_   Grade: _Choice_ Date: _____

Pieces: ___1___   Weight: _22_ Lbs. __8__ Oz.

Total Cost: _$31.50_   At: _$1.40_   Per: _lb._   Purveyor: _____

1	2	3	4	5	6	7
Breakdown	Weight Lb. Oz.	Value Per Lb.	Total Value	Cost of Each Lb. Oz.	Portion Size Cost	Cost Factor Per Lb. Portion
Bones	4 —	.00	.00			
Fat	6 —	.00	.00			
Hamburger	4 —	.80	3.20			
Tenderloin	1 8	3.90	5.85			
Striploin	7 —		22.45	3.21 .21	12 oz. 2.49	2.29 1.78
Total	22 8		31.50			

Portion Size: _8 oz. Steaks_

Cost Factor = $\dfrac{\text{Computed Cost Per Pound Ready to Eat: \$3.21}}{\text{As Purchased or Market Price Per Pound: \$1.40}}$ = _2.29_ Cost Factor Per Pound

Cost Factor/Portion = $\dfrac{\text{Computed Cost Per 12-Oz. Portion Ready to Cook: \$2.49}}{\text{As Purchased Price/Lb.: \$1.40}}$ =

_1.78_ Cost Factor Per Portion

Chart 11-1 Yield Test Form

   If you do your own meat cutting (generally not a recommended practice), you probably buy meat in wholesale cuts. You have to perform pre-prep work on the meat before you have meat that is Ready to Cook. You need to know what yield in number of portions you will get and you need to know cost per portion. To obtain this information, you have to do yield tests.

   Say, for example, you are going to perform a yield test on several short loins to see what average yield of strip steaks you get from them. Assuming you are cutting your own meat, set a time with the meat cutter and whoever is going to do the yield test so that it is mutually convenient for them. Several short loins should be cut at the same time so the final results can be averaged.

Chart 11-1 shows sample results of a simple yield test. In the chart, a short loin is broken down into fat, bones, hamburger meat, tenderloin, and strip loin. The strip loin is cut into 12-ounce steaks. Assign the current market value for the hamburger meat and tenderloin (Column 3). Multiply the market value of each of these (Column 3) by the amount you get of each of these (Column 2) to get the total value for each item (Column 4).

In Chart 11-1, the market value of hamburger meat is 80 cents per pound (Column 3). You get four pounds of hamburger (Column 2). So you multiply 80 cents by four pounds of hamburger. This gives you a total value of $3.20 for hamburger meat (Column 4). For tenderloin, market value in the chart is $3.90 per pound (Column 3). You get one and a half pounds of tenderloin (Column 2). So you multiply $3.90 by one and a half pounds. This gives you a total value of $5.85 for tenderloin (Column 4). You do not assign any value for fat or bones.

Subtract the total value for the hamburger and tenderloin from the total cost of short loin. This gives you a value for the strip loin. Total cost of short loin $31.50 (Total Cost at top of chart) minus total value hamburger $3.20 minus total value tenderloin $5.85 equals total value strip loin $22.45 (Column 4).

In Chart 11-1 you purchased a short loin for $1.40 per pound. After you have cut the loin, the price of the strip loin is $3.21 per pound. We found this value of $3.21 per pound for the strip loin by dividing the total value of strip loin $22.45 by weight of strip loin seven pounds. You get nine 12-ounce steaks from the strip loin, with four ounces of strip loin left over. Ignore the four-ounce remainder. Divide nine into the cost of the strip $22.45. This gives you $2.49, which is the cost per individual 12-ounce steak.

This whole process is called performing a yield test. You want to find out how many 12-ounce steaks you can get from a short loin and what they cost you. You find your cost per steak when you purchase a short loin, bone out the short loin, and cut the strip loin into individual 12-ounce strip steaks.

The cost you get this way is the cost of steak only. It does not include the cost for labor for the employee who boned out the short loin. It does not take into consideration the fact that you must set aside space in your establishment for cutting meat and you have to have the necessary meat-cutting equipment on hand.

The cost of the steak you cut should be lower than a cost per individual steak quoted to you by meat purveyors. Your purveyors add in their overhead costs and labor costs. We have not done this. If you add in these two costs—*your* overhead and *your* labor—the cost of the steak from the purveyor is apt to be comparable to or lower than what it costs you to cut your own.

Yield tests are important. They make it clear to you and your employees that a lot of the items you purchase are not ready for immediate use by your cooks. Yield tests point out to you that the costs of items go up as you alter them by pre-preparation.

Cost Factors

When you have performed yield tests on any item and found the cost per portion, you can calculate cost factors per pound or per portion.

A "cost factor" is a ratio between what you originally paid for an item As Purchased and your computed cost per pound and/or per portion after you have done a yield test. If you use cost factors, you can determine your cost for an item when that item's price increases or decreases without having to do yield tests again each time the price changes.

Cost Factor Per Pound

To obtain a cost factor per pound, do the following (we will use figures from Chart 11-1):

COMPUTED COST PER POUND STRIP LOIN $3.21 divided by AS PURCHASED PRICE PER POUND SHORT LOIN $1.40 equals COST FACTOR PER POUND 2.29.

If meat prices go up or down in the future, you can simply multiply the new market price per pound for short loin by what it would cost you to buy a short loin at a higher or lower price. Suppose the short loin increases in price from $1.40 per pound As Purchased to $1.50 per pound As Purchased cost to you. Multiply $1.50 by your 2.29 cost factor per pound. You get a new cost of $3.44 per pound for strip loin. Note that the price you paid per pound for short loins increased by only 10 cents per pound; the cost of your steak increased 23 cents per pound ($3.44 minus $3.21 equals 23 cents). This is because your cost factor has taken into consideration trim loss and useful by-products—hamburger and tenderloin.

Cost Factor Per Portion

You might want to go directly to a per portion cost. To obtain a cost factor per portion, do the following (using figures from Chart 11-1):

COMPUTED COST PER PORTION (12-ounce strip steak) $2.49 divided by AS PURCHASED PRICE PER POUND SHORT LOIN $1.40 equals COST FACTOR PER PORTION (12-ounce strip steak) 1.78.

In our example we computed a cost factor of 1.78 per 12-ounce strip steak portion. You can multiply your new higher market price for a short loin As Purchased $1.50 by the cost factor per portion 12-ounce strip steak 1.78. You get $2.67 new cost per portion 12-ounce strip steak. Note: In this example the price increased 10 cents per pound for short loins, but your steak increased 18 cents each ($2.67 minus $2.49 equals 18 cents).

Depending on the item, you might want to compute a cost factor per pound or per portion. It will depend on how you are going to use the information. For most meat items, you will probably find it is to your advantage to use the cost factor per portion. But suppose you buy potatoes in 100-pound sacks As Purchased. You have to peel them. You want to know the cost per pound after they are peeled. To find this you should probably use the cost factor per pound. You do a yield test and get the cost per pound after they are peeled. You could use your cost factor for potatoes to determine what is the cost per pound after they are peeled whenever the market price changes—without having to do additional yield tests on potatoes.

Whenever you use a cost factor, it will hold true for you only as long as you do not change your style and method of cutting meat or peeling potatoes or whatever methods of pre-prep you do. If we are talking about peeling potatoes, you have to buy the same type of potatoes and remove approximately the same amount of peel. If you change anything in the whole process in your method of pre-preparation, you should do additional yield tests to determine new cost factors.

Cost factors are a tool. They can tell you your costs as prices increase and decrease throughout the year and over periods of time. We have experienced considerable price fluctuation in recent years. If you apply cost factors as prices increase or decrease, you know your costs without having to do new yield tests. You can adjust selling prices more readily and pass on increased costs to your guests quicker.

As we said earlier, you should get *averaged* results from yield tests. If you are doing yield tests on short loins, test 8 to 10 loins. Results will vary between individual short loins. Averaged results from 8 to 10 loins will be much closer to what it will really cost you for your steaks. If you test only one loin, it may be an unusually lean short loin and you will get an unusually high yield. Or you may happen to test a very fat loin and get an unusually low yield. It averages out when you test several.

Another thing to consider is human variability. If you are doing tests on meat, meat cutters may suddenly get extraordinarily accurate if they know you will watch them and there will be only one yield test on one loin. A meat cutter is apt to unconsciously go slowly and be very careful. But if the meat cutters are specifically asked to do 8 or 10 loins at normal speed in the normal, routine way just as they would do with no one watching, they will probably come closer to performing like they would if no one were there watching them and writing down results. The same things are true for any yield tests—tests on peeling potatoes, preparing rib roasts so they're oven-ready, and so on. Do several tests on numbers of items and take the average. And emphasize to your employees that they should work in their normal way during yield tests.

Pre-Costing a Recipe (Chart 11-2)

If you cut your own meat, you will need yield test information when you pre-cost your recipes. You may need to do yield tests on other items besides meat and a few vegetables to get information to pre-cost recipes.

To pre-cost a recipe, you write down each ingredient and its cost. Chart 11-2 illustrates how you pre-cost a recipe—for beef stew, in this example.

1. Column 1: Ingredients.
   In this column list every ingredient you need to make beef stew.
2. Column 2: Weight, Volume, or Count.
   Here you list weight, volume, or any other appropriate type of count of every ingredient.
3. Column 3: Cost per Unit Ready to Use.
   List cost of each unit when it is Ready to Use.
4. Column 4: Total Cost Items Used.
   This is the total cost of all items used in the stew.

Total cost $56.30 divided by the number of portions 100 equals the cost per portion 56.3 cents. This 56.3 cents cost per portion assumes ideal conditions. Even the cost of spices is included in this recipe. Costing is theoretical. It assumes ideal conditions and accuracy. You list explicit measurements of ingredients and assume they will all be followed precisely. When it comes down to actual performance, however, your cooks may measure with their eyes instead of using exact measurements for a lot of their cooking. The more careful they are in measuring, the more accurately your pre-costing will work out in reality. Your cooks will not get the exact results you have pre-costed unless they do measure everything precisely. In baking, items must be precisely measured or failure can result in many products, but in cooking, slight variations in the amount of ingredients used do not have such a noticeable effect in the food. Variations can have some effect on the accuracy of your pre-costing, however. (There is more discussion on this in Chapter 17.)

Watch the yield closely when you are costing a recipe to be sure the recipe will give you the exact number of portions you want. If you get only 90 portions instead of 100, your cost per portion increases from 56.3 cents per portion to 62.5 cents per portion. The total cost you arrive at in your formal written pre-costing is the minimum cost you can get. This is the standard or potential portion cost in dollars and cents. Your costs will not be lower than this without adjustment of the recipe. If actual costs come in higher, employees are not following recipes accurately. You are not achieving your standard or potential cost. And you may not be getting the number of portions you had costed and had planned on.

Food Cost Percent Per Portion

To find your food cost percent per portion, do the following: PORTION COST divided by SELLING PRICE PER PORTION multiplied by 100 to convert to percentage equals FOOD COST PERCENT PER PORTION.

Menu Item: <u>Beef Stew</u> Date Prepared: _____ Recipe Multiplied: <u>/ Time</u>

Number Portion: <u>100</u>　　　　　　　　　　Size of Portion: <u>8 oz.</u>

Cost Per Portion: <u>$.563</u> Selling Price: _____ Percent Food Cost: _____

1	2	3	4
Ingredients	Weight, Volume or Count	Cost/Unit Ready to Use	Total Cost Items Used
Beef Stew Meat	35 lbs.	$1.25　lb.	$43.15
Flour – All Purpose	1 lb. 4 oz.	.072 lb.	1.44
Tomatoe Puree	1½ qts.	.72 qt.	1.08
Meat Stock	1½ gals.	1.08 lb.	.32
Roux <Flour / Fat	6 oz. / 6 oz.	.072 lb. / .20 lb.	.03 / .08
Frozen Stew Vegetables	35 lbs.	.273 lb.	9.56
* Spices	—	—	.04
Total Cost			$56.30

* Salt, Pepper, garlic Powder, Bay Leaves, Thyme, Casmel Color

Cost Per Portion: = $\dfrac{\text{Total Cost: } \$56.30}{\text{Number of Portions: } 100}$ = $.563

Chart 11-2 Pre-Costing a Recipe

If the item costs you 56.3 cents per portion to prepare and you sell it for $1.40 à la carte, you have a 40.21 percent food cost ($0.563 divided by $1.40 equals .4021 multiplied by 100 equals 40.21 percent). If the item costs you 56.3 cents per portion to prepare and you sell it for $1.70, the food cost is lower—it's 33.12 percent.

You can lower your per portion food cost percent for an item by:

1. Raising the price you charge for the item.
2. Lowering the amount you pay to purchase the ingredients in an item. If you buy lower quality beef, for example, and reduce the actual per portion cost to 50 cents, and sell it for $1.40 à la carte, the food cost is 35.71 percent. You have lowered your per portion cost and you've lowered your per portion food cost percent.
3. A third way to reduce the cost would be to serve a smaller portion for the same price. This reduces the cost per portion because you get more portions from the same amount of food. Instead of 100 portions, you squeeze 110 portions from the same amount of food (TOTAL COST $56.30 divided by NUMBER OF PORTIONS 110 equals COST PER PORTION $0.512). Sometimes cutting portion size is okay, sometimes it is not a good idea. Customers may not like it at all, and sales can go down if you are not careful about this.
4. A fourth method (not recommended) is to use lower quality *and* raise your prices.

All four of these methods are used by food service operations.

The best method is to use ingredients of a quality that your customers would reasonably expect from your type of food service. Make portion sizes as close to what your guests want as you can. And make prices reasonable in relation to the portion size you serve, to the quality of ingredients you use, and to the type of food service operation you have.

"Reasonable" is vague, and there is, unfortunately, no mathematical formula to help you know what "reasonable" is in your case. You simply have to use common sense and learn by experience what is "reasonable" in your own operation. A study of your competition may help you make your own judgments. If your operation is in difficulty, reexamine your ideas about "reasonable." For a general guideline, if you are "reasonable" in all areas, you *should* be getting the total food cost percent and profit you want.

Potential Cost

When you have completed your pre-costing, you are ready to estimate your potential costs. Potential cost is the food cost percent you get under perfect, theoretical, ideal conditions. Look at Chart 11-3. In Chart 11-3 you are estimating the number of sales of each item listed on your menu. Estimated and actual sales are put in Chart 11-3 deliberately to show both. Do your chart the same way as shown in the Chart 11-3 example so you can compare your estimated and actual sales.

1	2	3	4	5	6	7
Menu Item	Base Period Average Market Price	Main Ingredient Standard Portion Size	Main Ingredient Cost Per Portion	Surrounding Dish Cost	Total Cost Item	Sales Price
Appetizers						
Shrimp Cocktail	$ 2.75 lb.	4 Lg.	$ .800		$ .800	$ 1.95
Melon Balls au Rhum	11.00 case	8 balls	.090		.090	.75
Soup du Jour	—	4 oz.	.040		.040	.35
Total Appetizers						
Entrees						
Stuffed Breast of Chicken	$ .90 breast	6 oz.	$ .900	$ .525	$ 1.425	$ 3.50
New York Strip Steak	3.25 lb.	12 oz.	2.813	.525	3.338	6.50
Top Sirloin Steak	2.35 lb.	10 oz.	1.469	.525	1.994	4.95
Prime Ribs of Beef	1.89 lb.	14 oz.	1.654	.525	2.179	5.95
Chopped Steak	.74 lb.	8 oz.	.370	.525	.895	3.25
Combination Steak and Shrimp	2.35 lb.(Stk) 2.10 lb.	6 oz. 4 oz.	.881 .840	.525	2.246	6.25
Rocky Mountain Trout	.69 ea.	1	.690	.525	1.215	4.25
Beef Brochette	1.50 lb.	6 oz.	.563	.525	1.088	3.95
Stuffed Shrimp	2.10 lb.	4 Lg.	.840	.525	1.365	4.25
Total Entrees						
Desserts						
Chocolate Creme de Menthe Sundae	$ 1.39 gal. 3.56 qt.	1 Scoop	$ .100		$ .100	$ .50
Cheesecake with Strawberries	2.16 pie 8.00 case	1/12 pie	.210		.210	.65
Total Desserts						
Grand Total						

Chart 11-3 Estimated and Actual Potential Costs

8	9	10	11	12	13	14	15
Estimated Number to be Sold	Actual Number Sold	Estimated Weighted Cost Value	Actual Weighted Cost Value	Estimated Weighted Sales Value	Actual Weighted Sales Value	Estimated Potential Food Cost Percent	Actual Potential Food Cost Percent
35	40	28.00	32.00	68.25	78.00	41.03 %	41.03%
20	15	1.80	1.35	15.00	11.25	12.00	12.00
25	25	1.00	1.00	8.75	8.75	11.43	11.43
80	80	30.80	34.35	92.00	98.00	33.48%	33.05%
50	51	71.25	72.68	175.00	178.50	40.71%	40.72%
80	83	267.04	277.05	520.00	539.50	51.35	51.35
50	62	99.70	123.63	247.50	306.90	40.28	40.28
60	51	130.74	111.13	357.00	303.45	36.62	36.62
25	33	22.38	29.54	81.25	107.25	27.54	27.04
60	59	134.76	132.51	375.00	368.75	35.94	35.93
15	20	18.23	24.30	63.75	85.00	28.60	28.59
25	24	27.20	26.11	98.75	94.80	27.54	27.54
60	58	81.90	79.17	255.00	246.50	32.12	32.12
425	441	853.20	876.12	2,173.25	2,230.65	39.26%	39.28%
50	43	5.00	4.30	25.00	21.50	20.00%	20.00%
50	36	10.50	7.56	32.50	23.40	32.31	32.31
100	79	15.50	11.86	62.50	44.90	24.80%	26.41%
		899.50	922.33	2,327.75	2,373.55	38.64%	38.86%

Chart 11-3 Estimated and Actual Potential Costs (continued)

First we will discuss estimated sales, then actual sales, and then we will compare the two.

Discussion of Estimated and Actual Potential Costs (Chart 11-3)

First we'll discuss Columns 1 through 8 and Columns 10, 12 and 14. These concern estimated potential cost (before any prices go on the menu). Later we will discuss Columns 9, 11, 13 and 15. These columns show the effects after the menu has been priced and used.

Estimated Potential Costs (Columns 1 through 8, 10, 12, 14)

The following is the procedure for finding estimated potential cost:

1. Column 1: Menu Item.
   Menu items to be sold, showing appetizers, entrees, and desserts.

2. Column 2: Base Period Average Market Price.
   In this column you list the base period average market price. This is usually the average price you paid for items the preceding month.

3. Column 3: Main Ingredient Standard Portion Size.
   Here you list main ingredients in standard portion size.

4. Column 4: Main Ingredient Cost Per Portion.
   In this column you list main ingredient, cost per portion. It's generally used for entrees.

5. Column 5: Surrounding Dish Cost.
   "Surrounding dish cost" means cost of items that will accompany the entree. This column should usually list an average cost. It will probably include potato, salad, salad dressing, roll, and butter. In Chart 11-3, beverage is extra. Surrounding costs for appetizers and desserts are included in Column 4 Main Ingredient Cost Per Portion.

6. Column 6: Total Item Cost.
   You get this by adding Column 4 Main Ingredient Cost Per Portion and Column 5 Surrounding Dish Cost.

7. Column 7: Sales Price.
   This is the price you intend to put on your menu for the item. If your potential cost is not what you want it to be, come back and adjust these selling prices here in Column 7 and change prices before you print menus.

8. Column 8: Estimated Number to be Sold.
   You have to make an estimate of how much you think you will sell of each item. Do this *before* you put the menu into effect and *before* you start fixing any food. *This step is the key to pre-control.* You make your estimates of how much you will probably sell of everything *before* you prepare and sell food. *Base your labor schedule, your purchasing, and your production on this estimate.*

9. Column 9: To be discussed later.

10. Column 10: Estimated Weighted Cost Value.
    You get this by multiplying Column 6 Total Item Cost by Column 8 Estimated Number to be Sold.
11. Column 11: To be discussed later.
12. Column 12: Estimated Weighted Sales Value.
    You get this by multiplying Column 7 Sales Price by Column 8 Estimated Number to be Sold.
13. Column 13: To be discussed later.
14. Column 14: Estimated Potential Food Cost Percent.
    You get this by dividing Column 10 Estimated Weighted Cost Value by Column 12 Estimated Weighted Sales Value.
15. Column 15: To be discussed later.

The figures in Column 14 Estimated Potential Food Cost Percent come out the same way whether you divide Column 12 Estimated Weighted Sales Value into Column 10 Estimated Weighted Cost Value or you divide Column 7 Sales Price (of a single item) into Column 6 Total Item Cost (of a single item). The reason for this is that you have multiplied the individual selling price and the individual total cost by the same number. Therefore the results will be the same.

In the following discussion, we will be talking about the sixth figure down in the columns mentioned. Look at Column 10 Estimated Weighted Cost Value. The sixth figure down in the column is $267.04, for New York strip steaks. Divide this by Column 12 Estimated Weighted Sales Value $520. You get Column 14 Estimated Potential Food Cost Percent 51.35 percent. Column 6 Total Item Cost of a New York strip steak $3.338 divided by Column 7 Sales Price of a New York strip steak $6.50 equals Column 14 Estimated Potential Food Cost Percent 51.35 percent.

In this example we multiplied both the Column 6 Total Item Cost $3.338 and the Column 7 Sales Price $6.50 by Column 8 Estimated Number to be Sold 80 New York strip steak dinners.

"Weighted" means we multiply (or weight) both the $3.338 and the $6.50 by 80. Both numbers have been "weighted" by our estimated sales of 80.

What interests you most is the total cost of all items to be sold and total revenue from all items to be sold.

Add all figures in Column 10 Estimated Weighted Cost Value. The total is $899.50. Add all figures in Column 12 Estimated Weighted Sales Value. The total is $2,327.75. Divide Column 10 Estimated Weighted Cost Value Total $899.50 by Column 12 Estimated Weighted Sales Value Total $2,327.75. You get Column 14 Estimated Potential Food Cost Percent Total— 38.64 percent. 38.64 percent is the estimated potential food cost percent for your estimated sales.

This potential estimated cost percent—38.64 percent—*has* taken into consideration the sales of various items and the costs for these items in relation to the estimated sales of these items. The estimated food cost percent you get by following this procedure should be within one percent of the food cost percent you want.

If your food cost percent is too high and is not within one percent of where you want it, you could consider raising the prices of certain items slightly. This could reduce the sale of those items. A higher price could cause some guests to switch from that entree to a less expensive entree—but maybe to an entree that would let you achieve a better food cost percent.

For example, if you were to raise the price of New York strip steak from $6.50 to $7, it might cause some customers to switch to top sirloin steak or prime rib of beef. This would mean higher sales of top sirloin steak and prime rib of beef and lower sales of New York strip steak. This could lower your total potential estimated food cost percent.

Notice that you have only considered changing the price of one item— raising New York strip from $6.50 to $7. Perhaps you want to consider raising the price of your top sirloin steak, too. If you raise top sirloin from $4.95 to $5.25, some of your guests might switch from the New York strip steak to the top sirloin steak because $5.25 is more than $4.95 but still considerably less than $7. This would have an additional effect of lowering your total potential estimated food cost percent.

The preceding discussion has concerned estimated sales of various items. This is a very important key in your overall control. Take steps to achieve your desired *food cost percent before* you sell anything. Take steps to adjust your *selling prices before* you sell anything. Don't just wait to see what actual sales will be. Suppose you are off in your estimates. You can adjust prices later. But it is better to have thought about problems and acted before-hand instead of waiting to see what happens and then trying to take action after something is wrong. Chances are your estimates will be better than you think they will be, and you will get better at making them with experience. Compare your estimates with actual results.

Actual Potential Costs (Columns 9, 11, 13, 15)

Real or actual cost is the figure on your profit and loss statement. "Actual potential cost" is the cost you figure for ideal conditions. There is no provision for waste or error.

In our preceding discussion of Chart 11-3, we ignored Columns 9, 11, 13, and 15. These columns are where you record your actual sales. These columns show effects after the menu has been used and after sales have been made.

Now we will discuss these columns.

9. Column 9: Actual Number Sold.
   Put this column next to Column 8 Estimated Number to be Sold so you can compare the results and accuracy of your estimates.

11. Column 11: Actual Weighted Cost Value.
    You get this figure by multiplying Column 6 Total Item Cost by Column 9 Actual Number Sold.

13. Column 13: Actual Weighted Sales Value.
    You get this figure by multiplying Column 7 Sales Price by Column 9 Actual Number Sold. Column 7 shows the figures that have been printed on your menu.

15. Column 15: Actual Potential Food Cost Percent.
    Get this figure by dividing Column 11 Actual Weighted Cost Value by Column 13 Actual Weighted Sales Value.

You can also compute actual potential food cost percent per individual item by dividing Column 6 Total Item Cost by Column 7 Sales Price. (We discussed this previously in this chapter.)

Note that Column 14 Estimated Potential Food Cost Percent and Column 15 Actual Potential Food Cost Percent have the same food cost percent for individual items but not the same food cost percent for the totals. It is the totals that are important to you.

To get the final total figure, divide Column 11 Actual Weighted Cost Value Total $922.33 by Column 13 Actual Weighted Sales Value Total $2,373.55. This gives you your Actual Total Potential Food Cost Percent of 38.86 percent (bottom of Column 15).

Note that in Chart 11-3 our total *potential estimated* food cost percent was 38.64 percent compared to our *actual* total potential food cost percent of 38.86 percent. The two figures are within .22 percent of each other. This is good. This is what you want—to get these two figures as close to each other as you can. The closer they are to each other, the closer you are to the food cost percent you want. The farther apart they are, the higher your food cost on your profit and loss statement will be and you will not get the profit you want.

Chart 11-3 is the chart you use to get your potential cost. It is *potential* cost because it's ideal figures. We have figured the *exact* portion cost and the *exact* surrounding cost per individual item. No provision was made for normal waste, and the like.

Add a "Tolerance" to Your Potential Cost

Always add a 1 percent "tolerance" to your actual potential food cost percent. This 1 percent is to cover the cost of waste, the cost of condiments on the table, and so on. In our example, your "actual potential food cost percent" is 38.86 percent. Add 1 percent tolerance and you get 39.86 percent. This means your actual potential food cost percent should be 39.86

percent. Your *actual* food cost percent (real, not potential) should not be more than 39.86 percent. When you compute your real food cost percent at the end of the month on your profit and loss statement, it should not be more than 39.86 percent. If it is more, something is wrong and it's probably too much waste in food production.

Put Chart 11-3 on column paper yourself and fill in your own figures. Ideally, you should change and update your chart (or start a new chart if you need to) every time you make any changes in your menu. Some operations make a new chart every month. Others may go as long as three months before they start a new one. You should prepare this chart at least every three months because your costs are apt to change within most three-month intervals.

As you develop skill with experience in working with this chart, your Column 9 Actual Number Sold figure and your Column 8 Estimated Number to be Sold figures should compare more closely with each other. The difference between the two figures is that Column 9 Actual Number Sold is historical—what you really did do. Column 8 Estimated Number to be Sold is a calculated guess—what you expect you will do. Look at your estimated potential food cost percent. If the food cost percent is not what you want (based on a sound estimate), you can change prices beforehand. This should have an effect on the number of items you sell in each category. Take steps ahead of time to help you arrive at your desired food cost *before* you sell items.

Don't just wait, hope, and find out what happens after it has already happened! Plan and act in advance of events. Estimate the amount of business you expect to do, check as you go, and make changes if you need to before the month has ended and it is too late to correct a situation.

Most operators do not do all this. Some do not do *any* of it. They think it is a lot of work. It is. But it *can* be done reasonably simply and quickly. The more you do it, the easier and more routine it gets. It is easiest to install a system of potential costing when you are putting in a new standardized menu, which you expect to use for a period of time.

Menu Pricing Mistakes

If you make your estimates before you have your menus printed, you can avoid or eliminate a lot of mistakes. You can probably avoid the necessity of having to print new menus with higher prices. If your costs change, there is no remedy but to change portion sizes or change prices on your menu. If you have printed prices on your menu which cut your profits and should be changed, do correct them. Cross out prices and write in new ones, or reprint your menus. A lot of operators refuse to adjust menu prices when they should. They ignore it and take a loss. Don't follow their example. If your costs are fluctuating and changing rapidly, fix your prices rapidly.

It is not uncommon for food service operations knowingly to leave several items priced incorrectly on their menus. They think it is too expensive to reprint the menus. But that can be false economy. You do not always have to reprint incorrectly priced menus, but do fix them somehow, and use common sense. Take all steps possible beforehand so menus will be priced correctly. Try to anticipate what you will sell in the different categories of entrees. Try to determine ahead of time what effect these different amounts will have on your total food cost. Adjust prices before you print your menus. Effective pre-costing can save you time, trouble, and money.

If you want true accuracy from a cost standpoint, you should include appetizers and desserts in your pre-costing procedures, too. When you break down costs for appetizers and desserts, the food cost percents for these items are usually quite low compared with the entree cost percents. For example, the Column 15 Actual Potential Food Cost Percent total figure for desserts in Chart 11-3 is 26.41 percent compared with Column 15 Actual Potential Food Cost Percent total figure for entrees 39.28 percent. You don't do as much dollar volume in appetizers or desserts as you do in entrees.

The selling price of appetizers and desserts is low compared to the selling price of entrees. On items with low selling price, the food cost percent should also be low. Appetizers and desserts sales can help reduce total food cost percent because of their lower food cost percent.

Forecasting

Forecasting is another pre-control technique. When you make a forecast, you make a prediction, an estimate, of how much business you expect you will do. A forecast can be for a meal period, for a day, a week, a month, or a year. Forecast ahead of time and then base your activities (purchasing, production, employee scheduling, and so on) on your forecast for the period of time involved. Make general forecasts for a week, a month, a year. Make specific forecasts for each meal period. Some operations forecast for every meal they serve. For breakfast, you may just want to forecast the total number of guests you think you will serve. Most breakfast items are cooked to order anyway. For lunch and dinner, however, you may want to know how much of each entree to thaw or do pre-prep on or actually prepare because here—lunch and dinner—is where overproduction, underproduction, and waste are more apt to occur than at breakfast.

Management Should Make the Forecast

Forecasting is an attempt to project, predict, and estimate the volume of business you think you will get. Forecasting should be done by someone in a management position. The more forecasting you do, the more accurate a forecaster you will become. It is better to forecast and be wrong than not to forecast at all.

Don't let your employees figure out by themselves how much food to prepare. They usually do not have the overall information that is available to you, and their forecasts probably would not be as accurate as yours can be. Your employees will usually not be in a position to know all of the factors involved in making a good forecast. You should be. Or it is up to you to train employees to do the forecasting. If you do, make sure they have all the information needed.

Two Ways of Forecasting

There are two ways to make a forecast—a calculated guess based on experience and a statistical forecast based on written records of past experience.

Some managers who have had a lot of experience in food production and who know their market well can make fairly accurate estimates of how much of each item on a menu will be sold. Individuals with a lot of experience may be quite successful in doing an intuitive type of forecasting of the number of each entree they will sell. They base forecasts on everything they have learned about the food service industry. They know their market, have learned their guests' preferences in food, and may understand seasonal fluctuations and other factors.

Statistical breakdown forecasting is more formal and has a better chance of being more consistently accurate. A statistical breakdown can be a useful tool for all food service operators, whether they have had years of experience in the food service industry or not.

Ideally, you should combine the two methods in your forecasting. Use your records *and* your experience, knowledge, and common sense.

Forecasting a Meal Period

Forecasting is usually done for each meal period. If you use standardized menus, you can do statistical forecasting. If you don't, you can't. But you still can and should make forecasts. They will be calculated guesses and they are not apt to be as accurate as if you use standardized menus and do regular statistical forecasting.

When you make a statistical forecast for one specific meal period, it means you are going to try to estimate the total amount of entrees you will serve and the total number of guests you will serve during that one specific future meal period. To get an accurate statistical forecast, you have to be using a standardized menu. If you don't use a standardized menu, your forecasts will not be statistical—they will be calculated guesses. Calculated guesses are definitely better than no forecast at all.

Keep records of sales every day. These records should include the number of guests you served, how many of each entree you sold, and the total number you sold of all entrees combined. These become your written historical records. You refer to them when you make a forecast for future meal periods.

Estimate the Total Number of Guests to be Served

To forecast the total number of guests for one meal based on past statistics, look at the total number of guests you served for that meal period the previous time that same menu was used. And look at the total served for the same meal period last week. And the same meal period on the same *day* last year—the second Wednesday in February, for example—not just the calendar date, which may not coincide. Don't look up February 16 last year to forecast for February 16 this year. Look up the corresponding *day*.

Are there any unusual events that could affect the meal you are now forecasting—a nearby store sale, a convention in town, a heavy storm coming, a holiday? Anything that could affect your business for this meal period? Say, for example, your food service operation is a downtown restaurant and there is a hotel across the street from you. You usually count on some guests from this hotel to eat lunch at your restaurant. You find out (because you make it your business to find out) that there will be a large convention taking most of the rooms in the hotel for the day. Try to find out if they are having a planned luncheon somewhere. If they are, you probably won't get the convention people in your restaurant or your usual number of guests from the hotel. You should take this into account in planning your meal. If the convention is not having a scheduled luncheon anywhere, you may get many more than your usual quota from the hotel because the hotel is full and a number of the convention people might eat in your restaurant.

What is the weather predicted for the day of the meal for which you are making the forecast? And how accurate are your weather forecasters? Be aware of how the weather affects your volume, if it does. On bright sunny days people may go farther from their offices to eat. But they may be apt to eat close to their work if it is cloudy, raining, or snowing, or they may bring lunch from home and eat in their offices. For many food service operations, weather can have a decided bearing on volume of business. Weather can affect different types of operations in different ways. Bad weather can hurt you or help you. Try to find out how weather affects your operation and include these factors in your forecasting.

Look at your records of actual figures of the business you did for the same meal period yesterday, a week ago, and a year ago. Adjust for varying factors such as weather, special events (or lack of them), and so on. Estimate the total number of people you think you will serve.

How to Get a Percentage Index for a Meal Period (Chart 11-4)

A "percentage index" is a method of forecasting how much of each menu item to prepare for a meal period. Chart 11-4 illustrates how to set up a menu forecast percentage index chart.

1. Column 1: Menu Item.
   Get these items from your standardized menu for the meal period you are forecasting.
2. Column 2: Total Number of Each Item Sold.
   This is the total number of each item you sold the last time the same menu was used. Get these figures from your records.

3. Column 3: Total Number All Menu Items Sold.
   To get this figure, add all figures in Column 2 Total Number of Each Item Sold.

4. Column 4: Percentage Index.
   You get this for each item by dividing Column 2 Total Number of Each Item Sold by Column 3 Total Number of All Items Sold. This is the percentage each item represents of the total items sold.

5. Column 5: Forecast of Total Number of Guests.
   This is the total number of guests you estimate will come to your food service establishment for the meal period you are forecasting. Make a calculated guess based on all the matters we have discussed (records, weather, and so on).

6. Column 6: Forecast Items Will Sell.
   You get this for each item by multiplying Column 5 Forecast of Total Number of Guests by Column 4 Percentage Index for each item. Column 6 Forecast of Items Will Sell totals 425. This figure should be the same number as Column 5 Forecast of Total Number of Guests—425.

1	2	3	4	5	6
Menu Item	Total Number of Each Item Sold	Total Number All Menu Items Sold	Percentage Index	Forecast of Total Number of Guests	Forecast Items Will Sell
Stuffed Breast Chicken	46 ÷	390	11.79X	425	50
New York Strip	73 ÷	390	18.72X	425	80
Club Steak	46 ÷	390	11.79X	425	50
Prime Rib	55 ÷	390	14.10X	425	60
Chopped Steak	23 ÷	390	5.90X	425	25
Combined Steak and Shrimp	55 ÷	390	14.10X	425	60
Trout	14 ÷	390	3.60X	425	15
Beef Brochette	23 ÷	390	5.90X	425	25
Stuffed Shrimp	55 ÷	390	14.10X	425	60
	390				425

Chart 11-4   Forecast of Items Will Sell
Based on a Percentage Index and a Standardized Menu

This statistical percentage index forecast shown in Chart 11-4 should give you a fairly good indication of what you will sell. Remember that you are trying to predict what human beings will do. You certainly can't be 100 percent correct all the time (if ever), but your forecast can give you a good indication of what quantities of each item you will sell.

If the number of sales you estimate for an entree turns out to be 53, don't tell your cooks to prepare 53 portions, because, for one thing, they would think you were crazy. Tell them to fix 50 or 55—depending on the cost of the entree and depending on the item. You will probably forecast on the low side to minimize leftovers. With effort, your forecasting can become fairly accurate, although there will be times when you are off, of course.

In Chart 11-4, the one item you would want to forecast most accurately would be the prime rib. You can use it as a lower priced leftover, but not as well as you can use it at full price when it is hot and fresh. The other items in Chart 11-4 are cooked-to-order items. You are concerned that you have enough items thawed for the meal period. But if you don't sell those today, they will keep in the refrigerator and can probably be sold tomorrow. Not all menus have the majority of items cooked to order. It is for items *not* cooked to order that your forecast is really important.

Problems of Overproduction and Underproduction

In Chapter 10 on the menu, we mentioned some of the problems of overproduction and underproduction. Forecasting is a tool that can help you reduce these difficulties. Consider the following factors:

1. Is the food an item that is cooked to order? Maybe you should prepare a specific, small number to start with and be ready to cook more to order.
2. If the item is frozen, can more of it be thawed quickly and used?
3. If it is ready today but it does not sell, is it likely that you can sell it tomorrow?
4. If it is an expensive item and involves a lot of time for preparation, what will you do with it if it is left over?
5. If you run out, what will you substitute?

Try to figure out reasonable answers to these questions and come up with a reasonable estimate of the amount of each item to prepare. These estimated figures are used in your production records, which will be discussed in Chapter 17.

REVIEW AND DISCUSSION QUESTIONS

1. What do the following stand for: AP, RTC, RTE, EP.
2. What are the steps in doing a yield test?

3. What are the steps in costing a recipe?

4. What factors should you consider when you make a forecast?

5. Why are estimated potential food cost and actual potential food cost different from each other?

6. You bought beef chuck for 89 cents per pound. A four ounce portion of trimmed beef stew meat costs 32 cents per portion. Beef chuck goes up to $1.03 per pound.

   a. What is the cost factor per portion for beef stew? (Answer: .36) Show how you arrive at the answer.

   b. What does a portion of beef stew cost at the new, higher market price? (Answer: 37 cents per portion.) Show how you arrive at the answer.

12

Menu Pricing

Objectives

This chapter discusses the methods and the importance of menu pricing. After you have read this chapter, you should know:

1. Why loss leaders are not recommended.
2. Various approaches to menu pricing.
3. A method for actually setting your own prices.

"Menu pricing" means deciding what you will charge for food and putting the prices on your menu. Unfortunately there are no clear-cut, exact procedures for doing this. Many factors affect menu pricing and they do not readily lend themselves to neat, unchanging formulas.

When you do menu pricing, you *can* be sure that you have to:

1. Cover all your costs.
2. Make prices reasonable for your guests in terms of the value they receive.
3. Make prices reasonable for your food service operation so you obtain a profit.

LOSS LEADERS

A "loss leader" is an item purposely sold below cost to attract customers. Don't ever use this idea.

Supermarkets, which have thousands of items for sale for customers, may occasionally feature a loss leader, and for them it can make sense. "Loss leaders" are items you intentionally sell for less than you pay for them. Supermarkets use them to try to attract customers inside where, they hope, the customers will buy other items on which the store does make a profit. Supermarkets may be subsidized by the manufacturer of the loss leader, who writes it off as sales promotion cost. None of this applies in the case of food and beverage operations.

Some food service operators try to use the loss leader concept in the food service industry, but it does not work. For a food service operation, there is no point in selling a lot of one item at a loss—and especially not on purpose—because for you it doesn't do a bit of good. A food service operation is not a supermarket and *your* customers will not take home sacks of other merchandise. They can just eat your loss leader and leave, and a lot of them may do just that. You may wind up with loss leaders, unfortunately, but you certainly shouldn't *try* to.

The lead item on your menu, and the one you are trying to promote, should not be a loss leader, it should be a profit leader. A "profit leader" is an item that contributes substantially to the profit of your food service establishment. Promote *it*.

MAXIMUM AND MINIMUM PRICE FOR SPECIAL ITEMS

Establish maximum and minimum prices you think your guests will pay for everything, including specialty items. You see items like "fresh fruit in season" on some menus. With air freight today, you can get fresh fruit (fresh strawberries, for example) most months of the year. But buy them only if and when your guests are willing to pay what you must charge for them. Today it is not so much a question of seasonality—it's a question of cost to you and to your guests.

When you *can* afford to buy food and sell it in a large enough quantity so that it is profitable to offer it, it's reasonable. When you have to pay a lot for an item, you are forced to charge a lot, too. So you probably can't sell much of it. If this is true, take the item off your menu.

Many food service operations used to sell fresh lobster but do not any more. The prices they had to pay and charge got too high. Some substituted lobster tail, which you can keep frozen and thaw only as you need it. Others stopped trying to sell lobster at all and switched to crab or shrimp instead.

This does not mean you have to quit selling lobster (or fresh fruit, or any other item). It does mean you must sell a sufficient quantity of most items to give you a profit on them or you cannot afford to go on carrying them. There are exceptions to this. Some foods serve a unique function by attracting guests you could not get if you didn't offer them. You may occasionally get a request for particular expensive items—lobster tail or fresh strawberries, for example. If you can offer these items in limited, carefully controlled quantity, ok. They can add flair to your menu, attract customers, and have an effect on the sales of your other items, such as steak. Some individuals may have persuaded the group they are with to come to your food service operation because they know you offer both steak and lobster. The rest of their party may order steak or less expensive items, but one or two individuals want lobster and they come to you with their party to get it.

If you find a few items that do make this unique type of contribution, keep them on your menu. If they stop serving their particular function of attracting extra guests and no longer pay for themselves, take them off your menu. You should determine when the price you have to charge is too high to justify carrying them on your menu.

FREE FOOD

A fallacy left over from the old days of the free-lunch counter and the nickel beer is the notion: "I'll make so much money on beverage that I can afford to give food away." This idea persists, although it should have passed into history when (alas) the nickel beer did. You cannot give food away (with the possible exception of a few tidbits at the bar during cocktail hour). Both food and beverage sales should contribute to your profit. Liquor sales can lead to food sales and food sales can lead to liquor sales—but you should get profits from both.

Some customers may come into a food and beverage operation just for dinner and not have any drinks at all. The sale of their food alone should contribute to the profit of the operation. Others may come in just for drinks, no dinner. The drinks they buy should contribute to your profit, too. You must sell enough of both liquor and food to cover costs and derive a profit.

APPROACHES TO PRICING

Copy Your Competition Exactly

One way (a very bad way) to set menu prices is to copy the prices of your competitors exactly—no matter what differences exist between your food service establishments. Even if operations seem quite similar, there are sure to be *some* differences. The costs your competitors face may be different from yours. Your competitors may be more efficient or less efficient than you are. They may have different atmosphere, type of service, different standards of quality and sanitation. To arbitrarily set your prices to match theirs *exactly*—without making any allowances for differences in establishments—is foolish.

The following true story is a case in point. Specialty Restaurant A was not making the profit it should have been for the volume of sales it was doing. The owner of Restaurant A was convinced he could not raise his prices at all. He believed he had to charge the very same prices as his competition. He felt that his competition was another restaurant in his community and he was right. But there was actually no basis for his feeling that he and his competitor had to charge exactly the same prices. The other operation served the same kind of specialty food, but the similarity stopped there.

Specialty Restaurant A (the one that wasn't making the right profit) was a 200-seat restaurant. It had a very pleasant atmosphere, very good service, and very good quality food. Specialty Restaurant B (A's competitor) served good food, but it only had 40 seats and it had an extremely plain atmosphere.

Restaurant A was a more expensive establishment to run. The manager should have raised his prices. But he was afraid to. He was worried that if he raised his prices, Restaurant B would take away all his customers. He failed to realize that:

1. There was quite a large market in their community for the specialty foods both restaurants served.
2. His competitor only had 40 seats and could not possibly take away enough business to hurt him.
3. His establishment was more luxurious and more expensive to operate.

He *should* have charged more. He did not look at his situation realistically. He was also intimidated by the fact that the owner of Restaurant B was his own cousin.

Don't ignore the ways in which your operation does differ from your competitors'. If you provide different atmosphere, different type of service, different decor, and so on, you can charge different prices (higher or lower, depending on circumstances) even though you and your competitors both specialize in similar types of food. Your prices should not, however, get *too* far out of line from your competitors.' That *would* probably help them and hurt you in the long run.

Economics Approach to Pricing

Another factor to consider in menu pricing is the economics of the food and beverage industry discussed in Chapter 4. Different types of demand curves have different effects on prices and quantities sold. In general the food service industry faces an inelastic demand curve. This means that when you raise or lower your prices within a specific, limited, reasonable range, it will not noticeably change the number of guests you get. If you and your direct competitors keep your prices within a reasonably comparable range, depending on the variables in your operations, guests are not necessarily attracted or repelled by price alone. Guests are not usually *accurately* informed about the prices you charge nor are they *accurately* informed about the prices your competitors charge, though they'll have an idea of yours and your competitors' general price *range*. Guests are more concerned about quality of food, how it's served, the atmosphere and service in the establishment, its location and accessibility, than they are about whether you charge slightly more or less than the comparable establishments which are your competitors.

Your food service is the supplier of food for your guests. The owners of your establishment are the ones who decide the general price level at which you will supply certain items. You, the manager, are the one who sets the actual pricing for the menu. The food you supply and the price you charge should be appropriate for the type of business you are running and appropriate for the general type of food service category you are in. The guest who comes to you is the demander of your product and you are the supplier. Your product is not just food, it's many things including service, atmosphere, convenience, and so on.

In the United States, people can buy a hamburger for as little as 30 cents in a fast-food operation or for $2.50 or more in a luxurious restaurant. The price you as a food service operator charge will depend on what you are supplying, where you supply it, and to whom. In the fast-food field you supply a hamburger and a bun, maybe for the customer to eat in the car or very informally if you have tables and chairs inside your establishment. In the luxury restaurant you probably offer expensive atmosphere, service by service personnel, and so on. Both establishments could be charging a reasonable price for a hamburger if the first charges 30 cents and the second charges $2.50. The fast-food hamburger drive-in and the luxury restaurant compete in different markets. They can charge very different prices for a hamburger and yet each can be charging a reasonable price.

Keep these factors in mind when you establish your prices.

Marketing Approach to Pricing

Marketing is everything you do to sell your product and attract guests to your establishment. It is also the promotion you do on premises to increase your average check.

The marketing approach to pricing is: sell, sell, sell. In order to sell, you need an efficient sales staff. You train your waitresses and waiters to be salespeople. You definitely emphasize to your staff that they should *sell* the food. Under this selling approach you charge the highest price the traffic will bear. You do not sell an item for less if you can charge more.

Your customers come to your establishment to buy a service and they are not at all concerned with your costs. They are only interested in what they get for their money. The customer wants value. You want to charge as much as you can.

The marketing approach is to charge the maximum price you can get for an item. You are after terrific volume any way you can get it. But there is danger in being concerned solely with volume. The following story illustrates this. Restaurateurs were told by their accountant, "Do you know it is costing you $1.05 for every $1 you take in?" They replied, "Yes, but look at the *volume* we're doing!"

Under the marketing approach, you may get a very low individual food cost percent or a very high individual food cost percent simply because the cost of the item divided by its selling price gives you a high or low item food cost percent. The item food cost percent depends not so much on what it costs you as on how much you can sell the item for.

It is unwise to set up your pricing using *only* an exaggerated marketing approach. Do use the marketing and selling approach in your pricing, but keep it sensible.

Product Competition Approach to Pricing

Try to figure out and understand why customers choose your establishment or your competitors. Perhaps you and your competitors both buy U.S. choice steaks. They use a gas broiler and you use a charbroiler. Your steaks may start out the same as your competitors' but may wind up different when they're served. The steaks are served in different ways and in different establishments. The steaks are differentiated products.

Under the product competition approach to pricing, you do not engage in price competition with your competitor—you engage in product competition instead. Maybe, for example, you advertise and stress the fact that "All Our Steaks Are U.S. Choice Prepared on Our Charbroiler for Your Enjoyment." You use the product competition approach and philosophy when you set prices for your food service operation. You advertise any way in which your product is unique. Since your product is unique and different from your competitors', you charge a reasonably different price from your competitors' prices.

Cost Approach to Pricing

We discussed how to cost a recipe in Chapter 11. You should itemize and identify the costs of all the ingredients that go into the preparation of a food item. The item may be a steak with all its accompanying items or it may be beef stew where you cost the standardized recipe.

Traditionally the food service industry has predicated menu prices on the basis of food costs. To follow the concept of cost pricing to the ultimate degree, though, would be a serious mistake. Some items would be priced too high, some too low.

Normally, in setting menu prices, you divide the actual material cost of a portion by the food cost percent you want. This gives you your selling price. For example, your food cost for a steak dinner is $2. You want a 40 percent food cost. $2 divided by 40 percent equals $5. You would sell the steak dinner for $5. Another method of computing this (and it'll give you the same result) is to divide 100 percent (total of all expenses) by 40 percent (food cost percent you want). This gives you a markup percentage of 250 percent. 100 percent divided by 40 percent equals 250 percent. Multiply 250 percent by $2. 250 percent multiplied by $2 equals $5. This gives you the same $5 selling price.

In this example we just discussed, if you used a pure cost approach you would multiply each item for sale by 250 percent or divide each item by 40 percent to get the selling price of each item. To follow this procedure with no modifications at all would probably be following a road to oblivion. Some items would be very underpriced and some items would be very overpriced.

Combined Approach to Pricing

What you must do is combine all approaches to pricing into one method. Combine economics, marketing, product competition, and cost approaches to pricing into one combined approach to pricing that works for your establishment.

In Chapter 4 on economics of the food and beverage industry, we showed some of the problems of price cutting and attempted to show how you define the group to whom you would like to cater. In this chapter we have examined the concept of selling, product competition, and the differentiated product, and we have discussed problems that might arise from using only a pure cost approach to pricing.

In the example we used when we discussed cost approach to pricing, your steak dinner sold for $5. But if you run an inexpensive steak house and analyze your market, you may find that the maximum price most of your guests would pay would be $4.50. Instead of the 40 percent food cost you wanted, the best you can come up with would be a 44½ percent food cost ($2 cost of steak divided by $4.50 maximum selling price you can get).

Suppose, for further example, you could prepare a cup of soup for three cents. Using a 250 percent markup percent, the cup of soup would be sold on the menu for 8 cents (rounded up from an actual 7½ cents).

In the first case, if you price your steak at $5 it is more than most of your guests will be willing to pay. In the second case, you may sell soup at 8 cents a cup when your guests would be quite willing to pay 20 cents a cup or more. Suppose you lower your price to $4.50 on the steak and get a 44 percent food cost. And suppose you raise the price of soup to 20 cents and get a 15 percent food cost for soup. The only sane conclusion from all this would appear to be: forget the steaks, sell soup! Solely from a cost standpoint, it's true. But from a practical standpoint, there is a limit to how much soup you can sell in any food service operation, even if you *specialize* in soup.

You cannot just consider individual costs of items on the menu. You also have to balance these costs in a way that will let you achieve the overall total food cost you want.

In Chapter 11 on pre-control and pre-costing the menu, we discussed pre-costing concepts and suggested that you consider the effects actual sales of different items would have on each other as part of a total product mix. "Total product mix" means what food items you will sell (steaks, salads, chops, pie, chicken), how much of each you will sell, and the combined total of all the items you will sell.

Under the combined approach to pricing, you have to consider everything.

For the economic aspect, you consider:

1. Can you afford to supply the items at the price you set?
2. Will your guests want the items and buy them at your prices?

According to the marketing approach to pricing, you must realize:

1. Your guests are not at all interested in or concerned about your costs.
2. Your guests are only concerned about receiving what they feel is acceptable value for the money they spend.

Under the product competition approach to pricing:

1. You emphasize that you have a product that is different from—and better than—your competitors'.
2. You advertise *how* your establishment is different and better.

Under the cost approach to pricing, you must be sure that:

1. All your costs are covered.
2. You will get a profit.

In the combined approach to pricing, you apply all the approaches and factors we've discussed above. If you feel you have priced an item too low and you can charge a higher price, do it. If an item is priced too high, consider lowering the price or not selling the item. The essence of the whole matter is not the individual price of one item. The vital issue to you is the combined prices of all items and the combined sales of all the items in your product mix. This is what gives you total revenue. You deduct total costs from total revenue to get profit. You want to maximize total revenue and bring in as many dollars as you can. You want to maximize the sale of the items that will provide the best overall profit for the business.

SETTING MENU PRICES

In setting prices in the food service industry, there is a lot of emphasis on food cost. When you consider probable sales of each individual food item in relation to total sales, be sure your food service operation will achieve its overall desired food cost even though the food cost percent will vary on individual items.

The easiest way to set prices is to divide your desired food cost percent into 100 to get a markup percent. This markup percent will be a useful tool in arriving at your actual menu price.

To set menu prices for entrees, for example, you do the following:

1. Determine the cost of the individual entree.
2. To this figure you add the cost of all surrounding and accompanying items.
3. Multiply this total by your markup percent.
4. This gives you a starting point for evaluating your selling price.

Can you charge more? If you can, raise the price. If your guests won't pay that much, lower the price to what they will pay. Now decide if you can afford to sell the item at this price and still make a profit. If not, take it off the menu. Don't sell it. You must keep your competitors' prices in mind. Do not get your own prices too far out of line from theirs.

Use this procedure for each item on your menu. Then try to estimate the sale of each item. Follow the procedure discussed in Chapter 11 for obtaining estimated weighted food cost and estimated weighted sales value (see Chart 11-3 in Chapter 11). Divide the estimated weighted food cost by the estimated weighted sales value to get your estimated potential food cost percent.

Is this estimated potential food cost percent the food cost percent you want? If it is a little lower, great. If it is high, reexamine the prices of all items. Items with high food cost percents might be raised slightly—by 5 cents, 10 cents—maybe up to 50 cents. What effect would these price changes have on the number of sales of *every* item? Maybe you would sell fewer of the higher-priced items. Guests might order other items for which you would charge less and which would have lower food costs for you. Prepare a new estimated weighted food cost and a new estimated weighted sales value using your new figures. Divide the new estimated weighted food cost by the new estimated weighted sales value. This should give you your desired food cost percent. If it doesn't, do the whole process again until you achieve your desired food cost percent based on your estimate. Be realistic in your estimate.

Here is where you have applied the concepts of pre-control in your pricing. You have planned before guests get there and you have tried to anticipate what they will do. As we have said, pre-costing can save you printing costs to change prices on menus. More important, it helps you decide ahead of time what prices you need to charge for your items in order to make money. You should have a better chance of making profits on items sooner without having to fiddle around adjusting prices and learning about pricing by trial and error —and loss.

There are two main things you can do to insure profit:

1. Reduce and control your costs.
2. Make sure you are charging the *right* prices for the items you have for sale. A "right" price is a price your guests are willing to pay and a price that gives you reasonable profit.

Costs can be reduced by increasing your efficiency, cutting portion sizes, and cutting quality. Costs can also be reduced in terms of percentages by increasing selling prices.

General Guidelines to Menu Pricing

A general guideline is: the higher the menu price is, the higher the food cost percent can be. This works because, although you spend more for food cost as a percent of sales, you are also achieving a greater contribution to labor, overhead, and profit costs in actual dollars and cents from the higher-priced items than you would from a lower-priced item.

Many food service operators make the mistake of trying to maintain too low a food cost on expensive items and too high a food cost on inexpensive items in terms of selling price. The following are two good guidelines.

1. The lower the selling price, the lower the food cost percent should be.
2. The higher the selling price, the higher the food cost percent can be.

Individual item costs are not so important. Overall costs are.

CONTRIBUTION TO PROFIT

Keep in mind how much money individual menu items contribute toward your profit, labor, and overhead. Some food service operators think they make more money on their $3.50 fried chicken dinner than they do on their $5.75 steak dinner. If your food cost is $1 for a chicken dinner and $2.50 for a steak dinner, it is true you do have a lower food cost percent for the chicken than for the steak. The food cost percent is 28.57 percent for the chicken dinner ($1 divided by $3.50 equals .2857 multiplied by 100 to convert to percentage equals 28.57 percent) and 43.47 percent for the steak dinner ($2.50 divided by $5.75 equals .4347 multiplied by 100 to convert to percentage equals 43.47 percent). That is not the whole story, however. If you deduct the $1 cost of food of the chicken dinner from its $3.50 selling price, you get $2.50 contribution to profit, overhead, and labor. If you deduct the $2.50 cost of food of the steak dinner from its $5.75 selling price, you get a $3.25 contribution to profit, labor, and overhead.

The labor cost for the two dinners should be comparable—or labor for the chicken dinner might be more expensive. A guest who orders steak and a guest who orders chicken both occupy a chair in the food service establishment, enjoy the same atmosphere, and probably stay about the same length of time. Your overhead costs will be about the same for serving both meals. So each steak dinner, despite its relatively higher food cost, is making a bigger contribution to your profit than each chicken dinner.

The individual food cost of any one food item is not the vital statistic here. The total food cost of all items sold deducted from total sales is what counts. What is left is where your profits come from.

We emphasized at the beginning of this chapter that your prices have got to be reasonable for your customers and for you. Your customers must feel they are getting good value for the money they are paying you. Your prices have to be reasonable for you, too, and give you profit.

REVIEW AND DISCUSSION QUESTIONS

1. Explain the following approaches to pricing:
   a. competitive
   b. economic
   c. marketing
   d. product
   e. cost
   f. combined
2. Which is the preferred approach? Why?
3. Should restaurants use loss leaders? Why?
4. Why is food cost the basis for setting menu prices?

13

Employees' Meals

Objectives

This chapter discusses employees' meals. After you have read this chapter, you should be aware of:

1. The importance of calculating a reasonable cost for employees' meals, and how this can affect your FICA tax.
2. Various methods for calculating the value of employees' meals.
3. The special importance of the deduction for employees' meals for hotels.

It is usually customary for food service operations to provide meals for employees who work in the food service department. There are three ways to handle employees' meals:

1. Give meals free to employees (most common method).
2. Deduct cost of employees' meals (full or partial) from their pay.
3. Have employees pay full cost for their meals in cash, as the operation's customers do (rare method).

Whichever method you use, providing employees' meals is a cost of doing business. The food you serve to your employees should be relatively inexpensive, but it must be food of good quality. It is false economy to scrimp on the quality of employee meals. If the food provided for them is really of poor quality, employees are much more apt to devise ways to get at the establishment's most expensive food without management's knowledge. Some employees may become so upset they will quit.

EMPLOYEES' MEALS AND THE LAW

There are laws that apply specifically to food service operations regarding employees' meals. Check with your tax accountant or tax lawyer to be sure you are doing everything correctly.

If you do supply food for food department employees at no cost or at partial cost to them, you should do the following three things.

1. Set policy on number of meals.

Set a policy on the number of meals to which employees are entitled. Most operations use the reasonable general guideline that employees receive one meal (free or at reduced price) for each four hours they work. In fact, that is stated in many union contracts.

2. Know the income tax law.

It's important that you make close estimates and assign reasonable cash values for your employees' meals. Income tax law states that when employees are served meals for the convenience of their employers, the employees do not pay income tax on the value of the meals. The cost of the meals is allowed as a tax deductible operating expense for the employer. It is almost always true that food service operations which provide food for employees do so for the convenience of the employer. It would not be very convenient for food service employers if their employees walked out around meal times and went to a restaurant to eat.

3. Know and obey the social security tax law.

Social Security (Federal Insurance Contribution Act—FICA) requires you, the employer, to include the value of employees' meals in your employees' pay when you compute the FICA tax for your employees. For example, you pay your employees a base pay. You add the value of meals they receive to this base pay to get the FICA base pay. The FICA tax is computed by multiplying FICA base pay by FICA tax rate.

Say, for example, an employee earns $2 an hour for a 40-hour week. Base pay is $80 a week. You value the meals the employee receives at $5 a week. FICA base pay would be $85 a week. You would figure FICA tax on $85 a week and deduct from the paycheck accordingly. But you would figure the employee's income tax on $80 a week because you have given the employee meals for your own convenience.

The law requires you to put a *reasonable* value on the food you serve as employees' meals. The law also requires that FICA tax paid on the value of each meal must be paid by both employer and employee. If you fail to put a reasonable value on meals, then you the employer—not your employees—may be liable for all current and back FICA tax that should have been paid in the past by both employer and employees. If you value meals too low, you may not be paying enough tax and may wind up having to pay a sizeable amount of money (some of which your employees should have paid). If you value meals too high, you and your employees may be paying more FICA tax than you have to. So make accurate valuations of the cost of the meals you give to employees free.

SETTING THE COST OF EMPLOYEES' MEALS

Average Costs

This is the easiest way to establish the value of employees' meals. Analyze what your employees eat for each meal. Figure out an average cost per employee for each meal period. For breakfast, some employees may eat a lot—cereal, pancakes, and eggs, for instance. Others will want only coffee. Most employees would probably eat the equivalent of two eggs, toast, and coffee. For lunch and dinner you might have pre-planned meals for your employees where you cook foods especially for them, or you may be using up various leftover items. Try to estimate (as accurately as you can) a reasonable average cost for the value of what employees are eating for each meal period.

It is best to estimate separate values for breakfast, lunch, and dinner. For example, say you estimate 50 cents for breakfast, 75 cents for lunch, 95 cents for dinner. Employees eat different foods and different amounts of food at different times of the day, and your costs will vary.

If you are cooking food especially for employees, you can determine costs. But if you are using up varieties of leftover items, it is next to impossible to figure what they are worth (three portions of beef stew, six portions of meat loaf, four Swiss steaks, assorted salads, assorted desserts).

To get the total cost for all employees' meals, multiply the number of meals served to employees by your estimated average cost per meal. Total all three meal periods. This gives you the estimated cost of employees' meals per day.

For example, let us suppose you serve your employees 20 breakfasts at 50 cents, 30 lunches at 75 cents, and 18 dinners at 95 cents. The total cost for employees' meals for the day would be $49.60 (20 meals at 50 cents plus 30 meals at 75 cents plus 18 meals at 95 cents equals $49.60).

Some food service establishments use this same procedure except they put the same value on all meals consumed—say, 75 cents per meal. If they serve 20 breakfasts, 30 lunches, and 18 dinners—every meal at 75 cents—their total cost for employees' meals for the day would be $51 (68 meals at 75 cents each).

Actual Cashier Total Per Meal Beyond Amount Allotted Free

Some food service operations—especially if they have a cafeteria— have employees go through the cafeteria line so the operation has a record of how many employees ate. Employees are allowed up to a specified amount of food free. If they eat more than that, they may pay regular customer prices (or discounted prices) for the extra food. They may just sign a guest check for the free food. If they ate more than the free food, they may sign the check and have the cost of the extra food deducted from their wages. Or they may pay cash for the extra food.

For the FICA base tax, you would use the value of the free meal per employee multiplied by the number of employees.

Discounts

Some food operations have employees sign guest checks for the retail value of the meal they have selected and allow them a discount (40 percent, for example) from the menu price. Actual payment is collected from the employees by deducting the amount for the food from their paychecks.

Some states may require employees to pay sales tax on the total or discounted value of their meals. Find out what the policy is on sales tax for employees' meals in your state.

DEDUCTING EMPLOYEES' MEAL COST

In Chapter 9 on food cost formulas, we discussed how you deduct the value of employees' meals from the cost of food used to find the cost of food sold when you do your food cost formula. If you provide free or discounted meals for your employees, you must be aware of the following facts:

1. It is costing you money to feed your employees if you give them food free or at a reduction.

2. Food consumed by employees is not available for sale to guests.

3. You should deduct the cost of employees' meals from the cost of food used to get the cost of food sold. This gives you a more realistic figure for the cost of food sold. Do, however, add the value of employees' meals back on your profit and loss statement as an operating expense.

Your *profit* will be the same whether you do or do not deduct the cost of employees' meals to get the cost of food sold and then add the value of employees' meals back on your profit and loss statement as an operating expense. It is a realistic business practice, however, to make the deduction for employees' meals and then add it back on to your profit and loss statement. This is true because food given to employees is not available for sale.

COST OF EMPLOYEES' MEALS FOR HOTELS

If you are a food service manager in a hotel, it is especially important for you to arrive at a realistic value for your employees' meals and to make sure that those meals are carefully accounted for. Many employees who do not work in the hotel's food and beverage department do eat free or discounted food in the hotel prepared by the hotel's food department staff. If, for example, front office desk clerks on duty are provided free meals, the cost of their meals should be charged to the front office department by interoffice memos. The food service department should take the deduction in its operating costs, and the front office department should take the increase in its operating costs. If this is not done, the front office is not charged for the food expenses of their own employees, and it should be. The food service department bears the expense instead, and it should not. There is no effect whatever on the overall final profit of the hotel whether such a transfer of charges is made or not. But if it is not done, the profitability of the food and beverage department will be reduced unfairly and other departments will show more profit than they should.

It is recommended, therefore, that the cost of feeding any other department's employees besides food service department employees should be transferred to the departments involved. The food and beverage department should be charged only for food consumed by food and beverage department employees, no one else. The food and beverage department manager should ask the accounting department to charge respective departments for the cost of meals for employees of the other departments. This is a correct way for food service managers to control their own department's costs. It also allows them to come up with a more accurate departmental profit and loss statement. And the procedure gives the hotel management a more valid view of what each department costs and makes. It permits better, more accurate cost analysis of all departments of the hotel.

EMPLOYEE REST AREA

Establish a specific employee rest area if you possibly can. Some food operations permit dining room personnel to eat in a section of the dining room but
make no provisions for kitchen and other personnel to sit down and eat a
meal.

It is good management to have a specific place where all employees
can go for their breaks—where they can smoke, have coffee, and eat their
meals in pleasant surroundings. This applies to all employees, and especially to
the cooks. Many food service operators expect cooks to work eight-hour shifts
and eat at their stations. Cooks cannot be fully productive if they don't get a
chance to get away from their stations to sit down, relax, and enjoy meals during their rest periods. If they taste and nibble all day, they may consume more
food than they would if they went to the employees' rest area and sat down
and ate proper meals. It is not good for their health or psychological well-
being to stay in the kitchen all day.

Provide a suitable place for all employees to rest and eat their meals.
It makes it much easier for you to control the cost of food for employees'
meals. It is also a very important morale factor for your employees.

The following does not precisely concern employees' meals, but it is
important. There is one special problem that is very common among food service employees. They are usually on their feet a lot of the time, and the
problem is aching feet. Consider installing a foot vibrator machine in your
employees' rest area. Sore feet can wreak havoc with anyone's disposition and
working capacities. A vibrator to relieve tired feet can help employees' feet
and morale. It is not a silly extravagance. Check into it.

REVIEW AND DISCUSSION QUESTIONS

1. How do you value employees' meals by:
   a. average cost.
   b. cashier total.
   c. discount.
2. Why are employees' meals costs deducted from cost of food used?
3. Why is it especially important for hotels to deduct for employees' meals?
4. How can you substantiate that your estimate of the value of your employees' meals is reasonable?
5. Why is it important that employees have a rest area?

14

Food Purchasing Control

Objectives

This chapter is concerned with the purchasing of food. After you have read this chapter, you should:

1. Be aware of the need for purchasing for use, and how to use purchase specifications.
2. Know the various methods of purchasing, and the various ways of placing orders.
3. Know the flexibility that the use of convenience foods might give to your establishment.

WHO SHOULD DO YOUR PURCHASING?

In many food service operations, the manager delegates purchasing to subordinates, regardless of whether the subordinates know much about it or not. Managers themselves do not necessarily have to be directly in charge of all purchasing. But purchasing is very important to the success of a food service establishment. Whoever is in charge of purchasing—manager or subordinate—has to know how to do it well and must be trained in the mechanics and procedures of effective buying. If you do delegate the job, assign someone who has had previous experience in purchasing, or train someone to do it.

Many food operation managers put their chefs in charge of purchasing. Chefs are usually responsible for preparation of food and for the overall organization and running of a kitchen. They have had training and experience in cooking, but few chefs have been specifically trained to do purchasing. Don't *assume* chefs know how to purchase. If you want your chefs to do the job, work with and/or train them to make sure they know how to purchase the way you want it done.

SPECIFICATIONS (CHART 14-1)

Any food service establishment that purchases foods in quantity should definitely use written specifications. Specifications should set down in writing the standard you want in a product according to the specific use you intend to make of the product.

A specification sheet or card should contain:

1. Name of product.
2. Use you intend for this product.
3. Grade or quality you want.
4. Basic unit (gallon, pound, case) on which prices are quoted.
5. Any and all specific factors necessary to exactly describe and identify the item you want.

Ideally, you should have an individual purchase specification sheet or card for each item you purchase. Some specifications may be only a phrase or a line. Others may be quite detailed, like the sample shown in Chart 14-1. Put all the information on the purchase specification necessary to insure that you will get the product you want.

You do not put the purchase price or the quantities you want on purchase specification sheets. Quantities will vary and prices can change, but you

Product:	Oven-ready beef rib.
Use:	Standing rib roast.
Grade:	U. S. Choice
Price Unit:	per pound
Other:	

7-rib roast.
18-20 lbs.
Cut 2" above eye.
No variance.
Chine bone removed
Cut between 5 and 6 rib on neck end.
Cut between 12 and 13 rib on loin end.
All aged surfaces trimmed off.
Aged approximately 2 weeks.
Surface fat trimmed to 3/4 inch.
Blade removed.
Remove edible meat from deckle.
Replace deckle fat.
Tie securely with 6 loop strings
    and 1 loop string around
    the 7 ribs.

Chart 14-1 Purchase Specification Card

seldom change your specifications. You determine the quantity according to how much you need, and it will vary from day to day. When you order steaks, for example, quality and detailed specification factors will be the same regardless of how many steaks you want. (You do put quantity and price on the Purchasing Agent's Market Quotation List, which is shown in Chart 14-2 in this chapter.)

There is good information on meat purchasing in *Meat Buyer's Guide to Standardized Meat Cuts.*[1] This booklet gives you descriptions and photographs of a variety of meat items. It is helpful for anyone who writes meat specifications.

[1]*Meat Buyer's Guide to Standardized Meat Cuts.* National Association of Meat Purveyors, Chicago, 1965.

Specifications Must be Written

A few years ago, if you had asked employees responsible for purchasing for a food service operation if they used specifications, they would probably have said, "Oh, sure. I couldn't do any purchasing without them." But if you had asked them to show you a copy of their specification sheets, chances are they would have said, "A copy? I don't have anything in *writing*. I keep it all in my head." Times have changed. This will not work any more, if it ever did.

No one should rely just on memory when it comes to purchasing for a food service operation. The person or persons in charge of your purchasing should put all specifications in writing. This is essential for transmitting purchase specifications to other people and departments concerned with purchasing. Written purchase specifications are an important part of overall food control.

There are two main reasons why you should have purchase specifications in writing:

1. The purchaser cannot possibly remember all details.
2. If the purchaser is absent from the establishment, whoever takes the purchaser's place should have specifications in writing so purchasing can continue exactly according to standards. If purchase specifications exist only in one person's head, that is the only person who can use them.

Specifications should be prepared in quadruplicate (or more). The copies should be distributed as follows:

1. One copy kept by the purchasing agent.
2. One copy to the manager to keep him or her informed of everything ordered by the purchasing department.
3. One copy to the receiving clerk, who uses it as a receiving guide for standards.
4. One copy to each purveyor who will fill specifications. If you work with your purveyors, they can usually give you some good suggestions and help you write more effective specifications, which in turn makes it easier for your purveyors to do their job of filling your orders faster and more efficiently. It is very important to you to be on excellent terms with your purveyors. Make up good specifications for their sake and yours. When your purveyors receive clear, easy-to-understand specification sheets from you, it is much easier for them to follow your instructions and get you what you want.

PURCHASE FOR USE

Some food service managers say, "I buy nothing but the best, only the top quality." If they buy nothing but top grades of every item, they are probably making expensive mistakes and wasting money. Buy food items appropriate for the use you will make of them.

Many food service managers buy top grade and use it where a lower grade with a lower price would be just as satisfactory. In some cases it would be better. For just one case in point, say you purchase U.S. Choice grade beef to use in stews. But less expensive U.S. Good grade would be just as satisfactory or better. Stewing is a method of moist cooking used to break down the connective tissue. The U.S. Good grade has a lower fat content. The less fat in stew meat the better. So, in this case, the U.S. Good grade beef would give you stew at least as acceptable as stew made from U.S. Choice meats— maybe better. And it costs less. Save money. Don't buy "top grade" if lower grade can give you the same product for less money. This applies to everything you buy, of course, not just beef stew meat.

Penny Business

You may save only pennies at a time by purchasing lower quality, less expensive items where it is appropriate. But the food service industry is a penny business. Take advantage of every instance where you can save pennies here and there by astute purchasing. Every saving, large or small, helps you. It is conceivable that in the course of a year you could save thousands of dollars this way if your establishment is very large. This in turn can mean more profit. Instead of lowering the quality of your food, in many instances you can actually improve it by buying wisely.

For most items purchased for food service operations, grades are established for the consumer market (the home), not for the institutional market (you). The factors that influence this grading may not apply to the institutional market. In the case of fresh produce, for example, apples are graded by "color, shape, and general appearance." This might apply for home use but not necessarily for restaurant use. Institutional purchasers should buy the best quality they can afford for the market they serve *and* quality that is appropriate for the products' intended uses.

"Quality" is nebulous. You have to define the term according to the market in which you operate and the prices you get for your product. There is a good, clear discussion of this in Dr. Lendel Kotschevar's book *Quantity Food Purchasing.*[2] Dr. Kotschevar goes into considerable detail about the specific grades and qualities of food.

[2]Dr. Lendel H. Kotschevar, *Quantity Food Purchasing,* 2nd ed. John H. Wiley & Sons, Inc. New York, 1975.

Evaluation of Samples (Can Cutting)

Occasionally food service operations will request samples from different purveyors in order to evaluate a product before they place an order. This is especially true for canned items. For example, they may request a can of tomatoes of the same grade from four different purveyors. They open each can, put it upside down on a screen, and let it drain for exactly two minutes. Then they weigh what is left on the screen. What is left is called the "drained weight" of the product of that can. There will be variations in drained weights of different brands. The drained weight of one firm's can of tomatoes will probably be higher than the other three.

The higher the drained weight, the more usable the product is and the more portions you can get from that can. The brand with the highest drained weight may cost the most per can but may turn out to have the lowest cost per portion if you get enough more portions from that can. This can be very important when you are dealing in large quantities.

The time to do can cutting tests is right after your purveyors have received their new supplies for the year—probably in the autumn. Ask your purveyors. Food service managers test and then usually specify by brand name whichever brand has tested best when they are ordering that particular item. You may need several purveyors to get you the different brands you decide on. One purveyor may get your order for one product and another purveyor for another product.

Evaluate samples of other items, too, not just canned goods. Perhaps you will want to compare quality of one type of convenience food versus another, or of different steaks from different purveyors, or different dessert items. Comparisons can help you learn about products and get a better product for every purchasing dollar you spend.

PURE FOOD AND DRUG LAWS

Food and drug laws are meant to help protect consumers. Government inspections help prevent disease. Billions of food items are prepared annually by mass production. These foods purchased by food operations very seldom contain dangerous levels of pathogenic organisms. Food and drug laws came into prominence in recent years, however, because botulism was found in a tiny percentage of food products. These instances made national headlines because botulism is extremely rare and it can kill.

Steps are being taken to make food and drug laws tighter. As food service operators, you are not equipped to test every food item coming in, but you should be aware of the very remote possibility that foods (canned beans, for example) can be contaminated before they reach you. Make sure your cooks are aware of possibilities of contamination and that they think twice before they use *any* food item that gives *any* suspicious signs (odor, color, consistency, general appearance, whatever).

THE FOUR W'S OF PURCHASING

The "Four W's" are the guides that your purchasing agent should use for effective purchasing. They are what, when, where, and why. These four are often ignored by food service managers, but they should not be. They can be most effective in helping you achieve organized and efficient purchasing.

1. What.

What items do you need? What do you need to buy? You will have to purchase everything you will use to prepare the foods you serve. Your menu and your recipes tell you "what." We discussed menus in Chapter 10, and recommended that you try to plan several days' menus simultaneously to help you achieve effective balance and variety. After you have planned your menus, buy the foods you need to prepare the items on the menus.

What quantities do you need? You must also know what quantities of all these items you will need. You determine quantities by referring to your basic recipes and forecast (discussed in Chapter 11).

2. When.

When do you need the food item? This depends on when you intend to serve it and on how long it can or should be stored. The item purchased should be on the premises in plenty of time to permit pre-preparation (if needed) and actual preparation. But it should not be there so long that it wastes through spoilage.

3. Where.

Where will you buy the food? Where will you store it? Where will it go when you take it out of storage?

4. Why.

Why do you need the item? Because it is an ingredient you need to pre-pare items on your menu. Why should you purchase this particular grade or quality? Because it is the best-suited grade or quality for the use you will make of the item.

PAR STOCK

You might want to consider a par stock system for your purchasing procedures. Par stock means you establish predetermined quantities for the items
you want on hand. Deciding on the predetermined quantities is a management
responsibility. The manager or a supervisor sets the maximum and minimum
quantities for items you purchase. You do not want to go below the minimum
or above the maximum you have set for all items. The judicious use of par
stocks can help you simplify your purchasing procedure. You just check to see
how much of an item you have on hand. If you are below maximum par stock,
you order enough to bring your supply of that item up close to maximum par
stock without going over the maximum. You should never get below minimum. If you do, get back up close to maximum. If, through error, you have
more of an item than your maximum par stock calls for, don't order any.

Say, for example, you have set par stock for canned peas—minimum
of 6 number 10 cans and maximum of 24 number 10 cans. In making up your
purchase order, you count how many cans of peas you have in your storeroom.
Say you have 9. Nine from 24 is 15—the maximum number of cans of peas you
might order. Canned peas come 6 cans to the case. So you would order 2 cases
(12 cans). This would bring you up to a total of 21 number 10 cans of peas.
You are above your minimum par stock of 6 cans and below your maximum
par stock of 24 cans. And you are buying by the case, which saves money.
You would not order 15 cans. You order by case lots to get you close to maximum par stock, trying not to go over.

Par stock procedures, properly applied, can reduce a lot of the work
in actually placing orders. Establish minimum and maximum quantities. After
that, just count what you have on hand and order what is needed to bring you
near the maximum. In our example above, you want to keep as close as you
can to having 24 number 10 cans of peas on hand at all times. You definitely
do not want to have less than 6.

Review your decisions about minimum and maximum amounts periodically and make adjustments in the amounts set as par stock if you need to.
As you change your menu and usage of items, check to see if you need to
change your minimum and maximum par stock amounts.

METHODS OF PURCHASING

There are many different ways you can obtain the food items you need. Some
of these are:

1. Open market quotations (recommended and most widely used).
2. Standing order.

3. Cost plus.

4. One-stop shopping.

5. Sealed bids.

6. Government acceptance.

7. Blank check.

Open Market Quotations (Chart 14-2)

Open market quotations purchasing (or variations of it) is the most widely-used method. In general, it works best for most operations and it's the recommended method.

According to this method, you get prices from two or more suppliers per product line (at least two meat purveyors, at least two vegetable purveyors, and so on). It would seem logical simply to select the purveyor who quotes the lowest price. Unfortunately, it is not that simple. You may wind up giving your order to a purveyor whose price is slightly higher than another purveyor's because that company will give you better service, better quality, better trim, and the like—all still within the grades of quality you have specified. You should not base your purchases on price *alone*. Consider other factors, too.

Chart 14-2 is an example of a purchasing agent's market quotation list. There are variations on how this sheet can be used in a food service operation. You can buy quantities of a standard form from a specialty firm supplying hotel and restaurant forms. Or you can compose your own forms and have them made up for you by a local printer. You can simply use a sheet of paper on which you put down relevant information and provide space for quotations. Do what works best for you.

In Chart 14-2, the columns are as follows:

Column 1: Article.
This lists the items you want to purchase.

Column 2: On Hand.
This is where you list what you have on hand. You may or may not feel it is necessary to complete Column 2.

Column 3: Want.
This is the amount you want to order. This is where you list the exact quantities you want to purchase.

Columns 4 and 5: Price Quotations and Other Information.

Columns 4 and 5 are for listing actual price quotations plus information about delivery schedules, price breaks, quality, service, and so on. You call purveyors and get this information. In Chart 14-2, we have put in only two columns for recording price and information from purveyors. You may want more than two columns for this—maybe you'll want five or six or more columns for this purpose—so you can do a lot of price and service information

1	2	3	4	5	6	7	8	9	10
Article	On Hand	Want	Price Quotations Plus Other Information Purveyor A	Price Quotations Plus Other Information Purveyor B	Article	On Hand	Want	Price Quotations Plus Other Information Purveyor A	Price Quotation Plus Other Informati Purveyor
BEEF					DAIRY				
Brochette					Butter - Cooking				
Chopped Steak					Butter - Patties				
Club Steak 10 oz.					Cream - Light				
Club Steak 6 oz.					Cream - Sour				
New York Strip					Eggs - Boiling				
Prime Rib					Ice Cream - Chocolate				
PORK					Milk - Whole White				
Bacon - Strip					BAKERY				
POULTRY					Cheesecake				
Stuffed Breast of Chicken					Rolls - Hard				
SHELLFISH					Rolls - Soft				
Shrimp - Stuffed					MISCELLANEOUS				
Shrimp					Cocktail Sauce				
FISH					Coffee				
Rocky Mountain Trout					Ketchup - Btl.				
VEGETABLES					Mustard - Btl.				
Carrots					Pepper				
Celery					Salad Dressing - 1000				
Green Peppers					Salad Dressing - French				
Lettuce					Salad Dressing - Roquefort				
Mushrooms - Canned					Salad Oil				
Onions Canned Baby Whole					Salt				
Onions - Bermuda					Soup Stock - Beef				
Parsley					Soup Stock - Chicken				
Potatoes - Froz. Fr. Fry					Steak Sauce - A1				
Potatoes - Whole Idaho					Tartar Sauce				
Tomatoes					Tea Bags				
FRUITS					Tea Instant				
Lemons					Vinegar - Wine				
Melon Balls									
Strawberries									

Chart 14-2   Purchasing Agent's Market Quotation List

comparison. It will depend on your own situation and on how extensively you want to go into this and how many purveyors you want to call.

Columns 6 through 10: These just repeat the first five columns.

The usual procedure would be to call a purveyor and get price quotations on items you would be apt to purchase from that purveyor and any other information you want. Write it in the Price Quotations and Other Information column where you have written the purveyor's name. Call as many purveyors as you feel necessary. On these preliminary calls, just get price, delivery, quality, price break information. Don't place orders.

After you have all the information and quotations you want, go back over the quotation sheet and put a check by the lowest price. If all other things are equal (quality, service, and so on, based on the information you have about the purveyors), you would buy from the purveyor with the lowest price. However, since "all other things" are usually *not* equal and there may be other circumstances to consider, go back and review prices, other facts, and your overall needs. Then circle the items you are going to order from each purveyor.

Use common sense throughout this procedure. For example, you need fresh produce. Purveyor A has lower prices on all produce items except parsley. Purveyor B has the lowest parsley price in town. Don't ask Purveyor B to deliver just parsley to you solely because B's price for parsley is lowest. Buy your parsley from Purveyor A. Divide your orders among your regular purveyors so you get the best cost. When you divide your orders, you should also consider that you have to make it worthwhile for the purveyors to make deliveries to you.

Chart 14-2 should be prepared in duplicate:

1. One copy kept by the purchasing agent after the order has been placed.

2. One copy goes to the receiving clerk so the clerk will know what was ordered, how much, and from whom.

Standing Order

Standing order purchasing is quite common in the food service industry, particularly with a couple of variations. "Standing order" usually means that a specified quantity and quality of an item is to be delivered by your purveyor at specified times, usually continuing over an indefinite period of time. The ordered items keep arriving until you give notice to the purveyor to stop. If your needs change, you must alter the standing order.

A variation of standing order is when one firm has a standing order to deliver an item to you but quantities are not standard and you vary them every day.

Standing order is usually used for highly perishable items such as bread and milk. Milk is almost always purchased on a standing order basis. It is usually a fair-traded commodity so the price charged by one dairy company is usually similar to the price charged by any other dairy in that area. Milk is not purchased on price factor. It is seldom bought on quality factor either because all dairies must maintain minimum standards set by the government. The major factor that influences your choice of a dairy is usually service. Choose the firm that gives you good service, can give you milk in the types of containers or packaging you want, and can deliver at times most convenient for your food operation.

The usual practice would be that the dairy which gets your standing order for milk will serve you on a continuing basis and will be the only dairy supplying your milk. This dairy delivers all milk to your premises on a continuing basis. But you can vary the quantity you want from day to day. And you can ask for different types of containers (four-gallon milk cartons for a dispenser, cases of half-pints, whatever).

It is generally a good idea to establish par stock on a daily basis for some standing order items. Take bread, for example. Suppose your establishment usually uses an average of 40 to 60 loaves of sandwich bread a day. You decide on a par stock of no less than 40 and no more than 60 loaves—aiming to stay as close to 60 as you can. Suppose for two days in a row you use only 25 loaves of bread. Each day your bread purveyor arrives to replenish your bread supply and bring it up to your par stock of between 40 and 60 loaves in accordance with your standing order. The bread already stored on the shelves should always be moved to the front and used first. Fresh bread should be stored behind it, to the rear of the shelf. If you have a set-up like this and no one notices or takes commonsense steps to remedy the situation and adjust the standing order until you start using more bread again, it is quite possible that for a while there you will consistently serve day-old bread in your sandwiches! This illustrates that, for standing order items, it is important to have reasonable par stocks—adjusted for each day of the week where variation is necessary, and adjusted to the delivery schedules of the suppliers, and adjusted if your business temporarily changes drastically (as the result of a severe storm, for example).

In general, food service establishments normally give standing orders to the various firms that supply their bread, milk, ice cream, pies, and so on. You give each firm the order to deliver the commodity you want to your premises. Usually you will see one driver-salesperson from the firm, one individual who takes your orders and also delivers the items to you. You can generally make changes in the quantities of any standing order item. Your invoice should reflect only the quantities you actually receive. You can usually also ask for different flavors of ice cream, different types of pies, and so on, by telling the driver-salesperson.

Cost Plus

"Cost plus" purchasing is a method that has been used very successfully by some food service operations, but others have tried it and found that it did not work for them at all. How well it works seems to depend on particular combinations of individual purchasers and purveyors. It could work for you and is worth knowing about and considering.

In cost plus purchasing, you set high standards for the products you want. Your purveyors must meet these standards. They charge you what they pay for the item plus an agreed-upon handling charge. The handling charge may be an agreed-upon percentage of your purveyors' costs or it may be an unchanging, flat service charge.

Under this method you select one purveying company for one product line—produce, for example. You never buy produce anywhere except from this one purveying company. You give your produce purveyor a list of specifications for the items you want—lettuce, tomatoes, fresh fruits. The purveying company agrees to provide the quality you specify (usually the highest quality the purveyor can get) regardless of what the purveyor pays for it. The purveying company gives you the invoice for the price they paid for the commodity plus their handling charge. With this method of purchasing, you are much more concerned with getting the highest quality product you can than you are with price.

Your produce purveying company has all of your produce business. No other purveyors are competing with them to get your produce order, and they are guaranteed a return for their effort. The method is meant to allow one purveying company to devote more time, effort, and care to selecting exactly what you want.

In theory, this sounds fine. In practice it may or may not work. Some purveyors find it difficult to operate in this manner. They, or their employees, may get lax or careless. They may deliver goods that are not quite up to the standards you called for in your specifications. The idea is good in theory, but in reality there is usually nothing like competing for your orders to keep your suppliers at their most efficient.

One-Stop Shopping

One-stop shopping is a method of purchasing advocated by purveyors. Under one-stop shopping, you give all of your business to a single purveying company. They then theoretically supply you with all of your needs. Theoretically they can give you lower prices because they are receiving larger orders, which makes economies for them. Purveyors refer to a "cost per stop." It costs them so many dollars to have their trucks stop at your establishment. If the purveying company has a small order, they have to mark up their merchandise more than they would for a large order to make sure that their cost per stop is covered and that they make their profit.

The name "one-stop shopping" is really a misnomer. From your viewpoint it should be called "buying more items from a smaller number of purveyors" or "fewer-purveyor shopping." There aren't many purveyors, if any, who can really get you all the items you need. One purveyor may be able to supply all your canned goods, all your paper goods, all your cleaning supplies, and some frozen meats, but not fresh meat or fresh produce, for example. "One-stop shopping" or "fewer-purveyor shopping" (or whatever you name the idea) just means to you that you buy from fewer purveyors. You buy a bigger quantity of goods from each of them. This saves you time checking in material when you receive it. It should also save you money because each purveying company provides you with more items and they can pass on their increased savings to you in the form of lower prices.

Sealed Bids

The sealed bids method is not used very much in the food service business. It is used most by government institutions, which usually are obligated by government procedures to take the lowest price offered. Some hospitals use this method, too. They may, for example, request sealed bids from meat purveyors for a meat contract for 30, 60, or 90-day periods. The purveyor who submits the lowest bid fulfilling specifications gets the order for the time period. As long as the specifications are followed exactly, the job goes to the lowest bidder. No other factors are considered.

Even if specifications are used, there can still be problems with the sealed bid method. Purveyors may meet the specifications but fail to deliver on time. Also there may be real or imagined vagueness in the wording of specifications which purveyors can feel indicates leeway for their own personal judgment and interpretation. Problems can result. This can happen with other purchasing methods, too, but it is worse if it happens with sealed bids because you have contracted for a period of time and cannot change purveyors.

There is valid insight into another possible defect in the sealed bid system in the caustic comment by an American astronaut who was about to embark into space: "It's comforting to know that the rocket we're about to use was put together by thousands of lowest bidders all over the United States."

Unless you are in a field where it is required policy, sealed bids is not generally a recommended method.

Government Acceptance

Government acceptance purchasing is an excellent method for purchasing meat, especially if you do not really know a lot about meats. For a nominal fee, government inspectors working for the Department of Agriculture at a purveyor's or at a meat plant will see to it that your specifications of grade and quality of produce are met. The meat is packaged and sealed under their supervision. It is accepted by them for you after they are satisfied that it has met your minimum qualifications for meat products. Some food service operations find this a very successful way to purchase meat. Inspectors will see to it that your specifications for meat are met. They will also help you write your specifications. You pay the Department of Agriculture for this service, and they pay the inspectors who do this work. But you pay only for the time the inspectors actually work for you. For further information about this, contact your nearest Department of Agriculture, Livestock Division.

This method is not used nearly as much as it should be, probably for two reasons:

1. Managers don't know it exists.
2. Managers are aware of the method but say, "I know so much about meat, I don't need to pay for government inspectors."

It is a rare food service operation manager who knows as much about meat as a government meat inspector does. Give some serious thought to using this method, especially if yours is a large food operation.

Blank Check

A final method of purchasing is blank check, which is definitely not advocated. This is where you need a commodity but you do not know the exact cost. So you send a signed check to the supplier for the item and the supplier fills in the amount of money. If you *must* use it, establish a special checking account with a specified maximum balance in the account. Don't use this method unless it is a very unusual situation where you absolutely have to buy something and cannot get it any other way.

ORDERING FOODS

Placing Orders with Purveyors

Years ago, food service managers or their purchasing agents went to the market and personally chose foods for their food service operations. From that time, purchasing evolved into other methods. Salespeople called on food service operations for orders. Today most food service operation orders are made by telephone.

It is still wise for you (and/or your employee who does the purchasing) to visit food markets or purveyors' warehouses occasionally. A visit can bring you up-to-date on varieties and qualities of foods available. It can be a source of new ideas. You certainly don't have to get up at 5 a.m. and go to the produce market every day to inspect and purchase fresh produce, as food operations managers did years ago. Today only very large food service operations can afford to hire their own full-time specialists to go the the market to do their purchasing. But it is a good idea for you to go to different purveyors' establishments once in a while, when it's convenient for you and them, to see their facilities, to work out ideas about how purveyors can serve you best, and to get new ideas about purchasing.

Give a lot of thought and care to the selection of your purveyors for all your product lines. Some food service operations use as many as eight or more purveyors per product line. For most operations, however, two or three purveyors per product line should be enough. It depends on the size and type of your operation. You probably should use at least two firms so you can get quotations from both of them. This will help keep you at least somewhat informed about market price conditions and help you use the idea of "fewer-purveyor shopping."

You have got to be ethical about your contacts with purveyors. Don't set out deliberately to get a price from one firm knowing you will use it to try to browbeat another firm into a lower price. Use care and good judgment in choosing your purveyors and treat them fairly and honestly. Purveyors are very important to a food service operation. You will have to rely heavily on the judgment and service of your purveyors. They can have a big influence on the success or failure of your establishment. Shop around until you find purveyors who work well with you. Buy from them. Your purveyors supply you with the quality of goods you need at a price you can afford to pay. They are also in business to make money, and they, too, have to be concerned about making reasonable profits.

Meetings with Salespeople

Establish times during the day when you will see salespeople. Try to stick to your schedule for this, although you will have to have some flexibility. You might try to establish particular days when you encourage them to call. For example, you could indicate to salespeople that Tuesdays are the best days for you to discuss their products with them. Of course, you must be flexible. You will get many sales calls that are simply courtesy visits by salespeople who want to maintain contact with you and see that all is going well in their relationship with you. If you are dissatisfied with the items you are getting from their companies, they want to find out about it and try to correct problems.

Some salespeople still call for specific orders—especially if they sell soap and detergent, paper products, or canned goods. Salespeople from other kinds of companies may stop by, too. Regular suppliers will drop in, and representatives of other companies will come in to introduce you to new products. These may be salespeople from large national organizations who want you to try their product, although you would actually order their product through your own local purveyors.

You have to be realistic and flexible in meeting with salespeople. You want to keep informed about the market, but you cannot spend so much time talking with salespeople that you don't get time to take care of everything you must do to run your food service operation.

Ordering by Telephone

You will place almost all of your purchase orders by telephone. You should work out a well-designed and thoroughly organized telephone purchasing procedure using written forms so you can utilize your own and your purveyors' time most efficiently. You may want to use the purchasing agent's daily market quotation sheet (Chart 14-2) for telephone orders. Write it all down. Use some form listing date, quality, quantity, date to be delivered, purveyor, what ordered, price, and so on.

For some orders you may not get competitive bids because you want the product regardless of price. When you place the order over the phone, you should still write down all the information so you will have written records and know that you ordered the item, quantity, from whom, price, date, scheduled delivery, and so on.

PRE-PORTIONED FOODS

In the past, food service operations bought large quantities of many items and converted them to fit their own needs. For example, they bought meat in large wholesale cuts and then cut it into steaks, roasts, stew meat, whatever, themselves. Today most meat purveyors can perform this meat cutting function for you. If yours is a small to medium-size operation, it is a good idea to consider this service.

Meat purveyors have trained employees who are specialists in cutting meat. If your own kitchen employees cut your meat, chances are they also have to pre-prepare it, cook it, and get it ready to serve. Even if they are capable of doing all these jobs, they probably cannot cut meat as well as the meat purveyor's employees can. And if your own employees make mistakes and cut steaks too small, for example, your operation may be forced to use them only as stew meat. On the other hand, if your meat purveyor's meat cutters make a mistake on your order and cut steaks too small for you, another customer of the purveyor will probably want that smaller size. Meat purveyors have many different customers and many different orders to fill, so they have alternatives if the accuracy of the meat cutters varies. You don't.

It would appear at first glance that it is more expensive for you to purchase pre-portioned meat. It raises your food cost because you pay for the purveyor's labor, storage facilities, and equipment. But if you buy meat that is not pre-portioned and cut it and portion it yourself, you will have to pay for your own labor, storage facilities, and equipment. Costs are less obvious but still present.

When you buy pre-portioned meats, your food cost may increase but your labor cost should decrease. Some operators have even found that using pre-portioned meat has helped to decrease their food cost. They pay more but can reduce waste considerably. For many food service operations, switching to buying pre-portioned meat can eliminate a lot of problems and may actually save them money. If you are not sure and you are cutting your own meat, analyze what it is costing you. Do a series of yield tests as discussed in Chapter 11. You can find out what your food cost is per meat portion. Add your labor cost to this, plus amounts for overhead, for the space of the butcher block, for extra storage facilities that may be needed for equipment, and so on. Then you can compare the cost of pre-portioned meat with the cost of portioning it yourself. Some food service operators say, "I have the cooks cut meat because they're there anyway." Maybe they *shouldn't* be there to do meat cutting. Maybe they should be doing something else where their time could be more profitable for your food operation.

CONVENIENCE FOODS

Today in the food service industry the term "convenience foods" is widely used and little understood. Generally it is accepted to mean a frozen entree ready to be heated and served. But convenience food really means any food that makes work easier.

One of the original convenience foods was canned vegetables. All you had to do was open the can, heat the vegetables, and serve them. Canned foods were a real "convenience" innovation when they were introduced years ago. Now there are convenience products coming out every day in ready-to-cook or ready-to-heat form. They range from foods that have simply been breaded to foods that are totally prepared, fully cooked, and only need to be heated and served. Convenience foods can also include dehydrated foods, freeze-dried foods, dehydro-frozen foods, boil-in-the-bag foods, and the like.

Food service operations usually buy convenience foods thinking they will save labor. This is true *if* using convenience foods means you need fewer employees. But this usually is not the case. It is not safe to assume that using convenience foods will permit you to reduce the number of employees or cut employee payroll or that you can get enough extra volume to cover the cost of the convenience foods.

You can, however, consider convenience foods as supplemental foods. Many can be heated and served in a matter of minutes. For many operations, they are just what is needed to give variety to a menu.

The cost for many convenience foods is high compared to what it would cost you to prepare the foods from scratch. But the price may be reasonable if supplemental convenience foods serve as valuable additions to your menu. A lot of people order roast beef or steak when they go out to eat. But people who eat out frequently may find that roast beef and steak get monotonous and they want some variety. They may occasionally welcome beef burgundy or coq au vin, for example. Such items may do a good job for you if you buy them in pre-prepared convenience food form and use them limitedly to add interest to your menu.

You should not build your whole menu on convenience foods. They are too expensive for that. Use them discriminately to help you offer variety to your guests and increase your profits. You can obtain variety by using convenience food items that are available and pre-prepared to meet your own standards. These foods can help your profits where they eliminate leftovers. When they are prepared in one-portion orders, there is no waste.

Many convenience food items can be obtained in larger sizes—such as 10 or 25 portions in a pan instead of a case of separate single portions. If you buy the larger units, though, you can lose many of the original advantages of convenience foods. Buying convenience foods in bigger size and quantity can also increase the possibilities of leftovers. If you have cooked leftovers, there may not be any savings.

Virtually all food service operations today use some kinds of convenience and supplemental foods, including beef or chicken base for soup stock, convenience entrees for menu variety, or even just cans of vegetables.

One criticism leveled against many convenience foods is that many food operations buy originally identical products and competing establishments can wind up serving identical dishes. Some food service managers complain, "I buy exactly the same beef stew as my competitor. When guests order beef stew from either of us they get the very same type of stew. We don't make our stew, we just buy the same kind and heat it up."

Even if you and your competitors do buy the same convenience items, you can vary them. They don't have to be exactly the same when you serve them. Your pre-prepared stew doesn't have to be just like your competitor's. You could serve yours in a casserole dish instead of just on a plate. You could add a garnish, like a border of duchess potatoes, for example. Or you could list it as "Old-Fashioned Beef Stew with Dumplings," and make the dumplings with a mix.

There is a definite place for convenience or supplemental foods in today's food service operation, as well as for those items which are prepared from scratch.

Convenience foods can add to your menu. They can increase or decrease your total cost depending on how effectively you buy them and how effectively you use them in your establishment. Some establishments purchase their convenience foods only in single portions. They pay more buying single portions, but they know their exact costs and they do not have to contend with the problems of leftovers.

Institutions have been big buyers of pre-prepared entrees that call for limited cooking or heating. They have found that they can reduce total costs by balancing work loads better. For example, one day's meal is prepared from scratch, and the next day a pre-prepared entree is used. The day the pre-prepared entree is used, they are doing pre-preparation for the next day.

Consider if and how convenience foods can help you increase your menu variety, balance work loads, and possibly reduce waste. You might find it feasible to use some items that will allow you to serve more guests without hiring additional personnel. Hundreds of convenience food items are available to food service operations. If is fairly sure that you can make good use of some of them if you buy and use them wisely.

REVIEW AND DISCUSSION QUESTIONS

1. What should be included in purchase specifications?
2. What are the "Four W's" of purchasing?
3. What are the seven methods of purchasing?
4. Why is the food service business considered a "penny" business?
5. Why isn't the concept of one-stop shopping feasible for most food service operations?
6. What are the possible advantages and disadvantages of purchasing pre-portioned and/or convenience foods?

15

Food Receiving Control

Objectives

This chapter discusses the importance of seeing that you receive the items that you want and will pay for. After you have read this chapter, you should:

1. Know the various types of equipment that you need for receiving control.
2. Know the standard receiving routine.
3. Know the various forms and records that a receiving clerk can use.

PURPOSE FOR RECEIVING CONTROL

There are two main reasons why you need receiving controls:

1. To make sure you get exactly what you ordered.
2. To make sure you get exactly what you will pay for.

Many food service operators put a lot of emphasis on purchasing. Managers may take direct charge of purchasing themselves or make sure employees in charge of the job do it properly. That's fine. But then they may quit right there. They allow anyone to sign for and "receive" incoming merchandise. They give little or no attention to real receiving procedures. This makes no sense and it neglects an important area of control.

In many food service operations, it is not uncommon for delivery people to shove invoices in front of the first kitchen employees they see and say, "Here, sign this." If this happens in your kitchen, don't blame the delivery people for it. They are in a hurry. And don't blame your employees who sign. Blame yourself for not setting strict receiving procedures or for having no controlled receiving procedures at all.

If you do not have planned receiving procedures, no one at your operation is examining goods coming in to see if they are what you ordered or to make sure they are the quality you want. Worse yet, it could mean that hours after food arrives, someone notices that the shipment has been sitting in a hot kitchen when it should have gone into refrigeration immediately.

COMPETENT RECEIVING PERSONNEL

Ideally, you should have one employee assume complete responsibility for all receiving and one alternate employee ready to fill in if the first person is not available. In a very large operation, this work can require a full-time specialist with several assistants. Small operations may have to get by with one individual who does all the receiving plus other duties.

In many instances, the person responsible for receiving is the same individual who does the purchasing. From a control standpoint, this is not good. From a practical standpoint, however, you may have to resort to this policy if you cannot afford to have two different employees handle the two jobs.

In most situations, the receiving clerk will do little more than check the invoices which accompany the goods delivered to see that all items listed on the invoices are really delivered and that they are exactly what you ordered. The person you select to do your receiving should know something about foods, though. Sometimes he or she may have to make technical judgments about foods and whether they are acceptable or not.

The person you select for this job should be someone who is reliable and interested in the duties of receiving. It must be someone who is willing to pay attention to detail, will help work toward the goals and objectives of your food service operation, and will make sure your standards are maintained.

FACILITIES

Your receiving facilities can be quite simple. If your set-up is ideal, you will have a loading dock where delivery trucks can back up and unload goods at a level that is the same height (or close to the same height) as the back of most trucks. If this was planned in the original construction of your building, you are fortunate because this arrangement greatly simplifies unloading and receiving procedures. Items can be wheeled in from the truck, examined, counted, weighed, and signed for (or rejected) by your receiving clerk and taken directly to their respective storage areas, which should consist of space for storing dry items plus refrigeration adequate for your needs.

Chart 15-1 shows three receiving process flow situations. Number 1 shows the best arrangements for receiving—everything is on one level. Number 2 shows a typical arrangement with storage on a lower level. Number 3 shows a bad arrangement where goods are received at the front door and storage is on a lower level.

If your building is not constructed to permit a set-up such as example Number 1 (and most buildings are not), you probably cannot do a great deal about achieving this ideal pattern. It is ideal to have your goods progress quickly and directly from receiving to the kitchen or the storage area, depending on where they should go. From storage they should be directly available to the preparation area. From preparation, the food products move to the guests in the dining area. The cost of reconstructing or rearranging your building to achieve this horizontal flow of goods would probably be prohibitive depending on your existing arrangement. But do whatever you can to come as close to the ideal physical pattern as possible. It is the most efficient arrangement.

Unfortunately, it is common for food service operations to have storage areas located on a lower level, usually in the basement. This probably gives you maximum space for preparation and service areas, but it makes the flow of goods more complicated and costly. Figure out and use the most effective and easiest method for moving your goods from one level to another, making the movement of products suitable to your own operation and as easy and efficient as you can.

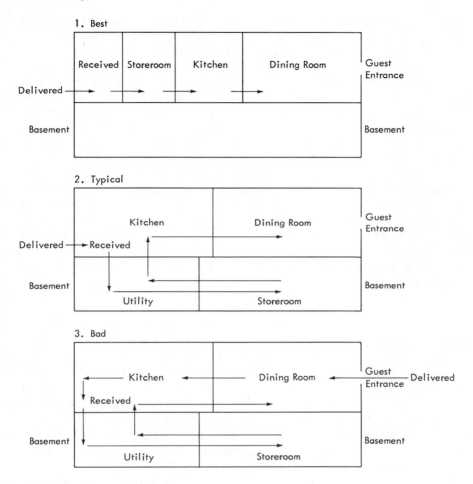

Chart 15-1 Receiving Flow Patterns

Equipment

For proper receiving procedures you will need some simple and comparatively inexpensive equipment, including:

1. Large scale.
2. Wheel.
3. Inclined plane and pulley.

Large Scale

Weighing incoming merchandise is an important part of receiving control. You need a scale capable of weighing any size package you purchase and receive. You may need a scale that weighs only up to 25 pounds if that is the heaviest item you purchase. Most food service operations, however, will probably need a platform scale capable of weighing up to 500 pounds. In very large operations it is not uncommon to find scales capable of weighing several thousand pounds at a time so that large quantities of items can be weighed together.

Figure out how big a scale you need so all items that come in to your establishment can be weighed. Your receiving clerk should check the actual weight of items or category of items on your scale and compare it with the weight on the invoice to make sure you receive the weight you ordered.

Dehydration of goods, thawing of meat, and the like can cause discrepancies between the weight stated on the invoice and the weight you find by actually weighing the items. Take note of discrepancies. You need to establish a point where you will call your purveyors concerning variations in weight. You should determine how much discrepancy on what items you will allow and how much you won't. Usually your purveyors can account for variations or they will make adjustments. Dishonesty is very rarely involved in the matter of weight variations.

The Wheel

There are some very basic principles of physics that food service operations do not use nearly as much as they should. You ought to have a two-wheeled hand truck, a four-wheeled dolly, or both—or several of both, depending on the quantity of merchandise you receive and the distance your employees have to move it. Human beings have been putting the wheel to excellent use for thousands of years—except in food service operations. Many food service establishments still require employees to do the backbreaking work of carrying crates and cases from one area to another even if it could be avoided. With a hand truck or dolly, employees can move goods along on the same level much more easily and quickly. Use the wheel lavishly in your establishment. Print the name of your food service operation on your hand trucks. Delivery people can easily mistake them for their own.

Inclined Plane and Pulley

Use the inclined plane (chute) and the pulley (dumbwaiter, elevator) wherever you can. The inclined plane can be very helpful for sliding items from one level down to another intead of carrying them downstairs to storage areas. An inclined plane can be a metal chute or it can be as simple as just a few heavy waxed planks nailed together. Usually items are moved to storage by the case or crate and come out of storage a few cans, bags, or small boxes at at time.

If your storage area is on a different floor from your receiving area (up or down), a pulley system (dumbwaiter or elevator) is, of course, most desirable. But if you don't have either, the cost of installation is usually prohibitive. An inclined plane or chute could be helpful for moving items down from one level to a slightly lower level. If the level is sharply lower, you might rig up planks at gentle levels with employees catching crates and cartons of unbreakable items and then sliding them carefully along down to the next level.

If your storage area is located on a floor or two above your receiving area and you cannot install any pulley device, goods will have to be moved manually, unfortunately.

Receiving Hours

Some food service operators set specific hours for receiving. They want all of their goods to arrive during a certain specified time—between 7 and 11 a.m., for example. Others prefer to receive deliveries in the afternoon so items will be on hand for the following day's production. They prefer afternoon delivery and feel things usually are not quite as hectic then as they might be in the morning. Some, especially those in very large cities, receive deliveries between the hours of midnight and 7 a.m. It is easier for delivery trucks to get in and out during these hours when they can avoid the congestion of daytime traffic.

Most food service operations will accept goods whenever their purveyors can deliver them. Many must accept delivery according to the schedules of their suppliers. Food suppliers plan schedules for sending loads to all the food establishments they serve. They have established routes. You cannot very well refuse delivery between 11 a.m. and 1 p.m. if your purveyor stops across the street at 11 a.m. and wants to deliver to you at 11:30 a.m. Purveyors will probably have to deliver your goods to you depending on where they can fit you into their schedule and routes. Some food service operators are in a position to specify when they will accept deliveries—from 7 a.m. to 5 p.m. with no deliveries between 11 a.m. and 1 p.m., for example. But many food service operators purchase very small quantities and are not able to dictate or negotiate any delivery scheduling at all.

Be as flexible about delivery hours as you can. If your purveyors have to make special trips or encounter special handling problems which increase their costs, they will have to pass these costs on to you.

Usually it is not the times of delivery (whether you can choose times or not) that create the real receiving problems. Receiving problems are frequently caused by improper planning by food service managers. You could probably do a lot to improve your situation by designing an effective receiving system and designating a reliable, trained employee to take charge of receiving deliveries whenever they arrive.

No matter what the conditions of your own receiving may be, take all possible steps to insure that your foods go through a thorough receiving procedure when they do arrive.

SPECIFICATIONS

We discussed purchase specifications in Chapter 14. Give a written copy of your purchase specifications (Chart 14-1 Purchase Specification Card) to your receiving clerk. This copy of the purchase specifications serves as the receiving specifications. It is imperative that you use a clear copy of your purchase specifications for receiving specifications. Purchase specifications and receiving specifications must be identical and legible. It is the duty of the receiving clerk to see that your operation's purchase specifications are adhered to exactly as receiving specifications.

A few years ago the food controllers of several hotels in a national chain debated among themselves whether food establishments should or should not accept delivery of goods that deviated from specifications. They concluded that they should not, and this decision makes sense. They discussed specific situations they knew about, including an incident where one of their hotels had placed an order specifying 10-inch ribs weighing 34 to 38 pounds. Some ribs that weighed 42 pounds were delivered. They were exceptionally good ribs—better than the specifications called for but still at the price originally quoted. Should the hotel have accepted the 42-pound ribs or should they have sent them back? They concluded that even in a case like this, specifications should be followed and delivery should be rejected. They decided that deviations from specifications should not be permitted and existing purchase specifications should be held to. The only exception might be if purveyors cannot get what the operation wants and the operation could be forced to accept substitute items.

Change specifications for the future if you want to, but stick to specifications you already have until you do change them. If you do not adhere to your purchase specifications in your receiving, the entire purpose for using specifications in receiving is defeated. If you do not use your written purchase specifications as a receiving control, you can usually expect higher costs and/or less desirable products for the use you intend to make of the goods you receive.

STANDARD RECEIVING ROUTINE

Your routine for receiving should be relatively simple. Establish a good, efficient pattern and follow it. All incoming items must be checked for:

1. Quantity (either by count or by weight).
2. Quality and/or brand.

The receiving clerk should check the purveyor's invoice, count the items (for such items as cases of canned goods), and compare items received with the purchase specifications. If quality is correct and the count and/or weight matches the purveyor's invoice, your receiving clerk signs the invoice. The receiving clerk keeps one copy of the invoice and returns one copy to the delivery person.

Some items (some meat and produce, for example) should be weighed. The receiving clerk checks the weight shown on the scale against the weight shown on the invoice and on the purchase order sheet (see Chart 14-1). The receiving clerk should check the purveyor's invoice price against the price quoted on the purchase order sheet. You and your receiving clerk should establish as policy ahead of time how much deviation you will allow on all items. Quite often your purveyors will load frozen meats on delivery trucks. By the time the truck reaches your food service operation, the meat may have thawed a little and there can be a blood-water loss. If the meat is delivered still frozen solid, just as it was when your purveyor weighed it, the weight should be exactly the same. Partial thawing on the truck, however, can reduce the weight of meat. Consider a factor like this (among others, such as dehydration of 100 pounds of potatoes, which could weigh 98 pounds when they reach you) when you define and establish tolerances and set limits inside of which you will accept the items and outside of which you will reject delivery and ask for an adjustment.

An item that is unsatisfactory to you because it is the wrong weight—or it fails to meet your specifications for any other reason—should be refused, returned to the driver, and taken back to the purveyor. A written record of this should be made so you are billed correctly. This is one of the major reasons why you need good receiving control. Receiving control is where you verify that you get the quantity and quality you ordered and will pay for. Prices may be checked by your receiving clerk and/or purchasing agent or just by your accounting department. Any items that do not meet your standards should be returned. Occasionally you will get the wrong things and you should return them. Errors will be made by purveyors and purveyors' employees. It is the responsibility of your own receiving clerk to catch these errors and ask for corrections.

Another thing to be aware of is that sometimes your purveyor may substitute items. Say you have ordered a specific item by brand name. The purveyor is out of that particular brand. The purveyor, trying to be helpful, sends a different brand of the same product. Your receiving clerk sees the different brand and calls the purveyor to check if it is an error or a substitution, and finds that it is a substitution. Whether you take the substitute items or not will depend on how important the item is to you and how fast you need it. If you have to have the item immediately, you may be forced to accept a substitute that is not precisely what you specified. If you do not need the item immediately, your receiving clerk can decide to refuse it and place a back order for the brand you originally ordered. Don't deviate from specifications if you don't *really* have to.

Substitutions or errors will call for judgment on the part of receiving clerks. Occasionally they may make mistakes and accept items that you do not want. If you do send items back, check the bill you will get later from your purveyor to make sure that you received credit for any items you returned. Do this because it is sensible and because mistakes do happen. They can occur in delivery and in billing. Your purveyors should promptly correct any mistakes they make. If they do not, or if there are more mistakes than you think reasonable, it is probably time to consider changing purveyors. If your receiving clerks make more errors or bad decisions than you feel are acceptable, you may need to re-train them or consider replacing them.

There is a problem of how much time you can delay delivery trucks while you check and weigh each item. Your clerks may be able to check all items quickly as they are unloaded from the truck. But if your receiving routines are going to delay the drivers very long, you may be able to work out special arrangements with your purveyors so you won't delay their drivers. You might be able to make arrangements with your purveyors so your clerks can go ahead and sign the invoices immediately and let delivery truck drivers go on their way. Then, at your receiving clerks' convenience and as they are preparing to store the items, they can weigh, count, check, and examine each item individually. If they find errors, discrepancies, or unacceptable items, you can notify your purveyors for a billing adjustment and exchange or return of merchandise later.

This arrangement can work well for all concerned. You can achieve your own goal of seeing that you receive exactly what you ordered and will pay for. Your purveyors' delivery schedules can proceed much faster. Purveyors have to be concerned with the cost per stop for their delivery trucks. If you delay them substantially, they must, in fairness to their other customers and for their own profitability, pass on a proportionate cost to you in the prices they charge you. In other words, it will cost you money if your receiving routines delay your purveyors' trucks. Try to work out a set-up with your purveyors to remedy this.

Many purveyors have delivery people who are prohibited by union contract from doing any work except placing items on a receiving dock or just inside a door where they will be protected from theft and weather. Usually you should not expect your purveyors' delivery truck drivers to take your items to a storeroom away from the immediate area of your receiving.

After you have received items, store them properly. Storeroom procedures are discussed in Chapter 16.

Your receiving clerk should record all invoices on a receiving sheet (Receiving Clerk's Daily Food Report Forms, Charts 15-1, 15-2, 15-3, 15-4). This sheet should be forwarded to your accounting staff office along with the invoice. In your accounting office, the receiving sheets should be used in preparing your daily food cost. Invoices should be checked for extensions (price multiplied by quantity) to see if they are accurate. Your purveyors' clerks could have made some errors in multiplication. The invoices should be checked further or spot-checked to make sure that the price on the invoice is identical to the price quoted to you by your purveyor. If you don't check all these things, you may get cheated by an unscrupulous purveyor who will quote you one price and bill you another. Most discrepancies, however, will be due to plain human error.

After the invoice has been checked and okayed, it should be paid, or filed until you do pay it.

Blind Receiving

Another receiving routine method is blind receiving. This is an excellent method. It gives you the best possible control you can have. But it is not recommended for everyone. It is an expensive and time-consuming procedure and just not practical for most operations, but it's something you might want to consider.

With the blind receiving method, there is no invoice accompanying the delivery. Your purveyors prepare regular invoices but they mail them directly to your accounting office. Usually a list will accompany the actual order, but the list may only indicate totals. It would say merely, "Forty pieces in this order," for example. Your receiving clerks have to make a complete listing of each item by counting and/or weighing and recording every article. This method forces your receiving clerks to do the job very carefully and exactingly. They cannot arbitrarily sign an invoice without actually inspecting the merchandise. They don't have an invoice. They have to write it themselves. They cannot weigh an item and say, "That's close enough," and let it go. They have to count and weigh each item and write it all down.

Your receiving clerks send the finished record to your accounting office. The accounting personnel compare the receiving clerks' records with the invoice that they received in the mail from the purveyors. The accounting office should also check prices and extensions as they would in a standard receiving routine.

From a control standpoint, blind receiving is excellent. Unfortunately, it is not workable for most establishments. It takes a lot of time for receiving clerks to get and record all the information involved, as opposed to just checking an invoice against a purchase order sheet. And this method takes a lot of time in the accounting department, where someone has to compare the receiving clerks' figures with those on the invoice mailed to the accounting office by the purveyors. Blind receiving also puts an extra burden on your purveyors. They have to make up a separate list of items for you. It is probably a nuisance for them to have to mail your invoice to your accounting department. This is not normal routine for purveyors. And special arrangements would have to be made so purveyors' delivery people do not have to wait around while your clerks go through the long blind receiving process before they okay a shipment.

Blind receiving is an expensive routine in time and money for you *and* your purveyors. You should be aware of the method, however, and decide whether or not it is feasible for you.

KEEPING RECORDS

Daily Food Report Forms

Many establishments make only one copy of the Receiving Clerk's Daily Food Report Form. It is completed and sent (along with the invoices) to the accounting department. This verifies to the accounting department that the goods on the invoice have been received. Then they can pay the invoice. The Receiving Clerk's Daily Food Report Form becomes a part of the daily food control system. The accounting department usually keeps the Receiving Clerk's Daily Food Report Forms for the current year and then throws them away. Other establishments may make two copies of the Receiving Clerk's Daily Food Report Form. One copy goes to the accounting department where the above procedure is followed. The second copy is kept in the receiving department for reference and is thrown away at the end of the month.

The Receiving Clerk's Daily Food Report, which the receiving clerk will need to use for receiving records and controls and for recording invoices, will vary from one food service operation to another. There are several types of forms, as discussed below.

Form 1 Receiving Clerk's Daily Food Report (Chart 15-2)

Form 1 is the one recommended for most food service operations. It is the simplest and fastest to use. Merchandise received is separated into two classifications:

1. Direct Purchases—Column 8 Distribution, Chart 15-2.
   These are items sent directly from the receiving area to the production area for immediate use. They never go to the storeroom and are not entered into the storeroom records. There are no requisitions for these items.
2. Storeroom Purchases—Column 9 Distribution, Chart 15-2.
   These are items entered in storeroom records, placed in the storeroom, and issued to production only by requisitions.

Individual food operations make their own decisions about which items should go in which category—direct purchases or storeroom purchases. It is up to you to decide which items should pass through the storeroom with requisitions prepared for issuing them and which should not.

Some operations will put almost all items on a storeroom purchase and storeroom issue basis. Other operations put most items on a direct purchases and direct issues basis with no requisitions involved. Make your own decision about which method works best for you. Remember that the more items you decide to have go through issuing from the storeroom, the more accurately you can prepare your daily food cost.

1	2	3	4	5	6	7	8	9
Quantity	Price Unit	Invoice Number	Description and Purveyor	Unit Price	Amount	Total Amount	Distribution: Direct Purchases	Distribution: Storeroom Purchases
175 lb.	lb.	36432	12 oz. N.Y. Strip-A	3.25		568.75		568.75
100 lb.	lb.		10 oz. Club Stk.-A	2.35		235.00		235.00
130 lb.	lb.		Prime Rib - A	1.89		245.70		245.70
25 lb.	lb.	60323	8 oz. Chopped Stk.-B	.74		18.50		18.70
25 lb.	lb.		Beef Brochette-B	1.50		37.50		37.50
20	bag	362	Dinner Rolls - C	1.25	25 per bag	25.00	25.00	
5	ea.		Cheesecake - C	2.16	12 per pie	10.80	10.80	
4	ea.	4232	Milk - D	1.34	6 gal. ea.	5.36	5.36	
6	450 Count		Butter Patties-D	.98	Box	5.88	5.88	
3	gal.		IceCream-Choc.- D	7.47	3- gal. container	22.41	22.41	
100 lb.	lb.	101314	Potatoes (bake)- E	.12		12.00		12.00
25 lb.	lb.		Potatoes (peeled)- E	.32		8.00		8.00
2	case		Iceberg Lettuce-E	.25	24 per case	12.00		12.00
1 case	#10	23268	Melon Balls - F	2.50	6 per case	15.00		15.00
50	ea.	12386	Trout - G	.69	25 per box	34.50		34.50
48	lb.	312	Coffee - H	1.12	12 per case	53.76		53.76
1 case	32 oz.	4636	Wine Vinegar - I	.88	12 per case	10.56		10.56
3 case	14 oz.	5981	Ketchup - J	.25	24 per case	18.00		18.00

Chart 15-2   Receiving Clerk's Daily Food Report—Form 1

Form 2 Receiving Clerk's Daily Food Report (Chart 15-3)

This form is frequently used, too. It demands more detailed breakdown of items. You classify items in separate columns (meat, poultry, fish, groceries, fruits, vegetables, and so on).

Form 2 has the advantage of giving you a more detailed breakdown of items as they come into your operation. With this form you can calculate the total cost of meat purchased, total cost of fish purchased, total cost of poultry purchased, and so on.

1	2	3	4	5	6	7	8	9	10	11	12	13	14
Date	Purveyor	Meat	Poultry	Fish	Vege-tables	Fruits	Butter	Eggs	Milk and Cream	Groc-eries	Ice Cream	Baked Goods	Total
	A	1,049.45											1,049.45
	B	56.20											56.20
	C											35.80	35.80
	D						5.88	5.36			22.41		33.65
	E				32.00								32.00
	F					15.00							15.00
	G			34.50									34.50
	H									53.76			53.76
	I									10.56			10.56
	J									18.00			18.00

Chart 15-3   Receiving Clerk's Daily Food Report—Form 2

There's a disadvantage to this form, though. It takes more time to prepare the columns in this form than it does simply to classify items as either direct purchases or storeroom purchases as you do in Form 1 Chart 15-2. But the main objection to Form 2 is not the work involved. The problem is that most managers who use it fail to do anything with the information they get from it. It's a waste of time and money to gather any records and collect any information and then file it and forget it. No form is worth any effort if you won't really use the information you get from it. If you do need this much information, however, and really do use it, fine.

Form 3 Receiving Clerk's Daily Food Report (Chart 15-4)

This form gives you an even more detailed breakdown than Form 2. In Form 3 (which should probably be used only in large food service operations), the items are broken down into still more detailed categories. Meat is classified separately as beef, veal, lamb, pork, variety meat, total meat, and so on. Fish and seafood might be put into two separate columns. The object is to determine what you are spending in each of these specific categories of meats, fish, seafoods, and so on.

| Date | Purveyor | Meat | | | | | | Fish | |
		Beef	Veal	Lamb	Pork	Variety Meat	Total Meat		
	A	810.00	40.00	100.00	49.45	50.00	1,049.45		
	B				30.00	26.20			

Chart 15-4   Receiving Clerk's Daily Food Report — Form 3

Form 4 Receiving Clerk's Daily Food Report (Chart 15-5)

This is the most specific detailed breakdown of all. There is a heading for beef and this is further separated into oven-ready ribs, 12-ounce strip steaks, fillets, hamburger, stew beef, sweetbreads, and so on. There is a heading for pork and it is further broken down into bacon, ham, liver, sausage, chops. Other meat classifications would also be broken down into specific cuts. The same applies to fish, seafood, and the like.

This form, with specific subheadings and item breakdowns and listings, can be used for anything, not just meat. For example, groceries could be broken down into specific categories for vegetables—tomatoes, peas, carrots. Carrots could be broken down into diced, sliced, crinkle-cut, tiny whole.

Obviously this is the form to use if you want maximum detail.

| Date | Purveyor | Beef | | | | | |
		Oven-Ready Ribs	12-Oz. Strip Steak	Filets	Hamburger	Stew Beef	Sweetbreads
	A	375.00	350.00	60.00	90.00	75.00	50.00
		Pork					
		Bacon	Ham	Liver	Sausage	Chops	
	A		49.45				
	B	30.00		26.20			

Chart 15-5   Receiving Clerk's Daily Food Report — Form 4

Use the Form That's Appropriate for Your Own Operation

The four forms we have just looked at and discussed show you how a food control system can grow and develop. The simplest is Form 1 Chart 15-2. If you need detailed information, use Form 2 Chart 15-3, Form 3 Chart 15-4 or, for most detail, Form 4 Chart 15-5. Keep in mind that additional detail costs money in terms of the time it takes you or your employees to gather information and complete these forms. This should not be the *only* deciding factor for you, however. Consider it in light of how much you really need detailed additional information and how you will use it. A very large operation may have thousands of dollars involved in many subcategories. They will probably want and use the information provided by Form 3 Chart 15-4 or Form 4 Chart 15-5. If yours is a large operation, it could be worth the additional expense to obtain the information because it could help you do a better job of managing your operation. If yours is a small operation and you try to gather too much detailed information, you will probably find that you don't have enough personnel to put together all this data and you probably don't need such detail anyway. If you are dealing in hundreds of dollars instead of thousands, you might scrap the whole system because you get bogged down in too much paper work that you don't really need. Use the form that's sensible for you and stick to it. You'll have to decide which form (or variations or combinations of forms) is best for you.

How to Use the Information

For an example of how you might use detailed information from Form 2 Receiving Clerk's Daily Food Report Chart 15-3, you could divide the cost of the total amount of money you spent for meat by food sales or by the total cost of food sold. If you do this over a period of time, it will give you an indication of how much money you are spending for meat and an idea of what proportion meat represents—either as a percent of your food sales or as a percent of your cost of food sold. This information can help you establish a standard for the amount you should spend for meat. If your standard starts to increase—as a percentage of food sales or as a percentage of cost of food sold —it should be a signal to you that you are using too much meat or that you need to adjust your selling prices. It is very apt to be the latter.

Perhaps you also want a more detailed breakdown of costs. Besides knowing how much you are spending for meat, maybe you also want to know how much you are spending for just beef, for example. If beef is a substantial part of your food cost dollar and you're spending thousands of dollars for it a month, this information could be useful to you when you are negotiating purchase price and quantities of beef.

USE THE RECEIVING PROCEDURE THAT IS BEST FOR YOU

Don't get too involved in a receiving function that bogs down in detail. Keep the whole system as simple as you can. Just gather information you will really use. If necessary, do special studies. Add up all invoices for meat items purchased in a month, for example. This will tell you the total dollars you spent that month for meat.

Do this occasionally and only on selected items. It is better to do simple studies occasionally to get information you need instead of devising detailed receiving procedures which you use all the time but don't actually need. You are not tying up your receiving clerks by asking them to do a lot of detailed work which you may not use. You are not going into a lot of detail on all items.

Decide which type of receiving form is best for you. Don't ask for detailed information unless the data will really work for you. Receiving information should make you more aware of where your dollar is going and why and what you can do to minimize the expenditures in these areas without sacrificing quality.

Use the type of receiving form that allows you—at the most reasonable cost to you—to get the information you must have to make necessary decisions about how you are spending your food cost dollars.

REVIEW AND DISCUSSION QUESTIONS

1. Why should you have receiving procedures?
2. What equipment is needed for receiving?
3. What is the standard receiving routine?
4. How does blind receiving differ from standard receiving?
5. Analyze the differences in the four Receiving Clerk's Daily Food Report forms. Who would use which form? Why?

16

Food Storeroom Control

Objectives

This chapter discusses the importance of maintaining a storeroom, and the procedures involved. After you have read this chapter, you should:

1. Know various ways of organizing storeroom facilities.
2. Know the mechanics of issuing food and pricing requisitions.
3. Know various methods for evaluating food inventory.

It is fairly obvious that you need storage space so you can:

1. Store goods and have them on hand when you need them.
2. Purchase in large enough quantities and sizes to give you the best price break.
3. Buy in large enough quantities so that you don't have to do excessive handling (which costs you money) and can avoid the expense of frequent deliveries (which also cost you money).

You need control systems for your storeroom for the following reasons:

1. To prevent theft from your storeroom.
2. So you can set up and use good routines to rotate stock and avoid having items spoil because they stayed in storage too long.
3. So you can easily determine what items you have on hand in your storeroom, can easily figure out what you have to purchase, and can avoid over- and underpurchasing.
4. So you know and record the cost of all the items you store and use.

Methods of handling the storage of food service operation goods are changing. The trend today is for food service operations to carry less inventory on their own premises. The cost of storage is high, so many operations let their purveyors carry the inventory instead. Many operations figure the cost of a storeroom on a square foot basis, and the cost of storage space per square foot is apt to be much greater for a food service operator than it is for a purveyor. Food service establishments are usually located in dense population areas where the cost of land and construction is high. Purveyors' warehouses, on the other hand, are usually located in areas near railroad tracks, trucking terminals, and the like where the cost of land, buildings, and thus storage space is lower. Zoning requirements and construction costs also make it possible for the purveyor to store goods at a lower cost than the food service operator can. Many food operators do, of course, store necessary amounts on their own premises, but they make special efforts to keep their own stored stock minimal without neglecting the price breaks in quantity purchasing or ignoring the cost of constant deliveries.

Besides the cost of storage space, another problem is the fact that storage space is just an afterthought in many food service operations. It is seldom really considered thoroughly in the building's original construction plans, and it is usually in an inconvenient location.

Use whatever storage space you have as effectively as you can. If you have too much goods in the storeroom, you may be tying up money in inventory, which you could use to better advantage for other things. If you don't store enough goods on hand, you may not be operating as efficiently as you should be. You do need to have enough items on hand to take care of your business.

Generally it is better to buy five cases of an item and have this supply last you two or three weeks than it is to buy one case every two or three days. For one thing, you should be able to get a better price on five cases than you could on one. You also pay extra delivery costs and pay for extra handling of goods by your own employees if you have to replenish the same items every two or three days.

Unless you deal in very large quantities, have plenty of storage space to handle goods, and use goods very fast, you should rotate your stock regularly. "Rotate stock" means to shift it and rearrange it so you always use the oldest first. Small operators who get involved in buying several months' supply of an item are really engaging in inventory speculation. They are probably also jamming their storerooms with a big supply of one item and do not have space for storing other items they need. And if they are not careful to rotate stocks so they take the oldest items first, items may spoil. It is best to keep rotating your stored stock to avoid having items deteriorate in your storage areas.

For most operations, a reasonable and sensible approach would be to try to use and replenish an item within one month's time. You will probably have to purchase some perishable items every few days. Other items, such as spices, may last several months.

THE STOREROOM

Location

Storerooms are usually located in the least expensive space in a building—probably the basement or lower level for the typical food service operation. Usually little or no consideration is given to the problem of how you move goods from the storage area to the production area. Goods are generally moved to a lower storage level by employees carrying them, and back up to the production area by the same method. If your storeroom is located on a lower level, figure out the fastest and easiest way to move your goods to your main production area, as discussed in Chapter 15. Put in elevators or dumbwaiters if you possibly can, or at least try to use an inclined plane when you want to move goods down.

In many food service operations, storerooms are located near utility areas where heat from furnaces or steampipes can cause very fast deterioration of goods. Don't store goods near excessive heat. Ideally, storerooms should be dry and moderately cool.

Physical Layout

Many food operators have practically no storage space—perhaps a small room or just a tiny area added to the building. If you can't do anything about this, you have to live with it, and it's difficult. The physical layout of whatever storage space you do have is very important. Chart 16-1 shows three storage arrangements.

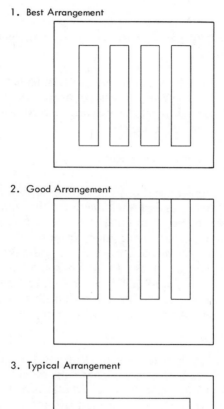

1. Best Arrangement

2. Good Arrangement

3. Typical Arrangement

Chart 16-1 Layout of Storeroom and Shelves

1. Number 1 (Best arrangement).

This shows the outside walls bare and open for passageways. Floor-to-ceiling shelving is clustered in the middle of the room. You can easily get at any shelf from any side. This is the best physical arrangement for a storeroom. It makes proper stock rotation easiest. You can get at both sides of a shelf, so you simply move the old goods forward and put the new goods behind the old ones. Change to this central shelving with passages around the outer walls if you can.

2. Number 2 (Good arrangement not as good as Number 1 but better than Number 3).

One end of each shelf is attached to the outside wall. You can still get at both sides of the shelves. You can still get proper stock rotation by moving goods forward. This is slightly more awkward than Number 1 because you can only walk around the shelves at one end.

3. Number 3 (Typical arrangement).

Many operations have shelves along the outer walls in the storeroom. They put items on the shelves and stack the rest in the middle of the room. This is an inconvenient arrangement and makes it hard to keep the storeroom clean. To rotate stock, you have to remove goods from the shelf, put the new goods on the shelf and shove them back toward the wall, then put the old goods toward the front of the shelf. It is a lot of work and a lot of employees won't bother to do it. Items are apt to be left on shelves for much longer periods of time than they should be. If you have a set-up like this, try to rearrange it. Set-up Number 1 is best. Arrange shelving like Number 1 if you can.

Sanitation and Pest Control

Your storeroom should be kept clean, neat, and orderly at all times. This makes it much easier to move goods in and out conveniently. Place food on shelves, or at least on pallets (raised platforms), never directly on the floor. You want air to circulate all around the goods to extend storage life. Try to arrange your storeroom so that it can be easily cleaned on a regular basis.

In handling goods, it is very easy to tear containers or damage bags and spill things on the floor. Spilled goods must be removed and the area cleaned promptly for the sake of sanitation and also to prevent the danger that employees might slip and fall.

Cleanliness can be a great help to you in controlling the pests that frequently inhabit storerooms. Pests can enter through conduits and other passageways and openings from the outside. Typical pests are mice, rats, and cockroaches. The pest you are most apt to have to contend with is the traditional restaurant pest, the cockroach.

You will have to have a constant and continuous pest control program. The typical cockroach is small and flat and can get in and out of almost any space. You should assume that all food services (including your own) do have—or can expect to have—cockroaches. You will always have cartons arriving from warehouses and entering your storeroom, and these can carry in roaches. The goods moving into your food service operation come from a lot of different places, many of which are not protected against pests. Cockroaches get into these goods in storage or transit and lay egg capsules. There will probably be some egg capsules attached to crates, cartons, and bags of goods that enter your storeroom. Each capsule is slightly larger than the period at the end of this sentence.

Each egg capsule can hatch and produce about 40 cockroaches. If these 40 grow and mature and are left unchecked for one year, they can produce about two million cockroaches. It's obvious you've got to have a careful pest control program to destroy capsules and roaches.

It is usually best to hire an exterminating company on a continuing basis and have them make regular periodic inspections of your premises. The place to start is in the storeroom. Decontaminate on a routine basis. This is your best insurance that cockroaches will not get beyond the storeroom and into other areas. If they do, you can have a really major problem and may even have to close down for a few days to decontaminate your entire establishment.

TYPES OF STORAGE FACILITIES

You need different types of storage facilities:

1. Temporary storage for food and beverage.
2. Temporary storage for miscellaneous equipment, accounting forms, and anything else you will use in the relatively near future.
3. Space for storing permanent records you have to keep on the premises.
4. Separate storage space for heavy equipment you use for banquets (special tables, chairs, and so on).
5. Space to keep cleaning equipment.

Ideally, each of these should have a separate area with different types of storage facilities, but few operations have space for this.

You should have specific kinds of facilities for food storage. Today the trend is to keep more and more items in the freezer because you are apt to have more pre-portioned and/or pre-processed types of foods. You must have proper refrigeration and you should have separate types of refrigeration where temperatures can be varied. It is usually recommended that meats should be stored at temperatures of 34 to 38 degrees Fahrenheit. If you stored fresh produce at the same 34 to 38 degrees temperature, however, some items (such as celery and tomatoes) might freeze because of their high water content. Fruits and vegetables need their own separate refrigeration at about 40 degrees Fahrenheit. In addition, you also need a dry storage area for canned goods, flour, sugar, and so on.

Storeroom Purchases and Direct Purchases

In Chapter 15 on food receiving control, we talked about classifying food items you receive as direct purchases or storeroom purchases. It is up to you to decide how you want to classify goods. Storeroom purchases are all items that go from receiving into the storeroom and leave the storeroom only when they are requisitioned. Direct purchases (also called direct issues) are all items that go from receiving directly into the production area with no storing and no requisitions involved.

PRICING GOODS IN THE STOREROOM

Any item moved out of the storeroom and sent to any other location should be issued only by written requisition. When you try to keep track of your daily food cost and work out your food cost formula, your biggest problem will be finding the cost of the goods so that the cost can be put on the requisition. The extension (cost multiplied by quantity) has to be written on the requisition and then the requisition has to be totalled. To help you do extensions on requisitions, you need records of prices paid for goods in the storeroom. Then, when the goods leave the storeroom, you (or your storeroom clerk or some other employee) can record the cost of the item being requisitioned on the requisition.

The following are ways to keep records of prices so you can find them and fill them in on your requisitions.

File Box or Loose-Leaf Notebook

You can use a small file box and 3 by 5 cards or a regular loose-leaf notebook for keeping records of prices. Have a separate card or sheet for each category of food. Many food service operations use this method but few really like it. You have to write down the price of the article and the date you are writing it down. It takes a lot of time and work to maintain cards or notebooks. If you don't keep them accurately, they can't give you accurate information when you need it to figure your food cost.

When you want to find out the price of anything, you have to look it up in your file box or loose-leaf notebook, which is a nuisance. The written record method (file cards or notebook) is not usually very effective in most operations. There is too much time and work involved. Prices are apt to be somewhat inaccurate because files are hard to keep up.

Rubber Stamp Price and Date

The best method for recording prices is the method used by most supermarkets and some food operations. More food service operations should use it. Use a rubber stamp to mark prices right on each food item, especially canned goods. Get the prices from your invoices. For example, say you pay $6 for a case of six number 10 cans of something. Divide the $6 cost per case by six cans per case. You get your cost per can—$1. You stamp $1 on the top of every can. Stamp the price on each item before you store it. Use a stamp that can be adjusted to print any figures. Or just print the price legibly on each item with a large black marking pencil instead of a stamp—just so the price is printed clearly and permanently on every item.

The big advantage to marking the price on each individual item in the storeroom is that as each item is requisitioned, you don't have to stop and go look up the price in a box of file cards or a notebook. You just write the item on the requisition—a number 10 can of tomatoes—and get the price right from the top of the can. You can record the price immediately on the requisition.

A second advantage in having the price stamped or written on each item is that it makes taking inventory much easier and faster. It is just as helpful for valuating inventories as it is for valuating requisitions. You just copy the price from the top of the item. You don't have to look it up in a card file or notebook.

A further valuable refinement in the procedure of putting the price on every item is also to put the date you receive it on the item. Get a stamp that puts price and date and that can be changed easily to print any price and any date, or just use a marking pencil. The date on the can or bottle or box will tell you precisely when the item arrived in your storeroom. This will help you in stock rotation and help to make sure that the oldest items are used first.

More Sophisticated Methods to Record Prices

We have just discussed two comparatively simple ways to keep records of items in the storeroom. There are also more sophisticated approaches:

1. A more complex system involves the use of special punch cards. You can code them so that when you insert a metal rod through all the cards, you can pull out only the cards for specific items about which you want information.
2. A still more sophisticated method would be to use a computer for keeping exact records of date, quantity, and price of every item entering and leaving the storeroom.

The more sophisticated systems can be expensive. Complicated storeroom record systems in very large establishments can require full-time personnel devoted solely to the care and pricing of inventory items. For the average and smaller food operation, the simple procedure of putting the price (and date received, if possible) right on each can, box, bag, or jug, is usually satisfactory and is recommended.

CONTROLLING THE STOREROOM

Take care to set up good procedures for issuing items from the storeroom. Generally it is smart to classify as many items as "storeroom purchases" as you can so they will be issued by requisition. The requisitions give you information that helps you keep track of your daily food cost more accurately.

If you can do it, it is ideal to have specific employees (one or more) assigned as storeroom clerks to take charge of your storeroom. It should be their responsibility to:

1. Keep records of everything in the storeroom.
2. Remove items from the storeroom.
3. See that all items are correctly recorded on requisitions.
4. Make extensions on requisitions.
5. Give requisitions to whoever keeps the food cost formula.

When the clerk is not at the storage area, the room should be locked to prevent unauthorized entry. It can be difficult to make this idea work. You and your food production personnel must make some plans and take some pains to make it work. It may help to have certain items in a kitchen emergency storage area. If the storeroom person is not immediately available to open the locked storeroom, employees can get items they need fast from the emergency area without having to get someone to unlock the main storeroom in the absence of a storeroom clerk. In general, you should keep very small amounts of items in an emergency storage area. These would probably be bulky and low-cost items (flour, condiments), and not the type of thing employees steal, so theft should not be a real problem in your emergency storage area.

Another way to alleviate problems that might be caused by locking the storeroom would be to have the head person in each production area of the kitchen (the head pantry person, for example, and the roast cook and the fry cook) examine tomorrow's menu at the end of their shifts every day. They should make a list of all items they will need first thing the next morning. They should list these on requisitions and give the requisitions to the storeroom clerk before they go home for the day. The storeroom clerk should arrive for work early—probably about an hour (or whatever amount of time is needed) before the rest of the crew—and start filling the requisitions turned in at the end of the previous day. As the cooks, pantry people, and so on, report to work, the storeroom clerk should be bringing (or should have already brought) the items the employees requisitioned to their stations. Any items that have to be kept refrigerated should go right into the kitchen refrigerators as the store-room clerk brings them in. When all food production employees start work, they should all have, right on hand at their stations in the kitchen or in the kitchen refrigerators, all of the items they will need for the day's food produc-tion.

When you start any new control system, there will be mistakes. When you start a locked storeroom control, employees will forget to requisition things they will need. Kitchen personnel and the storeroom clerk will still have to do some dashing back and forth carrying needed items for a while. No system will ever work perfectly at all times, of course, but the system should get better and easier when you have used it for a while. All employees should eventually learn to try to do their own pre-planning and avoid last-minute realizations that they need supplies. A lot of emphasis on pre-planning is the key to the success of any control, including this one.

You should decide what times of the day the storeroom should be open for issuing items. Normally this should probably coincide with your day shift because in most operations that is when maximum production takes place. And purchased items are usually received during the day shift. If a shortage of a necessary item develops and kitchen personnel need immediate access to the storeroom but the storeroom clerk is not there at the moment to unlock it, many food service operations would require that the assistant mana-ger (or anyone else designated by the manager) should open the storeroom, get the needed items, and fill out the requisitions. Employees will prefer not to have to go to the trouble of getting the assistant manager, telling him or her what item they need and why, and asking the assistant manager to unlock the storeroom for them. The assistant manager should strongly recommend to them that they start planning ahead. Most employees probably will then make an effort to do so next time and avoid the whole routine.

Have certain clearly-designated and well-understood times established for when the storeroom will be open. Anyone who needs or will need items from the storeroom should learn to try to plan accordingly.

Mechanics of Issuing

The actual mechanics of issuing are relatively simple. You do the following steps:

1. Individuals (authorized by you) give completed requisitions, which they have signed, to the storeroom clerk.
2. The clerk finds items in the storeroom, always taking the oldest stock and issuing it first. (This is correct stock rotation and helps prevent spoilage.)
3. The clerk finds unit prices marked on the items, records them on the requi-sition, and gives the items to the individuals who requisitioned them. If you don't have prices marked right on the items, clerks will have to look up prices in card files or notebooks after they have given the items to the employee who requisitioned them.

4. As soon as the clerk has time, he or she completes the extensions on the requisition.

5. The clerk forwards completed requisitions to the individual in charge of keeping up the food cost formula sheet.

Requisition Forms (Chart 16-2)

Chart 16-2 is an example of a food requisition form. Requisition forms are stock items you can buy from many printing companies, or you can make up your own and have them duplicated.

The form should have spaces to write in the quantity, description of the article, unit price, and dollar value for the total of each item. There should also be a space for the signature of the person who requisitions the items. And there should be space for the signature of the person who did the issuing from the storeroom and a place to put in the date.

The manager, working together with food production personnel, should decide who is authorized to sign a requisition and who is not. There should always be one person or more in the kitchen with the authority to sign requisitions. There should also be a person from the service area authorized to sign requisitions for replacements of sugar, salt, ketchup, steak sauce, and such common condiments needed by guests in the dining room, if you don't have a supply of these items in your emergency storage.

For smaller operations, a definite schedule of times when the storeroom is open is a good idea because it gives the storeroom clerk time to perform other duties. Many small operations never lock their storerooms. Consequently they have little or no storeroom control. They may ask employees to write down everything they take from the storeroom, but this doesn't really work. Employees will forget or else probably skip the nuisance of making a record.

Storeroom control should help you avoid having unnecessary items in the kitchen. Most items not needed for current production should be kept in the storeroom. "Current" production usually means today. Sometimes items should be in the kitchen undergoing advance preparation for the following day. If you don't pay attention to controlling what belongs in the storeroom and what belongs in the kitchen, you will probably have too much food in the kitchen that shouldn't really be there. Some of it will spoil or be wasted.

INVENTORY

Inventory Valuation

The reason you valuate (figure out the worth of) an inventory is to establish a dollar value for all goods on hand. You use this value when you are determining your food cost on your profit and loss statement. You also use this value in the asset section of your balance sheet.

Required of Storekeeper the Following Supplies			
1	2	3	4
Quantity Size of Unit	Article	Unit Price	Extension (Total)
4 10-lb Box	Shrimp	2.10 per lb.	84.00
1 Can	Melon Balls	2.50 ea.	2.50
51	Stuffed Breast of Chicken	.90 ea.	45.90
83	N.Y. Strip	3.25 per lb.	269.75
62	Club Steak – 10 oz.	2.35 per lb.	145.70
59	Club Steak – 6 oz.	2.35 per lb.	138.65
60 lb.	Prime Rib	1.89 per lb.	113.40
33	Chopped Steak	.74 per lb.	24.42
10 lb.	Beef Brochette	1.50 per lb.	15.00
20	Trout	.69 ea.	13.80
58	Stuffed Shrimp	2.10 per lb	121.80
140 lb.	Potatoes – Whole	.12 per lb.	16.80
3	Green Peppers	.37 per lb.	.20
1 Can	Mushrooms	1.20 ea.	1.20
1 Can	Baby Onions	.40 ea.	.40
1 Bag (5 lb.)	French Fries	.19 per lb	.95
30 Pints	Tomatoes, Cherry	5.25 per Case	12.63
1 Case (12 lb.)	Coffee	1.12 per lb.	13.44
		Total Cost	1,020.54

Ordered by: (chef's Signature)

Issued by: (Receiving Clerk's Signature)

Date: (March 19, 19—)

Chart 16-2 Food Requisition Form

General accounting theory recommends that you value your inventory conservatively. According to accounting theory, you do not want a high price on your balance sheet for your inventory because if in the unlikely event that you were to try to sell your inventory supplies as anything except food served in your food service operation, they would not be worth much.

Accounting procedures generally tell you that:

1. Any adjustments in cost should be included in current costs.
2. You want your current cost always to reflect the high cost of doing business.
3. You want your inventory stated conservatively.

The most commonly used method of valuation in food service establishments is to use any price you know or have a record of or can find out.

If you are a typical food service operator, the value of your inventory is relatively low in relation to the volume of business your operation does, and your inventory will consist of a wide variety of items. You may have many dollars represented in your total inventory, but you do not usually have a large dollar amount tied up in any one category of items, except some entrees.

You have to decide (probably by trying different methods) which method of inventory valuation will work for you and use it consistently. The Actual Cost method below is best for most food operations. You can find details in most elementary accounting books about methods for inventory valuation.

There are several ways to valuate (put a value on) your inventory:

Actual Cost

Actual cost is always correct. Use it if you can. The only time you would ever use anything else is if you cannot find out what the actual cost is and have to resort to the other methods described below. Actual cost is the recommended method. You should already have marked the actual cost on the item before you store it so you have the exact actual cost right there when you want it for valuation purposes and for requisitions.

First In First Out (FIFO)

You use prices of your newest, most recently acquired items for inventory valuation. (Charge your oldest price to your current food cost.) Value inventory at your newest price. This is the least conservative approach to inventory valuation on your balance sheet in times of rising prices.

Last In First Out (LIFO)

Use prices of your oldest items for inventory valuation. (Charge newest price to your current food cost.) Value inventory at your oldest, earliest price. This gives you a more conservative valuation for inventory on your balance sheet in times of rising prices.

Lower of Cost or Market

You use the lowest figure you can get for inventory valuation. Use the cost figure or the market figure—whichever is lower. Cost figure means the price you really paid. Market figure means the current market price you would pay if you bought the item today. The inventory states the lowest price, whether it is your cost price or the current market price. (Charge the highest possible cost to current food cost.) This is the most conservative approach to inventory valuation on your balance sheet.

Perpetual Inventory

We have not mentioned perpetual inventory as a means of storeroom inventory valuation, and there is a reason why we have ignored it. Perpetual inventory is not generally recommended for handling foods. Perpetual inventory means you constantly keep records up-to-date throughout the entire month for the number of items you have on hand and for the dollar value of all items you have on hand.

Food service establishments usually handle a very large variety of items. The work of maintaining a perpetual inventory in a food establishment would cost quite a bit in time and money. Perpetual inventory *is* recommended, however, for liquor operations and for handling liquor.

Perpetual inventory is used by warehouses and others who have to maintain a constant, totally accurate count of items on hand and their dollar value. But items in warehouses are in case lots, which makes it much easier for warehouse personnel to maintain perpetual inventory than it would be for the average food establishment personnel to do so.

Perpetual Inventory on High Cost Items

A lot of food service operations can, however, use a modified version of a perpetual inventory just on high cost items—just for meat, for example. Say that you buy 12-ounce strip steaks. You count the number of steaks you have on hand. Add this figure to the number of steaks you receive. This is your new total on hand. From this total you subtract the number you issue to the cook. This should give you your ending inventory of the number of steaks you have on hand. Do this every day. Instead of trying to keep track of all items in the storeroom in terms of dollars, you just keep track of selected items by item count, not dollars.

Cooks in the production area can follow the same routine. They count the steaks on hand at the beginning of each day and add the number of steaks issued to them. This is the total number they have available. After a meal period they count the number of steaks left to find out how many steaks were used. You compare the total number of steaks used with the number of steaks actually sold. Get the figure for the number of steaks actually sold from your sales analysis (which we will discuss in Chapter 20).

It is easier to establish perpetual inventory on certain selected items. It may get you the information you want with considerable savings in time and effort on the part of your employees. Except for certain high-cost items (like meat and liquor) where perpetual inventory may be feasible and desirable, it is usually not recommended for food service operations.

Tag System

Another version of perpetual inventory and storeroom control technique is a tag system. It is only worth using on highest-cost items. You attach a two-section tag to a 12-pound loin of pork, for example, when you receive it. You fill in both sections of the tag, writing "One 12-pound loin of pork received," and total cost and date received. You tear off the bottom half of the tag and send it to your accounting office or food controller. The half-section tag remains on the meat until the whole 12-pound loin has been requisitioned. (There may be partial requisitioning.) When the meat is completely requisitioned, the second portion of the tag, which has been attached to the meat, is forwarded to the accounting office or food controller. The two sections of the tag are compared. At this time, the meat is charged to cost.

The tag system is generally not recommended. It is too involved for the benefit you get from it. You should be aware of it, however, because you might want to adapt it to your operation.

Daily Storeroom Inventory Control (See Chart 9-2, Chapter 9)

You should establish and maintain a daily control for your storeroom in dollar amounts. The formulas for doing this are:

1. OPENING FOOD INVENTORY BEGINNING OF DAY DATE 1 plus STOREROOM PURCHASES DATE 1 equals TOTAL FOOD AVAILABLE STOREROOM DATE 1.

2. TOTAL FOOD AVAILABLE STOREROOM DATE 1 minus FOOD REQUISITIONS DATE 1 equals OPENING FOOD INVENTORY BEGINNING OF DAY DATE 2.

In Chapter 9 on food cost formulas, Chart 9-2, look at Column 3 Opening Food Inventory Beginning of Day Date 1. The amount is $1,985.07. Add Column 4 Storeroom Purchases Date 1 $319.67. This is your Column 5 Total Food Available Storeroom figure for Date 1—$2,304.74. This Column 5 figure is the dollar amount of food in your storeroom for Date 1.

From this Column 5 Total Food Available Storeroom Date 1 figure $2,304.74 you subtract Column 6 Food Requisitions Date 1 $327.15 (dollar value of all items requisitioned during the course of Date 1). This gives you Column 3 Opening Food Inventory Beginning of Day Date 2—$1,977.59. Opening Food Inventory Beginning of Day Date 2 is the closing inventory figure for Date 1. Follow this procedure every day for the rest of the month.

At the end of the month, take a physical inventory. Compare the results of your physical inventory of what *really* is on hand in your storeroom with the results of your computed dollar amount of inventory (bottom figure in Column 3, Chart 9-2).

In Chart 9-2, we started with a Column 3 Opening Food Inventory Beginning of Day Date 1 figure of $1,985.07. Add Column 4 Storeroom Purchases Total for Month (bottom figure Column 4)—$13,181.39. You get $15,166.46. This is Total Food Available Storeroom for the Month. (The $15,166.46 is not on the chart.)

Subtract Column 6 Food Requisitions Total for Month (bottom figure Column 6) $13,249.69 from the $15,166.46. You get $1,916.77. This is the figure at the bottom of Column 3 Opening Food Inventory Beginning of Day.

The actual physical inventory figure you get from actually counting and making extensions of the items in the storeroom should be very close to this $1,916.77 figure. Ideally, it should be within one percent of this amount—either above or below. If it is within one percent for this example in Chart 9-2, the range for inventory could be from $1,897.77 to $1,935.77. ($1,916.77 plus or minus 1 percent—$19.00.)

Why Physical Inventory and Calculated Inventories May Not be the Same

The following factors can cause the dollar amount figures for physical inventory and calculated inventory to differ from each other:

1. Requisitions were not completed (most common cause).
2. You received some items but failed to add them into your "storeroom purchases" record.
3. Items were stolen from the storeroom and obviously not recorded.

Theft is a possibility. If it did occur, obviously you have inadequate storeroom procedures.

If your physical inventory figure and your calculated inventory figure are not within one percent of each other, find out why. Check into the three possible reasons listed above. Make sure storeroom purchases are recorded in storeroom purchases records. Make sure requisitions are filled out and nothing leaves the storeroom without a requisition. Make sure only authorized individuals are allowed in and out of your storeroom. If other efforts to correct the situation do not work, put different employees in charge of your storeroom.

Minimize and Organize Storage

Minimize what you keep on hand in your storeroom. You have to have items you need to use to carry on your business and you have to have enough in storage so that running out of items doesn't interrupt your business. But don't store more than you really need. It is not necessary and it is expensive in terms of the space and capital which storage ties up. Carrying too much in storage is inventory speculation and it's not a good idea for a food service operator. The volume of business your establishment is doing should be your major criterion for deciding on quantities of items you should store. And, of course, you may be restricted by the amount of storage space you have. The main thing is to try to get proper storage space and organize it so you have enough goods on hand to take care of your volume of business.

When your goods have been properly recorded, organized, and stored in the storeroom, they are ready to be issued from the storeroom for use in food production.

REVIEW AND DISCUSSION QUESTIONS

1. Why should you have storeroom control?
2. Why is pest control especially important for storerooms?
3. What types of storage space are apt to be needed by most food and beverage establishments?
4. What are the methods for valuing inventory?
5. How can you compute a dollar value for what ending inventory should be?
6. Why is storeroom layout important?
7. What kind of problems could you experience if you have too much or too little in the food storeroom?
8. What problems can you encounter if you do not mark the cost of items on the items in the storeroom?
9. Why is perpetual inventory not generally recommended for the food in the storeroom?

17

Food Production Control

Objectives

This chapter concerns planning food production and minimizing overproduction and underproduction. After you have read this chapter, you should know:

1. How to write your own standardized recipes and how to use them.
2. Various ways to do portion control.
3. How to plan and schedule your food production.

A major key to successful food production (or anything else in the food service industry) is good organization. Proper organization makes food production easier and more efficient. Over the past 20 years there has been a definite change in kitchen organization.

In the past, large establishments had "executive" chefs and smaller establishments had "working" chefs in charge of running their kitchens. In recent years there has been a trend toward having a "food production supervisor" run the kitchen, particularly in institutional food service.

Old-time chefs were skilled craftspeople. They had eventually worked into jobs as kitchen chefs because they knew how to prepare all the items the establishment wanted prepared. Today's food production supervisors may be individuals who have only limited knowledge of food preparation and cooking but who know techniques of management. They use management skills to schedule and plan work in the kitchen.

No matter who runs your food production—executive chef, old-time general cook, food supervisor—your food production department must be well organized. The chain of command should be carefully planned by you and the head of your food production department. Authority and responsibilities should be clearly defined so all kitchen personnel understand their duties and know who their immediate superior is.

We looked at organization charts for different types of food service operations in Chapter 2. You will have to make up and use your own organization chart. You will not find charts ready-made anywhere that will precisely suit your own food service operation. The charts in Chapter 2 should give you ideas about how to set up your own chain of command system. Do set up an organization structure and chain of command and make sure everyone understands it. It is important that your employees know whose directions they should follow.

Today the trend is toward simpler menus, as we discussed in Chapter 10. Many cooks are not as skilled now in all aspects of food preparation as cooks were a few years ago. They don't have to be, but they must be able to do a good job of preparing the items the food service operation will sell.

The degrees of skill necessary for cooks will vary from one food service operation to another. In an operation that uses a lot of convenience foods, or foods prepared in a commissary, cooks will not have to be as skilled as they would in food service establishments that prepare all of their own food items from scratch. When you plan your own menus and food production, don't lose sight of what type and degree of cooking skill your cooks will need to do the job.

The most important rule to remember in food production is: *if you want good food to come out of your kitchen, you have to buy good food to begin with.* We talked about purchasing in Chapter 14, and emphasized that you should purchase for use. The production area is where food items are actually prepared and produced. The items you buy and use should be of the correct quality for the foods you want prepared and appropriate for your own recipes.

RECIPES AND FOOD

Standardized Recipes

During recent years many articles have appeared in food industry trade journals on the importance of standardized recipes. Standardized recipes are an extremely important tool you should use in your food production control. Virtually all food service operations can use standardized recipes and/or standardized procedures in food production.

Get recipes from any source you wish—quantity cook books, cook books for the home, magazines—and make them "standardized" yourself. A "standardized recipe" just means a recipe that you have worked out and set up formally in terms of yield and quality for your own establishment. When you have your recipes standardized, your cooks should stick to them exactly unless you and they working together decide you ought to adjust them. If you do change them, then stick to the new ones exactly.

A standardized recipe should list:

1. All ingredients, including spices.
2. Exact quantities of everything (except spices, for which approximate amounts will suffice).
3. Methods of preparation for everything.
4. Size of portions.
5. Total number of portions to be obtained from recipe.

The names of all spices should be included in each recipe, but it is probably a good idea to list just approximate amounts of them. Cooks *should* taste foods as they are preparing them and adjust final seasonings to taste. Strength and flavor of spices can vary with brand and age. For example, a new beef base for soup could be saltier than the previous brand. If cooks do not taste the soup but just add the same amount of salt called for in the standardized recipe, the soup may be too salty. Your standardized recipes should be flexible when it comes to amounts of spices. Final seasoning of all foods should be done to taste.

Write All Recipes Down, Standardize Them, and Follow Them

Some old-time chefs can present problems if they will not be flexible in cooking methods. You might even find one who will refuse to reveal "secrets" about a favorite recipe. You certainly cannot standardize a recipe if you cannot even start by writing it down accurately. Maybe you can work diplomatically with chefs like this. You will have to convince them it's important that you know each recipe. If you can't convince chefs that you've got to have standardized recipes written down and followed for all the foods they prepare, you may have to find new chefs.

One big advantage in having standardized recipes is that it permits you to train new cooks in exactly how you want items prepared. If you don't have standardized recipes, cooks will probably prepare items the way they did in the last place they worked. Maybe the food will be better than your own recipe produces. Maybe it will be worse. The point is, *you* should control the recipes so your food is consistently good and you know what it costs.

Make sure your recipes do produce good food. Your establishment's recipes should be followed accurately and should produce the quality you want. Some dishes (such as Beef Stroganoff, for example) can be prepared many different ways by different food service operations across this country— and across the world, for that matter—but everyone still calls the dish "Beef Stroganoff" (or a translation thereof). It is important to you that any cook in your food operation, including a new one, should prepare it exactly the way you want it prepared and use exactly the ingredients you want used. Use standardized recipes and make sure they're followed.

To illustrate this point, let us say that one day your relief cook makes your cream soup for the first time. You taste it and you don't like it; it's not nearly as good as it is when your regular cook makes it. You complain to the relief cook, "What's the matter with the soup? Did you follow the recipe? This sure doesn't taste like it does when the regular cook makes it." Your relief cook answers, "No, it sure doesn't. I followed the standardized recipe exactly. I just used milk like the recipe says. The regular cook always uses real cream." Of course the regular cook's soup tastes better! It tastes better but it is costing you more to make it than you had planned and set a cost for. If you are not aware of the higher food cost cooks can cause by altering standardized recipes and if you don't charge your customers more for soup made with cream instead of milk, it will definitely raise your food cost and cut your profit for the soup.

You definitely need standardized recipes and they have to be followed. Soup is, of course, just one item—just one very small example of what we are talking about. Consider the large number of food items you produce and sell every day, week, month, year. Slight changes made in recipes without your knowledge or your planning in controlling costs and setting prices can mount into tremendous increases in your costs.

To return to our soup example, go ahead and use cream if you want to. Put cream in your standardized recipe. Plan on it, cost it, and price the soup so guests pay accordingly. The point is, base your costs and your selling prices on your standardized recipes, have good recipes, and make sure the recipes really are followed.

One main reason why standardized recipes are recommended is that they list all ingredients and quantities, which means you can figure the cost. To find out what each portion you produce is costing you, divide the total cost of the ingredients by the number of portions the recipe yields.

A standardized recipe should also give very clear directions for preparation and should spell out cooking methods. It should state amounts of all ingredients and how the item is to be put together and prepared—braised, broiled, boiled, simmered. It should give temperatures, times, and anything that needs to be done while the food is cooking (cover it, uncover it, add water, stir). It is important to make all preparation and cooking directions detailed and explicit so they are easy to use and a substitute cook can use them with no trouble. If meat should be boiled vigorously, for example, or simmered gently, a recipe should say so. For just one example, meat boiled vigorously will not be as tender as the same meat slowly simmered. High heat causes connective tissue in meat to contract quickly. Slow simmering causes a gradual breakdown of connective tissue. Different meat products with different uses and different yields result from different cooking methods. Your standardized recipe should give very detailed and specific instructions so you get just the result and the quantity and quality you want.

Occasionally there will be mistakes in the written standardized recipes. Or perhaps the recipe was written correctly but your cooks think it could be improved with different ingredients or quantities or cooking methods. Cooks should call these things to the attention of your food production supervisor. They should change and correct a recipe together. The food supervisor should be aware of any resulting changes in the cost of the item and should tell you so you can adjust the menu price if necessary. If a standardized recipe is altered in any way, you must know so you can alter your costing and pricing accordingly.

Hot Foods

It is not enough just to prepare food properly. You must provide proper care and safe sanitation procedures for the food after it has been prepared and while it is waiting to be served to guests. Hot foods should be kept constantly hot and cold foods constantly cold—right up to the moment the guests eat them. Sometimes guests probably wonder whether their food is meant to be hot or cold. Often it is in between and not appetizing.

Hot foods that are not served immediately after preparation should be kept in a steam table or in a bain marie (a pan resting in hot water) or under infrared lights. The steam table can be heated by either moist heat or dry heat, whichever you prefer for your own food service operation.

The temperature at which hot foods are held is very important. Hot foods *must* be held at temperatures *above* 140 degrees Fahrenheit. At temperatures above 140 degrees, most harmful food organisms will be killed. At temperatures from 140 degrees down to 50 degrees, harmful organisms can grow. To prevent serious germ growth and possible danger to guests, you've *got* to keep hot food at a temperature above 140 degrees Fahrenheit. Foods being kept in the steam table should be checked periodically with a thermometer. Buy thermometers from your local food service equipment dealer.

Employees should regularly check the temperatures of foods with ther-mometers and make sure correct heat is *always* maintained.

Aside from the very important factor of germ control, the tempera-ture of hot food is also an important factor in taste and appeal to your guests. If food is supposed to be hot, guests want it *hot.* Taste studies have shown that when the temperature of hot food falls below 120 degrees Fahrenheit, guests consider the food cold and distasteful. It is extremely difficult to get food to the guest while it's still at a temperature of at least 120 degrees if the steam table is holding the food at only 120 degrees or less.

Holding Foods

Frequently you will have foods cooked and all ready to be eaten but will have to keep them ready until someone orders them. Some foods hold up better than others if there is a delay. In general, the less time any food item is held, the better it will be. Ideally, a steak should be taken off the broiler, put right onto a plate, and served to the guest immediately. Creamed items (like chicken a la king) may have to be held in the steam table.

Many foods do not hold up well at all if they are not eaten soon. Green frozen vegetables tend to break down and lose their color if you keep them in the steam table longer than half an hour. Try to cook small batches of green vegetables at a time and avoid keeping them in the steam table very long.

Proper planning by the cooks can help prevent the necessity of holding foods too long. Instead of one pan or pot for cooking vegetables, they should use two or three. As they take one small cooked batch off the stove, they should put another batch on to assure a small but continuous supply. They should also have two containers for the steam table so they do not mix freshly-cooked green vegetables in with green vegetables that have been held in the steam table for even a short time. There is a noticeable color difference when freshly-cooked green vegetables are mixed in with the old. First use all the food already in the steam table. Then put in the food just cooked. From a sanitation standpoint, this is a good idea for all cooked foods that are held for a time—not just green vegetables.

Cold Foods

We have said it's important for you to keep hot food hot. That's the way guests want it. And it minimizes the danger of organism growth. These same factors apply to cold foods. Keep cold food cold because that's the way guests want it. And really cold temperatures, too, can reduce the danger of or-ganism growth. Ideally, cold food should be served at a temperature of about 40 degrees Fahrenheit. Salads should not be much colder than that, though, or they can freeze. If you hold cold foods at temperatures below 50 degrees, it retards the growth of organisms.

Cold foods should be served cold and they should be served on cold plates. Salads put on plates still hot from the dishwater can turn soggy. Ice cream or jello put on plates still hot from the dishwasher can turn into disasters.

Put plates for cold food in a refrigerator ahead of time—overnight if you can—so they are really chilled. Many food service operations that feature self-service salad bars have special refrigeration units right at the salad bar for chilling plates. Some of these units keep plates so cold that they almost hurt the hands. That's good and cold! Salads and other cold foods are much better if they are served on cold plates.

Portion Control

"Portion control" is everything you do to control the exact size of a portion. There are three ways of doing portion control. They are:

1. Buy items already pre-portioned.
2. Buy items in bulk and portion them yourself ahead of serving time.
3. Portion items at the last minute as you serve them.

Buy Items Already Pre-Portioned

More and more food service operations are buying and using pre-portioned items. Meat is one item classification where this is especially true. You can buy steaks pre-cut to size, hamburger patties pre-formed, cheese pre-sliced, and so on. This assures uniform portion size to every guest. The advantage with this method is that your portioning has already been done for you.

Buy Items in Bulk and Portion Them Yourself Ahead of Serving Time

Many food service operations buy items—some meat items, for example—that have not already been pre-portioned. They do their own precise portioning.

Here is one rather small example of how individual pre-portioning can work for you. Assume that you sell corned beef sandwiches. First you decide how many ounces of corned beef you will put in each sandwich. Should you use one ounce, one and a half ounces, two ounces, three ounces? Decide definitely before you ever make the first corned beef sandwich. The amount of corned beef you put into each sandwich will definitely affect the price you should charge for each sandwich. (So will the type of bread you use and whatever else you use to finish and garnish the sandwich.) Let us assume you will sell a lot of corned beef sandwiches at lunch every day. In many food operations corned beef is just sliced and given to the sandwich maker, who grabs handfuls of corned beef and slaps it between two slices of bread during busy lunch periods. If this is what happens, no one really knows how much corned beef is put into each sandwich. Sandwich makers probably won't have time to weigh every portion of corned beef during the lunch hour. They are almost sure to be too busy. The sandwich makers try to portion by judging the amount by eye and by feel. But this certainly is not exact portioning. Amounts actually used will vary, and your costs will vary, too.

Do the following instead. During pre-preparation and set-up time, have your kitchen personnel weigh each portion of corned beef on a portion scale, making up individual portions according to the weight you have decided you want in each sandwich. After the corned beef has been weighed, each portion should be separated by hamburger patty papers. Have stacks of weighed individual portions—one portion for each sandwich—ready to go before lunch. Cover the entire pan with a plastic sheet to keep the corned beef from drying out in the refrigerator. When the lunch rush comes, sandwich makers grab a patty paper with pre-portioned corned beef, put the meat between two slices of bread, and finish the sandwich. This method controls the amount of corned beef used in each sandwich. It is faster, too. If you *don't* do this pre-portioning and your sandwich makers grab corned beef by the handfuls, they will probably try consciously or unconsciously to do some judging of amounts on their own as they go—but their well-intentioned efforts will probably just slow them down and decrease their efficiency during peak busy periods.

You don't just pre-portion corned beef, of course. You do the same pre-weighing and individual pre-portioning with all the cold sandwich meats you can (ham, roast beef, turkey). Your own portion control and pre-portioning system is most vital to you if you buy items that do not come already portioned. Then be sure to weigh or measure and make up individual portions ahead of time where feasible.

We've just given one example for meat. Use the same *idea* everywhere you can, not just for meats.

You Portion Items at the Last Minute as You Serve Them

Teach your employees how to use portion control. Say you want a three-ounce portion of peas. This may mean something very clear to you, but it may not mean a thing to your employees if they don't know how big or small a three-ounce portion of peas really is. Weigh out a three-ounce portion of peas and show it to your employees so they know how much it is before they start dishing up portions. During busy times, employees cannot stop and weigh each three-ounce portion of peas, but if they have a mental picture of how large a portion three ounces is, they can come closer to serving that amount.

Use the same idea for other vegetables and items you want served. Make up samples so employees know what size portions they should be serving. Have employees use all the measuring devices you can think of—cups, ladles, scoops. And have them judge by eye how much of the dish used should be filled by the portion size wanted.

Some operations get an instant color camera and take photographs of various items on their menus, such as a shrimp salad plate, a fruit plate, a roast beef dinner. The pictures are posted near the appropriate stations and used as guides by employees so they know what their finished product should look like in general appearance and quantities of items. It is still very true that a picture is worth a thousand words. Pictures can help give employees ideas about appropriate portion sizes.

For meat items, keep a portion scale at the carving station so meat portions can easily be weighed as they are sliced. It may not be feasible to weigh every portion of meat, but a spot check of every third portion or so will help keep the carvers accurate in their portioning. For meat, you should:

1. Slice it.
2. Weigh it.
3. Serve it.

It would be ideal if you could weigh each portion. For example, consider the standing rib roast. If your meat carver slices a portion too thick, the guest who eats the oversized portion pays the regular price. The meat carver may try to make up for the extra thick cut by cutting the next one too thin, and the guest who gets the skimpy portion also pays the regular price. Portions should be the same size and price for all guests (children, women, men) unless guests specifically request small or large cuts and pay accordingly. Many operations list different size portions of items at different prices on their menus. This is the *only* case where different portion sizes are acceptable.

Use portion control wherever you can. Meat is a high-cost item so be particularly sure you pre-portion it wherever possible. Establish portion sizes and show employees what you want ahead of time. Use a size ladle for soups, sauces, and so on—one ladle equals the portion you want. Use sized ice cream scoops for ice cream (number 20, 16, 12, depending on the size portion you want). Scoops can also be used for meatballs and croquettes. They help to pre-portion as well as speed up production. Determine how many portions you want from a pie—six, seven, eight. Determine all of these things ahead of time. Make charts of portion sizes and post them at appropriate stations so employees can see them, know them, and follow them.

Portion control should be an integral part of food production. You are making sure that you are not serving too little and upsetting guests or too much and upsetting your costs.

PLANNING FOR PRODUCTION

In Chapter 11 on pre-control and pre-costing the menu, we discussed forecasting for production. Here is where you use that forecast (Chart 11-4 Forecast of Items Will Sell) in your daily food production planning. Food production supervisors should use the forecast when they tell cooks what amounts of items to prepare.

Many items are prepared to order in food service operations today, so you probably should not have as many problems with leftovers as food service operations had in the past. Today most luncheon menus offer many sandwiches and the ingredients for these can usually be used tomorrow if you don't use them today. But even in the case of comparatively simple sandwich production, if you forecast and estimate the quantities you will need in advance, it can help you avoid problems.

For example, if homemade soup is on the menu, you or your kitchen supervisor should decide—basing the decision on your forecast—how much soup to prepare. Don't leave it up to your cooks to make whatever amount of soup they think you will need. Do estimate sales and see that the kitchen staff makes the amount you have estimated you will need. You may be one of the unfortunates who has cooks who make three gallons of soup because when they reach up to the rack to get soup pots they happen to grab the three-gallon pots instead of a different size. Yes, that sounds nutty. It is. But it happens. Your whole food production can evolve out of an astounding variety of assorted nuttinesses you will never know a thing about if you don't take charge. See to it that your total food production evolves from reasons *you* decide on. Keep on checking up and keep on enforcing your decisions. You and your supervisors should be aware of what is going on in all departments.

All production should be geared according to the sales you have estimated. Steaks should be cooked to order. But how many steaks should be pulled from the freezer? With good refrigeration, a thawed steak can be held for several days. But in a lot of food operations, stew (or a fancy name for stew) appears for sale unplanned in order to use up steak meat before it goes bad—simply because someone pulled too many steaks from the freezer without planning ahead or using a valid forecast of sales.

Each department head in the kitchen should have some say in preparing work schedules for his or her own department. Work with your head pantry person, your head fry cook, your head roast cook. Help each figure out a schedule that is workable and satisfactory for her or his own staff—all depending again on how big or small your own operation is.

Use a Production Schedule Sheet

The process of preparing a work schedule sheet forces your supervisors to think ahead of time about the work that needs to be done in their departments. Ideally, your production work schedule should be made out the day before the items are to be produced to facilitate delivery of items from the storeroom and to simplify the day's production. As employees report for work, all the items they will need that day should have been brought to their work stations by storeroom clerks, as we discussed in chapter 16. Ideally, they can start right in on production because they know what to prepare, how to prepare it, and how much to prepare. They will know what to make and how much to prepare because the food production schedule sheets for the day should already be posted in the kitchen. If the items they are to prepare call for standardized recipes (and most items should), copies of the standardized recipes they will need should be posted for them to use.

Many food service operations (particularly institutional food service operations, such as hospitals or college food services) find it a good idea to prepare production work schedules a week ahead of time. They buy very large quantities of certain items and use the production work schedules as guides in purchasing these items.

Food production schedule sheets can be very complex or quite simple. Make yours according to your needs, but be sure you do the following three things:

1. Make them up ahead of time.
2. Always put them in writing.
3. Write them so they are easy to read and easy to understand.

Employees should be able to read posted production schedules immediately when they come to work. They should know right away what foods they should prepare and be able to go right ahead and prepare them without confusion or questions.

How to Prepare a Food Production Schedule in Portions (Chart 17-1)

The key to food production control planning and organization is the food production schedule sheet (also called a cook's worksheet). Chart 17-1 includes only entrees, so this chart would be used only by a department that prepares entrees. You would need a chart every day for all other production departments in the kitchen, too—salad, vegetables, desserts—depending on the size and complexity of your operation. These charts should be prepared by the kitchen supervisor for each day. You may want to add additional columns for directions for your employees, such as how much meat to thaw, which standardized recipe to follow, and so on.

Chart 17-1 is an example of a food production schedule sheet in portions. This sample chart lists entrees on the menu for the day. It gives a breakdown of entrees and quantities to be prepared.

1. Column 1: Item.
   These entree items are taken directly from your menu for the day. In this entree chart, menu items include items which were purchased already pre-prepared or which were pre-portioned and cooked to order.
2. Column 2: Forecast in Portions.
   This column tells the entree cooks how many portions of each item they should prepare. This information comes from your forecast sheet (Chapter 11, Chart 11-4).
3. Column 3: Original Amount to Prepare in Portions.
   This is the amount forecasted. This column tells cooks how many portions

1	2	3	4	5	6	7
Item	Forecast in Portions	Original Amt. to Prepare in Portions	Additional Amount Prepared	Total Preparation in Portions	Sales	Left Over
Stuffed Breast of Chicken	50	50	3	53	53	O
New York Strip	80	80	—	77	77	3
Club Steak	50	46	—	46	46	4
Prime Rib	60	3 roasts 60 lbs. Total	—	60	45	15 lbs.
Chopped Steak	25	25	10	35	34	1
Combination Steak & Shrimp	60	60	—	60	60	—
Trout	15	15	4	19	19	—
Beef Brochette	25	Marinated 25 portions	—	25	24	1 portion
Stuffed Shrimp	60	60	—	54	54	6

Meal: *Dinner*   Day: Date:

Chart 17-1   Food Production Schedule Sheet in Portions Cook's Worksheet.

to make. In the chart, this column tells them to roast 60 pounds of prime rib and marinate 25 portions of beef brochettes. It also tells them the number of portions of all other meat items to prepare.

4. Column 4: Additional Amount Prepared.
   This column shows how many extra portions were prepared beyond those forecasted (Column 2) and originally prepared (Column 3).

5. Column 5: Total Preparation in Portions.
   This column lists the number of portions cooked or cooked to order. It is the total of Columns 3 and 4. Note: Club steak is less than the 50 forecasted. But club steak should be cooked to order, so you should not have leftovers.

6. Column 6: Sales.
   This shows how many portions you sold. Fill this column in after the meal period has ended.

7. Column 7: Left Over.
   This column is used to list any items left over. This shows you how accurately you forecasted.

FOOD PRODUCTION TIPS

Garnish

After food has been prepared, it is, as we have said, important to serve it hot if it should be hot or cold if it should be cold. It should be attractive in every way. Aim to make it the best food your total operation can produce. Be sure food is appropriately and properly garnished. Garnish can be the plus that makes an average dish more attractive, and it is important that food be attractively presented. People *do* "eat with their eyes."

There are other garnishes besides parsley. Use them. For example, use spiced crabapples, different kinds of pickles (not *just* pickle chips), a vegetable relish, kumquats, and so on. Use imagination and create unique, tasty, different types of garnishes. The cost of the garnish can be more than offset by good revenue. If you present an item attractively, it may be reasonable for you to charge a higher price.

Serve Promptly

After the food has been prepared, it should be held correctly and served as soon as possible. Prompt service is important. Make sure your waiters or waitresses get the food as soon as they can after it is ready and take it to your guests as fast as possible. Many food service operations have installed infrared spotlight "holding areas" to keep food hot in case the service personnel are delayed in the dining room and cannot get the food quickly when it is ready. Some operations have installed bell systems, light systems, or pocket buzzers to notify service personnel that their orders are ready.

Avoid Squabbles

It is extremely important that you achieve good coordination and cooperation between your production personnel (cooks) and your service personnel (waitresses and waiters). Both jobs exist only to serve the needs of your customers. This fundamental fact is often forgotten. If you permit squabbles to go on between cooks and service persons (or among any employees), it can do a great deal of damage to your whole establishment. It is part of your job to help personnel work together as an efficient team. It is up to you to convince bickering employees that they must help each other. If you can't and they won't, it is up to you to create a harmonious crew by rescheduling or replacing employees so they will work together successfully.

Service people do get mad at grumpy customers. Cooks do get hot, tired, and disgusted. When furious waiters or waitresses dash to the kitchen and demand special orders of meticulously prepared fried eggs from hot, tired, disgusted cooks for the satisfaction of cranky guests, it is usually up to you, the furious, hot, tired, disgusted, cranky manager to soothe everyone involved. Do everything in your power ahead of time to avoid the reasons for cook-waiter/waitress-customer explosions.

Special Requests

There is one fairly common occurrence that can create dissension among your staff. It is when guests order items that are not on the menu or ask to have something prepared differently from the way it is listed on the menu. Pre-planning can help you here. You should realize ahead of time that your staff *will* get outlandish requests for food. Guests *will* order unusual foods cooked in peculiar ways. You and your staff should know these things will happen and be ready to handle them.

Working with your staff, establish guidelines ahead of time concerning what types of requests will be refused and what types will be fulfilled. Set up clear policies on these matters and make sure your entire staff knows them. Make your policies feasible for your staff to follow and as satisfactory for your guests as you can. If unusual requests can be handled without disrupting total service, they should usually be fulfilled. Give satisfactory service and make special allowances in your procedures to please individual guests to as great an extent as you possibly can. But make these decisions ahead of time and make them jointly with your staff so they know what will be or will not be expected of them.

Once in a great while you may get an extremely inconvenient request from a guest which you *should* fulfill, although it is not feasible and it does interrupt production. The following true story illustrates this. In a large nightclub many years ago, a nationally known newspaper columnist ordered ham and eggs and fried potatoes for dinner. Ham and eggs and fried potatoes were not on the menu. The nightclub was right in the midst of one of its most frantically busy nights of the whole year. But the order was filled. The columnist was pleased and appreciated the special service. He was so pleased, in fact, that he mentioned the incident and the name of the nightclub in his column. The nightclub received some totally unexpected and very nice publicity. The reward for performing beyond the normal bounds of duty was repaid 1,000 percent in this particular case. Usually there will be no reward except one ordinary customer who got what he or she wanted. But do use discretion. Special cases should get special reactions. All customers (not just famous ones) should receive the very best service you can muster. And there may be rare and special occasions when you should be prepared to do the impossible—and not just for "important" guests.

SUMMARY

Production work schedules can help you avoid problems. They are an important and useful tool. You should try to achieve the quality of food and service you want by improved supervision and increased cooperation between departments.

Written work production schedules can be a big help here. Food should be prepared according to predetermined standards. It is up to you to decide exactly what these standards will be and up to you, in the final analysis, to see that they are met and maintained.

Overproduction and underproduction need to be evaluated in terms of satisfying guests. At the same time, you must keep your costs of operation in mind so you get the food cost you want. You have to try to arrange for satisfactory solutions (in advance) for problems of overproduction and underproduction. You have to keep customers satisfied and arriving in large enough numbers at your food service operation. You have to teach, cajole, direct, motivate, wheedle, encourage, threaten, inspire, and kid your staff into becoming an efficient team. And, while you do all this (plus a thousand other things), you must also get the food cost and profit you want. As we will discuss in the following chapter, you have to see that the food is courteously and correctly served, too. It's a handful.

REVIEW AND DISCUSSION QUESTIONS

1. What should a standardized recipe include?
2. Why are the temperatures at which you hold foods important?
3. Why should a kitchen supervisor prepare and use a food production schedule sheet?
4. What portion control methods were discussed in this chapter? What other portion control methods could food service operations use?
5. Under what circumstances should your food service operation prepare special requests for foods?

18

Food Service

Objectives

This chapter discusses the various ways that food is served, and how methods of service vary from one establishment to another. After you have read this chapter, you should know:

1. The different types of service and table settings you can use.

2. Why you should train employees to provide the proper service.

3. Why tips may vary with the way you establish employee stations.

Organize your food service operation so you can serve food properly and promptly after it has been prepared. When food is ready for guests, get it to them quickly. This is especially true of items that are cooked to order. Steaks will get cold and omelets can fall if they aren't served to guests immediately. If food is supposed to be hot, guests don't like it cold and they don't like to wait. Good, quick service is very important.

There are different kinds of service and different types of table settings appropriate for different kinds of food service operations. Simple service and table settings are typical of most food establishments in the United States. Choose personnel and the type of service suitable for your own operation. A coffee shop would not use French service, for example, but a very elaborate and finely appointed restaurant with an expensive à la carte menu certainly might.

The type of service you select should be appropriate for your menu, your atmosphere and the type of guests who patronize your food service operation. The type of service you choose does, in turn, affect your menu and helps create your atmosphere. It is a case where factors influence each other. In general, there is a trend in the United States today toward less elaborate, less expensive, more informal service because currently this seems to be what more guests prefer. The public's attitude about this can vary from time to time and from place to place.

It is difficult to get good service personnel for any type of food operation. If you want elaborate service, be prepared to work hard training and supervising your service personnel. Also, if you use elaborate service, your service personnel will have to serve fewer guests than they could if you used simpler service. It is a question of whether you are qualified and willing to spend the time and money necessary to train your employees to provide elaborate service if that is what you want. It is a question, too, of whether you have (or can find) employees who can or will successfully provide formal service.

Good service is an important factor to guests when they select a place to eat out. In Chapter 10, The Menu, we said that good service means more to guests than price does (within a limited category of competitively priced establishments). But don't confuse good service with elaborate and formal service. Guests want waiters and waitresses who are pleasant and prompt, and who bring them the food and drink they want when they want it. They want attention and courteous concern. They definitely do not want to be ignored. Even when your food service operation is at its very busiest, your personnel should politely acknowledge your guests' presence immediately and assure them that they will receive service as quickly as possible—and then follow up and provide it.

Good service does not mean *fancy* service. If you don't have the facilities or personnel to carry out formal service correctly, don't try. Give good (prompt and courteous) service, whether it is very simple or very elegant.

TYPES OF SERVICE

There are guidelines for service. Usually, forks go to the left of the plate, knives to the right of the plate, and spoons to the right of the knives. Utensils should follow the order in which courses will be served so the guest always takes the fork farthest to the left from the plate or the knife or spoon farthest to the right from the plate in sequence as courses are served.

Another general guideline is that food is usually served from the left and cleared from the right and beverages are usually served from the right. There are exceptions for different types of seating arrangements (booths, counters, and so on). In some of the types of service described below, food is served from right or left depending on the type of service and the course.

Some restaurant dining room layouts make it very difficult to follow one set, traditional way, so use common sense when you train your service people to serve food.

Following is a brief discussion of different types of service used in the United States today. For more details on types of services, *The Essentials of Good Table Service*[1] is highly recommended.

The services to be discussed are:

1. American service.
2. French service.
3. Compromise service.
4. Banquet service.
5. Russian service.
6. English service.
7. Smorgasbord and buffet service.
8. Cafeteria service.
9. Family service.
10. "Hash house" service.

American Service (Chart 18-1)

American service is the type used most in the United States today. Chart 18-1 shows how to set a table for American service.

Table Setting

The knife and spoon are placed to the right of the plate, and one or more forks are placed to the left. Beverage is placed to the top of the plate and

[1]*The Essentials of Good Table Service,* rev. ed. The Cornell Hotel and Restaurant Administration Quarterly. School of Hotel Administration, Cornell University. Ithaca, New York, 1966.

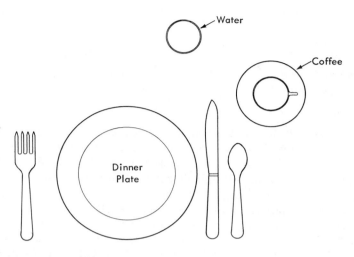

Chart 18-1 American Service

slightly to the right of the center of the plate. The coffee cup usually is pre-set. American service does not normally include a pre-set wine glass. The dinner plate is not pre-set.

Food Handling

The entree is usually dished right onto the plate in the kitchen, and the vegetable and potato are put on the same plate with the entree. Some food service operations put a steak by itself on a steak platter and use a vegetable dish (called a "monkey dish") for each accompanying potato and vegetable. They also use a separate salad plate. In recent years, many operations have omitted vegetables except for potatoes, and main meals usually consist of entree, salad, and potato. The salad is served first. Then the entree and potato are served. The plate is placed in front of the guest from the guest's left and removed from the guest's right. All items are presented to the guest from the guest's left side and removed from the guest's right.

Beverages are usually served from the right. Guests are usually asked if they want coffee with the meal or after it or both. Coffee service varies considerably in different parts of the United States.

Pros and Cons

An advantage of American service is that it is fast, simple, and comparatively inexpensive. If you use this service, you can serve more guests with fewer service personnel than you can with any other type of service. It can be used either at counters (the service person serves the food across the counter) or at tables.

French Service (Chart 18-2)

French service is the most elaborate type of service. It is the most formal, elegant, and expensive, and it is the slowest.

Table Setting

The dessert fork and spoon are pre-set on the table at the top of the plate. All eating utensils are pre-set. Usually the table setting will include one or more pre-set wine glasses, placed to the right of the plate above the knives and spoons. It is assumed with French service that your guests will have wine with their meal. The coffee cup is not pre-set.

A service plate is used in French service. (Russian, compromise, and banquet service may also call for the use of service plates.) The service plate is usually a highly decorated plate on which other plates are placed. That is all it is used for. No one eats from a service plate and no food is put on it. A service plate is pre-set on the table in front of the guest and other plates are placed on top of it.

Chart 18-2   French & Russian Service

Food Handling

For proper French service, food is prepared in the kitchen, placed in silver dishes and covered, and put on a formal serving cart called a *gueridon.* The cart is wheeled into the dining room to the guest's table. The entree is dished from the platter onto the dinner plate at the cart.

If meat is to be carved (Chateaubriand for two, for example), the service person carves it on the cart while the guests watch and puts it on the guests' plates. If there are sauces to be poured over the entree, the service person should have the sauce on the cart in dishes and pour the sauce on the entree while guests watch. Then the service person puts potatoes and other vegetables from other platters on the cart onto the plate and serves the plate containing all the food items to the guest.

In French service, the entree is served from the right, salad is served from the left, and beverages are served from the right.

Entree, vegetables, and salad are usually wheeled to the guest's table on the cart. The service person may perform final steps in preparing some of the food items. Service persons may do some cooking, or flaming, using chafing dishes, for items such as peach flambé or crepe suzettes. They may toss the salad, sautée the mushrooms, and complete the cooking of an entree right at the cart in front of the guest. (Oriental food service operations may also do considerable food preparation at the guest's table, but they seldom use the cart.)

French service involves a lot of showmanship in the actual serving of the food. Service personnel may do quite a bit of work—carve meat, pour sauces, cut bread, flame special dishes or desserts—at the cart at the guest's table in the dining room and serve the plate to the guest with flourishes.

Wine would be served from the right, after the entree has been served. In French service it is not uncommon to have two main courses—a fish course and a meat course. White wine is traditionally served with a fish course. Red wine is traditionally served with a meat course if the meat course is a red meat. (See Chapter 24 on wine and beer for some comments about wine traditions.)

Coffee would be served at the end of the meal. First the table is cleared and then, with very formal service, the table is "crumbed." An empty cup and saucer are placed in front of the guest. The coffee may be served first, or the dessert may be served first. It varies. With formal French service, coffee is poured into the cup from a silver pot.

Pros and Cons

Real French service is usually much slower than other types of service. It is more expensive from a payroll standpoint. Service persons are actively involved in formally presenting (and perhaps partly preparing) food, and this takes time (as well as skill). They cannot serve many guests.

French service takes more time and it also requires more floor space. You have to have room between the tables for service personnel to maneuver the carts through the dining room and set up near the guest's table and serve the dinner. If you use French service, the total seating capacity of your dining room will therefore be less than it would with other types of service. With French service, it is not uncommon for each service person's station to consist of just eight guests—probably two tables of four, or a table of four and two tables of two. With American service you can probably plan a station of 16 guests for each service person.

French service is elegant and expensive in personnel and equipment. It is suitable for luxury operations where costs can be covered.

Compromise Service

This is a variation of American service. It is called "compromise" because it brings in an element of French service—a service cart.

Table Setting

Same as for American service.

Food Handling

Same as American service except that the service person may wheel the entree (roast beef, for example) to the guest's table on a cart, carve the beef in front of the guest, put the meat on a plate, and serve it to the guest immediately. The service person brings the salad and vegetables into the dining area and serves these to the guest. A variation would be to have the service person do the tossing of the salad right at the cart, too.

Pros and Cons

The whole procedure is a merchandising and sales tool as well as a technique of service. Compromise service is less showy than French service, but more so than American.

Seating capacity may be reduced because of the room you need to wheel the cart around. It may not reduce seating if you just bring in a tray instead of the cart and place it on a stand near the guest's table to toss the salad, for example.

Banquet Service

Banquet service is usually just a variation of American service. You can use special round or rectangular banquet tables, or you can just push your regular tables together.

Table Setting

The table setting and placement of silver are the same as for American service. Any extra eating utensils that will be needed are pre-set (a soup spoon to the right of the teaspoon if soup will be served, a cocktail fork to the left of the dinner fork if shrimp cocktail will be served, a dessert spoon—an additional teaspoon nearest to the knife—if ice cream will be served.

Food Handling

Food is pre-dished onto the plates in the kitchen. Plates are served from the guest's left and cleared from the guest's right. Beverage is served from the right, usually with the dessert.

Pros and Cons

This is an efficient type of service. Large numbers of people can be served by comparatively few service personnel in a relatively short time.

Russian Service

Russian service is a simpler, less expensive, and faster variation of French service, but it is still showy. Carts are not used.

Table Setting

It is the same as French service except the dinner plates are pre-set. Wine glasses are pre-set. Coffee cups are not. Eating utensils are pre-set. If service plates are used, they are pre-set.

Food Handling

In Russian service, foods are put on platters (usually silver) in the kitchen. The service person carries the platters to the guest's table and serves food onto the dinner plate, which is pre-set in front of the guest before the entree is presented. Guests see the big, garnished platters before the service person starts serving. This provides showmanship without using carts. The service person serves all the guests at the table. Food is served from the guest's left. Right-handed service persons will hold the platter in the left hand and serve food onto the guest's plate with the right hand, using a fork and spoon both held in the right hand. Left-handed service persons will reverse the procedure.

With Russian service, entrees and vegetables are served from platters or serving dishes. Salad may be pre-dished or may be served onto a plate. A service plate may or may not be used with Russian service. It may be used for the first or second course but is usually removed before the main entree is served.

Pros and Cons

Some guests confuse Russian service with French service. Unless you are serving connoisseurs in an haute cuisine restaurant, it should not matter much what you call it or what your guests think it is, as long as you do it properly and well and make it pleasant for the diners. An advantage of Russian service is that it does add a lot of showiness and merchandising appeal to food presentation. Most guests enjoy having the service person dish up their food with a spoon and fork in one hand. Most get a kick out of the flourishes and attention. You do not use carts, so you don't have to leave extra spaces around the tables. Russian service can be carried out much more quickly than French service, and service persons can serve more guests.

Russian service costs more money for proper serving utensils. It is slower than American service. But it is still faster and less expensive than French service and it is ceremonious enough to please most guests. Russian service (or variations of it) is sometimes used at banquets.

English Service

This is seldom used in the United States. English service can be an innovative and attractive alternative type of service. It is an interesting idea to know about and perhaps experiment with in terms of your own food service if it (or your variation of it) is at all applicable to your establishment for special occasions.

There are a few distinctive features about English service. It is generally used in a private dining room for a small group of guests, usually about 10 to 20. The host or hostess may carve and/or serve the meat, and the whole dinner is set up very much as if it were taking place in someone's home. Depending on the entree, the host/hostess may ask you to pre-carve the meat in the kitchen and bring it in all sliced.

English service could be used, for example, when people invite a group of friends to dine out with them to celebrate some special occasion, or a large family gathers for a Thanksgiving or Christmas dinner at a restaurant. What it amounts to is a small banquet presided over by one of the guests who is the host or hostess.

Table Setting

The table setting is comparable to American service—knives and spoons to the right, forks to the left. The number of utensils needed and pre-set will depend on the meal ordered and the number of courses. Wine glasses would be pre-set if wine has been ordered. If wine has not been ordered, coffee cups may be pre-set. Dinner plates are placed in a stack to the right of the host or hostess, or they are handed one at a time to the host or hostess while he or she is carving.

Food Handling

Say, for example a group has reserved your private dining room for a banquet of roast turkey for a party of 16 people, and you will use English service.

Your service person brings in a whole roast turkey on a platter and places it in front of the host or hostess. Plates have been stacked or are placed one at a time by the service person to the right of the host or hostess. The host or hostess carves the turkey, asking each person his or her preference for white meat, dark meat, or both, just as they would do at home. Then the meat is put on a plate and handed to the service person, who dishes up vegetables and all other accompanying items from a cart or side table. Your service person then places the fully served plate in front of a guest, serving from the guest's right.

This procedure—the guest in charge carving and serving turkey, the service person dishing everything else onto the plate from the cart or table and serving the plate to a guest—is followed until all the guests (including the host or hostess) have been served. The hostess or host may ask if anyone wants seconds and will follow the procedure again, or carve extra portions and put them on serving platters and ask the service person to serve anyone who would like seconds.

Pros and Cons

As its name might imply, English service (or variations of it) is more popular in England than elsewhere. There are some problems with English service in the United States:

1. It is slow and time-consuming for your service personnel and for your guests.

2. It is usually not very popular with Americans who are not pleased with their own carving skills and would rather not take any part in carving and serving food.

3. It is expensive for the person who is paying. Your service person will have to bring in generous amounts of food on a cart, and there is bound to be some waste in this type of meal. The host and/or hostess pre-order the meal and you should do everything possible to make as close an estimate as you can concerning how much food will really be used for the number of guests in the party. But is is important to have enough food ready for the group. There is almost sure to be food left over and the host and/or hostess will have to pay for it. For example, they would be charged for the entire turkey, whether it is consumed at the dinner or not. Any leftovers may be wrapped and given to them to take home, or at least you should offer to do this since they are usually paying for the entire turkey.

Smorgasbord and Buffet Service (Chart 18-3)

In the United States, these two terms are generally used almost interchangeably and, to most Americans, there is not much difference between them. Perhaps the word smorgasbord may indicate to Americans that they will get Scandinavian foods. To many, "smorgasbord" or "buffet" may just mean a variety of foods they get from one big table.

Smorgasbord is a popular term in the United States for "self-service" eating, helping yourself from a big table full of various foods. The actual definition of "smorgasbord" is "Hors d'oeuvres or appetizers, especially as served buffet style at a long table."[2]

[2]*Webster's New Twentieth Century Dictionary of the English Language,* unabridged, 2nd. ed. World Publishing Company. New York, 1969.

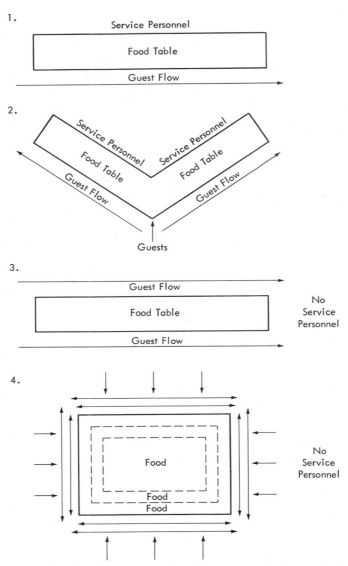

Chart 18-3 Smorgasbord and Buffet Food Table Arrangements

According to ancient Scandinavian tradition, smorgasbord means large varieties of Scandinavian foods (including many, many varieties of items —especially hot and cold fish—plus other hot and cold foods such as meatballs, puddings, hard-boiled eggs, salads, fruits) set up on one huge table from which guests help themselves. Smorgasbord in the United States usually includes an appetizer course (usually cold fish and salads), a hot meats and vegetables course, and a desserts course.

Buffet is a French word meaning "a counter or table where refreshments are served."[3] To be formally correct, a buffet should offer foods prepared in the French style of cooking. It is also self-service.

Table Setting

The table setting at the table where the guest sits would be the same as for American service. Salad plates (if used) and dinner plates are on the buffet table. Eating utensils are pre-set at the guest's table. These usually include two forks, one knife, and one or two spoons, depending on what is included with the dinner.

Food Handling

Sometimes an appetizer is served at the table before the guest goes to the big table. This quickly gives the guest something to eat and something to do. Heavy soup is often used as an appetizer at the table before the meal. It curbs appetites and may mean that guests will take less food from the buffet or smorgasbord table.

Some food service operations (which may or may not offer an appetizer) put tossed salad as the first item on the buffet table. It takes up a lot of room on the guest's plate and limits the amount of space left for other, more expensive food items.

Appetizers and/or salads (both comparatively low-cost items) can have the effect of reducing the amount of the higher-cost food items guests take from the buffet or smorgasbord table. Some operations may provide a separate salad plate as well as a dinner plate at the buffet table.

At a buffet or smorgasbord meal, guests are usually served the appetizer (if there is one) at their table and eat it. Then they walk to a big central table (or tables) laden with food and help themselves to the various selections. Some establishments have service personnel at the buffet table to carve and/or serve the main entrees (prime rib, ham) for each guest. This provides additional service and helps control entree cost.

Chart 18-3 shows different ways to set up your main food table(s) for easy access by guests. It illustrates the guest traffic flow pattern in relation to the table set-up as guests serve themselves.

Chart 18-3 Number 1 and 2 illustrate table arrangements where service personnel are used. Number 1 is a single line. Number 2 shows two identical lines where guests go either to the left or to the right. The same food is served to both lines.

Chart 18-3 Number 3 shows one table where guests may go down both sides of it. Some foods may be duplicated on both sides of the table. There may be only one dish of certain items—usually placed in the middle of the table—from which guests on either side may help themselves.

---

[3]Ibid.

Chart 18-3 Number 4 illustrates a large rectangular arrangement with tiers of different sizes stacked on top. Food is placed on different levels all the way around and guests proceed any way they want around the entire set-up.

Guests should get clean plates at the start of a table each time they go back for more food. You will need service personnel to clear used plates from their tables while guests have gone back to the buffet table and also to bring beverages to the tables. Desserts can be brought to the guests at their tables or put on the buffet table.

Pros and Cons

Some buffet-smorgasbord managers set a limit on the number of times each guest is permitted to take food from the table. Some just put a limit on the amount of entree each guest can take. Some set no limits whatsoever. Your pricing will depend on your policy.

Compared to other types of food service where all foods are brought to guests who remain seated at their tables, a buffet or smorgasbord usually has a high food cost but a somewhat lower service person labor cost. Fewer service personnel are needed. This may be offset, however, by increased labor cost in the kitchen. Fairly large varieties of items are usually offered, and it takes time to prepare the foods and garnish everything for proper display at a buffet or smorgasbord.

Depending on your own operation, buffets and smorgasbords could be an idea to consider, perhaps something to feature on slow business nights to help increase sales.

Cafeteria Service

Cafeteria service is self-service. It is similar to buffet and smorgasbord but is usually much more informal. Buffet and smorgasbord are usually served for one, all-inclusive price. In cafeteria service, guests pay a separate price for each item they take. Foods are usually simpler and more apt to be pre-dished at the counter and served to the individual in portions.

Table Setting

No dishes or silver are pre-set on the tables. There may be some condiments on the table. Guests get tray and silver at the counter as they enter the line. Silver may be pre-wrapped in napkins or set up in canisters or racks, and guests take what they need. At the counter, food is dished onto plates and handed to guests.

Food Handling

There is no service at tables—except perhaps service personnel who go around refilling coffee cups. Many cafeterias now have coffee stations in the dining area where guests can go to refill their own coffee cups.

Usually guests do not select their table until they have gotten their food. They go directly to the start of the cafeteria line, pick up tray and silver, and proceed through the line, selecting items they want. Foods are usually set up with salads first, then hot entrees and vegetables, then desserts and beverages.

Guests get to the cashier at the end of the line, pay there, and then go find a table. Or they get to the checker at the end of the line, get their check, find a table, eat, and pay on their way out. This second method can encourage guests to return to the food line (maybe for another vegetable, more dessert). Some cafeterias have service persons in the dining area who will go through the line for the guests and bring them extra items. They will take guests' receipts, go to the serving line for them, and bring them forgotten dessert, more milk, or whatever. This can help increase sales, because the guest may not want to "buck the line." The cost for these additional items is added to the receipt. Then guests go to the cashier and pay on their way out.

Types of Cafeteria Service

There are three basic types of cafeteria service (Chart 18-4):

1. Straight line service (Chart 18-4, Number 1).

All items are placed on one long counter. All guests walk along in one long counter. All guests walk along in one line and select what they want.

2. Island service (Chart 18-4, Number 2).

One long counter is used but guests can go just to the area or areas of the counter they want, select what they want, and go to a separate place to the food cashier or food checker to pay or get their check. They don't have to wait in a long line for all other guests buying all items.

3. Scatter (or scramble) service (Chart 18-4, Number 3).

Scatter means that you have several separate, distinct counters not attached in a row but scattered apart. You might have one counter just for sandwiches, another just for hot entrees, a third just for desserts, a fourth for beverages. Guests go to any area or areas they want and then to a separate area to the cashier or checker.

The island service or the scatter service arrangements work much more quickly and efficiently than the one long straight line set up and are particularly useful where there is a large volume of business. Guests do not have to plod along waiting in one long line if all they want is a sandwich and coffee.

Family Service

Family service is not used very often any more. In some places in the United States, it is against state law to use it.

1. Straight Line

2. Island

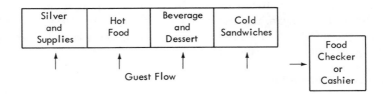

3. Scatter

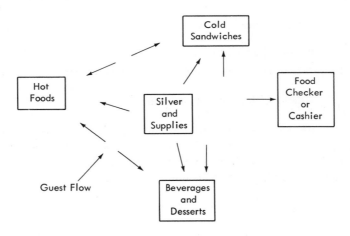

Chart 18-4 Cafeteria Arrangements

Table Setting

The table setting is the same as for American service. Normally all that is pre-set is the plate, knife, fork, spoon, napkin, water glass, and usually the coffee cup. Occasionally a soup spoon or salad fork may also be pre-set.

Food Handling

In the kitchen, food is pre-dished on to platters and into bowls. Service persons place the platters and bowls in the center of guests' tables. Guests help themselves, serving themselves from the platters and bowls and passing them on to the others sitting at the same table. Usually many guests sit at each large table, not necessarily just people who are together or in the same party.

Pros and Cons

Family service may or may not be legal in your state. Some no longer permit it because of sanitation problems.

There are also problems of waste—more food may be dished on to the serving platters and dishes than will be consumed. The food cannot be reheated because of sanitation regulations. Even without the sanitation factor, reheating typical family service food items (platters of pancakes and fried eggs, for example) would be hard to do successfully.

Because of these reasons, family service is seldom used today. But it is a very fast way to serve a lot of people in a very short period of time.

"Hash House" Service

"Hash house" is a slang term for all-around terrible service. This service exists in many food service operations, but it shouldn't—ever. It is found in any type of food service operation—truck stops, coffee shops, expensive restaurants. It is largely a matter of employee attitude—loud, careless, belligerent, or downright nasty. Silverware is slammed in front of the guest. Food is banged down onto the table or counter. Coffee is served in a cup and in the saucer and on the table simultaneously. Menus, tables, floors, and silverware may not be clean. Food may not be good. Service personnel will not walk a few extra steps. Instead they yell orders across the room. They are not interested in serving guests and they make sure everyone, including the guests, knows it.

Where hash house service exists it is management's fault for permitting it. Unfortunately it can exist, slightly or overwhelmingly, in all kinds of operations. Sometimes it thrives where guests least expect it. It can develop and take over in any food service operation if management does not obliterate any sign of it immediately.

TRAINING EMPLOYEES TO PROVIDE SERVICE

No matter what type of service you use, you must train your employees to carry it out correctly and efficiently. Unfortunately, new employees are often told, "Just follow so and so there. She (or he) will tell you what to do." And that's the end of it. Maybe new employees will figure out how to do their jobs. Maybe they won't. Real training and follow-up supervision are essential.

In many food operations, the employees who are told to train new employees have no interest in training, do not know a thing about how to do it, do not want to do it, and *do not* do it. Consequently, new employees are not trained at all. The persons you assign to administer training should care about providing the kind of service you want and should know how to train people to do the serving correctly. And persons who do the training should be compensated for the job of training. After new employees have been trained, supervisors should continue to check on them, including eating at their stations or at least observing them as they serve guests.

When service employees are trained, they should be taught how to set tables and serve food from left or right and clear dishes from left or right, according to how you want it done. Make sure they are instructed in all the basics of service so they provide your guests with the type of food service you want.

Teach your service personnel how to take guest orders. The service person should "key" on one guest (probably easiest if they always choose the guest sitting closest to the front door, or closest to the kitchen, or whatever, as the "key" person) and then proceed around the table from that individual to the right or left. They should always do this the same way so it is routine and becomes habit for them when they take orders.

When they arrive at a table with a tray full of dinners, "keying" should help them avoid the business of, "Who gets the medium steak? Who ordered chicken? Who wants the fish?"—a waste of time for the service person and a nuisance for guests. If service persons use the "key system" when they write orders, they will know which guest ordered first. This should give them a quick, easy system for going around the table serving guests. This may sound minor but it can irritate guests if it is not done correctly—particularly when service persons plop plates of food between guests or the wrong dinners in front of guests and then disappear, leaving guests to shuffle plates back and forth. These service persons are generally the same ones who wonder why they don't get good tips.

Bad service probably is not just the service person's fault. It is also very likely the manager's fault for failing to make sure that all service personnel are trained to do their jobs correctly and failing to insist that standards of good service are upheld.

Keep Ordering Simple

Train your service personnel so they can help reduce the number of decisions guests have to make when they order food. Do everything you can to make it fast and easy for guests to order food from service persons.

The following dialogue might be appropriate for a 1920s vaudeville routine, but variations of it (some even longer and sillier) currently do occur in food service operations every day.

Waiter: "What would you like to order?"
Customer: "Steak, medium."
Waiter: "How would you like it—rare, medium-rare, medium, or well done?"
Customer: "Medium."

Waiter: "You want French fried potatoes or a baked potato?"
Customer: "Baked."
Waiter: "You want sour cream on that?"
Customer: "Yes."
Waiter: "You want butter on that, too?"
Customer: "Yes."
Waiter: "You want green beans or carrots?"
Customer: "Green beans."
Waiter: "You want fruit salad or tossed salad?"
Customer: "Tossed salad."
Waiter: "You want French, thousand island, or blue cheese dressing on that?"
Customer: "French dressing."
Waiter: "You want dinner rolls or bread?"
Customer: "Rolls."
Waiter: "Butter? Jelly?"
Customer: "Jelly."
Waiter: "You want anything to drink?"
Customer: "Plain black coffee."
Waiter: "You want cream in that?"
Customer: "No."
Waiter: "You want sugar in that?"
Customer: "*No.*"
Waiter: "Dessert?"
Customer: "Just *plain* apple pie."
Waiter: "Blueberry, cherry, peach or apple?"
Customer: "APPLE."
Waiter: "A la mode?"
Customer: "#$%¢&* + !!"

Service personnel do have to ask *some* questions, but keep it to a minimum. And train service persons to pay attention to what a guest says so the same question is not asked more than once.

Perhaps (if your costing permits) the service person could bring all items such as cream, sugar, sour cream, and butter to the table and let guests serve themselves. Perhaps the service persons could ask questions about the ensuing courses after they have already brought one—between courses, instead of taking the whole order at once—if this does not mean delays.

Do what is feasible in your operation to minimize the questions and decisions for the guest. Try to speed up service and improve merchandising by avoiding long, involved interrogations of guests by the service person.

Teach your service personnel to take orders using the key system. Teach them (and help them) to reduce the amount of questioning, and train them to listen so they don't repeat questions. And train employees to work quietly. These areas are generally overlooked in training. Think of additional specifics to teach service personnel. Really analyze your service procedures and really train your service personnel to do the job nicely and efficiently. If you don't do the training yourself, make sure the person who does do your training knows what you want done.

New employees need a lot of encouragement—particularly during their first few days on a new job. Many of them decide to quit during their first *hour* at a new job because they are ignored and lost in the shuffle. Start good training right away. New employees should be greeted immediately, welcomed, oriented, and *trained*. It is important. (This means all your employees, not just your service personnel.)

Employee Appearance

The personal grooming and physical appearance of your service personnel are important, too. If you supply uniforms, provide attractive ones. If employees supply their own uniforms or outfits, their appearance should conform to the atmosphere of your establishment. Uniforms should fit well and be appropriate in style and color for your food operation. Too often uniforms or outfits worn by employees do not enhance the atmosphere of the establishment.

Personal cleanliness and neatness are essential. All service personnel should look well groomed. Some managers limit the amount of jewelry worn by service personnel.

Employees' Rest Periods

Schedule employees for the dining area according to your overall forecast of business for each day. Service personnel should be scheduled so they have regular rest periods. Their stations should be taken care of by someone else when they are on breaks. Employees should not go on breaks until their stations are clean and organized so someone else can easily fill in and take care of customers. While an employee is on break, another employee should be able to step right in and go to work with the least amount of inconvenience.

Try to provide a separate, specific area for employees' meals and breaks. It is ideal if you can set up space near the kitchen (or perhaps on a lower level) where all employees can eat and take their breaks away from the dining room and the guests. As we said in Chapter 13 on employees' meals, employee break time is particularly important in the food service industry. Employees should be able to take breaks in pleasant surroundings, or at least in an area away from their normal work area.

Employees' Stations

A frequent problem for service personnel is the station they are assigned in the dining room. The size of the station will vary depending on the type of service used, the capabilities of the employees, and the physical layout of the food service establishment. If employees have to walk long distances to get food and supplies, they cannot serve nearly as many guests as they can if items are close at hand and distances involved are short.

When you establish stations, it is probably a good idea to divide the dining room into areas and assign stations on a rotating basis, usually changing weekly. Some stations are better than others in terms of where guests want to sit. Employees working in better stations will usually make better tips. Make sure the host or hostess responsible for seating guests uses discretion so all service personnel have an equal share in the work of serving guests and earning tips. Service personnel used to have to bribe the host or hostess in order to get the chance to wait on rich-looking guests. Fortunately, this situation no longer exists in most food service establishments.

Tips

Service personnel generally depend on tips for most of their income. Good food service operations are apt to have higher average checks and/or more volume, which probably means more and better tips. You should want your service personnel to make maximum tips. Service personnel work for money. The more money they make, the more willing they usually are to put forth extra effort. The two seem to go hand in hand—better service means better tips and better tips mean better service. When employees are making a reasonable salary and reasonable tips, you can impose reasonable standards for reasonable services. It all ties together.

When it originated, the word "tips" meant "to insure prompt service." Today guests expect prompt service as a matter of course, although they don't always get it, of course. But the practice of tipping continues. For years, clubs and some other types of food service businesses have imposed service charges instead of tips. In Europe, a service charge is usually charged and sometimes tips are still expected in addition.

It is up to you to decide what to do about this in your own operation. A major objection by many employees to the service charge idea is that in some establishments the service person may get only part of it—or none of it. Maybe managers will use the service charge money to pay better wages to service personnel, and maybe they won't. From a guest's standpoint, many guests are not aware that a service charge has been imposed on them even if the check states that it has been included. Many will not notice this and will leave a tip, too. To make matters even more expensive for guests who don't know that they are paying a service charge included in their bill, they may use the total amount of their check including the service charge when they figure out how much tip to leave!

The idea of a service charge has not been widely applied in most American food service operations. The question of a service charge versus no service charge in America will take more time to be resolved on an industry-wide basis and on an individual operation basis.

SUMMARY

Serving food to guests is the reason why food service operations exist. You buy food, prepare and cook it, and serve it to guests who have come to your establishment because they want good food served well. It is important to you to have your guests really receive what they want. One thing they want is good service. It is one very important part of the overall reasons why guests come to your establishment.

After service persons have served the food and guests have eaten it, there is the matter of collecting money. That is the subject of the next chapter.

REVIEW AND DISCUSSION QUESTIONS

1. What are the types of food service?
2. Why should ordering by guests be kept simple?
3. What is the "key" system for taking orders?
4. How can service people minimize the number of questions they ask when they take guests' orders?
5. How would you look at the question of tips versus service charge if you were:

   a. a service person.

   b. a manager.

   c. a customer.

6. A guest in your cafeteria has just paid for his tray full of food and is walking toward a table. He drops the whole tray. Would you offer to replace his meal free? Would it make any difference if another of your guests had bumped him and caused the tray to fall?

7. Two guests at your cafeteria with trays of food they have paid for bump into each other. Both drop their trays and get food on each other's clothes. What do you do?

19

Sales and Cash Control

Objectives

This chapter discusses various methods of recording sales and ensuring that you receive the cash from each sale you make. After you have read this chapter, you should:

1. Know why guest checks should be treated the same as cash.
2. Know the various types of cash registers available, and how they can relate to your cash control.
3. Know different ways to establish cashier's banks, and procedures for handling cash.

SALES CONTROL

After you have made a sale, you need procedures to insure that you:

1. Bill for the proper amount of money.
2. Collect it.
3. Get it into the cash register.
4. Get it into the bank.

GUEST CHECKS (CHART 19-1)

Most commercial food service operations use some kind of printed guest check for writing orders and collecting payment. A sample of a typical guest check is shown in Chart 19-1.

Guest checks used by service personnel need tight control procedures. If you have lax control over guest checks, unscrupulous service personnel can take advantage of the situation and steal.

Treat guest checks just as carefully as you treat cash. Very few food service operations leave money lying around, but a lot of them handle guest checks very carelessly. You need a systematic and thorough approach to handling all guest checks.

When guest checks arrive on your premises, lock them in a safe storage place where no unauthorized person can get at them. Checks should be taken as needed from the storage area only by you the manager (or by someone you specifically designate) and given directly to the individual or individuals (usually cashiers or hosts or hostesses) who will be responsible for issuing them to service personnel.

In most food operations, the employees in charge of issuing guest checks to service personnel are usually either the cashiers or the hosts or hostesses—and it is probably best to have your cashiers do it if you can. Cashiers have a set station and should be at that station when business is brisk. When things are busy, hostesses or hosts have to move around greeting and seating guests and cannot stay in one place to oversee the issuing of guest checks.

Guest Check Signout Sheet (Chart 19-2)

Chart 19-2 shows a sample guest check signout sheet. Provide these (or a similar sheet appropriate for your own operation) for your cashiers. They should use these sheets to keep records of guest checks.

Your guest checks should probably be printed with space for the initials and/or code number of the service person. Many food service operations assign code numbers to service persons for use on guest checks. It is faster for them just to write in a code number instead of their name, and it simplifies the procedures for control of guest checks.

NAME OF RESTAURANT		
Sales Person: Name: _____ Code Number: _____	Number of Guests: _____	Guest Check Number: _____
ITEM		AMOUNT
SUB-TOTAL:		
TAX:		
TOTAL AMOUNT DUE:		

(detachable stub optional)

Guest Check Number: _____

NAME OF RESTAURANT

TOTAL AMOUNT DUE: _____

Note: Detachable stub is guest receipt. Guest keeps this.
Carbon copy of the guest check itself (not stub) is the DUPLICATE CHECK.

Chart 19-1 Guest Check

Guest checks should also have chronological numbers printed on them. When cashiers give guest checks to service personnel, they should record the name of the service person (and his or her code number if you use that system) on the signout sheets and the chronological numbers printed on the checks each service person gets.

Printed Name of Service Person	Code Number of Service Person	First Check Number	Last Check Number	Signature of Service Person	Missing Checks

Chart 19-2 Guest Check Signout Sheet

The signout sheets should have a space for cashiers to write the numbers of the first and last checks in the sequence of checks they give to each service person. There should also be space for the service person to sign his or her name next to the check numbers, all on the same line. And there should be space to note missing checks by the individual service person.

Have service persons personally sign their names for checks they receive. This pinpoints responsibility and indicates that the service person has received the checks listed on the signout sheet.

The usual procedure is to have the service person write the customers' orders on guest checks, total the amount, and give them to the guests so they can pay.

The most commonly used ways to collect payment from guests are:

1. Service persons give guest checks to customers. Customers take guest checks to cashier, pay, and leave.
2. Service persons give guest checks to customers, take guest checks and money from customers to cashier, and bring change back to customers at their tables.

The second method means extra walking for service people, but a lot of them prefer this method. They tend to get bigger tips if they return the change to the guests. Wise service persons can make sure that the change they return to guests is in a good assortment of coins and bills to make good tipping fast and easy for guests. Many guests will not have much change. If the first method is used, guests go to the cashier themselves and pay their bills. If they did not have change for a tip before they left their table, they will have to go back to the table to leave a tip, and a lot of guests will not do it. They will leave nothing or whatever small change they happen to have, get up, leave the table, go to the cashier, pay the bill, and leave—without walking back to the table to leave an appropriate tip.

Both systems for collecting payment are widely used. It is up to you to decide which method you want and why and then follow it. One method is not advocated over the other. Managers should, however, be aware of and concerned about the tips that their service persons get. You want them to get good tips.

Cashiers Verify All Checks Returned to Them

When checks are returned to cashiers with guests' payments, the amount should be rung on the cash register and the check should be cancelled by the register. The best register is the kind that prints the total on the check and on the cash register tape. This verifies that each check was rung and totalled.

During slow business periods of the day, cashiers should be responsible for sorting the checks according to the service person's name or code number. Then the cashier should take one service person's checks at a time and put them in numerical order for each service person.

Some food service operations find it a good idea to have a file box with a slot for each service person's guest checks at the cashier station. Chart 19-3 shows this type of file box. Each slot is just large enough to hold one service person's series of guest checks. As checks are rung, they are put directly into different slots according to the individual service person. This makes it fast and easy for cashiers to sort guest checks as they go. Each slot can be marked with the name and/or code number of service persons on duty.

At the end of the shift all unused checks should be returned by the service personnel to the cashiers. Cashiers correlate these returned, unused guest checks with the name or number on the signout sheet. They sort any late checks into numerical order by service person and verify that all checks are accounted for.

Missing Checks

Every time there is a missing check, take immediate action and investigate. This notifies service personnel that you will not tolerate missing checks. Any missing check that cannot be traced or accounted for should be reported to you or to whichever management person is on duty. It is management's responsibility (not the cashier's) to follow up on missing checks.

If checks are sorted by cashiers during each shift, you know immediately if any checks are missing and should have time to ask questions about a missing check before service people have left for the day. Service people may be able to remember, while it is fresh in their minds, which customer did not turn in the missing check, if that is what happened. Sometimes it might even be possible for you to trace the person who walked out without paying. Occasionally guests *will* walk out without paying. One advantage in having the service

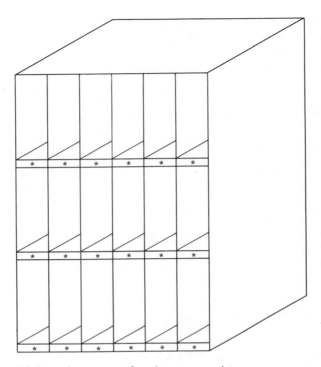

* Code number or name of service person on duty.

Chart 19-3 Cashier's File for Guest Checks

person present the check to the guest and collect the money is that there are fewer of these "walkouts." If guests are supposed to go to the cashier to pay the bill, some may just get up and walk out without paying, perhaps while the service person is in the kitchen and has no way of knowing that the guest did not pay. Cashiers can miss this, too. Some guests will leave without paying no matter what method of collecting cash you use. Some will purposely walk out without paying. A few will be just plain absentminded and wander outside, never realizing that they did not pay.

Fines for Missing Checks

Some establishments impose fines on service persons who have checks missing. This practice may be illegal according to the minimum wage law. And usually it is not a good idea anyway. It can tempt retaliation. Say, for example, you impose a $10 fine for each missing check. The first time a service person has a missing check, it may have been a case of a forgetful or dishonest guest walking out without paying. The second time that same service person has a missing check, it may not be an accident. Perhaps the bill is $20. The service person, resenting that $10 fine which he or she felt was unfair, collects the $20 from the guest, tears up the check, and reports it as missing. He or she pays the $10 fine and pockets $10.

Don't impose fines. A service person who wants to can probably figure a way to get back the fine plus interest. Take all precautions to see that missing checks don't happen. Be very sure you have good control procedures to prevent customer walkouts. Do keep track of which service persons have missing checks. If some have too many, find out why.

If you do have missing checks, usually you will get a smattering of checks missing from all personnel. If one individual service person has many more missing checks than anyone else, you had better investigate to see if that person should be discharged. This employee may have devised his or her own system for making extra money, or may be extremely careless. You should not tolerate either situation.

Even if you have excellent control systems, unscrupulous service persons may still devise ways of cheating. Take, for example, the true case of a very busy waiter in a restaurant. He gave extremely good service, and he served a lot of customers. But his recorded sales level was lower than that of some of the less busy service personnel in the establishment.

He had gone to a printer and had had copies of the restaurant's guest checks made for himself. He was occasionally substituting his own checks for those of the restaurant, presenting his checks to his customers, and collecting and pocketing the money. Most of the time he used the restaurant's checks and turned them and the money in to the cashier, as all other service persons did. He would use a limited number of his own checks each evening and simply keep the checks and the money. In this case there were no missing checks, but the waiter was definitely cheating the restaurant. Eventually he was discovered when one of his customers gave one of his privately-printed guest checks to the cashier instead of to him. The cashier caught it because the number on the waiter's own private guest check did not correspond with any of the guest check numbers currently being used by the restaurant.

Dishonest service personnel can dream up imaginative ways to cheat you. The more you know about tricks they can use, the better you can watch for them and act to prevent a dishonest employee from trying them or getting away with them.

Duplicate Checks System

Some food service operations use a system of duplicate checks in the kitchen as a means of control. The duplicate check system is an excellent control device. The waiter who printed his own private guest checks in the example we just discussed could not have used his theft technique if there had been a duplicate check system in use in the restaurant where he worked. In a duplicate check system, someone in the accounting office (or whomever management designates) compares each duplicate used for ordering food with the guest check to make sure they are both there and they are both the same. And service persons must give a duplicate check to the kitchen staff before they pick up their orders of food. The waiter's phony guest check system would not have worked. Without a duplicate, he could not have received any food from the kitchen. Guest checks and duplicates must both be used and both have to go through the accounting office.

In a kitchen duplicate check system, the check number for the food order must be put on all duplicates. Duplicates must be turned in by service persons when they pick up an order from the kitchen. Cooks must not give any orders to any service person until they get a duplicate check. Some food service operations have their checks printed with a duplicate attached. The duplicate is torn off and turned in to the kitchen when orders are picked up. A duplicate check is a carbon copy of the guest check.

One problem with the duplicate check system is that all the duplicates have to be put in order and compared against the checks turned in to the cashier to make sure they agree. This takes some time and work, and some payroll expense.

Duplicates Just for High-Cost Items

Some food service operations use a variation of the duplicate check system, using it just for high-cost entrees. The service persons give to the broiler person (for example) a slip of paper on which they have written the number of specific high-cost items ordered and signed their name: "4 steaks— 1 rare, 1 medium-rare, 2 medium. George." This keeps track of high-cost items where control is most essential. At the end of a shift, the broiler persons should have all the steaks they started with minus only those for which they have slips of paper.

It is the broiler persons' responsibility to see that they get a slip listing each steak they prepare. It is their responsibility to count all steaks before they start and after they end their shifts. They are responsible for missing steaks. If you make the broiler persons responsible for missing steaks, they will be much more diligent about making sure they get an order slip for each order from each service person. Then it is a simple matter for you (or someone else) to check "George's" guest checks to make sure that the four steaks listed on his order slip in our example have really been accounted for on his guest checks for that day.

The advantage with this system is that only expensive entrees are watched and comparatively less expensive accompanying items (salads, appetizers) are not. Of course, this is not as complete as a full duplicate system, but it does pinpoint selected expensive items.

The duplicate system has another advantage. It can reduce the noise in the kitchen. Service people just put the duplicates on a spindle. Cooks can work from the checks on the spindle without having to call out orders. This can reduce noise and confusion in the kitchen. Some operations still have the order called out before the duplicate is put on the appropriate spindle. If the order is called, the cooks do not have to stop to read. For example, if "four steaks" is called, they can put them on the broiler immediately. Before those four steaks leave the kitchen, however, cooks should verify that they received a duplicate slip for them.

Food Checkers

Instead of a duplicate check system, some large establishments use a food checker system. This helps them to make sure that everything called for on the check (no more and no less) is on the tray when the tray goes into the dining room. Service persons in the dining room may write in food items ordered on the guest check. A food checker in the kitchen may use a pre-check machine or register to put in the prices. A pre-check register looks like a cash register. It records the price of the entree or dinner on the guest check and it will total the guest check. The pre-check machine may also perform other work—perhaps print the entree on the guest check. The guest check is then returned to the service person and the check is paid to the cashier. If the system is working correctly, the total on the guest check register should be the same as the total on the cashier's register.

In the past, food checkers were used more often than they are today, and some were very strict. If an ordered item was left off the tray, or if more items than the ones ordered were put on the tray, the service person was alerted to the fact and notified that it should not happen again. The system worked effectively in general. But payroll for a food checker is expensive and many operations cannot justify the extra cost. Many food service establishments use other methods of control (duplicate check system, duplicate check system for high-cost items, sales analysis) to cover the job formerly performed by the food checker.

THE CASH REGISTER

There are many different types of cash registers available. If possible, get a cash register that:

1. Maintains a perpetual balance that should not be cleared.
2. Cancels guest checks by printing the total amount paid on them.
3. Has two cash drawers—one for the cashier and a different drawer for the relief cashier.

This recommended register is more expensive than those that do not perform all these functions, but it is the best type to have.

Someone other than the cashier should do the cash register reading. Cashiers do not have to know the total on the register. If they don't read the register, how can they know how much money to turn in? They turn in all the money in the register minus the amount of their cashier's bank (the amount cashiers start with and use for change-making purposes). The office is the place where the amount of the cash turn-in should be compared with the amount of the actual register reading, and this job should not be done by a cashier.

The person responsible for reading the register and computing the turn-in should not handle the cash. There is an old saying in accounting: "Anyone who handles records should not handle cash." Someone should be responsible for cash handling. Someone *else* should be responsible for determining what the amount of the cash turn-in should be.

Over and Short

To determine the amount of cash turn-in, subtract the opening balance figure from the closing balance figure on the cash register. This figure is the amount of cash you should have in the register. The net amount of cash in the register (total cash minus cashier's bank) should equal the amount shown on the cash register. If your cashier has paid out cash for invoices, add the value of these invoices to the cash for reconciliation purposes. If the amounts don't agree, you are over or short. If there is more cash in the register than the amount shown on the register, your cash is over. If there is less, it is short. Cash over is frequently caused by failing to ring or by underringing the amount of a guest check. Cash short is frequently caused by ringing too large an amount for a guest check or by giving too much change to the customer. Two examples to clarify:

1. Your cash is over: Your cashier receives $5 in payment for a $5 check but rings it up as 50 cents.
2. Your cash is short: Your cashier receives $5 in payment for a $5 check but rings it up as $15.

Some food service operation managers insist that the cash turn-in every day must be identical with the register reading, right to the penny. It is not usually a good idea to insist on this. If you do, cashiers will probably personally keep all overages and make up all shortages out of their own pockets. Unless you have extremely exacting control procedures, cashiers can take artificial steps to see to it that money is not over or short if that is what you want. This is bad because you should be aware of overages and shortages and find out why they happen. And the cashiers should not be able to pocket overages and make up shortages. If there are inaccuracies, you want to learn why, not have them artificially fixed and covered up by cashiers.

Uniform System of Accounts For Hotels[1] and *Uniform System of Accounts For Restaurants*[2] both recognize that over a period of time cash will

---

[1] *Uniform System of Accounts For Hotels,* 6th ed. rev. Hotel Association of New York City, Inc. New York, 1963.
[2] *Uniform System of Accounts For Restaurants,* 4th ed. rev. National Restaurant Association. Chicago, 1968.

probably be short. Both books recommend that you have an account called "cash short" listed under administrative and general expenses. If guests are short changed, they will tell the cashier if they notice it. But some guests will not tell the cashier if they get too much change. So, over a period of time, you are apt to be short.

It is better when you, not your cashiers, keep track of overages and shortages. If your cash overage or shortage exceeds a certain amount (say $5, for example), you should immediately analyze all checks to find the discrepancy. Some food service operations would not bother to investigate anything less than a $10 discrepancy. Others would consider that much too large a variation and insist on investigating if they are $1 over or short. The important thing is to set a specific appropriate amount and investigate any variation (overage or shortage) from that amount.

Overages can occur when checks are not rung or when guests do not get enough change. Guests will be unhappy if they notice that they did not get enough change.

Shortages can be caused by an overring, which means the cashiers hit the wrong key and ring up more money than they really receive. For example, they receive $1 and hit the $10 key instead. According to the register, they will be short $9.

Explain your policy on overage and shortage to your cashiers and make your rules very clear. Someone other than the cashier should calculate overage and shortage every day. Cashiers who are inaccurate too frequently should be retrained and warned. If they continue to be inaccurate, you should probably consider replacing them.

CASHIER'S BANK

Your cashier has to have funds available for making change. These funds are called the "cashier's bank" or "imprest funds."

There are two ways to set up a cashier's bank:

1. Individual cashier's bank.
2. Revolving cashier's bank.

Individual Cashier's Bank

Some food operations issue an individual bank to a cashier when the cashier is originally hired. The cashier is responsible for that bank as long as he or she is employed as cashier. If you use this method, you should provide a place where the bank can be locked up safely. Nobody (not the manager, not the assistant manager, not the auditor) except that one cashier has access to it without that cashier's knowledge.

An advantage with the individual cashier's bank is that the bank does not have to be made up every day. Cashiers are responsible for seeing that they have proper denominations for making change. They buy change and bills from the head cashier or manager.

A disadvantage is that if a lot of cashiers are employed, each one has to have a separate bank and a separate safe locked place to store it so that no one else can get at it.

Individual cashier's banks should be audited periodically. Periodic audits insure that the correct total amount of cash that is supposed to be there really is there. This can be done by inspecting the bank with the cashiers just before they go on duty.

Revolving Cashier's Bank

Another procedure to provide funds for the cashier to use for making change is a revolving bank. If you use the revolving bank method, you only have one bank—not one for each cashier. The bank goes from one cashier to the next. A revolving bank is a bank made up from money in the register. A cashier going off duty gives it to the next cashier coming on duty. This can be used where there is continuous operation and always a cashier on duty.

The cashier who is about to go off duty makes up a bank of a specific amount (established by management) out of the money in the cash register and gives it to the cashier coming on duty. During the time the incoming cashier is counting, the cashier who is about to go off duty uses the receipts taken in to make change for guests. The cashier coming on duty counts the money in the bank and verifies that the cashier going off duty has handed over the correct amount of money. If the register has liftout trays, it is a simple matter to take a reading. You tear off the tape, switch the trays, and the new cashier is ready to go on duty. It takes about one minute to do this.

Revolving banks do not normally need auditing because they are checked every time they go to a different cashier. You would have revolving banks audited, however, if you suspected collusion between cashiers.

Policies and Procedures for Change-making and Records

With either method—individual cashier bank or revolving cashier bank—cashiers should have all loose coins rolled in coin wrappers if there is enough to make a roll (50 pennies, 40 nickels, 50 dimes, and so on). Change that is less than a full roll should be kept in the bank (individual or revolving). Cashiers should do the job of rolling coins in wrappers so that large amounts of change do not have to be wrapped in the office. Cashiers can wrap coins during slow times.

Have a supply of change in a safe in your office. Your cashiers may need a lot of quarters or a lot of dollar bills, for example, quickly. You sell these to your cashiers. Cashiers give money to you and specify what change they need. You put the money received from the cashiers in the safe and give them the bills and coins they need.

You, the manager (or someone you designate), should keep permanent records of cash turn-ins by cashiers. Make sure the records agree with the actual reading of the cash register tape. If perpetual balance is maintained on the register, it is not possible to tamper with machine totals and falsify daily readings.

Paid-outs

Occasionally cashiers (with your authorization) may make a "payout" from the register for something—a freight charge which must be paid right away for something delivered to the operation, for example. Set a policy on this. Decide when it is or is not correct for cashiers to do this and make sure they are following your policy. Cashiers should get receipts for all pay-outs. They should put the receipts in the register. These should become part of the cash turn-in for that day. Receipts for pay-outs should be counted and treated just like cash.

Many food service establishments have found that it is better to make pay-outs from the cash register and record them later as expenses instead of having a separate petty cash fund and using that for pay-outs. In many food operations where there is a petty cash fund, it is not kept under very good control. As a result petty cash funds are apt to have less money in them than they are supposed to.

If you do maintain a separate petty cash fund, have it audited periodically.

I.O.U.s

Periodic audits should be made of individual cashier's banks because there may be less cash in them than there should be. Instead of cash, there may be I.O.U.s. Cashiers may have personally run short of private cash and borrowed $10 or $20 (or whatever amount), which they intend to repay at payday, and left I.O.U.s in their bank. *Do not permit this.*

Determine how much cash is needed in the bank for change-making purposes. Set a definite amount. That amount should always be there. If cashiers need a private cash advance, they should ask the manager for it. Cashiers should not be allowed to take any money from their individual cashier banks.

Credit Cards

Today any restaurant where guests can run up a large dinner tab is pretty much expected to allow guests to charge it on a national credit card. The drive-in and the coffee shop may still require cash, but larger establishments are generally expected to permit guests to use credit cards. These include Diners' Club, Carte Blanche, American Express, and more recently Mastercharge and BankAmericard, plus others.

When your guests use their credit cards to charge meals at your establishment, the credit card company is performing a service for your restaurant and will charge your restaurant a percentage of what the guest has charged. Food service operations have to pay the credit card company a fee every time they let a customer use a credit card to charge a meal. Some credit card companies charge the individual a fee to get a credit card, and some also charge cardholders interest if they do not pay the amount due when it is due.

The cost for this credit service can vary from, say, 4 percent to 7 percent of the total bill. Each credit card company has its own rules and rates. Usually the more volume of business your food operation does with one credit card company, the lower the rate will be that you will pay to that company. For example, the rate might be 7 percent on $1,000 worth of sales and 4 percent on $5,000 worth of sales. That is why some businesses—including food service operations—will accept one or two credit cards and not others.

Your service person should fill in the credit card form according to the credit card company's directions. The credit card and bill are inserted into the credit card machine to stamp the bill. Then the service person returns the card to the guest with the completed credit form for the guest's signature. The guest's copy is torn off after the form has been signed and given to the guest; the restaurant's copy is returned by the service person to the cashier.

Keep your copy of the completed form in the register and treat it just like cash, whether you follow the practice of ringing up the sale or not. You may or may not attach the guest check to the credit billing slip. If you do attach the guest check to the credit card billing slip, your cashier should make a record of the check number and the name of the service person. You need this information so you can account for the guest check at the end of the day. You also need the information when you make a tally of missing guest checks.

As we said above, treat completed credit card forms just like you treat cash. At the end of the day, these charged forms should be turned in just like cash as part of the total sales for the day. The forms should be separated and recorded according to credit card companies. They should be kept in a very secure place—preferably in a safe. Follow the procedures that the credit card company requires when you fill in the forms to get your money. Careless handling of completed credit card forms can result in a substantial loss to you.

Bill Direct

Some food service opeations will not let guests charge a meal on any national credit card. Some restaurants have their own private credit cards and do their own billing of their own customers who use them. If you do this and bill your customers direct, you have to pay for the time, work, and materials involved in mailing the bills. Even if you have a very efficient billing system, it is hard to do the job for much less than 3 percent of the sale. There is time and payroll cost involved in preparing bills, stuffing envelopes, plus the actual cost of postage, and you absorb losses on uncollectable accounts. It all adds up to an expense for your food operation.

Advantages to having your own credit cards may be good public relations and it could cost you less than having your guests use their own national credit cards.

Credit Cards Just as I.D.

Some food operations will accept national credit cards just for identification purposes and mail a bill to the customer. If you do this, you can expect losses. The credit card that the customer uses just for identification purposes may be outdated, not valid, stolen, or whatever, and you may never receive payment.

Other Controls

There are other machines available to handle cash and guest checks besides the cash register described earlier in this chapter. Some large food operations use guest checks that are really computer punch cards and feed the cards directly into a computer. Analysis of sales, totalling of receipts, and gathering of additional information can all be done quickly by the computer. This type of system is expensive to install and normally is not feasible for smaller units.

There are also transistorized machines now becoming more readily available. In some of these, you can set keys to print your prices of items you sell. For example, if you tap the key that says "hamburger," 30 cents (or whatever amount you set it for) is recorded. You do not have to touch number keys at all. This is speedy. It lets you accumulate totals for several different types of food products sold (hamburger, fish sandwich, milk shake). This is especially useful in drive-ins.

Many drive-ins have also developed and used an extensive paper control system. They count cups at the beginning and end of a shift. The number of cups used during the shift should equal the number of soft drinks or milk shakes sold. The number of cups used should correspond to the revenue received from the sale of the drinks.

The best control is where you put combinations of controls together. For example, you use a machine control *plus* a duplicate check system control *plus* a paper control *plus* guest check signout sheets *plus* you verify check revenue against the machine total.

The secret of good cash control is a realistic series of checks and balances combined to help you get the results you want.

BONDING EMPLOYEES

A final precaution and safety measure in the area of cash control is to bond all employees who handle cash. Bonding is a relatively inexpensive form of insurance. If a bonded employee steals cash, and you can verify the amount stolen and who took it, the bonding company will reimburse you for your loss. Then they will try to collect from the employee who took the money.

Your controls should be set up to detect the guilty, protect the innocent, and prevent theft. If theft does occur despite your controls, bonding can still help to protect you—if you have tight written records and can give proof to a bonding company showing which employee took what amount.

REVIEW AND DISCUSSION QUESTIONS

1. Why is guest check control important?
2. How can you find out how many checks are missing?
3. Why is cash turn-in more apt to be short than over?
4. How can you maintain cash control if you do not use a duplicate check system?
5. A guest wants to charge a meal on a credit card that your food service does not honor. What would you do?

20

Sales Analysis

Objectives

Sales analysis is the final step in the food cost control cycle. After you have read this chapter, you should:

1. Know why you should perform a sales analysis.
2. Know various ways in which you can gather sales analysis information.
3. Know what to do with sales information after you get it.

Sales analysis is the final step in your food control cycle. This is where you examine, analyze and evaluate your sales. Here is where you break down your sales and look at all aspects of them.

Sales analysis should be a learning device. What you learn may cause you to decide to make some changes and try to improve your sales—either total sales or sales of certain items. Through sales analysis, most operators get information they can use to strengthen their operation.

How frequently you should do a sales analysis will depend on how you use the information you get. Some operators do an analysis for each meal period. If they use a duplicate check system, they may want to compare each duplicate against the original check right at the end of meal periods. Some operators do weekly sales analysis. Others may do an analysis only occasionally.

WHY DO A SALES ANALYSIS?

You do a sales analysis because you want to know what food items were sold, what amount of each item was sold, where items were sold (in case you have more than one dining room), what time of day they were sold, and who sold them. It depends on your own operation. Get whatever information you need to have so you can analyze your sales.

Use the information you get from sales analysis to review your current menu. Maybe you will find that you should make some changes in your menu. Sales analysis can help you plan your production to avoid over-and under-production. Sales analysis can help you make better forecasts of the total number of guests to be served and what they will order. This in turn affects your production.

You need sales analysis information to establish your potential costs. The number of customers served and the items they ordered affect your total revenue and your food cost. If you are not getting the food cost you want, you can adjust some menu prices and change some menu items (product mix) to get the food cost you *do* want. When you have decided what you are going to sell and have planned your production accordingly, you can purchase more effectively.

You can also use sales analysis information to determine the revenue you should be receiving from your sales of individual items. Total sales of all items combined should equal total revenue received. Total sales compared to total revenue is part of your checks and balances control.

Sales analysis tells you how you are doing. With sales analysis information you can compare customer count for different periods of time—from month to month and year to year. This could be particularly useful information during inflationary periods when you will probably want to know whether your business has increased (more customers) or you are serving fewer customers but at higher prices.

Sales analysis tells you what time of day which items are selling and who is selling them. You can learn how much revenue is brought in by each service person. This can help you establish norms and standards for sales by service persons. These norms and standards can be used as guides for planning future staff schedules.

A lot of information can be generated from sales analysis. For some uses—such as reconstructing sales per service person or total revenue for permanent records—you want very accurate and precise information. For other uses—menu changes, for example—a general indication of how well an item sold might be adequate.

To do your sales analysis, you will probably want to gather the following information (maybe more, maybe less depending on your own needs):

1. What menu items you sold.
2. How much of each item you sold.
3. What service persons sold what items.
4. How many guests you served.
5. What items sold during which meal periods (breakfast, lunch, dinner, supper).
6. What items sold in which dining areas (in case you have more than one dining room).
7. Does total revenue on guest checks equal total revenue in the cash register.
8. What is the amount of your average check.

METHODS OF GETTING SALES ANALYSIS INFORMATION

Following is a discussion of ways to collect information you will need in order to perform a sales analysis. Some methods will give you complete information, some only partial information. You can combine the procedures to get the information you want.

Guest Checks

A very common method for gathering information is to go through all your guest checks (for a meal or a day) and mark the number of each item sold on a menu. Add up the marks on the menu for each item. You know what items you sold and you know the quantity of each item you sold. You will also see which menu items *did not* sell.

Multiply the number of each item sold by its selling price and you have revenue for each item. Add totals for all items and you have the total revenue you should have received.

If you separate guest checks by time of day, you can find out what items sold at lunch, dinner, any meal period. (If you have more than one dining room, use different colored guest checks for each room.)

The person going through the guest checks can mark items sold on a menu and can simultaneously record the number of guests on a separate sheet of paper, or go through the guest checks twice, first checking items on a menu and then using an adding machine to tally the guest count.

Going through all guest checks this way is a good, complete method to gather information for your sales analysis, but it takes time. This method is fine for a restaurant with limited numbers of guest checks. It would work, for example, for dinner establishments where guests come in to dine and spend an hour and a half to two hours for dinner. It is not so simple for coffee shop types of restaurants, which use a lot of checks—some with just sandwiches, just desserts, just entrees, or just beverages. Coffee shops will have a lot more guests and a lower average check. For them, this method will take much more time.

Duplicate Check System

This is very similar to the guest check method just described except that the information is further compared against a duplicate check so there is more time and work involved. Compare all duplicates against the original checks to see that all items on the duplicate check are recorded on the guest check. This is to insure that you are receiving the proper revenue—so you know that guests are not being charged for hamburgers when they have been served steaks, or vice versa, for example.

A variation of the duplicate check system is duplicate checks—also called chits—for high-cost items only. For all high-cost items, chits must be turned in to the broiler person. Chits for high-cost items are compared against the guest checks. The advantage of this high-cost-item chit method is that you can tie it easily into a perpetual inventory (discussed in Chapter 19) for additional control.

Pre-set Register

In Chapter 19 on sales and cash control, we talked about a type of cash register you can pre-set to record the sale of individual items. When you sell a hamburger, for example, you don't have to hit number keys to record the hamburger. You just hit the key with "hamburger" printed on it. The daily total recorded by the "hamburger" key would be your total hamburger revenue for that day. Divide this total by your price per hamburger and you know how many hamburgers were recorded on the register. Compare this figure against a perpetual inventory on hamburgers.

This type of register can be set to record any foods you want. At the end of the day, get your totals from all your pre-set food item keys and you have some of the information you want for your sales analysis. This method is especially useful in drive-ins.

Computer

If you have access to a computer, you can put it to excellent use in sales analysis. Your guest checks could actually be computer cards. These can be punched or marked so a computer can read them and tabulate the results as part of your sales analysis. It takes time to prepare the guest check computer cards so that they can be inserted into a computer. But after you have done this, a computer can do your complete sales analysis in less than a minute. Computers can give you all the information you want. A computer can:

1. Tell you sales of individual items.
2. Give you total sales of all items.
3. Figure what your receipts should be.
4. Give total number of guests served.
5. Give average check.
6. Calculate sales revenue and average check for each sales person.

A computer system is comparatively expensive now. But in the future, sales analysis by computer may become more feasible for more operations.

Food Checker

Some establishments, particularly cafeterias, still use food checkers. These employees add up the total price for each tray. For service to a dining room, they might also check a tray to make sure the correct items (no more, no less) are on it. Usually a food checker will also fill in the guest check and put the price of the meal on it, by hand or by machine. Some food checking machines are set so that totals can be recorded for some items. Usually, however, there are not enough totals on a food checker's machine to record all the information you want.

The food checker could use a regular food checker's machine plus a separate odometer to record each menu item. A food checking odometer is similar to an odometer in a car, which records each mile traveled. For food checking, it records each menu item you sell. It is set up so that every time you hit a key, the total advances by one. Most operations that use odometers need several of them—one for entree items, one for appetizers, one for desserts, and so on—all items priced separately. The food checker surveys each tray before it goes to the dining room and records each item on the appropriate odometer. This can give you a three-way check of your revenue:

1. The food checker's register total.
2. The cashier's total receipts for food.

3. The odometer numbers multiplied by selling prices (if all items are kept track of).

All three of these methods can tell you total receipts, although usually odometers are not used for beverages.

Perpetual Inventory

Another way to find out what was sold (just for some items) is to keep perpetual inventory on selected high-cost items, which we discussed as part of a duplicate check system or with the use of a pre-set register. You can use perpetual inventory, however, if you have no duplicate check system at all and no pre-set register. You can combine perpetual inventory with a paper control. Count the number of cups you have for soft drinks, for example, before and after a meal period. The difference should be the number used during the meal period. Multiply the number used by the selling price of each drink and you know what revenue you should have received and the number you should have sold.

In our earlier discussion, we said that perpetual inventory should be maintained on hamburgers to make sure the register figure and the perpetual inventory figure agree. Perpetual inventory means that you always know the amount you have. The number you have on hand when you start plus any you add minus your closing inventory (and minus any items eaten or wasted by employees) should equal the amount you sold.

Combine Methods to Get the Information You Want

Some of the methods to obtain information for sales analysis are very complete and time-consuming. Others tend to be somewhat incomplete (such as the perpetual inventory method), but should be a part of your production control. The method you use should give you information that you can and will use. It may not be possible for you to afford to go through guest checks every day to get all of the information described above. But if you do it occasionally, it can provide you with useful information.

Go through guest checks where service persons can watch you. Just tell employees that you are "gathering some information." If you have had problems with unrecorded items or other errors (due to carelessness or dishonesty) on guest checks, your unexplained activity can be a control all by itself until you devise means of *really* improving guest check routines. Thorough analysis should provide you with information to help you stop wrongdoing, improper pricing, careless procedures, and the like on guest checks.

What to Do With the Information You Get

After you have gathered your information about sales, you analyze the information. This can help you make decisions about many areas.

Evaluate Your Menu

You have learned how much you sold of each menu item. After a period of time, you will see what sells and what doesn't. Maybe you should change your menu. Probably some items sold well and some didn't. If an item does not require much preparation and it gives you a good cost, you may want to keep it on your menu even if it doesn't sell very well. But if it *does* require a lot of preparation and doesn't sell well, maybe you should take it off the menu —or at least try to find out why it doesn't sell well. Maybe you should change the recipe. For example, if your beef stew sells poorly, you might want to omit it because it requires preparation time and it is going to involve more problems if you have it left over than items that are cooked to order. On the other hand, you may have a cheese omelet on the menu that doesn't sell well. But it is cooked to order, and you have cheese and eggs in the kitchen anyway, so you may decide to keep it on the menu.

Generally items should be kept on the menu if:

1. Guests like them.
2. You can produce them easily.
3. They sell well.
4. They make money for you.

Some items will obviously be your top sellers. Some you should obviously stop offering. For other items, it will be harder to be sure. Sales analysis gives you insight into guest preferences. This can be very useful in planning future menus and production.

Forecasting

Sales analysis information can help you do better forecasting. If you are using a standardized menu, it is easy to use the percentage index (discussed in Chapter 11) because you have the actual figures of what items were sold. This is the basis for planning future production based on what people actually ordered the last time the menu was used. By using statistical information for planning production, you can eliminate some of the problems of under-and overproduction.

Adjusting Menu Prices

In Chapter 11, Pre-Control and Pre-Costing the Menu, we discussed potential cost based on estimated sales of items and actual sales of items. Sales analysis information gives you the actual count of items actually sold. The number of items sold multiplied by their selling price tells you the total dollar amount you should receive. Use this to compute the potential food cost you should be able to get. If you are not achieving the food cost you want, you may want to change some menu items or adjust some prices. If you increase the selling price of one item, it may cause guests to switch from that item to another item that will give you the revenue and food cost you want. Sales analysis information gives you the actual figures you need in order to make these decisions.

Revenue

Sales analysis information can help you check on your revenue. The number of items sold multiplied by their selling price should equal the amount of money received and in the cash register. Information from the sales analysis can also tell you the sales per individual sales person. Add up the guest checks for each sales person and the number of guests each sales person served. These totals for all service persons should equal the total revenue you should have in your cash register and the total number of guests served. Divide the total sales by the total number of guests. This tells you the average check per guest served. This gives you an indication of the revenue you are receiving from each guest. If you are satisfied, fine. If not, you may want to devise ways to try to increase the revenue per guest.

Keeping track of guest count can give you useful information. This is especially true during inflationary times. Check your records. Are you serving your normal number of guests? Are you serving more? Perhaps your dollar revenue is increasing but you are actually serving fewer guests—your dollars are higher but your guest count is lower. If so, maybe your expenses are down because it is taking fewer people to bring in the same revenue. This usually does not happen, however. You may want to increase advertising to bring back more guests.

From your guest checks you can compute the average revenue brought in per service person. Divide the total sales by a service person by the number of guests served by that service person. This gives you the average check for each service person. Compare this average against the average check for the establishment. Some service persons will be above and some will be below average. Find out why some are doing well and others poorly. Those below the average may have a poor station or they may not be doing a good job of selling.

You can also divide the total revenue of all sales people by the number of sales people on duty. This will tell you the average sale per service person. Compare the total sales of each service person against the average sales per service person and see how they compare. Some will be doing better than others. Maybe it is the station or maybe these people need additional training in service.

After you have determined the average sales per service employee, this information can be useful for planning work schedules for service people. Divide the estimated sales for a meal period by the average dollar revenue per employee. This will tell you how many service employees you will probably need for that meal.

AFTER SALES ANALYSIS

The information you get from your sales analysis is the final step in your food control cycle. You take the information you get from your sales analysis back to the beginning of the cycle—your menu—and start applying it. Make any changes you should along the way in the cycle, all the way back from selecting menu items and on to pre-costing, pre-control, purchasing, receiving, storing, planning production, and collecting revenue, right through sales analysis again, and repeat the whole circle.

The cycle of control goes on and on and doesn't stop. You go back to the beginning and start again, carrying on the entire checking, correcting, and controlling procedure continuously.

REVIEW AND DISCUSSION QUESTIONS

1. What can you learn from sales analysis?
2. What are the different methods for doing sales analysis?
3. What do you do with sales analysis information?
4. When should you leave an item on your menu? When should you take an item off your menu? Give some examples.
5. You would like to get all the sales analysis information a computer could total and calculate for you, but you don't have a computer. How could you get this same information without a computer?

21

Beverage and Bar Control

Objectives

This chapter shows how the bar contributes to the profitability of your total business. After you have read this chapter, you should:

1. Know what a standard drink list is, and why it is important.
2. Know how to calculate drink costs and prices.
3. Know about different types of beverage dispensing equipment.

BEVERAGE CONTROL

In the area of beverage control, one of your main jobs is to control your beverage cost. Beverage cost may be high due to poor practices by your bartender —overpouring, for example. Mistakes in any steps between buying beverage and selling it can cause high beverage cost and reduce your profit. Poor methods, errors, or lack of good controls in purchasing, receiving, storing, issuing, preparing, pricing, collecting money, and analyzing sales can cost you money. You can be cutting your own profits if you fail to apply standard control procedures—and a very important one among these procedures is your system to control theft.

Some operators are satisfied with the profits they get from their beverage operation and some are not. Almost all of them could get better profits if they improved their complete beverage operation control system.

Divide the Work

Most bartenders are honest. If bartenders do try to steal, it is up to you (management) to prevent them from succeeding. It is your fault if bartenders have the opportunity to steal and are not detected if they try it.

It is your job to divide work and responsibility in all phases of food and beverage control so opportunity for stealing is at least reduced or—ideally —eliminated. It is particularly important for you to divide work and responsibility in the area of liquor control. If you put one bartender in charge of purchasing, receiving, storing, issuing to the bar, mixing drinks, collecting money for drinks, and recording sales—in complete charge of your total beverage operation—you are making stealing extremely tempting and easy for a bartender who is less than 100 percent honest. Try not to put one person in complete charge of your total beverage function. If you do, you have no right to be surprised if you don't get the profits you want from your bar.

Apply checks and balances to your beverage system and pinpoint responsibility. The work of purchasing, receiving, storing, and issuing beverages should be kept completely separate from the work of mixing drinks and collecting cash. The more you can divide the whole beverage operation into small jobs handled by different people, the better your chance for controls will be. Usually, however, it is difficult to do this. For most operations, volume of business is too small to cover labor costs that would be involved in having several different employees handle separate, divided tasks in the whole beverage procedure. Most businesses have to run on a system of having the bartenders mix the drinks and also collect the money for them. This is normal practice, but it makes it very difficult to put in complete beverage controls and eliminate stealing. Temptation is built in.

It is more difficult for a bartender to steal from a beverage operation if the work is divided. Even in small operations, the bartender should not have complete control. There is usually a manager and a bartender, and the manager can at least issue the liquor to the bar.

Ideally, you want to pinpoint responsibility at each level. Have one person receive beverage and another person issue it if you can. It is ideal if you can have just the bartender, no one else, mix drinks, and just the cashier, no one else, collect money for the drinks. Unfortunately, staffing arrangements like this are not possible in most bars because they cannot afford it.

Most bartenders are honest. But, from a management standpoint, controls should be established anyway. If the bartender is honest, all is well. If the bartender is not honest, controls can help cause this fact to show up in increased costs and make it much easier for you to uncover dishonesty.

Try to divide work so more than one person is involved. If a bartender has complete charge and steals, he or she has only himself or herself to worry about. But if other employees handle other areas of work, the bartender will have to have the help of the other individual or individuals in order to steal, and this does a lot to reduce the temptation. It is collusion if more than one person is involved in theft, and it makes theft more complicated to perform, harder to hide, and riskier.

Many employees figure that if a bartender wants the employee to help steal, the bartender is crooked, can't be trusted as a partner, and would probably blow the whistle on the employee if caught. Most employees would not take the risk. This is why it is so important to establish controls and set things up so that the only way an employee can steal is if there is collusion. It should be pointed out, however, that where collusion does exist, you are apt to be taken for a lot more than you probably would be if only one lone individual is stealing—mainly because the stolen money has to be split more ways, so they will take more.

The number of individuals who actually do steal is small. Unfortunately, they have been given a rather bad reputation in general to all who handle liquor. You need to protect the innocent and detect and dismiss the guilty.

Whether you can or cannot split beverage jobs among several people, there are other beverage controls you can and should use.

Liquor Control

Liquor control is similar to food control. Many of the routines and methods discussed in previous chapters on food control apply to liquor control. In the following chapters on beverage control we will emphasize some of the differences.

Beverage control is easier to maintain and simpler to do than is food control. But beverage control has to be tighter than food control and it has to be more strictly enforced because:

1. It is easier for beverage employees to steal money than it is for food employees to steal money.
2. Liquor is more tempting to many employees than food.
3. Liquor is more expensive than most food items.

Beverage control is simpler than food control because you are dealing with a much smaller number of items. Even if you have quite a large variety of beverage items in inventory, it is still small compared to the very large number of items involved in a food operation.

Another reason why beverage control is simpler than food control is because beverages always come to you in standard-size bottles and containers. For commercial use, the minimum size of liquor container purchased is a fifth (4/5 of a quart). Many establishments also use quarts, half-gallons, and so on. Beer is purchased in bottles, or by quarter-barrel or half-barrel, and such. It is simpler to keep track of bottles or half-barrels as they move from storage through a beverage department than it is to keep track of 10 pounds of flour, 15 pounds of sugar, 30 pounds of stew meat. Food items may be purchased and stored in standard sizes of 50 or 100 pound bags for flour, sugar, and so on, but you don't use them in this form. The small operator usually takes broken amounts (less than a 100-pound bag) from the storeroom, so theft is simpler and less noticeable for these items than it would be for beverage.

Beverage control needs to be tighter than food control because it is not generally a great temptation to steal 10 pounds of flour. It can be a great temptation to steal a bottle of liquor, however—especially if employees feel they can get away with it.

Employee Theft

There is a peculiar thing to consider about beverage theft control. Some employees don't think it is really stealing to take a drink of whiskey from their employer without paying for it. They can convince themselves that there is so much liquor at the bar that a shot or two—or a bottle or two—won't be missed. Some employees who will steal your liquor if they can would not steal your money even if it would be rather easy to do it. Somehow they see a difference.

A true story illustrates this. A manager wanted to test this theory that employees are more likely to take liquor than money. He left a $5 bill and a bottle of whiskey in plain sight of all employees. In a very short time the whiskey was gone but the money was still there. Later on the money disappeared, too. An employee had taken the bottle of whiskey. Later the same fellow had come back and taken the money. He was reluctant to steal the money, but he couldn't find a way to steal more whiskey so he took the money so he could go buy some.

Some employees seem to think it is all right to take your liquor. Some really do not seem to feel it is stealing. Most will not take money, or if they do they will be much more hesitant about it. That is one reason why you have to devise thorough and strict beverage control procedures.

Unfortunately no beverage control system is 100 percent perfect, but you've got to keep beverage theft to a minimum. Try to convice all employees of the importance of working towards the common goal of making money for the whole establishment and making money for themselves legitimately in the process. And see that your employees—especially your beverage employees —do make good money for their work.

There is a notion that liquor "evaporates." If you are in an extremely dry climate and bottles are not sealed tight, evaporation can occur. If a very small amount disappears from opened bottles, it could have evaporated. If more than a *little* "evaporates," it did not evaporate. It was probably stolen or wasted by overpouring or careless handling. When a bottle is opened, topped with a pour spout, and left sitting on a shelf for a long time, a little of it could really evaporate. But liquor in unopened bottles with unbroken seals does not evaporate, and neither do glass bottles. If your liquor seems to disappear into the air, 99.9 percent of the time it is not evaporating. It is vanishing because of bad beverage controls. Install tight beverage controls to stop it. If whole un-opened bottles disappear, you certainly can't blame "evaporation." Blame yourself for bad controls.

STANDARD DRINK LIST

If there are problems in your beverage operation, don't simply condemn your bartenders and blame all bar problems on them. Work with your bartenders.

Many bars carry a much larger inventory than they need to. Don't tie up money unnecessarily in inventory. A good way to analyze your inventory is to sit down with your head bartender and develop a list of probably about 25 mixed drinks, the ones most requested in your beverage operation. (It doesn't have to be precisely 25, of course—more or less depending on your operation.) In the United States, martini and manhattan will probably head the list. After that the list will vary depending on what part of the country you're in, although generally popular drinks such as whiskey sour, tom collins, old-fashioned, or stinger are apt to be included in your list.

You will probably find that more than 90 percent of your mixed drink orders come from this list you have made. The remaining 10 percent of your sales will consist of a variety of drinks. But you will know what most of your mixed drink orders will be. After you have prepared your list, you and your head bartender should develop a standard recipe for each one of these mixed drinks. Write each recipe down in a card file or notebook and have this avail-able for all bartenders. Make sure all bartenders use these. Each recipe should clearly specify the exact amount of each ingredient to be used.

If you don't have standardized recipes, bartenders will make drinks according to their own whims or the way they learned to make them at the last place they worked. If you ask five martini drinkers how to make a martini, you will probably get five different martini recipes. There is even one old recipe (which wouldn't go over well today) that calls for a proportion of three parts of gin to one part of vermouth. Today most people would consider this too much vermouth. Have your own regular recipe for martinis (and everything else).

The standard for a martini today is probably six or eight parts of gin to one part vermouth. When customers ask for martinis, some of them would prefer it if your bartender would lightly spray vermouth in the general direction of the gin with an atomizer, or, better yet, wave the vermouth bottle cork very briefly over the gin. A lot of customers who order "dry!" martinis really want straight gin.

Figure out what proportions of gin and vermouth you should put in your standard martini. Otherwise your bartender will be tempted to serve gin and no vermouth to everyone who asks for "A very, very dry martini," but just charge them for a standard martini. Gin is more expensive than vermouth. If your bartender pours extra gin but does not charge extra for it, you lose money. Some beverage operations put "martini" on the list at one price and put "extra-dry martini" on the list at a higher price. Guests can get their extra-dry martinis with more gin, but they will pay more. You and your bartender have to work out decisions like this for all drinks, not just martinis. If you do, you can set selling prices that are fair to you *and* your customers.

Decisions need to be made about how you will prepare all your mixed drinks, when and how you will change your recipes, and what prices you will charge. For example, in a brandy alexander or a grasshopper, the standard recipe calls for light whipping cream. But today very few establishments use real cream in either of these mixed drinks. Most use half-and-half. If yours is the unique establishment that does use light whipping cream in these drinks, though, you should come out with a better product than half-and-half would give you and you should charge more. Whipping cream incorporates air better than half-and-half and you might get more overrun (larger volume) because of the air. Maybe you could use less whipping cream than half-and-half. It may still cost you more to use whipping cream than it would cost you to use half-and-half. But if the end product is better, your customers may not object to paying a bit more. Unfortunately many beverage operations say they use real whipping cream and charge a whipping cream price but use half-and-half.

This is just one example of the type of thing you should know about, think about and make decisions about. Set your prices so you get the profit you want. Go through every item that goes into every drink on your list of 25 (or however many) standard drinks. You will have to make decisions that will affect your costs. Consider every detail before you establish your selling price.

Other Drinks

There is still the problem of the remaining drinks not on your most-requested list of 25 or so. Make sure your bartenders have a book—or several books—available to them at the bar on how to prepare varieties of drinks, including rare and unusual ones. Some beverage companies put out books on how to mix good drinks. Their recipe books will tell you to use their own brands, but you can substitute other brands if you wish. Check with beverage companies about getting copies. You can get other books on drinks from book stores and industry publishers. Recipes in these can serve as guides to your bartenders for making drinks not included in your own standardized list of drink recipes.

Of course, an excellent source of information on how to prepare a particular new or unusual drink may be guests who order it. If they just arrived from a different area where a new or different drink is a favorite, they will probably be glad to explain to the bartender how to make it. They will usually also be quite willing to pay a good price to get this special drink. Special order drinks should not be bargains, but they shouldn't be exhorbitant, either. If special new drinks really catch on and become popular with your guests, develop standardized recipes for them and add them to your other standardized recipes.

We suggested at the outset that you establish a list of about 25 drinks. Revise this list periodically as you need to and add popular new drinks to this list of recipes. This will help train future bartenders and help control overall beverage costs.

Specify Brands

Work with your bartenders. Establish what ingredients they should use. You should probably also list specific brands by name. Decide what brands you will use for bar whiskey, bar gin, bar scotch, and so on. A brand used as "bar" whiskey in one beverage operation may be used as "call" whiskey in another. The term "bar" whiskey (or "bar" gin, or "bar" anything) is a brand you can get for less cost than some other brands. It is the brand you use if no brand is specified by the guest. When customers ask for whiskey, gin, scotch (anything) without naming a specific brand name, they get your bar brand. It can be a brand that is not especially well known, but it should be good quality. To many people, the term "bar" whiskey (gin, scotch, etc.), means cheap and inferior. Some bars do serve cheap bar liquors. Don't use really inferior quality liquors for your bar brands. Bar brands should be comparatively inexpensive for you to buy but they should be good quality.

"Call" whiskey (or "call" gin, "call" scotch, etc.) means guests ask for the item by special brand name. Normally you will sell call liquors at a higher price than bar liquors. If guests just say, "Give me a whiskey and water," give them your bar whiskey at your set, standard price. But if they say, "Give me Brand X Whiskey and water," give them Brand X Whiskey and water. They should pay a reasonably higher price for this than they would if they had just ordered whiskey without naming a brand. You are justified in charging more for call whiskey because it costs you more than your relatively less expensive bar whiskey and the guests have asked for a specific brand.

Make good decisions about your choices of liquors and beverage recipes. Serve a product which is of a quality that is suitable for your type of beverage operation. Use good qualities for bar whiskey, bar gin, bar scotch, and so on. You will use these in mixed drinks when guests don't specify brand names. They should be good drinks and they should bring you a good profit.

Use a Shot Glass

We've discussed your list of 25 standard, most common drinks. You work out exact proportions for these. But there are a lot of other details you have to work out, too. For example, when someone orders whiskey and water, what size shot glass will you use? One ounce? One and a fourth ounce? Seven-eighths of an ounce? Decide on a specific size shot glass (or other measuring device) and insist that it is used at all times. Many bartenders claim they can pour accurately without measuring, and perhaps some can. But there is danger of overpouring or underpouring unless they use an exact measurement every time.

In a bar operation there will be many details to consider. Rules and routines must be established and followed. Your bartenders should not set these policies and make these decisions. You, the manager, working with the bartenders, should. Set bar operation procedures ahead of time. Then make sure they are followed.

THE BAR CONTRIBUTES TO THE PROFITABILITY OF THE TOTAL BUSINESS

The fact that you have liquor for sale does not mean you will *automatically* make profit. There is profit to be made in operating a bar, but you have to set a correct price for each drink in the first place, you have to collect properly for each drink, and you have to have volume. Many people entering the food and beverage industry have the idea that their bar is sure to make plenty of money, so their food can be sold at breakeven or loss. Wrong. Both beverage and food must contribute to the profitability of the food and beverage operation.

An average food and beverage establishment will normally take in about $1 in beverage sales for every $3 it gets in food sales. This average is somewhat slanted by the fact that some operations sell only food and no beverage and some sell mostly beverage and very little food. Beverage laws of most states require beverage establishments to sell food. Some beverage operators who do not want to get into much food service solve this by selling pizza for $7.50, a cold roast beef sandwich for $3.50, and a hamburger for $2.50. They intentionally overprice their food so they won't get many orders for it.

But an average food *and* beverage operation which wants to sell as much of both food and beverage as possible should try for a reasonable balance of food and beverage sales.

How Costs Are Computed

One reason why a bar can *look* like it is making a lot of money even if it really isn't is the way bar costs are computed. In most food and beverage operations, the bar is charged only for:

1. Material cost—this can run anywhere from 20 to 40 percent of the sales dollar.
2. Direct payroll—this includes the salaries and wages of bartenders and cocktail waiters and waitresses and can run from 12 to 20 percent of the sales dollar.
3. Direct bar overhead—this includes glassware, cocktail napkins, giveaway items, and so forth, and can run from 3 to 10 percent of the sales dollar.

A typical bar might, for example, have beverage cost 30 percent, direct payroll cost 15 percent, and direct overhead cost 5 percent. If you look at it this way, the bar makes a 50 percent profit. But the items just mentioned are direct charges only. Heat, light, and proportionate rent and taxes (among other things) are not charged to the bar. These expenses should be charged against combined food and beverage sales. They should not be charged just to the food department or just to the bar department. Don't arbitrarily try to allocate these expenses as a proportionate amount to either department. Charge direct costs affecting the food department to the food department. Charge combined total indirect charges against combined food and beverage sales.

If all costs for heat, light, rent, and so on are charged just to food and none of it to bar, it looks at first glance like the bar has a 50 percent net profit. But it really doesn't. Actually it has a 50 percent operating profit, which is not net profit. The bar contributes to the total profitability of the entire food and beverage operation. The bar helps you sell food. Food helps you sell beverage. Both should contribute to your profitability.

The cost of service personnel is one to examine closely, for instance. Many beverage operations do not have separate cocktail service personnel. They use the regular food service personnel to serve drinks to guests in the dining room. This cost is usually just charged against total combined food and beverage sales, and it should be. This is recommended accounting procedure and it is fine—but it may make the bar's departmental profit look better than it really is. The bar's direct costs (such as cost of beverage sold, direct labor, and direct overhead) should be charged to the bar and computed and compared against beverage sales. If special cocktail waiters or waitresses are used, their wages should be charged directly to the bar operation. This will help define a norm for the bar to use in setting its standards. The bar operation should compare itself to its own norm. All *direct* bar costs should be charged to the bar so you have the actual facts on the bar profit, not just part of the picture.

The bar should be expected to contribute substantially to the overall profitability of the business and it should be analyzed realistically according to its real expenses and its real profits.

Costing and Pricing Drinks

Work out potential costs for liquor. You can apply the concepts we discussed for potential food cost to potential beverage cost. (See Chapter 11, Chart 11-3.)

Say you buy a quart of whiskey to sell in your operation. You pay $6.30 for it. You estimate that you expect to get 30 drinks from this quart. Divide $6.30 (total whiskey cost to you) by 30 (number of drinks). This tells you that the whiskey costs you 21 cents per drink.

Next you figure out the average cost to you for mix and all other ingredients (garnish, soda, ice) per drink. These additional items (not including the main ingredient which is whiskey) are called "surrounding costs." Say you find the average you spend for surrounding costs is 3 cents per drink. Add the 3 cents to the 21 cents and you get your total average beverage cost per drink— 24 cents per drink.

It is probably better to find an average figure for your surrounding cost. Some guests will order whiskey and soda (soda is surrounding cost), some will order whiskey and water (no surrounding cost for water). So whiskey and water won't cost you exactly the same amount of money as whiskey and soda do. Normally, however, you will sell both drinks for the same price. You figure the average cost per drink including averaged surrounding cost.

To get the selling price, you decide what beverage cost percent you want and divide it into 100 percent. Suppose, for example, you want a 25 percent beverage cost percent. You divide 25 percent into 100 percent. Your markup percent is 400 percent. You multiply the 24 cents average cost per drink we just discussed by the 400 pecent markup. You get a selling price of 96 cents per drink. Normally you price everything on a 5-cent basis. So you decide (based on your own market) whether to round this off at a price of 95 cents or $1. Most beverage operations would probably charge the $1.

Not all beverage items (or food items either) are priced by the same standard markup. You should probably use a markup lower than 400 percent for some items and higher than 400 percent for others. Suppose, for example, you compute the cost and markup for a brandy alexander. According to your calculations, you should sell it for $1.05. Many operations might price a brandy alexander at $1.25. They add 20 cents as a nuisance value cost because there is extra work involved in cleaning the mixer after a cream drink is prepared. When special extras in time and work are involved in a particular item, allow for them in your pricing. Adjust prices individually when you need to so you will get the beverage cost you want.

Working with your bartender, decide (ahead of time) what you will do about pricing drinks that are not on your standard drink list. For instance, you could set guidelines for pricing—bartenders should charge a specific amount per ounce for cordial, for whiskey, for gin, for vermouth—plus a set amount per drink for surrounding cost. Bartenders should have recipe sources plus pricing guidelines for drinks not on your standard list.

Prices should be in line with your other prices. Drinks not on your drink list should be profitable for you. It may take extra time for your bartenders to make them (they may have to look up a recipe, get special ingredients). Keep prices reasonable for you *and* for your guests. Guests will usually be primarily concerned with getting what they want. The 25 cents extra for a special drink, for example, may not mean very much to your guests, but that 25 cents (or whatever amount) extra for many special drinks you serve can mean a lot to you. It could mean better profitability for your total food and beverage operation.

DISPENSING MACHINES

There are many types of liquor dispensing machines on the market. They range from very simple to very sophisticated. In many, you set the machine's controls on the amounts you want, invert the bottle into the machine, and the machine will measure and dispense the portions you have set on the machine. Some will keep count of how many drinks they measure out.

Advantages of Dispensing Machines

The following are advantages with most beverage dispensing machines:

1. Drink size is pre-set.
2. Drink is automatically measured, so there is no overpouring or underpouring.
3. Yield per bottle is consistently better because the bottle drains completely into the dispenser.
4. Each portion is precisely and accurately measured.
5. Besides dispensing liquor, some machines can meter each drink. They can count and keep visible records. This helps to take inventory.
6. Machines can be especially useful for mixing martinis, manhattans, or the like, where the precise amounts of vermouth and gin or vermouth and whiskey are measured into a standard drink.
7. Properly set up, some machines can do the whole drink-making job faster than a bartender can.

8. There is no spilling.

9. If machines meter drinks, it cuts theft. Bartenders can't alter the number sold. The bartender should have money in the cash register for each drink metered by machine.

10. Some machines are so sophisticated that they can measure, dispense, count the drinks, print the guest check, and maintain a perpetual inventory.

11. Machines never drink on the job, steal, or give drinks to their pals.

Disadvantages of Dispensing Machines

There are some disadvantages involved with dispensing machines.

1. Expense.
   A major disadvantage of beverage dispensing machines is the cost of buying them. Decide whether you should or should not get a beverage dispensing machine on the basis of what it can and cannot do for you. Can you offset the cost of buying or leasing a dispensing machine by tighter controls, higher yield per bottle, better revenue? Is it worth the price? Normally you should have high volume in order to justify buying (or leasing) and installing some of the more expensive, sophisticated types of dispensing equipment.
   Equipment for automatically measuring and/or dispensing beverage has improved considerably in the past few years. You can get very simple devices that you attach to a bottle to measure the exact shot. You can get many types of devices ranging all the way up to very sophisticated machines that measure the drink and record it on a guest check and in a memory bank. Operations which have high volume, transient clientele, and transient employees (racetrack bars, for example) might give very serious consideration to installing sophisticated measuring and dispensing machines.

2. Unpopularity in some operations.
   A luxurious private club with about, for example, 400 members might do better *not* getting complicated equipment. The atmosphere and requirements of a private club are very different from those of a racetrack bar. Members of a private club might prefer to have their own bartender for the comradery and individual personal service that a bartender in a small club can provide. There have been instances where private club members have thoroughly disliked automated drink dispensers and have rejected them where they have been tried. The management of a private club should bow to members' preferences in a matter like this.

Investigate Equipment Available

Many food and beverage operations have installed various kinds of automatic beverage measuring and dispensing equipment, and many are extremely satisfied with them. The range of available equipment is changing constantly. If you are contemplating installing equipment, check the market carefully. Find out what is available, what it costs, and whether you can justify the expense or not. The equipment has improved mechanically and also in terms of design. A lot of the new equipment looks better these days and can be bought in size, shape, color, and design to fit in with the total decor of different kinds of establishments.

The equipment also works better. Operators who put in dispensing systems several years ago sometimes found that the equipment was slow, which caused real problems during rush periods. Some also found that they needed more than one unit. The equipment they had was inadequate or slow, so they did not use it and went back to hand pouring. When they needed their systems the most—during busy times—they didn't use them because they were too slow. As a result the equipment was of limited value. Today most of the previous problems and deficiencies in the equipment have been resolved. The equipment available today is fast, efficient, and more attractive than it was several years ago.

Automatic beverage dispensing equipment today usually comes with a total program of beverage control. The equipment company usually provides forms they have devised that help you take inventory and compute your bar costs. A standardized program used with machines can help you get the beverage cost you want.

Evaluate the pros and cons of installing dispensing machines as you would evaluate advantages and disadvantages of purchasing any new equipment. Analyze what an automatic beverage dispensing machine can and cannot do to help you run your operation more efficiently and help you get the profits you want. As a guideline, the cost of installing and maintaining the beverage equipment should be returned to you through increased efficiency, lower labor cost for your volume of business, and a reduced beverage cost percent. The savings should be converted to dollar amounts, and these savings should pay, over a period of time, for the cost of installing the equipment. The dispensing machines should at least pay for themselves. Ideally, they should increase your profits.

SUMMARY

As we said at the beginning of this chapter, the fact that you have a bar does not automatically mean that your bar will make profit. You have to have volume. You have to control costs. Like every other facet of your food and beverage business, your bar has to be managed. It has to be controlled. Work with your bartender. A bar is unique because, unfortunately, in many instances it has to be set up so that the bartender is responsible for mixing drinks and collecting money. This creates opportunities for unscrupulous bartenders to take advantage of the establishment. In the following chapters we will discuss procedures to minimize this.

REVIEW AND DISCUSSION QUESTIONS

1. Why should liquor control be tighter than food control?
2. How does the bar contribute to the profitability of the total business?
3. How are drinks costed and priced?
4. What drinks would you put on a standard drink list?
5. Under what circumstances would you want liquor dispensing equipment if you were:
   a. the manager.
   b. the bartender.
   c. the customer.
6. A guest "calls" for a particular brand of whiskey. It happens to be your "bar" whiskey. Should you charge the guest a higher price?

22

Bar Cost Formulas

Objectives

This chapter discusses various formulas used in bar operation. After you have read this chapter, you should:

1. Know how to maintain beverage storeroom control.
2. Know how to compute daily or weekly bar cost.
3. Know how to compute your potential sales revenue based on quantity of liquor used.

There are three different formulas for computing daily or weekly beverage cost. Use one or more of them or use variations of all three so that they are adjusted for your own needs.

Formula 1 tells you your bar cost for the day or week based on adjusted issues. It should be used completely or partially by all beverage establishments. Any operation that does not use all of Formula 1 should at least use part of it—the part that pertains to storeroom control (Columns 1 through 6, Chart 22-1).

Formula 2 tells you your weekly bar cost based on bar inventory. This formula is used at the bar.

Formula 3 tells you the amount of revenue you should receive based on the quantity of liquor you sold.

Some beverage operations use variations and combinations of all three of these formulas or parts of them. In general, most operations will use one formula and part of another. Smaller operations are apt to use Formulas 1 and /or 2. Larger establishments may use Formula 2 or 3 plus the storeroom control part (Columns 1 through 6) of Formula 1. Very large establishments might, for example, use part of Formula 1 (Columns 1 through 6) for storeroom control; Formula 2 to find out how much liquor they used in terms of cost; and Formula 3 to find the amount of revenue they should have received.

Combine or adjust the following three formulas in any way you want so that you come up with a bar cost formula or revenue formula that suits you best.

BAR COST FORMULA NUMBER 1 (ADJUSTED ISSUES FORMULA) —CHART 22-1

Formula 1 is also called the "Adjusted Issues Formula" because:

1. The basic key to this cost formula is issues from the storeroom.

2. Issues from the storeroom (which are the basis for daily, weekly, or cumulative cost) are adjusted to make allowances for transfer of items to and from the bar.

This formula is the easiest one to do. For Formula 1 you don't have to take inventory of open bottles at the bar. But Formula 1 tells you less than Formula 2 or Formula 3 do.

There are four equations in Formula 1. They are:

1. OPENING INVENTORY BEVERAGE STOREROOM BEGINNING OF DAY plus BEVERAGE STOREROOM PURCHASES equals TOTAL BEVERAGE AVAILABLE STOREROOM.

2. TOTAL BEVERAGE AVAILABLE STOREROOM minus BEVERAGE REQUISITIONS equals CLOSING INVENTORY BEVERAGE STOREROOM.

1	2	3	4	5	6	7	8	9	10	11	12	13	14
Date	Day	Opening Beverage Storeroom Inventory Beginning of Day	Beverage Storeroom Purchases	Total Beverage Available Storeroom	Beverage Requisitions Storeroom	Transfers from Kitchen to Bar	Transfers from Bar to Kitchen	Today Cost of Beverage Sold	Today Beverage Sales	Today Beverage Cost Percent Per Dollar Sale	To-Date Cost of Beverage Sold	To-Date Beverage Sales	To-Date Beverage Cost Percent Per Dollar Sale
Mar. 1	M	3041 42	317 39	3358 81	154 13	6 57	2 19	158 51	388 25	40 83	158 51	388 25	40 83
2	T	3204 68	212 51	3417 19	97 87	8 23	1 58	104 52	367 40	28 45	263 03	755 65	34 81
3	W	3319 32	-0-	3319 32	138 33	4 19	-0-	144 52	536 10	26 58	405 55	1291 75	31 41
4 Th		3180 99	-0-	3180 99	149 17	3 28	-0-	152 45	479 80	31 77	558 00	1771 55	31 50
5	F	3031 82	346 47	3378 29	119 42	6 51	3 47	122 46	621 60	19 70	680 46	2393 15	28 43
6	S	3258 87	-0-	3258 87	166 76	8 13	1 86	173 03	559 30	30 94	853 49	2952 45	28 91
7	S	3092 11				-0-	-0-	-0-	-0-				
Total Week I		-0-	876 37	-0-	825 68	36 91	9 10	853 49	2952 45	28 91			
8	M	3092 11	332 14	3424 25	147 38	7 14	5 12	149 40	404 75	36 91	1002 89	3357 20	29 87
9	T	3276 87											

Follow Same Procedure for Rest of Month

Chart 22-1 Bar Cost Formula Number 1 (Adjusted Issues Formula) Bar is closed Sunday.

3. BEVERAGE REQUISITIONS plus TRANSFERS FROM KITCHEN TO BAR minus TRANSFERS FROM BAR TO KITCHEN equals COST OF BEVERAGE SOLD.

4. COST OF BEVERAGE SOLD divided by TODAY BEVERAGE SALES multiplied by 100 to convert to a percentage equals TODAY BEVERAGE COST PERCENT PER DOLLAR SALE.

The easiest way to use this formula is to prepare a chart on column paper as shown in Chart 22-1 and do the following steps:

1. Column 1: Date.
   You always start a new chart the first of each month, so your Date column always starts with 1.

2. Column 2: Day.
   In the Day column, put whatever day the first of the month happens to fall on. (S if it's Saturday, W if it's Wednesday, and so on.) In our sample Chart 22-1, we say you are starting on March 1, and we say it is a Monday. COLUMNS 3 THROUGH 11 ARE TODAY FIGURES—JUST DAILY, DAY BY DAY—NOT INCREASING AND NOT ACCUMULATING AS YOU GO.

3. Column 3: Opening Beverage Storeroom Inventory Beginning of Day.
   This figure is the total dollar value amount of all beverage in your beverage storeroom on the first day of the month—Monday, March 1 in our chart. You get this figure from your closing physical beverage storeroom inventory for the last day of the preceding month. Or get the figures from your perpetual inventory totals—the totals of all bin cards. Or you could take the bottom figure in Column 3 from your Formula 1 February chart if you did not take a physical inventory at the end of February.
   In Chart 22-1, on Monday, March 1, your Column 3 Opening Beverage Storeroom Inventory Beginning of Day figure is $3,041.42. On Monday, March 1, you start the day with $3,041.42 worth of beverage in your storeroom.
   Column 3 always has one figure more than it has days in the month. That is because you are using Column 3 to record both opening and closing inventories for the month. Your closing inventory figure for Monday, March 1 is your Column 3 Opening Beverage Inventory Beginning of Day figure for Tuesday, March 2.
   Closing inventory for Date 1 is $3,204.68. Put this in Column 3 Date 2 because closing inventory for Date 1 is Opening Beverage Inventory Beginning of Day for Date 2.
   To get Date 2 for this Column 3, you do the following steps:

   a. Add Column 4 Beverage Storeroom Purchases Date 1 $317.39 and Column 3 Opening Beverage Storeroom Inventory Beginning of Day Date 1 $3,041.42. You get $3,358.81. This $3,358.81 is your Column 5 Total Beverage Available Storeroom Date 1.

   b. Subtract Column 6 Beverage Requisitions Date 1 $154.13 from Column 5 Total Beverage Available Storeroom Date 1 $3,358.81. You get

$3,204.68. This $3,204.68 is Column 3 Opening Beverage Inventory Beginning of Day Date 2.

4. Column 4: Beverage Storeroom Purchases.

On Monday, March 1 you received Beverage Storeroom Purchases of $317.39 worth of beverage. You put the beverage in your beverage storeroom. This beverage should not leave the storeroom unless it is requisitioned in writing.

You get this figure by adding the dollar value of all beverage invoices for the beverage you put in the beverage storeroom each day. This figure is all beverage items that will go into the beverage storeroom. When they leave the beverage storeroom, requisitions will be written for the items and then they will go directly to the bar.

5. Column 5: Total Beverage Available Storeroom.

To get this figure for Monday, March 1, you add Column 3 Opening Beverage Inventory Beginning of Day Date 1 $3,041.42 and Column 4 Beverage Storeroom Purchases Date 1 $317.39. You get $3,358.81. This $3,358.81 is your Column 5 Total Beverage Available Storeroom Date 1 figure (Monday, March 1).

This figure is the dollar amount of your total inventory plus items you received and put into the storeroom that day.

This is the value of beverage you had to start with on Monday morning March 1 plus what you received Monday—the total value of beverage available to you on Monday, March 1.

6. Column 6: Beverage Requisitions.

You get this figure by adding up all your beverage requisition slips for Monday, March 1. The Date 1 (Monday, March 1) figure on Chart 22-1 is $154.13. Add up all beverage requisitions for the day to get your total dollar cost of all beverage items removed from your storeroom that day. $154.13 worth of beverage was removed from your storeroom on Monday, March 1. Requisitions were written for all this beverage. All the beverage went directly to the bar.

If you want to use only part of this Formula 1 Chart 22-1 for storeroom control, you would just use Columns 1 through 6. This would tell you what you started with, what you have added to the storeroom, what you have taken out of the storeroom, and what you have left. You can do the chart daily or weekly. Columns 1 through 6 of Formula 1 can be used in conjunction with Formula 2 or Formula 3. This will help give you tight security and control in terms of dollars for your beverage storeroom. If you also use bin cards (discussed in Chapter 23) besides this, you should get maximum control of your storeroom.

7. Column 7: Transfers from Kitchen to Bar.

This means items you transfer from the kitchen to the beverage department. The bar can requisition cream, milk, eggs, oranges, lemons, limes, cherries, olives, and such from the kitchen. They are sent to the bar and used in drinks. These are food items taken from the kitchen and used in drinks. Don't charge these to food cost. Charge them to the bar.

If bartenders need food items to use in drinks at the bar, they write requisitions for the food items and give them to the kitchen personnel—probably cooks or whomever you designate. Whoever is keeping the bar cost formula chart gets these requisitions from the cooks, adds them up, and puts the figure in this column every day.

8. Column 8: Transfers from Bar to Kitchen.

Transfers from bar to kitchen are bar items needed in the kitchen in food production. These are items transferred to your kitchen from your bar. The chef (or anyone you designate in the kitchen) makes requisitions for items the kitchen wants from the bar and gives the requisitions to the bartender. Whoever makes up the bar cost formula chart gets the requisitions from the bartender and puts the dollar amounts of transfers to the kitchen for the day in this column.

Examples of transfers from bar to kitchen would be beer requisitioned from the bar and used in the kitchen to make welch rarebit, wine requisitioned from the bar and used in the kitchen for cooking, and so on. These are bar beverage items. But they are not beverage items available for bar beverage sale. They are used in the kitchen as ingredients in food. Charge their cost to food cost, not to bar or beverage department cost.

Some operations ignore transfers to kitchen and transfers to bar because they don't think there is enough money involved to bother with making the calculations and putting them in the chart. It is up to you to decide if you think it is worthwhile for you or not. You should, however, be aware that food items taken from the kitchen and used at the bar in drink preparation cannot be sold as food, and beverage items taken from the bar and used for food preparation in the kitchen cannot be sold as bar items, so there will be an effect on bar and kitchen costs if there are transfers. How much these transactions can alter your cost of beverage sold depends on how much transferring goes on and how much the items cost. If enough transfers take place to affect your cost of beverage sold, you should be aware of it.

9. Column 9: Today Cost of Beverage Sold.

If you don't calculate transfers from kitchen to bar and transfers from bar to kitchen, then your Column 9 Today Cost of Beverage Sold figure for a day will be the same as that same day's figure in Column 6 Beverage Requisitions. If you don't calculate transfers, you have not adjusted your issues. You are just using issues as the only basis for calculating your beverage cost—instead of using "adjusted" issues, which means you *do* include all transfers.

We will assume you do make calculations for transfers and go on to the next step.

To get your figure for Column 9 Today Cost of Beverage Sold Date 1, you add Column 6 Beverage Requisitions Date 1 $154.13 and Column 7 Transfers From Kitchen to Bar Date 1 $6.57. You get $160.70 (which does not appear on the chart). You subtract Column 8 Transfers From Bar to Kitchen Date 1 $2.19 from this $160.70 (total of Column 6 Date 1 and Column 7 Date 1). You get $158.51. This $158.51 is your figure for Date 1 in Column 9 Today Cost of Beverage Sold.

Follow this procedure through the rest of the month.

Note: Back in Chapter 9 on food cost formulas, we told you to deduct for "employees' meals" from cost of food used. Here now in your bar cost formula we have *not* told you to deduct for "employees' beverages" from cost of beverage used! There should be no drinking by any employees on duty. They should not be permitted to buy drinks, get them free, or bring any drinks in from outside.

If you do have a free-drinks-for-guests policy, and your bartenders are permitted to give a few drinks a week free to customers, you might want to consider adding another column for "Giveaways" to Chart 22-1 Bar Formula 1 to recognize and allow for the fact that there is a cost for doing this.

10. Column 10: Today Beverages Sales.

This is your total beverage sales for Monday, March 1. You get this figure from your closing cash register tape for Monday. In Chart 22-1 you had $388.25 in beverage sales on Monday, March 1.

Get the closing figure from your cash register tape every day for this column.

11. Today Beverage Cost Percent Per Dollar Sale.

You get this figure by doing the following: Divide Column 9 Today Cost of Beverage Sold Date 1 $158.51 by Column 10 Today Beverage Sales Date 1 $388.25. You get .4083. Multiply by 100 to convert to a percentage. You get 40.83 percent. This 40.83 percent is your Column 11 Today Beverage Cost Percent Per Dollar Sale Date 1 figure.

Follow this procedure for the rest of the month.

COLUMNS 12, 13, AND 14 ARE TO-DATE FIGURES. THESE COLUMNS *DO* INCREASE AND *DO* ACCUMULATE FOR THE MONTH AS YOU GO ALONG.

12. Column 12: To-Date Cost of Beverage Sold.

For Date 1, your Column 12 figure is the same as Column 9 Today Cost of Beverage Sold Date 1 $158.51.

To get Column 12 Date 2, do the following: Add Column 12 To-Date Cost of Beverage Sold Date 1 $158.51 and Column 9 Today Cost of Beverage Sold Date 2 $104.52. This gives you Column 12 To-Date Cost of Beverage Sold Date 2 $263.03.

To get Column 12 Date 3, do the following: Add Column 12 To-Date Cost of Beverage Sold Date 2 $263.03 and Column 9 Today Cost of Beverage Sold Date 3 $142.52. This gives you Column 12 To-Date Cost of Beverage Sold Date 3 $405.55.

Follow this procedure for the rest of the month.

13. Column 13: To-Date Beverage Sales.

For Date 1 your Column 13 figure is the same as Column 10 Today Beverage Sales Date 1 $388.25.

To get Column 13 Date 2, do the following: Add Column 13 To-Date Beverage Sales Date 1 $388.25 and Column 10 Today Beverage Sales Date 2 $367.40. This gives you Column 13 To-Date Beverage Sales Date 2 $755.65.

To get Column 13 Date 3 do the following: Add Column 13 To-Date Beverage Sales Date 2 $755.65 and Column 10 Today Beverage Sales Date

3 $536.10. This give you Column 13 To-Date Beverage Sales Date 3 $1,291.75.

Follow this procedure for the rest of the month.

14. Column 14: To-Date Beverage Cost Percent Per Dollar Sale.

To get this figure you do the following: Divide Column 12 To-Date Cost of Beverage Sold Date 1 $158.51 by Column 13 To-Date Beverage Sales Date 1 $388.25. You get .4083. Multiply this .4083 by 100 to convert to a percentage. You get 40.83 percent. This figure is your Column 14 To-Date Beverage Cost Percent Per Dollar Sale for Date 1.

Follow this same procedure for the rest of the month.

Note: When you compute Column 14 To-Date Beverage Cost Percent Per Dollar Sale, it is especially important that you *always* divide Column 12 To-Date Cost of Beverage Sold by Column 13 To-Date Beverage Sales. Don't ever try to average your cumulative beverage cost percents. It will not be accurate.

In Formula 1, to arrive at cost of beverage sold, requisitions are adjusted to allow for transfers to and from the bar. Transfers were added to or subtracted from the costs on the requisitions. This adjusted cost is your beverage cost when you use Formula 1. It assumes that whatever is requisitioned is used.

On a daily basis, this formula will not be very accurate because it assumes that your cost was only the cost of items removed from the storeroom that day and adjusted by transfers. Actually, though, you may be using many items which were already on hand at the bar and which you don't replace at the bar that day.

Over a period of several days, the cumulative to-date columns (Columns 12, 13, and 14) begin to indicate the trend your cost is taking. It is a simple procedure to set up and maintain Formula 1. The only adjustments you make in the dollar value of your requisitions are for transfers to and from the bar.

At the end of the month, closing storeroom inventory for the last day (shown as last figure for the month in Column 3 Chart 22-1) should exactly equal physical inventory, which you should take the last day of the month. A physical inventory is recommended so that you can be sure your perpetual storeroom inventory has been maintained accurately.

On the last day of the month, physical beverage storeroom inventory and perpetual beverage storeroom inventory should be identical. If they are not, find out why they don't agree. Possible reasons are:

1. Items were removed from storeroom without requisitions.

2. Items were stolen from the storeroom.

Check your perpetual inventory cards (discussed in Chapter 23) and try to find out if requisitions for items taken from the storeroom were lost or misplaced, or if there were no requisitions made out at all. If you cannot find a requisition for a missing bottle and there is no record on your perpetual inventory card to indicate where the bottle went, assume the bottle was stolen. Take action to assure that all items will be properly requisitioned and accounted for. Tighten control so no one can steal liquor from the storeroom. If any liquor is not exactly where it should be and all is not in absolutely correct order, you should automatically assume the worst (theft), act accordingly, and put even stricter controls into effect immediately.

BAR COST FORMULA NUMBER 2 (DAILY BAR INVENTORY)—CHART 22-2

Bar Cost Formula Number 2 is much more accurate than Formula Number 1, but Number 2 is more work. It involves taking inventories and making extensions (which Formula 1 does not).

This formula is based on the idea of taking physical inventory at the bar. Large-volume operations may take inventory every day. Small-volume operations may find it satisfactory if they take inventory just once a week. Your figures will be affected depending on whether you take inventory daily or weekly. If you do the formula daily, you will get day-to-day variations, which will appear in your cumulative beverage cost for the week. If you do the formula weekly, you will get week-to-week variations, which will appear in your cumulative beverage cost for the month.

For most smaller operations who use Formula 2, it would probably be better to do Formula 2 just once a week, unless their liquor costs are way out of line. Then they should do a daily formula chart.

Whether inventory is daily or weekly, your figures should be cumulative for the entire month. Weekly figures should still include all transactions that affect your bar during the week. For smaller operations, weekly inventory is probably more feasible. For them it may not be worth the time and work to take physical inventory and make extensions every day. If you take inventory on a weekly basis, your cumulative to-date figures from your weekly (instead of daily) columns can still give you cumulative costs for the month—not as up-to-the-minute as the daily system would, but still timely enough to help a small operation.

In Formula 2 you do take actual physical inventory at the bar.

There are three equations in Formula 2. They are:

1. OPENING INVENTORY BAR plus REQUISITIONED BY THE BAR plus TRANSFERS FROM KITCHEN TO BAR equals TOTAL BEVERAGE AVAILABLE.

2. TOTAL BEVERAGE AVAILABLE minus TRANSFERS FROM BAR TO KITCHEN minus CLOSING INVENTORY BAR equals TODAY COST OF BEVERAGE SOLD.

1	2	3	4	5	6	7	8	9	10	11	12	13	14
Date	Day	Opening Inventory Bar	Requisitioned by the Bar	Transfers from Kitchen To Bar	Total Beverage Available	Transfers from Bar To Kitchen	Closing Inventory Bar	Today Cost of Beverage Sold	Today Beverage Sales	Today Beverage Cost Percent Per Dollar Sale	To-Date Cost of Beverage Sold	To-Date Beverage Sales	To-Date Beverage Cost Percent Per Dollar Sale
Mar. 1	M	357 16	154 13	6 57	517 86	2 19	405 91	109 76	388 25	28 27	109 76	388 25	28 27
2	T	405 91	97 87	8 23	512 01	1 58	409 62	100 81	367 40	27 44	210 57	755 65	27 87
3	W	409 62	138 33	4 19	552 14	-0-	404 61	147 53	536 10	27 52	358 10	1291 75	27 72
4	Th	404 61	149 17	3 28	557 06	-0-	423 11	133 95	479 80	27 92	492 05	1771 55	27 78
5	F	423 11	119 42	6 51	549 04	3 47	374 93	170 64	621 60	27 45	662 69	2393 15	27 69
6	S	374 93	166 76	8 13	548 82	1 86	394 28	153 68	559 30	27 88	816 37	2952 45	27 65
7	S	394 28	-0-	-0-		-0-		-0-	-0-				
Total/Week I		357 16	825 68	36 91		9 10	394 28	816 37	2952 45	27 65	-0-	-0-	-0-
8	M	394 28	147 38	7 14	431 04	5 12		112 64	404 75	27 83	929 01	3357 20	27 67
		Follow Same Procedure for Rest of Month											

Chart 22-2 Bar Cost Formula Number 2 (Daily Bar Inventory) Bar is closed Sunday.

3. TODAY COST OF BEVERAGE SOLD divided by TODAY BEVERAGE
   SALES multiplied by 100 to convert to percentage equals TODAY
   BEVERAGE COST PERCENT PER DOLLAR SALE.

The only difference between Bar Cost Formula Number 1 and Bar
Cost Formula Number 2 is that in Bar Cost Formula Number 1 you *do not* include opening and closing bar inventory; in Bar Cost Formula Number 2 you
do. However, this is an important difference. With Formula 2 you know the
actual quantities of liquors used. With Formula 1 it is assumed that all liquor
issued to the bar is used immediately, but in reality that is not always true.

Usually you take inventory at the bar in terms of tenths of a bottle.
You examine the bottles and estimate how many tenths remain in each. You
record the information on your inventory sheet. Later you compute the actual
cost of the dollar value each bottle represents by doing extensions (multiplying
the cost of a full bottle by the number of tenths of a bottle you have).

It takes time to take a physical inventory. It takes even more time to
make the extensions. You can take inventory and prepare your bar cost formula chart on a daily or weekly basis. Many beverage operations that use Bar
Cost Formula Number 2 take inventory and make extensions on a weekly
basis.

Many beverage operations are closed on Sundays. For some it is their
own decision; for others state law prohibits the sale of liquor on Sunday. Some
are closed on a different day of the week. No matter what day you have for
your last day of the week, the last thing you do each week right after you have
closed your bar on the day that ends your week is to take physical inventory.
The inventory figures you get are your closing inventory figures for that week
and your opening inventory figures for the following week.

Bar Cost Formula Number 2 is set up in column form. Set up Columns 9, 10, and 11 as your "Today" or your "This Week" figures, depending
on whether you do daily or weekly inventory.

The last three columns—12, 13, and 14—are for "To-Date" figures.
These columns are where you accumulate your daily (or weekly) figures as you
progress into the month.

If you are keeping your books on a monthly basis (as most bar operations do), you should start a new chart the first day of each month.

Some beverage operations maintain bar records on a quarterly basis.
They start a new chart every quarter (three months). They would probably
keep their bar records on a weekly (instead of daily) basis and come up with
weekly figures. Then they would accumulate weekly figures on a weekly basis
for the rest of that quarter.

The easiest way to use this formula is to prepare a chart on column
paper as shown in Chart 22-2 and do the following steps:

1. Column 1: Date.
   If you do daily computation, Date is the first of the month—always 1. If

you do weekly computation, Date is the date on which you start your recordkeeping week. It can be any day. Most commonly a beverage operation's week runs from Monday to Saturday, because a lot of bars are closed on Sunday. They would start their week on Monday morning, so the first date they would put in their Date column would be the date of the first Monday in each new month.

2. Column 2: Day.

   If you do the formula daily, the Day will be whatever the first day of a new month is. If you do the formula weekly, Day will be the first day in the new month when you start your new week.

3. Column 3: Opening Inventory Bar.

   Get this figure from the result of the physical inventory you took on the last day of the month that just ended. You wrote this figure on last month's inventory sheet and called it "closing inventory" for the month. To get the figure in this column for Date 2, you do the following: Your Column 8 Closing Inventory Bar Date 1 figure $405.91 is your Column 3 Opening Inventory Bar Date 2 figure. The Column 8 Closing Inventory Bar Date 1 figure $405.91 is your Column 3 Opening Inventory Bar Date 2 figure $405.91. These figures are the same. Just take the Column 8 figure each day and use it for the next day's figure in Column 3.

   Follow this procedure for the rest of the month.

4. Column 4: Requisitioned By The Bar.

   To get this figure, you add up all requisitions for items from beverage storeroom to bar for the time period involved. If you do it daily, add up the one day's requisitions. If you do it weekly, add up the week's requisitions. Enter this figure in Column 4 Requisitioned By The Bar. For Date 1 the Column 4 figure is $154.13—the total value of items requisitioned by the bar from the beverage storeroom on Date 1.

   Follow this procedure for the rest of the month.

5. Column 5: Transfers From Kitchen To Bar.

   Items requisitioned from the beverage storeroom by the kitchen would go directly to the kitchen and would be included in the amount of beverage requisitioned for that day. This amount would then be included in your transfers from bar to kitchen.

   This column is for items you transfer from the kitchen to the bar. These are food items used in the preparation of drinks. These food items become a part of bar cost because they cannot be sold as food items. Bartenders write requisitions for food items they need and give them to the kitchen personnel you designate. Whoever is keeping the bar cost formula chart gets these requisitions from the kitchen personnel, adds them up, and puts the figure in this column every day (or week).

6. Column 6: Total Beverage Available.

   To get Column 6 Total Beverage Available you add Column 3 Opening Inventory Bar and Column 4 Requisitioned By The Bar and Column 5 Transfers From Kitchen To Bar.

   For Date 1 you add Column 3 Opening Inventory Bar Date 1 $357.16 and Column 4 Requisitioned by the Bar Date 1 $154.13 and Column 5 Transfers from Kitchen to Bar Date 1 $6.57. You get $517.86. This $517.86 is your Column 6 Total Beverage Available Date 1 figure.

Follow this procedure for the rest of the month.

7. Column 7: Transfers from Bar to Kitchen.

Transfers from bar to kitchen are items you use in the kitchen in food production. These are beverage items that should be charged to food cost since they are no longer available for sale at the bar. The chef (or anyone you designate in the kitchen) makes requisitions for items the kitchen wants from the bar. Whoever makes up the bar cost formula chart gets the information from the bar and puts the dollar amount of transfers to the kitchen for the day in this column. The Column 7 Transfers from Bar to Kitchen Date 1 figure is $2.19.

Follow this procedure for the rest of the month.

8. Column 8: Closing Inventory Bar.

You get closing inventory bar figure by taking an actual physical inventory of all beverage items at the bar by tenths of a bottle. Make the extensions. Multiply quantity (the number of tenths in a bottle) by cost of the bottle. Add up all your extensions for all beverage items to get your total. This total is your closing inventory bar figure. Enter this figure on the chart in Column 8 Closing Inventory Bar every day (or every week).

If you do a daily chart, you have to take inventory every day and make extensions every day. If you just do the chart once a week, you take inventory once a week and make extensions once a week. Enter your figures in Column 8 every day or once a week. The Column 8 Closing Inventory Bar Date 1 figure is $405.91.

COLUMNS 9, 10, AND 11 ARE TODAY COLUMNS—THEY DO NOT INCREASE AND THEY DO NOT ACCUMULATE AS YOU GO.

Columns 9, 10, and 11 can be either daily or weekly columns. Chart 22-2 shows daily figures for eight days. If you were doing this chart on a weekly basis, you would enter figures only once a week. Your "This Week" figures would be the same as your "To-Date" figures for week 1. But in week 2, they would not be the same. If you do it weekly, follow the same procedure to get the second week's figures that you would use to get the second day's figures if you do it daily.

9. Column 9: Today Cost of Beverage Sold.

To get this figure, subtract Column 7 Transfers from Bar to Kitchen and Column 8 Closing Inventory Bar from Column 6 Total Beverage Available.

Column 6 Total Beverage Available Date 1 is $517.86.

Subtract Column 7 Transfers from Bar to Kitchen Date 1 $2.19 and Column 8 Closing Inventory Bar Date 1 $405.91 from the $517.86. You get $109.76. This $109.76 is your Column 9 Today Cost of Beverage Sold Date 1 figure.

Follow this procedure for the rest of the month.

10. Column 10: Today Beverage Sales.

This is the total beverage sales for each day. Get the closing figure from your cash register tape each day for this column. For Date 1 this figure is $388.25.

11. Column 11: Today Beverage Cost Percent Per Dollar Sale.

You get this figure by doing the following: Divide Column 9 Today Cost of Beverage Sold Date 1 $109.76 by Column 10 Today Beverage Sales Date 1 $388.25. You get .2827. Multiply by 100 to convert to a percentage. You get 28.27 percent. This 28.27 percent is your Column 11 Today Beverage Cost Percent Per Dollar Sale Date 1 figure.

Follow this procedure for the rest of the month.

COLUMNS 12, 13, AND 14 ARE TO-DATE FIGURES. THESE COLUMNS DO INCREASE AND DO ACCUMULATE FOR THE MONTH AS YOU GO ALONG. (This is true whether you are doing this chart on a daily or a weekly basis.)

12. Column 12: To-Date Cost of Beverage Sold.

For Date 1, the Column 12 figure is the same as Column 9 Today Cost of Beverage Sold Date 1 $109.76.

To get Column 12 Date 2, do the following: Add Column 12 To-Date Cost of Beverage Sold Date 1 $109.76 and Column 9 Today Cost of Beverage Sold Date 2 $100.81. You get $210.57. This $210.57 is your Column 12 To-Date Cost of Beverage Sold Date 2 figure.

To get Column 12 Date 3, do the following: Add Column 12 To-Date Cost of Beverage Sold Date 2 $210.57 and Column 9 Today Cost of Beverage Sold Date 3 $147.53. You get $358.10. This $358.10 is your Column 12 To-Date Cost of Beverage Sold Date 3 figure.

Follow this procedure for the rest of the month.

13. Column 13: To-Date Beverage Sales.

For Date 1, the Column 13 figure is the same as Column 10 Today Beverage Sales Date 1 $388.25.

To get Column 13 To-Date Beverage Sales Date 2, do the following: Add Column 13 To-Date Beverage Sales Date 1 $388.25 and Column 10 Today Beverage Sales Date 2 $367.40. You get $755.65. This $755.65 is your Column 13 To-Date Beverage Sales Date 2 figure.

To get Column 13 To-Date Beverage Sales Date 3, do the following: Add Column 13 To-Date Beverage Sales Date 2 $755.65 and Column 10 Today Beverage Sales Date 3 $536.10. You get $1,291.75. This $1,291.75 is your Column 13 To-Date Beverage Sales Date 3 figure.

Follow this procedure for the rest of the month.

14. Column 14: To-Date Beverage Cost Percent Per Dollar Sale.

To get this figure, you do the following: Divide Column 12 To-Date Cost of Beverage Sold Date 1 $109.76 by Column 13 To-Date Beverage Sales Date 1 $388.25. You get .2827. Multiply by 100 to convert to a percentage. You get 28.27 percent. This 28.27 percent is your Column 14 To-Date Beverage Cost Percent Per Dollar Sale Date 1 figure.

Follow this same procedure for the rest of the month.

Note: When you compute Column 14 To-Date Beverage Cost Percent Per Dollar Sale, it is especially important that you *always* divide Column 12 To-Date Cost of Beverage Sold by Column 13 To-Date Beverage Sales. Don't ever try to average your cumulative beverage cost percents. It will not be accurate.

Compare Formula Number 1 Chart 22-1 and Formula Number 2 Chart 22-2. Many figures are the same in both charts. Note, however, that the Today Beverage Cost Percent Per Dollar Sale (Column 11 in both charts) and the To-Date Beverage Cost Percent Per Dollar Sale (Column 14 in both charts) vary from one chart to the other. This is because the cost in Formula 1 is computed *just* on the basis of adjusted issues. Formula 2 uses this same adjusted issues information, *plus* it takes opening and closing inventory at the bar into consideration. The today and to-date beverage cost percents vary between Formula 1 and Formula 2 because of inventory—Formula 1 does not use inventory, Formula 2 does.

Formula 1 has provisions (in Columns 1 through 6) for storeroom control. Formula 2 does not include storeroom control.

If you use Formula 2, it is recommended that you also maintain a separate sheet for Formula 1 Chart 22-1 Columns 1 through 6: Column 1 Date, Column 2 Day, Column 3 Opening Beverage Storeroom Inventory Beginning of Day, Column 4 Beverage Storeroom Purchases, Column 5 Total Available Storeroom, and Column 6 Beverage Requisitions. This gives you beverage storeroom control if you use this in conjunction with Formula 2. Formula 2 already has a more accurate today and to-date beverage cost percent because you take inventory changes into consideration. (If you use Formula 2 but also use a separate chart for Columns 1 through 6 from Formula 1, follow the procedures discussed under Formula 1 for these 6 columns.)

At the end of a week you know your cost of beverage sold for the week. You also know what your beverage cost percent is. This tells you how much of your sales dollar you spent for liquor. This is an actual figure because you have allowed for the changes in inventory at the bar.

If your beverage cost percent is higher than you want, it means you are using too much liquor for your sales. Maybe your bartender is overpouring. Or you are failing to collect for drinks. Or your bartender is drinking on the job. Or you are not charging high enough prices for your drinks. There are quite a few possible reasons. Check and find out why your beverage cost percent is too high. The sooner you get this information, the sooner you can take corrective action to solve whatever problems you may find. First you have to find out *if* there is a problem. If there is, you have to find out why. Then do everything you can to eliminate the problem.

You have to know the trend of your beverage cost percent as you go so that you can take effective action before it is too late to solve problems.

BAR COST FORMULA NUMBER 3 (POTENTIAL SALES REVENUE, SOMETIMES CALLED RETAIL ACCOUNTABILITY)—CHART 22-3

Formula 3 is called the Potential Sales Formula because it tells you (based on quantity of liquor used) what your revenue should have been. Formula 3 is also called the Retail Accountability Formula because it tells you how much

Bar Cost Formulas   343

Date: _____ Day: _____

Brand	Size of Bottle	Selling Price Per Drink	Beginning Bar Inventory in 10's of Bottle	Issues to Bar in 10's of Bottle	Total Available at Bar in 10's of Bottle	Ending Inventory in 10's of Bottle	Amount Used in 10's of Bottle	Revenue Per Bottle in 10's of Bottle	Potential Revenue Bar Should Receive	Date	Day
Scotch A	Q	$.90	42	50	92	18	74	$2.70	$199.80		
B	Q	1.00	6	10	16	9	7	3.00	21.00		
C	Q	1.00	8	20	28	7	21	3.00	63.00		
D	5th	1.25	14	−0−	14	12	2	3.00	6.00		
Bourbon A	Q	.90	12	60	72	16	56	2.70	151.20		
B	Q	.90	16	10	26	6	20	2.70	54.00		
C	Q	1.00	23	−0−	23	5	18	3.00	54.00		
D	5th	1.25	9	−0−	9	7	2	3.00	6.00		
Brandy A	Q	1.00	8	−0−	8	6	2	3.00	6.00		
B	5th	1.25	12	−0−	12	12	−0−	3.00	−0−		
Rum A	5th	.90	4	10	14	3	11	2.16	23.76		
B	5th	1.00	13	−0−	13	8	5	2.40	12.00		
C	5th	1.00	7	−0−	7	5	2	2.40	4.80		
Gin A	Q	1.00	48	60	108	22	86	1.50	129.00		
B	5th	1.25	26	20	46	16	30	1.50	45.00		
C	Q	.90	8	20	28	12	14	1.35	18.90		
D	Q	1.00	15	−0−	15	9	6	1.50	9.00		
Sub-Total Liquor									803.46		
Wine A	Gallon	.75	24	20	44	5	39	1.50	58.50		
B	Gallon	.75	33	40	74	12	62	1.50	93.00		
C	Gallon	.75	27	30	57	8	49	1.50	73.50		
Sub-Total Wine									225.00		
Beer A	12 oz.	.75	53	48	101	31	70	−0−	52.50		
B	12 oz.	.75	64	72	136	47	89	−0−	66.75		
Sub-Total Beer									119.25		
Total									1,147.61		

Chart 22-3 Bar Cost Formula Number 3 (Potential Sales Revenue-Retail Accountability) Start a new cha everyday.

sales you have to account for at retail prices. Retail Accountability means the same thing as Potential Sales. Formula Number 3 tells you how much money you ought to get in cash (or credit card) sales.

This formula can be used on a daily or weekly basis. Daily is recommended because it is more accurate than weekly. In this formula you count the amount of each item used. Multiply the total of each item used by the item's individual selling price. This tells you the total revenue you should receive for the total amount of each item sold. Add the totals of all items sold to get the overall total sold.

For Formula 3, you follow the same procedures described in Formula 2. You take inventory of each brand. Quantity used of each brand is determined by the following three formulas:

1. BEGINNING BAR INVENTORY IN TENTHS OF BOTTLE plus ISSUES TO BAR IN TENTHS OF BOTTLE equals TOTAL AVAILABLE AT BAR IN TENTHS OF BOTTLE.

2. TOTAL AVAILABLE AT BAR IN TENTHS OF BOTTLE minus ENDING INVENTORY IN TENTHS OF BOTTLE equals AMOUNT USED IN TENTHS OF BOTTLE.

3. AMOUNT USED IN TENTHS OF BOTTLE multiplied by REVENUE PER BOTTLE IN TENTHS OF BOTTLE equals POTENTIAL REVENUE BAR SHOULD RECEIVE.

Divide the amount used by the number of drinks per bottle. For example, say you used two and a half quarts of a brand of liquor. Divide two and a half by 30 one-ounce drinks per bottle. (To allow for spillage, use 30 drinks per quart instead of the actual 32 you get if pouring is totally accurate.) The result is that 75 one-ounce drinks of this particular brand were used. If the drinks were sold for $1 each, you should have gotten $75 in revenue from this particular brand.

Add all the totals of all items sold during a specific period of time to find total revenue you should have received from the sale of liquor during the specific period of time you are examining.

Make adjustments for bar whiskey and bar gin if you sell large numbers of martinis or manhattans. In Chart 22-3, two ounces of gin are used per martini.

For example, say you use a one-ounce shot of whiskey for a highball, but you use one and a half ounces of whiskey in a manhattan and two ounces of gin in a martini. Some beverage operations adjust the whiskey used for manhattans based on the relationship of the amount of sweet vermouth used. If you use a four-to-one ratio for manhattans, four parts of whiskey should be used for every one part of sweet vermouth. Four bottles of whiskey should be used for every one bottle of sweet vermouth. Most operations have a different selling price and different revenue received from whiskey used for manhattans compared to the whiskey used for highballs. When you sell manhattans, you will receive less revenue for the quantity of whiskey used than you would if the same quantity of whiskey were sold in highballs.

Bar Cost Formula Number 3 takes more time and is more work than Formula 1 or Formula 2. But it does tell you what your retail sales dollar should be. Formula 3 establishes "potential sales," which means the amount of bar revenue you should have received.

You need a new chart for each day (or each week, depending on whether you use the formula daily or weekly). It is more accurate if you do it every day instead of once a week.

Potential Sales can serve as a guideline for you concerning the amount of revenue you are supposed to get for the quantity of liquor used. The potential sales figure you get from Formula 3 can serve as a check on how accurately your bartenders are pouring liquor and how accurately they are doing their job. You can also use it as a way to check and make sure you are getting the money you are supposed to be getting.

To use Formula 3, Chart 22-3, prepare a chart on column paper and do the following steps (daily or weekly):

1. Column 1: Brand.
   In Column 1 list every brand of alcoholic beverage you sell. It is recommended that you separate the brands into categories such as scotch, bourbon, brandy, rum, gin, cordials. Separate wine and beer, too. List wines and beers separately so you can compute separate sub-totals for liquor and wine and beer, and a total for all three. Chart 22-3 illustrates the procedure you should follow. This sample chart is not complete and does not show all the items you might carry—it does not include vodkas or cordials, for instance. On your own chart, list *every* item you sell.
   List items by their actual brand names. In Chart 22-3 we list Brand A, B, C, D, and so on, instead of actual brand names. When you do your chart, put in real brand names.

2. Column 2: Size of Bottle.
   It is important to list the size of bottle because this is what determines the number of drinks you should get per bottle. A quart actually is 32 ounces and a fifth actually is 25.6 ounces. But to make calculations for the number of one-ounce drinks, count a quart as having 30 drinks per bottle and a fifth as having 24 drinks per bottle. You do this to allow for any spillage, evaporation, overpouring, and so forth. We have assumed one-ounce drinks. You may use larger or smaller drinks. You should adjust to sizes you actually use.
   Chart 22-3 shows wine as gallon bottles (128 ounces per gallon) and it shows that 20 six-ounce portions are obtained from a gallon. Beer is purchased in 12-ounce bottles and is counted as number of bottles. Beer is the only item not counted in tenths of bottles.

3. Column 3: Selling Price Per Drink.
   This is the actual price you charge for each drink. If you have a drink list, just take each price right from your drink list and put it in this column. If

you don't have a drink list, take the prices you have instructed your bartenders to charge and put them in this column.

4. Column 4: Beginning Bar Inventory in Tenths of Bottle.
   These figures come from actual physical inventory. You actually count the bottles of each brand at the bar, including full and partial bottles. A full bottle is counted as 10 tenths, a partial bottle is counted as whatever number of tenths remain in that bottle. For example, in Chart 22-3, Scotch Brand A has a beginning inventory of 42 tenths of bottle. This means you have four full 10-ounce bottles and one bottle which has two tenths in it.

5. Column 5: Issues to Bar in Tenths of Bottle.
   This means full bottles brought from the storeroom to the bar. But the figures in this column should always be entered as tenths. For example, Scotch brand A has 50 tenths of bottle. This means that you issued five full bottles to the bar.

6. Column 6: Total Available at Bar in Tenths of Bottle.
   You get this figure by adding Column 4 Beginning Bar Inventory in Tenths of Bottle and Column 5 Issues to Bar in Tenths of Bottle. In Chart 22-3, Column 4 Beginning Bar Inventory in Tenths of Bottle Scotch Brand A is 42. Add this to Column 5 Issues to Bar in Tenths of Bottle 50. You get 92. This 92 is your Column 6 Total Available at Bar in Tenths of Bottle figure for Scotch Brand A.

7. Column 7: Ending Inventory in Tenths of Bottle.
   You get this figure by taking an actual physical inventory of bottles at the bar in tenths of bottle. Column 7 for Scotch Brand A is 18. This means that when you took inventory, there was one full bottle of Scotch Brand A at the bar plus one bottle of Scotch Brand A at the bar with 8 tenths left in it.

8. Column 8: Amount Used in Tenths of Bottle.
   You get this figure by subtracting Column 7 Ending Inventory in Tenths of Bottle Scotch Brand A 18 from Column 6 Total Available at Bar in Tenths of Bottle Scotch Brand A 92. You get 74. This 74 is your Column 8 Amount Used in Tenths of Bottle Scotch Brand A.

9. Column 9: Revenue Per Bottle in Tenths of Bottle.
   To get this figure, multiply the number of ounces per bottle by the selling price per drink. Then divide by 10.
   Column 2 Size of Bottle for Scotch Brand A was a quart. You count on 30 drinks per quart. Column 3 Selling Price Per Drink for Scotch Brand A is 90 cents per drink. Thirty drinks multiplied by 90 cents per drink equals $27 per 10 tenths bottle. $27 divided by 10 equals $2.70. This $2.70 is your Column 9 Revenue Per Bottle in Tenths of Bottle figure for Scotch Brand A.
   To further illustrate this, look at Scotch Brand D. Column 2 Size of Bottle for Scotch Brand D was a fifth. You count on a fifth as 24 one-ounce drinks per bottle. Column 3 Selling Price Per Drink for Scotch Brand D is $1.25 per drink. Twenty-four drinks multiplied by $1.25 per drink equals $30 per 10 tenths bottle. $30 divided by 10 equals $3. This $3 is

your Column 9 Revenue Per Bottle Per Tenth of Bottle figure for Scotch Brand D.

10. Column 10: Potential Revenue Bar Should Receive.

To get this figure, multiply Column 8 Amount Used in Tenths of Bottle by Column 9 Revenue Per Bottle in Tenths of Bottle. Column 8 Amount Used in Tenths of Bottle Scotch Brand A 74 multiplied by Column 9 Revenue Per Bottle in Tenths of Bottle Scotch Brand A $2.70 equals $199.80. This $199.80 is your Column 10 Potential Revenue Bar Should Receive figure for Scotch Brand A.

Follow this same procedure for each brand to get the figures for Column 10.

When you have completed all the columns, add up Column 10 for liquor. The sub-total in Column 10 Potential Revenue Bar Should Receive is the amount of money you should have received in liquor sales for this day.

Wine and Beer

Follow the above procedure to get your wine sales for this day. Add up the total of all wine sales to get a separate sub-total for wine sales.

Beer is handled differently. In our example Chart 22-3, beer is purchased in 12-ounce bottles and sold by the 12-ounce bottle. (If you buy beer in other than 12-ounce bottles, adjust your chart accordingly.) Beer is the only item on the chart not counted or computed in tenths of bottles. To get your beer sales for Beer Brand A, do the following:

1. Column 1: Brand.
Write in the name of the brand. We call it Beer Brand A, which we will discuss in the following.

2. Column 2: Size of Bottle.
Always 12 ounces.

3. Column 3: Selling Price Per Drink.
75 cents.

4. Column 4: Beginning Bar Inventory in Tenths of Bottle.
You don't list beer in tenths of bottle. The 53 in this column means you have 53 12-ounce bottles of Beer Brand A. You actually count the bottles to get this figure for beginning inventory.

5. Column 5 : Issues to Bar in Tenths of Bottle.
This figure is not tenths of bottle for beer. You count bottles, and you have 48 12-ounce bottles of Beer Brand A—number of bottles issued to the bar. The 48 goes in this column.

6. Column 6: Total Available at Bar in Tenths of Bottle.
Add Column 4 Beginning Inventory 53 12-ounce bottles and Column 5 Issues to Bar 48 bottles. (No tenths at all for beer.) You get 101 12-ounce bottles Beer Brand A. This 101 is the number of 12-ounce bottles of Beer Brand A available at the bar.

7. Column 7: Ending Inventory in Tenths of Bottle.
   No tenths for beer, just 12-ounce bottles. For Brand A, you have 31. You count 12-ounce bottles of Beer Brand A left at the bar at the end of the day. In our example, we say it is 31. Get this figure by actual physical count.

8. Column 8: Amount Used in Tenths of Bottle.
   There were 70 12-ounce bottles of beer used. You get this figure by subtracting Column 7 Ending Inventory from Column 6 Total Available. Subtract Column 7 Ending Inventory Beer Brand A 31 from Column 6 Total Available Beer Brand A 101. You get 70. This 70 is the number of 12-ounce bottles of Beer Brand A used this day—70 bottles are gone and *should* have been sold.

9. Column 9: Revenue Per Bottle in Tenths of Bottle.
   There is no figure in this column for beer. You sell beer only as 12-ounce bottles, so you do not have to compute a figure for tenths of bottles for beer.

10. Column 10: Potential Revenue Bar Should Receive.
    For Beer Brand A the figure is $52.50. You get this figure by multiplying Column 3 Selling Price per Drink Beer Brand A 75 cents by Column 8 Amount Used Beer Brand A 70 12-ounce bottles. You get $52.50. This $52.50 is your Column 10 Potential Revenue Bar Should Receive figure for Beer Brand A for this day.
    Follow this same procedure for all other brands of beer you sell.
    Get a separate sub-total for beer. Add all your sub-totals—sub-total for liquor, sub-total for wine, sub-total for beer. The figure you get is the total potential sales revenue your bar should have received for this day.

Now compare this total potential sales revenue bar *should* receive figure with your *actual* bar total revenue figure you get from your closing cash register tape for this day. The two figures should be within 1 percent of each other. If they are not, you are not getting the bar revenue you should be getting.

In our example the bar *actually* received $1,137.80. The potential revenue bar *should have* received (grand total, Column 10) was $1,147.61. The difference between the two figures is $9.81. The bar received $9.81 less than the Potential Revenue Bar Should Receive figure. This $9.81 figure is .86 percent of the $1,137.80 *actual* revenue received figure. This .86 percent *is* within the 1 percent guideline.

If the potential sales figure you get in Column 10 Potential Revenue Bar Should Receive Total Figure is more than 1 percent higher than your actual total sales revenue figure (day's closing figure on cash register tape)—and there is no mathematical error anywhere—then you are not getting the revenue you should. We already adjusted for average spillage in Formula 3. We counted on 30 drinks (instead of the actual 32) per quart bottle and 24 drinks (instead of the actual 25.6 ounces) per fifth bottle. So, if the two figures are not within 1 percent of each other, find out why. If your actual revenue is higher than your potential sales revenue, it may be that your bartenders are pouring too little liquor. If your actual revenue is lower than your potential sales revenue, it could be carelessness, theft of liquor or money, overpouring, failure to collect money, negligence in keeping records. Investigate until you find out what is wrong. Correct what's wrong.

Bar Cost Formula Number 3 (Potential Sales Revenue Formula) has proved very effective for many who have used it. And it is not difficult to computerize this formula if you want to. After you have written your computer program, just insert the issues to bar and ending inventory figures into a computer. A computer can do the rest of the computations and can print Chart 22-3. Programs can be written for daily and/or cumulative records for computers.

SUMMARY

Use Bar Cost Formulas 1 or 2 to determine daily, weekly, and monthly bar costs. Bar Cost Formula 3 tells you the amount of liquor used and the revenue you should have received. Formula 3 is a procedure you use to calculate the potential revenue you should have received based on quantity of beverage used.

Each of the three formulas will give you guidelines to use in setting standards. Compare your operation's current activities and performances with these standards. Keep track of how well you are doing as you go along and make changes if you need to.

If your beverage cost is higher than you want, or if you are not getting the money you feel you should be getting from beverage sales, it means you are using too much liquor for your sales. Maybe your bartender is overpouring or failing to collect for drinks. Or maybe you are not charging enough for your drinks. Check to find out *why* your beverage cost is too high and your revenue is too low.

As you go along, these formula charts will help you find out if you do or do not have problems. If you *do* have, find out why. Then do everything you can to eliminate the problems so your costs *will* be what you want them to be and you *will* get the revenue you should get.

REVIEW AND DISCUSSION QUESTIONS

1. What are the differences between the three bar cost formulas?
2. If you use Bar Cost Formula Number 2, why should you also use the first six columns of Bar Cost Formula Number 1?

3. A bar operation uses Bar Cost Formula Number 1 on a daily basis. Bar cost percent fluctuates several percentage points each day. Should the manager be worried?

4. Would your answer to question number three be different if the operation were using Bar Cost Formula Number 2 instead of Bar Cost Formula Number 1? Why?

5. How would you devise a system of bar control using parts or all of the three formulas?

23

Beverage Purchasing, Receiving, Storing, and Issuing Control

Objectives

This chapter discusses differences between food and liquor purchasing, receiving, storing, and issuing. After you have read this chapter, you should know:

1. Ways to purchase liquor.
2. The records needed for receiving liquor.
3. How to organize a liquor storeroom.
4. The mechanics of issuing liquor to the bar.

When you purchase, receive, store, and issue beverages, you use control systems very similar in concept and method to the systems used for purchasing, receiving, storing, and issuing foods, which we discussed in Chapters 14, 15, and 16. Refer to the records and charts for foods in those chapters. Most beverage purchasing, receiving, storing, and issuing forms will be the same with just a few changes in the wording.

In this chapter we will emphasize the differences between control systems for foods and control systems for beverages.

PURCHASING BEVERAGES

Purchasing beverage is much like purchasing food. Buy beverages (like foods) that are appropriate for the uses you will make of them. Buy the best where it is needed. Save money by buying less expensive items and brands for ingredients if you can still get the quality you want in the finished product you sell.

Use your list of about 25 most commonly ordered drinks (see Chapter 21) when you purchase. You will need everything in all the recipes on that list. You will need call whiskeys, call gins, bar whiskey, bar gin. You will need extra items that may not be included as ingredients on your list of 25 drinks. And you will need a careful selection of ingredients on hand so that you can offer other drinks besides the ordinary. Avoid buying quantities of anything you are not sure you will sell.

Normally you purchase beverages in case lots. But there are certain cordials and liqueurs you will use limitedly. Buy these items one or two bottles at a time. For some cordials and liqueurs, a case would be a five-year supply or more. Be very careful not to overbuy *anything*—particularly cordials and liqueurs. It can tie up too much money.

How Many Brands Should You Carry

Your bar whiskey, gin, scotch, whatever, should be good quality, but they do not have to be well-known brands. Your call whiskeys, gins, and so on should be popular and well known.

You have to decide how many scotches, how many gins, whiskeys, and others you will carry for bar and call drinks and what brands you want. For example, say you decide to carry one bar scotch and eight call scotches. If guests come in and order a scotch you don't carry, chances are they will not walk out and go somewhere else just because you don't carry their brand—as long as your eight call scotches are recognized name brands of good quality. The same holds true for other types of liquor. You may have eight, twelve or only four call scotches. You decide how many in each class (gin, scotch, whatever) and how many brands of each of these you will carry.

If something sells, carry it. If it doesn't sell, don't buy any more and stop carrying it.

After you have decided which general types of liquors to carry and which brands of each, it is a good idea to establish a par stock for each brand.

Par Stock

As we said in Chapter 14, par stock means staying between a predetermined minimum and maximum quantity. Stay as close to the maximum as you can without going over. You set a minimum amount that you will not go below (two cases or 24 bottles of Scotch Brand A, for example) and a maximum you won't go over (six cases or 72 bottles of Scotch Brand A, for example). You keep your supply of Scotch Brand A within these two limits. You should always have at least 24 bottles and never have more than 72 bottles of Scotch Brand A in your storeroom. Set predetermined quantities with minimum and maximum levels of how much of each brand of each beverage you want to carry.

It is usually less expensive to buy in case lots, so it is advisable to set up your par stocks with this in mind. As you purchase each item, specify how many cases you want. You should be able to get better prices on some items if you buy more than just one or two cases at a time. Sometimes you pay a set price for one or two cases but less per case if you order, say for example, five cases. If that is the situation, decide whether it is worth it to tie up money and storage space for five cases of liquor to get the saving on the purchase price. In general, it is okay to buy up to a six-month supply if you get a good price reduction. If you have to buy much more than a six-month supply to get the discount, you will probably be better off buying smaller quantities more often and not tying up too much money in inventory.

Buy It By the Bottle

You may want to buy some items by the bottle instead of the case because they are specialty items and you don't want much. Recognize the fact that you cannot have every item every guest wants. You don't try to on your food menu; don't try to in your beverage operation either.

You may want to special-order a bottle or two of a particular item for one or two individual guests who happen to prefer a special brand of, say, a scotch you don't normally carry. If these few guests are regular customers, you could order it by the bottle. Maybe other guests will order it, too. But if the guests you order it for know that you went out of your way to get what they want (tell them), they will appreciate it and will be apt to keep coming to your establishment instead of another. They may recommend your establishment to their friends. You cannot special-order liquor for all your guests, but you can for a very few, and sometimes it's a good idea.

Purchasing Responsibility

The bartender can and should recommend what is selling over the bar —what guests want—to the person who does the purchasing. But the bartender should not make up the order *and* do the purchasing alone. You, or whomever you put in charge of beverage purchasing, should make up the purchase order and place the orders with the purveyors.

In most medium-size and small operations, liquor purchasing is done by the manager or the assistant manager. Managers or assistant managers know the firms they deal with. They should know when to take advantage of a quantity discount and when not to. Bartenders do not have all the information about the financial condition of a business that managers or assistant managers should have. Bartenders might order more than they should. Managers and assistant managers should have a more complete picture of the operation's total liquor consumption and usage. And if they do the buying, there is less danger of bartending skulduggery.

Periodically check on how your various liquors are selling. A drink that is popular for a while may decline in popularity. Liquor should move at a reasonable speed from the storeroom to the bar to the guest. Don't buy too much of anything. You don't want large quantities sitting unused in your storeroom for long periods of time. If it doesn't move, don't carry it—except special ingredients you need for unusual drinks. Keep very small amounts of these on hand.

Legal Restrictions on Beverages

There are quite a few legal restrictions imposed on handling liquor in many countries. In the United States, we have federal and state regulations.

When Prohibition was repealed, it again became legal to sell liquor in most states. But some states continued to prohibit the sale of liquor. Some decided to allow it if certain state requirements were met. Some states still prohibit selling beverages containing more than a certain percent of alcohol. In some states, counties, and cities you can buy and sell beer and wines only if they are below a set alcoholic content.

There is much variation in state liquor laws. No two states agree 100 percent on precisely how you legally buy and sell liquor within their own borders. You have to find out exactly what is legal and what is not in your own area.

In some states, liquor is sold but the states themselves are their own wholesalers. Some states did this for prohibition-type reasons. Most did it to make money. In many states today, some of the state's general fund comes from profits from the sale of liquor within that state. The state makes a profit on the sale of liquor and also gets revenue from additional taxes imposed on liquor.

Purchasing from the State

In some states you will have to buy your liquor from the state itself. Check the situation in your own location. You must follow the procedures your state requires. Some states require the following:

1. You must pay cash.

2. You may purchase no more than once a week.

3. You can only inspect liquor and get adjustments and changes when you receive the liquor. You probably cannot do so later.

Some states have open liquor sales and you can buy liquor from distributors. It is vital that you comply with your state's requirements, whatever they are.

Purchasing from Distributors

If you are in a state that permits distributorships, you contact the distributor for each brand of liquor you want. The distributor becomes your supplier for a particular brand. When you want that brand, you must purchase it from that distributor because no one else has it. Most distributors will have a fairly complete line of items for sale from one or more distillers but these items will not be in competition with each other. For example, a distributor may carry one brand of scotch, one brand of bourbon, one brand of cordial. If you want a different brand of any of these, you have to go to the distributor who handles it.

RECEIVING BEVERAGES

Procedures for beverage receiving should be much the same as they are for receiving food, as discussed in Chapter 15. Check to see that you are getting the items you ordered. Also check to make sure you get exactly what the accompanying invoices say you get.

When you receive beverage, inspect cases for broken bottles. Beverage bottles do break—especially if they have been shipped a long distance— particularly imported scotches, champagnes, and the like. Check for possible loss due to leaks and spillage even if there is no obvious evidence of breakage.

Beverage receiving is usually handled by the same person who does the purchasing, usually the manager or assistant manager. From a control standpoint, ideally the person who receives the liquor should not be the same person who purchases it. From a practical standpoint, this is not always feasible.

The person in charge of beverage receiving should know what was ordered and what quantities were ordered. Most liquor is ordered by brand name. This simplifies the receiving procedure.

You may or may not need special beverage receiving forms. It is up to you to decide. Look at Charts 15-2, 15-3, 15-4, and 15-5 in Chapter 15. You could probably adapt these to serve as beverage receiving forms. The invoice that accompanies beverage received is apt to be adequate for use as a receiving form for most establishments. *Do* be sure to record beverage items you receive on bin cards (Chart 23-1). Do this whether you do or do not have separate beverage receiving forms.

After everything has been checked out with the invoice and the order has been okayed, the invoice can be signed (to be paid later) or the liquor can be paid for right then and there—depending on your own financial arrangements with your beverage purveyors. Then the liquor should be taken directly to the storeroom.

The manager or assistant manager should do the receiving. Actually moving the cases of bottles into the storeroom is usually done by bar or utility personnel. This should be personally supervised by the manager or assistant manager to prevent theft.

After the beverage shipment has been accepted and placed in the storeroom, specific storeroom procedures should be followed.

STORING BEVERAGES

Liquor should be moved into the storeroom immediately after it is received to avoid theft. Bottles should be removed from the cases and placed on shelves, ready to be issued from the storeroom to the bar.

If you have a lot of bottles, it may not be feasible for you to put them all on shelves. You may have to stack some in cases. If you do stack liquor in cases in your storeroom, you should check these cases periodically to make sure they are really full of bottles. Bottles can be stolen. In a beverage operation, no one bothered to inspect stored cases. When they finally started using the cases, they found each bottom case contained only four bottles—a bottle in each corner of each case to support the cases above them. They never did find out what happened to the missing bottles. This could happen to you if you don't check your cases.

When a case is opened and the first bottle is removed from a case, the entire case should be emptied right away and all the bottles should be placed on shelves. This will help prevent the potential for theft just described.

If you put liquor bottles on shelves, be sure the shelves are strong and substantially built. If they are not, they can collapse under the weight of liquor—as many beverage operators have learned the hard way. Bottles of liquor can add up to a good deal of weight. A lot of money can be lost if the shelves collapse and the bottles break.

Perpetual Inventory (Chart 23-1)

Items should be arranged and organized by brands and sizes when they are stored on the shelves. This makes taking inventory and issuing from the storeroom much easier. Rotate stored liquor just as you would stored food, using the oldest first.

Normally, perpetual inventory (discussed in Chapter 16) should be maintained on all liquor in the storeroom. You can use a three-by-five card file, a notebook, or bin cards for this. It is recommended that inventory be maintained perpetually both in terms of dollar value and in terms of the

Item: __Whiskey__   Cost: __4.80__   Month: __March__

Supplier: __A. Beverage Co.__   Phone: __700-0007__   Size: __5ᵗʰ__

Date	Number of Bottles Beginning of Day	Received		Issued		Balance	
		Number of Bottles	Cost	Number of Bottles	Cost	Number of Bottles End of Day	Cost
1	26	36	172.80	6	28.80	56	268.80
2	56			8	38.40	48	230.40
3	48			5	24.00	43	206.40
4							

Chart 23-1 Bin Card

number of bottles on hand. It is advisable to do both. You will want to know the dollar value at the end of the month when you compute your closing inventory for your profit and loss statement. You will also want an inventory by bottle count so you know every bottle is accounted for.

You should have a separate sheet (or card) for every brand of liquor. Write the cost and the size of the bottle on the sheet or card. The sheet or card should have space to record items received and issued every day of the month—in dollar amounts and bottle count. There should also be space to record the total number of items on hand in terms of dollar amount and bottles (see Chart 23-1).

Some operations have cards printed on both front and back. They use one side of the card for one month, then turn it over and use the other side for a different month. If you do this, put January on one side of a card and July on the back of it; February on one side of a card and August on the back of it, and so on. Don't try to put January on one side and February on the other side of the same card because it will be a nuisance. Someone will probably need the February side in your storeroom at the same time someone else needs the January side in the accounting office. Someone has to bring all the cards up-to-date at the end of the month and into the first few days of the following month. It is much easier to do this work in an accounting office instead of in a liquor storeroom. Your accounting employees will want to take cards to the accounting office. So some inventory cards are apt to be missing from the storeroom when your storeroom employees need them there. It is best to have a completely separate card or sheet for each month.

The best time to bring in new cards and take the old to the accounting office for verification and any last-minute updating of inventory values is the end of the month when actual physical inventory is taken and cards are checked to make sure they are in balance.

Some beverage operations compute the dollar value of their inventory only at the end of the month. But they do maintain their perpetual inventory on a bottle count basis throughout the month. Every time an item is received or issued, they record the information on the bin cards.

To compute beverage inventory, do the following:

1. For each brand, multiply the cost of each bottle by the number of bottles you have. This gives you a total cash value at cost for each brand.

2. Add the total cash value of all brands of beverages to get your total dollar value of your beverage inventory. This figure is used on your profit and loss statement and it is also used in Bar Cost Formula Number 1 (see Chapter 22, Chart 22-1, Column 12 To-Date Cost of Beverage Sold).

Beverage Inventory Turnover

You should also compute turnover of your beverage inventory. The formula for beverage inventory turnover is:

BEVERAGE INVENTORY TURNOVER equals DOLLAR VALUE OF COST OF BEVERAGE SOLD divided by DOLLAR VALUE OF AVERAGE BEVERAGE INVENTORY.

Cost of beverage sold is your liquor cost for the month. Average inventory is your opening beverage inventory plus your closing beverage inventory divided by two.

As a guideline, the dollar value of your beverage inventory should be approximately equal to what you pay each month to buy beverage. This means that 12 times a year there should be a turnover of close to the dollar value of your monthly beverage inventory.

Dollar value of beverage inventory will not necessarily turn over as fast as you want dollar value of food inventory to turn over. There is not as much danger of spoilage in beverage as there is in foods. Beverage has a longer shelf life than food. Therefore you can buy beverage in larger quantities (so you get a price break) without fear of spoilage.

The dollar amount represented by beverage (especially if you have a lot of wines on hand) adds up to quite a large investment in comparison to the amount of beverage used—but you still want to have your beverage inventory turn over as often as possible. Some beverage operations turn over their dollar value more than 12 times a year. On the other hand, establishments with very extensive beverage inventories (particularly wines) might find their inventories turning over as little as eight times a year or less.

Beverage inventory turnover tells you how fast you are converting your beverage inventory into cash. If your beverage inventory is not turning over and you do not have a large inventory of wines, you are probably carrying too much stock. Chances are you would be better off if you reduced your inventory and put the money to use elsewhere in your business. It takes space to store beverages. There is seldom enough beverge storage space set aside when a food and beverage operation is originally planned and built. Ideally, your liquor storage area should be located by itself in a place separate from all other storage areas. Ideally, only alcoholic beverages should be stored in the beverage storeroom.

Beverage Storeroom Key Control

There should be limited access to the beverage storage area. There should be at least two keys to the beverage storeroom. All but one of these keys should be locked in the office safe. One key should be kept by the manager or assistant manager. They receive liquor, see that it is stored, and issue it to the bartender. Probably one of the last things the person with the key should do before he or she goes off duty is to check to see if the bartender needs anything form the liquor storeroom.

Sometimes it may be necessary for bar personnel to get into the liquor storeroom after the manager or assistant manager has left the premises. Perhaps they need a particular brand of liquor in a hurry and unexpectedly—if they run out, for example, and need more than would normally be expected. You might want to have a key available for the bartenders or some other individual so that they can get into the liquor storeroom under these special circumstances. The key should be used very rarely—only for emergencies. Make it clear to whomever keeps the key (and everyone else) that you do not want many emergencies.

The cashier or bartender could be in charge of the emergency key. Don't give anyone the key, however, without taking precautions. Put it in an envelope. Seal the flap. Write your name across both the envelope and the flap. Then completely seal the flap with clear tape. No one can get at this key without destroying the envelope. It is impossible to slip a pointed object like a pen, pencil, or paper clip in at the end of the envelope and fish out the key because you have written your name on the envelope in your own handwriting.

Check the envelope every day. If the envelope is torn or in any way tampered with, start asking questions. Find out (rather loudly perhaps) who had to get into the liquor storeroom, why, what they took, whether they marked it down on requisitions. If you do all this, you have accomplished two things:

1. You have shown that you know or suspect that someone went into the beverage storeroom when you were not there.
2. You have shown that you don't like it and don't expect it to happen often.

Check into the reason why they went into the storeroom, why they needed the item, why they had not requisitioned ahead of time. Let everyone know that you investigate when anyone uses the emergency beverage storeroom key.

You have made the point that you want that beverage storeroom kept under *very* strict control. Employees will realize that you will investigate whenever anyone goes into the beverage storeroom when you are not there. Any time your special key in the sealed envelope is used, make quite a to-do about it. Go through the procedure every time so that employees know you are not getting careless. Show that you expect beverage employees to requisition from the storeroom when you are there and not use the storeroom otherwise unless there is a very good reason.

Another thing you should do is plan ahead with your bartender so the bar does not run out of anything when you are gone. You might consider increasing bar inventory of selected items so that the bar won't run out and employees won't have to go into the storeroom. Do everything you can to avoid emergency situations where someone would have to get an additional supply of liquor for the bar when you are not there.

ISSUING BEVERAGES

In most small to medium-size food and beverage operations, issuing from the beverage storeroom is usually done by the manager or assistant manager. (See Chart 16-2, Chapter 16, Food Storeroom Control, and modify the chart for beverage.) This is certainly better control than having the bartender do everything. The normal procedure is to have bartenders write requisitions for items they want from the beverage storeroom. Then you (or your assistant manager) go to the storeroom, make a written record of what you are taking on the perpetual inventory bin card, and remove the items. You (or a utility worker supervised by you in person) take the items directly to the bartender.

Mark it Down

As each item is removed from the storeroom, record the number of bottles issued on the perpetual inventory brand bin card. Have a bin card for each brand.

You probably won't have an adding machine in the storeroom for calculating and maintaining up-to-date records of dollar amounts. You don't really need one if you keep records on the perpetual inventory sheet by bottle count. The important thing is to maintain records in the storeroom and keep them up-to-date. Nothing should leave the storeroom without a correct written record of the fact that it did.

Full Bottle for Empty Bottle

A common method of issuing from the storeroom to the bar is to allow one full bottle to leave the storeroom for every empty bottle of the same brand returned to you for you to dispose of. With this method, a bottle has to be completely empty at the bar before it is replaced. This calls for a larger inventory at the bar with backups of extra bottles, one or more, for each brand so that the bar does not run out. When a bottle is empty, bartenders open a full new bottle, which should already be at the bar in reserve supply, and put the pouring spout in it. They set the empty bottle aside and turn it in later in exchange for a full bottle of the same brand.

Check your own state beverage laws. Many states require that liquor bottles must be removed from the premises within 24 hours after they are empty. Some states require you to destroy an empty bottle immediately by breaking it. Where this law exists, you cannot use the ''exchange a full bottle for an empty bottle'' method, so you issue a full new bottle when the bottle at the bar is, say for example, less than one-fourth full.

You can dispose of empty bottles by using a hammer for a bottle breaker, but there is danger of flying glass. Or you can order a bottle-crushing device from your equipment dealer.

Two reasons for breaking bottles are:

1. You are complying with your state law if your law requires you to break bottles.

2. You can get a lot more bottles in a trash receptacle if they are smashed into pieces instead of left intact.

The practice of destroying liquor bottles within 24 hours is acceptable in most states. It renders bottles ''unfit for refilling,'' which is what a lot of states require.

Whatever issuing method you use, all issuing should be recorded in writing. Issuing from the storeroom should be done by someone other than the individual who mixes drinks. This is part of your checks and balances system. It is vital to divide the responsibility so that no one person has complete charge of the total beverage function.

REVIEW AND DISCUSSION QUESTIONS

1. What is the difference between buying beverage from a state and buying it from a private distributor?

2. How can you control the liquor storeroom key?

3. Why must empty liquor bottles be removed from the premises?

4. Why is perpetual inventory recommended for liquor but not for food?

5. Your perpetual inventory records state you should have 17 bottles of Brand X Whiskey in your beverage storeroom. Physical inventory count shows that there are only 14 bottles of Brand X Whiskey really there.

   a. How would you find out what happened to the three bottles?

   b. What steps would you take to see that this type of situation does not happen again?

24

Wine and Beer

Objectives

This chapter discusses why wine and beer should be handled separately, and differently from the way liquor is handled. After you have read this chapter, you should know:

1. The various classes of wines and how to price, promote, and sell wines.
2. How to price, promote, and sell beer.

Wine and beer can give you extra sales. Sometimes they will sell when stronger beverages won't. Some people classify beer and wine as foods. They can be consumed before, during, and after meals—much more so than other types of alcoholic beverages.

Handling wine and beer calls for special considerations. Storing, serving, and keeping track of them are important. It is best to keep separate costs on wine, separate costs on beer, and a separate cost on all your other alcoholic beverages. Then combine the three categories for a total beverage cost. Different and separate factors govern the pricing of wine and beer and the other alcoholic beverages.

WINES

Classification of Wines

Classifications for wines fall into four general categories:

1. Appetizer (aromatic) wines.
2. Table wines.
3. Sparkling wines.
4. Dessert or fortified (arrested fermentation) wines.

For good detailed information about wines, consult *Grossman's Guide to Wines, Spirits, and Beers.*[1] It is an excellent reference book on all alcoholic beverages.

Wine consumption in the United States has grown considerably in recent years. Many Americans have traveled to Europe where they enjoyed the wines of the countries they visited and developed a taste for wine. Many young people learned to enjoy wine. It is one of the oldest alcoholic beverages and it is mentioned throughout the Bible. Wine is consumed by many people who will not drink any other alcoholic beverage.

In the past, wine sales have not been as big as they could have been in the food and beverage industry in the United States. They still aren't. This is probably due to several reasons, including:

1. Overpricing of wines.
2. Snobbery about wines.
3. Poor wine selections available.
4. Lack of good promotion efforts by managers of food and beverage operations.

[1]Harold J. Grossman, *Grossman's Guide to Wines, Spirits, and Beers,* rev. ed. Charles Scribner's Sons. New York, 1955.

The most popular wines are table wines. There are two categories:

1. White wines, which can be clear, pale, yellow, but have no red in the color.
2. Red wines, which can be any of varying shades from the very pale pink of a rosé to the dark purple of a burgundy. There is always some red in the coloring.

Wine is usually made from grapes. It can also be made from other things, including dandelions, rhubarb, and rice. Most countries have some type of local wine, or they can get wine from a country that does have vineyards and wine production. Native or imported wine is available in most nations, including the United States.

Wines can also be classified as domestic or imported. From an American viewpoint, American wines (domestic) tend to be a blend of many fermentations. Imported wines (most of which come from Europe) tend to consist of individual fermentations from a particular vineyard. This can get so narrowly defined that in some instances wines are made exclusively from grapes picked from a certain slope in one vineyard at a particular time of year.

Both domestic and imported wines can be good or bad. Use discretion when you develop your wine list. Use the best of domestic or imported which will satisfy the wine preferences of your guests. There's always the story of the American snob who was in France and ordered nothing but American wine. He wouldn't drink anything that wasn't imported.

Excellent wine lists can be made up using only domestic wines or only imported wines or using both.

Promote Wine Sales

Wine should be promoted and *sold.* Wine can be a definite plus sale for any food and beverage operation that takes the time and trouble to promote wine sales. In this country most of the wine sold is table wine which is consumed with food.

Promote wine in your food and beverage establishment. When you sell wine, it is a source of revenue for you. Table wines can be enjoyed with food. Many people think it helps digestion and adds to the total enjoyment of a meal.

Wine has two competitors in the United States—water and coffee. In some European food and beverage operations, it is easier to get wine than water. This is not true in the United States. In most American food service operations, guests have to inquire about and ask for wine—it is not offered automatically. If they get wine in America, it may be poor quality and high priced. Most American food service operations automatically give their guests free ice water. Most guests who ask for wine will want coffee, too. Wine does not cut into your sale of coffee and usually it won't cut your sale of liquor. It is to your advantage to sell wine with a meal. It can bring you extra revenue.

Many food and beverage operations promote wine sales by having wine glasses already pre-set on the dinner table when guests are seated. Have a wine list already on the table when guests sit down, or have your service person present it to the guests. Some food and beverage operations use their regular menu for promoting wine. You can use combinations of all of this to promote wine.

It is also a good idea to have your service personnel promote wine when they take the dinner order—perhaps say to the guest, "What type of wine would you like to enjoy with your meal?" This tells guests that you do have wines available. Maybe they had not thought of it and will appreciate having it suggested. They may say, "None, thank you," or they may order a wine, or they may ask the service person, "What do you have?" "What do you recommend?" People who have not consumed much wine generally prefer sweeter wines. Connoisseurs may prefer drier wines. There are wines for all types of tastes. Your service personnel should know something about wines. When guests ask them for suggestions or help, they should be ready and able to recommend wines and promote their sale.

Do Not Overprice Your Wine

A lot of food and beverage operation managers make the same mistake about wine. They think, "Here's where I make money. I'll buy wine for $1 a bottle and I'll sell it for $5 a bottle." It doesn't work.

If your guests are wine connoisseurs (or at least knowledgeable about wine), they will know something about wines and their prices. They may buy wine retail and drink it at home. Perhaps they also drink wine when they dine at your competitors'. You can't fool them. They will know whether your wine price is reasonable or not. If your prices are out of line, they probably will not buy your wine.

If your guests are not connoisseurs and know little or nothing about wines and wine prices, unreasonably high wine prices can scare them off. They may decide, "I don't know much about wine and for $5 a bottle I'm not going to find out!"

Unreasonably high wine prices will get you nowhere. Price wine reasonably so it will sell. If you buy wine for $1 a bottle, perhaps you could reasonably sell it for $2.50 to $3.50 a bottle. Perhaps wine that costs you $4 a bottle could reasonably be sold for $8 a bottle. You will get a lower beverage cost percent on the more expensive wine, but you can also get more dollars. Subtract $4 cost from an $8 selling price and you have $4 left to contribute toward your labor, overhead, and profit. Subtract $1 cost from a $3.50 selling price and you have $2.50 left for labor, overhead, and profit. On the $8-a-bottle wine you have a 50 percent cost. On the $3.50-a-bottle wine you have a 28.5 percent cost. But in the final analysis it is dollars, not percentages, that count.

Keep records of wine costs and sales separate from beer and liquor records.

Charge prices that are fair and reasonable for your guests and that give you a profit. Serving wine involves costs for you. You have to store it properly and see that it is served at the proper temperature and in the correct type of glassware. All this means some expense for you, but actually rather minimal expense considering the potential revenue wine can bring you. It takes a little time for a service person to present and serve a bottle of wine to guests correctly. But there can be money in it for both the service person and the establishment. From the service person's standpoint, wine service increases the total check, and thus the tip.

Bonus for Wine Sales

Many operators find it profitable to have a bonus system for the sale of wine. You might consider the idea. Establish a minimum quota of wine sales per service person per month. This quota should be reasonable—say a number between 6 and 10 bottles. This should cover your basic cost for buying, storing, and maintaining wine in your wine inventory. After your employees have sold the quota number of bottles of wine, they get a percentage of the retail price for each bottle of wine they sell. This is extra, besides tips and basic wage. This wine bonus can add up to a fair amount of money at the end of the month for employees. It can mean increased revenue for your operation, too. There should not, of course, be any penalty for service persons who cannot sell the minimum quota number of bottles of wine a month. The idea is to reward those who *do*, and thus create incentive. But do not encourage pressure selling by service personnel.

Sell Your Guests the Wines They Like

Wine purists and connoisseurs (plus a lot of people who like to think that is what they are) may enjoy following "tradition" when they drink wine with their meals. They will want white wine with white meat (chicken, fish) and red wine with red meat (steak, roasts). That is fine. Most of your guests, however, will not be connoisseurs. Sell all your guests *any* wines they want if you have them—no matter what color or type of wine they want with whatever it is they are eating. Your guests should drink any type of wine they want and enjoy. Sell it on that basis. Don't be stuffy about "connoisseur's wine traditions"—and don't let your beverage service personnel or wine stewards or anyone else in your operation be intimidating toward guests about wine. A lot of people would prefer white wines with steaks and roasts, red wine with chicken, an appetizer of dry vermouth with no gin, a rosé with fish *and* red meat. Sell them what they want. There are millions of food service guests who know little or nothing about wine but would be willing to try some varieties if they were treated warmly and not condescendingly by beverage service personnel in restaurants.

No guests should ever have their own wine requests or preferences questioned. You should stress the enjoyment of drinking wine. Some guests will want champagne before, during, and after a meal. Or red wine. Or white wine. That is up to your guests. It is not up to you or your service personnel or bartenders.

Serve Wine at Proper Temperatures

Serve white wines *well* chilled, at a temperature between 40 and 50 degrees. Serve red wine at a temperature between 60 and 70 degrees, no warmer. If you have heard the old tradition about serving red wine at "room temperature," forget it. The old tradition originated in Europe centuries ago when "room temperature" was pretty sure to have been below 70 degrees.

Today some beverage operations store all their wine in the basement—maybe, unfortunately, near the furnace. In some operations wines are stored in areas where it is hot—maybe even 95 degrees. Most operators chill white wine down to a correct 40 to 50 degrees before they serve it. That is right. Do that. But some feel obliged by tradition to serve red wine at room temperature—even if the wine comes to the guest direct from a 95-degree room! Be sure your red wine is not warmer than 70 degrees when you serve it.

Sell Wine by the Glass or Carafe

Many guests might like a glass of wine with a meal, but not a whole bottle. You can probably buy wine for your beverage operation in splits, half-bottles, and so on. Serving wine by glass, half-liter, or liter in a carafe is popular in some parts of the United States. Inexpensive red and white wine is available on this basis. Guests who may not want to spend several dollars for a bottle of wine can still have some wine with their meals and pay a reasonable price.

One problem with this idea—and a reason why more operations don't do it—is the restrictions placed on establishments by some state beverage laws, which may prohibit food and beverage operations from selling wine in carafes. It would be worth your while to check with your own state liquor control board to see if there are any such restrictions that affect you or if it is all right for you to sell wine in carafes. Some states do allow you to dispense wine from gallon containers into carafes. Other states do not. If you are allowed to do it, you might consider the idea of selling wine by glass, half-liter, or liter. It could be a way to bring in extra revenue.

Wine-Tasting for Employees

Many establishments have wine-tasting sessions for invited customers to make them more familiar with different types of wines. It is customary to charge a small fee to cover the cost. And many establishments also have wine-tasting sessions for their own service personnel (no charge to the service personnel), and it, too, is a good idea. Your service personnel sell wine to your guests. Some of your guests will expect your service personnel to be walking wine encyclopedias.

Occasionally you should hold wine-tasting sessions for your service personnel so they can taste the different wines they serve guests. If you hold regular employee meetings with your waitresses and waiters (which is a good idea), these could be excellent times to incorporate wine-tasting. Inform them about the different wines they sample so they will know what they are talking about when guests ask them about wines. Wine-tasting for employees should not take much wine. It should be wine-tasting, not wine-guzzling.

Wine Service

As part of total wine presentation to guests, the wine service personnel should present the wine bottle to the person who ordered it for inspection and then open it with a flourish. The cork should be placed in front of the guest who ordered the wine to sniff it and examine it to make sure it is not dry. The person who ordered the wine should be served first. A small quantity of wine should be poured into his or her glass to sniff, taste, and decide if it is all right.

Guests will very seldom reject a wine. But you should have a well-established policy concerning whether guests will or will not be charged for a bottle they reject. When the guest says the wine is okay, the service person pours the wine—first for the other guest or guests at the table and last for the person who ordered it.

Wine Glasses

Use wine glasses big enough so guests can appreciate the full bouquet of the wine. The wine glass should be approximately twice the size of the wine portion poured. Many beverage operations use an eight-ounce glass and fill it half full. This allows the guest to sniff and enjoy the bouquet of the wine.

Some beverage operators still use wine glasses someone sold them 25 years ago, when enterprising wine glass salespeople were promoting four-ounce wine glasses. If you have four-ounce glasses, you could use them for serving two ounces of sherry. Table wines should be served in larger glassware.

Corks

If you store wine bottles stoppered with real corks, the bottles should be stored on their sides so the corks stay wet. If the corks dry out, air and bacteria can get in and ruin the wine. Ruined wine may look cloudy. It can have a sour or vinegar-like taste. It is possible to store wines upright for very short periods of time, just briefly while they are being chilled. Today many wine bottles have plastic stoppers. If you use plastic, it is not necessary to keep bottles on their sides at all.

How Many Wines?

How many wines should your beverage operation carry? It varies from one operation to another. Some very exclusive hotels and restaurants carry several hundred varieties of wines and have a most elaborate wine list. Others may carry an intermediate number and have 70 to 80 varieties of wines available. Many beverage operations will, of course, carry a much smaller number. Beverage operations that do want to serve wines but don't want a large inventory of different varieties might find that 10 to 20 different wines would be fine. Most beverage operations probably fit into this last category.

You should probably have two or more red wines, two or more white wines, a rosé wine, a sherry, and a champagne. Most of the wines should probably be in the red and white table wine categories. The number you will need will depend on how strongly and successfully you promote wine sales. Maybe you will want just one red wine and one white wine and serve them in bulk.

For the typical beverage operation, it is best if you carry fewer wines and make sure they are good quality. Sell and promote these at reasonable prices so your guests can enjoy them with their meals. *Sell* what you offer. And offer primarily only what you really do sell. Don't carry a large variety of high-priced wines that you can't sell.

BEER

Beer, like wine, calls for special handling. Most people who drink any kind of alcoholic beverages do drink beer sometimes. When guests buy beer, it should be properly presented and served to them. Beer, like wine, can be classified as a food. It can be consumed before, during, and after a meal.

Beer is perishable. It comes in a sealed container but must still be handled properly to insure the maximum enjoyment by your guests. If beer is not properly handled, you can have problems with it. It can develop an off taste if it is old and has been around too long. Or, worse, it can acquire a "skunky" odor, and then it is called "light-struck beer." Most beer comes in cans or in dark brown bottles to prevent light from getting at it. Beer that is exposed to bright sunlight in a clear bottle or glass for as little as fifteen minutes can develop the "skunky" odor, which is extremely objectionable.

Serve Beer Cold

Preferences in the temperature of beer vary in different countries. Most Americans like beer very cold. In England, warmer beer is preferred by many. Generally, beer at a temperature of 40 degrees is acceptable for most Americans. Some want it colder. Very few want it warmer. You can usually get help and ideas from your local distributor about the right temperature for you to serve beer in terms of your own market, area, equipment. Your customers will let you know, too.

As we mentioned earlier, many consider beer as a food. It can, of course, be promoted as a beverage to be consumed with food. Many people like beer and a sandwich. Many beverage operations merchandise beer today as an accompaniment to foods. Beer contains B vitamins and it's a nice way to get them.

Beer Should Be Reasonably Priced

Beer, like wine, should be priced reasonably for your operation. Beer is a very common drink in the United States. It is seldom overpriced because competition won't allow it. Sometimes, however, beer is underpriced. A luxury food and beverage operation that maintains a very formal atmosphere and gets high prices for mixed drinks should also charge a reasonably high price for beer. It should charge more for beer than the neighborhood bar does.

Take, for example, the cocktail lounge that charged a minimum of $1 for bar brands of liquor and more for call brands. But this same bar sold nationally known brands of beer for 55 cents a bottle. The minimum they should have charged (considerering the status of the national and local economy at that time and the type of establishment) was 75 cents a bottle—perhaps more. Seventy-five cents would have been a reasonable amount for the guest to pay. At 55 cents, the guest was getting a real bargain. Fortunately for this particular cocktail lounge, most of its clientele were not beer drinkers so there was not much of the incorrectly priced beer sold. But this cocktail lounge did not collect as much revenue as it should have from its beer sales. It should have priced its beer reasonably for its customers and for itself.

Draft Versus Bottled Beer

It is up to you to decide whether you should sell draft beer or bottled beer. Many guests prefer draft beer to bottled beer. If you sell large quantities of beer, it could be profitable for you to have one or more brands of draft beer available. If you sell limited quantities of beer, you will probably be better off selling only bottled beer.

Beer is packaged in units figured on the basis of a barrel containing 31 gallons. The standard unit for most draft beer is the half-barrel (15½ gallons). As a general guideline, you should sell a minimum of a half-barrel a week or more before you are justified in trying to sell draft beer.

If you do sell beer in these quantities, it is possible for you to make more money selling draft beer compared to the same amount of bottled beer. Bottled beer usually contains 12 ounces per bottle (although some firms do bottle different quantities in different size bottles). If you use a 10-ounce glass for serving draft beer, the glass might contain only 7 ounces of beer and 3 ounces of foam. You can get more glasses of beer from draft beer than you can from the same amount of bottled beer because of the foam. Foam is part of draft beer. Take this into consideration when you decide what price you should charge and what size and shape of glass to use. The glass most commonly used for beer is larger at the top than it is at the bottom. A small amount of foam at the top takes the place of a few ounces of beer. In the United States, foam is also an important factor in guest enjoyment. Most Americans seem to enjoy beer more if it does have foam, or a "head," on it.

Pour Beer Properly

If you pour beer down the side of a glass so there is no foam, the carbon dioxide in the beer has not been released. If you serve beer this way—without having released the carbon dioxide—it will give your guests who drink it a full, stuffy feeling. They will be less apt to enjoy the beer and they probably will not be able to drink very much of it. Make sure your bartenders pour beer (draft or bottled) into the center of the glass, not down the side. This releases the carbon dioxide and gives the beer a head. There is an old saying about draft beer—"If the white (the foam) is the same price as the brown (the beer), give them a little more of the white and make money." Some beverage operations get carried away with this idea and take it to extremes. But do make sure the carbon dioxide has been released and there is a head on the beer. Most guests prefer it this way.

Occasionally guests will insist on having their beer poured down the side of the glass so that there is no head on it. If that is the way they want it, that is the way they should have it.

Washing the Beer Glass

When we discussed wine, we said it was important to have the proper size glass for wine enjoyment. For beer, the way you take care of the glass it is served in is much more important than the size of the glass. The handling of the glass can definitely affect the taste and action of beer.

Most beer companies will be glad to teach you and your staff how to handle beer glasses properly. A glass that has gone through your dishwashing machine may be clean, pass health inspections, and be perfectly ready for any beverage—except beer. Glassware has to be "beer clean" for beer.

Use the cleaning procedure described below. Correct washing of beer glasses calls for a three-compartment sink and the following procedures:

1. First sink.

   The first sink should contain a special detergent for washing beer glasses. Check with your local beer distributors and see what they recommend. Many still recommend the use of trisodium phosphate because it will not leave any residue. There should be brushes in the first sink with the special detergent. The beer glasses should be washed and rotated over the brushes so the inside of the glass is thoroughly scrubbed to remove any film that might adhere to the glass.

2. Second sink.
The second sink should contain cool, plain water to remove all traces of detergent and trisodium phosphate.

3. Third sink.
The third sink should contain cool water plus a sanitizer in the proper proportion recommended by the manufacturer of the sanitizer and in accordance with local sanitation laws.

4. Drain.
After the glass has been washed and rinsed and sanitized, it should be placed on a drain rack—preferably stainless steel—and left there for at least 30 seconds. This allows the water to drain off and gives the sanitizer time to do its job.

This four-step procedure will give you a "beer clean" glass. A glass that is beer clean allows the foam or head to stay on the beer much longer than a glass that is not beer clean. A glass with grease or any other substance on it will cause beer to lose its foam almost immediately. You can tell if a glass is beer clean by how it looks as beer is consumed from it. The head should not disappear. There should be traces of foam left in rings on the glass as beer is drunk from the glass. In a glass that is not beer clean, the foam just dissipates.

We said that the beer glasses should be put on a stainless steel rack to drain and dry. Beer glasses should never be placed on wood, paper, plastic, linen—or anything except stainless steel—to dry. Beer can absorb taste and odor from glass that is drained on practically anything except stainless steel, and this can destroy the taste of the beer. Beer is sensitive enough to pick up these effects from glass. Beer is so sensitive it can pick up taste and odor from anything that touches the glass it is in (hand lotion, for example). Beer can even pick up odors from the air (cooking, smoke) in the establishment.

Beer glasses aren't the only things to be kept clean. Don't forget to clean the beer tap and beer lines to the keg, too. Take them apart and wash them in baking soda or a solution recommended by your beer company. Rinse well. If beer lines and taps are not cleaned properly, they will give the beer an off taste.

Beer is very fragile. The taste and odor of it can easily be ruined. Take pains to avoid this. Beer that's properly protected and served can be enjoyed by many and give you good sales.

Keep Beer Cost Separate from Liquor Cost

Keep all your beer costs and sales records separate from your liquor costs and sales figures. Keep separate wine costs and sales records, too. You will probably want to maintain a beer markup that is different from your wine or liquor markup. This will depend on the volume of your beer sales in relation to your total beverage sales. High-volume beverage operations that sell lots of beer tend to price their beer quite reasonably and sell lots of it. Some beverage operations, however, may not *want* to sell much beer. They offer it only as an accommodation to guests and purposely price it quite high.

Whatever you decide to do about this, you should probably use a markup percentage for beer that is different from your liquor markup percentage. You should compute a beer cost percent, a wine cost percent, a liquor cost percent, and a total beverage cost percent. Compute separate costs for each area so you know your gross profit on sales in each category. You can adjust selling prices of an item in one category as you need to and thus adjust gross profit in total beverage sales. You do not have to resort to just raising all prices in order to get more gross profit from beverage sales. Total beverage cost percent and the dollars you earn are the figures that are important to you.

Keep Track of Empty Beer Cases

If your beverage operation handles beer, you should keep track of empty beer bottles and empty half-barrels just as closely and carefully as you keep track of them when they are full. You have to pay deposits on most of these bottles and barrels, so be sure you do return them and get credit. Getting refunds on empty beer bottles and barrels is not the only reason you should watch them closely, however. Another reason is to help prevent theft of full barrels or bottles.

If you possibly can, store your empty bottles in their cases away from the area where full bottles are stored. Consider this story about storing beer bottles. A beverage operation stored all its beer bottles, full and empty, together in one area. A beer delivery man wheeled five cases of beer into the beverage operation on his cart. He intentionally took out four cases containing full bottles of beer, with one case of empty bottles on top as camouflage. This is a remote example of what can happen, but it *can* happen. This beer delivery man was caught, reported, and fired by the company he worked for.

It will pay you to keep your full and empty beer bottles clearly separated. It will help to protect you from theft and also make it much easier for you to keep total inventory of your full bottles and count your empty bottles. Don't mix them together.

Beer and wine can be profitable items. They are both part of the total beverage operation of many food and beverage establishments. Both have to be correctly handled, cared for, stored, and sold in order to bring you profits.

REVIEW AND DISCUSSION QUESTIONS

1. What are the classifications of wines?
2. What other beverage items are wine's competition in your establishment?
3. What is the "best" rule to follow when you are promoting wine to your guests as an accompaniment with their food?

4. Why are wine bottles stored on their sides? Is it always necessary?

5. How should beer be poured into a glass so it does have a head? So it does not?

6. Explain the procedures for getting a glass "beer clean."

7. Why should separate costs be computed for liquor cost, wine cost, and beer cost?

25

Problems of Bar Operation and the Law

Objectives

This chapter discusses various state and federal laws that pertain to liquor operations. After you have read this chapter, you should know about:

1. Who can get a license.
2. How you could lose your license.
3. Illegal activities as well as required procedures.

WHO CAN GET A LIQUOR LICENSE?

Bar and liquor licenses are usually controlled by the local community—town, city, county—perhaps state. A community usually restricts the number of licenses issued. Frequently, the number of licenses issued is based on the population in the area, perhaps one liquor license for every 1,000 population. The community may also restrict the number of licenses by charging very high fees for the right to sell liquor.

Communities may apply further restrictions. They may specify "No liquor establishment within 300 feet of a church or school." Some communities modify this rule so that no bar *entrance* can be located "within 300 feet of the main entrance of a church or school."

When they issue licenses, most communities are concerned about the type of establishment requesting the license. They do not want beverage operations that will create any problems (noise, drunkenness, fighting, crime, whatever). Many communities require that beverage operations must also serve food. Many do not want "old-time saloon" types of establishments.

Individuals applying for licenses must be of legal age. They must not have been convicted of a felony. If you want to apply for a license in a community, contact a lawyer who can advise you of local and state laws.

LEGAL RESTRICTIONS IN THE UNITED STATES

There are many restrictions imposed on the beverage industry by state and federal laws. If you are a beverage operation manager, you are legally responsible for the on-duty job activities of all of your employees, whether you are aware of what is going on or not. Ignorance is dangerous.

Following is a sample list of some types of illegal activities. If these apply in your area, it can cost you your liquor license to disobey them. If you are convicted of violation, your establishment can be closed temporarily or permanently. Restrictions vary from state to state in the United States and they vary in other nations.

In the United States, contact your State Liquor Commission and find out details on local, state, and federal liquor laws that apply to you. If you are outside the United States, check with appropriate government agencies. Learn and carefully follow every restriction that affects you.

1. Refilling liquor bottles.

It is smart to return refillable beer bottles for refunds, and it is *essential* to remove all empty liquor bottles from your premises *fast*. Dishonest bartenders can pour an inferior brand of liquor (or even moonshine) into expensive brand bottles and charge guests top, brand-name prices and pocket the money (if your inventory, sales analysis, and other controls are not tight). This is why there are legal restrictions preventing you from keeping empty liquor bottles on the premises. Get rid of empty bottles immediately, doing it precisely the way the law states if a law about this applies to you.

It is also illegal to pour two bottles of the same brand together into one bottle. This can give you one full bottle instead of two partially full bottles. The practice is quite common, but don't do it. If this is done in your operation, you are the one who is held responsible. It makes no difference to the law if you do or do not know about it, or if you have or have not tried to stop the practice. If it happens, you are guilty. Make sure it is not done.

When a liquor bottle is empty, get rid of it. You don't want old-looking or soiled and worn-looking bottles. Plainclothes government inspectors do keep surveillance on beverage operations. If they notice that a bottle has a torn label or appears to be soiled, it can indicate to them that this bottle has been used for a longer period of time than is normal and liquor may have been mixed or transferred. Even though they may not identify themselves, or warn you, or give you any indication that you are being checked, they may return. Soon.

2. Absence of federal tax strip stamps on bottles.

When you first open a bottle of liquor, do not remove the federal tax paper strip stamp from the bottle. The federal serial number should stay right on the bottle and the number should remain clearly legible. Government inspectors can come in with no warning and check this. If they find a bottle without the legal federal seal or stamp, they can close your establishment.

3. Watering of liquor.

Bartenders who have given away too much liquor or pocketed too much money may decide to help the cost picture by adding water to the liquor. This practice can close your establishment very quickly indeed. Inspectors can check the alcoholic content of liquor with a hydrometer. If the alcoholic content is not precisely what it is supposed to be, you can lose your license.

4. Pre-mixing drinks.

Some establishments mix cocktails ahead of time—pitchers of martinis, manhattans, whiskey sours. In many states it is illegal to pre-mix any drinks and pour them into any container. Some states will permit you to pre-mix drinks when you have a specific order for them (for a banquet, for example).

Check the laws in your state. *Never* pour pre-mixed drinks into a liquor bottle. That would violate federal law.

5. Displaying license.

Most states require you to "prominently display" your license to operate a bar. This means hanging in plain sight at the bar. Many beverage operation managers don't know this and hang their licenses to operate their bars in their offices, or they don't put them up at all. In a lot of states, they are violating a state law.

6. Gambling on premises.

Many states are very strict about *any* kind of gambling in an establishment where alcoholic beverages are sold. Don't permit any gambling. Enforcement agencies are more concerned with flagrant violations than they are with small-scale instances (guests matching to see who buys, or playing a friendly game of dollar-bill poker). But, as a matter of fact, *any* gambling—insignificant or not—is illegal in most states.

The above are just a few of the laws that can cause you to lose your liquor license if you are found in violation of them. It is essential that you do a thorough investigation into laws that apply to you, wherever you are, so you can take precautions against violating any of them. Be sure you know your local ordinances (hours of operation, and so on), state laws, and federal laws.

In this chapter we have discussed some of the legal ramifications involved in operating a bar. If some of the activities described go on in your operation—even if you are completely unaware that they go on—it can put you in jeopardy of losing your license. Know all laws and obey them. You have got to be aware of what is going on in your beverage operation. You must be on your toes and in control. If your are not, it can cost you money—or even your license.

REVIEW AND DISCUSSION QUESTIONS

1. What factors could prevent you from obtaining a liquor license?
2. Why is it important that you know state and federal liquor laws?
3. What could cause you to lose your liquor license?
4. The bar whiskey you use is less expensive for you if you buy it in half-gallon bottles. Half-gallon bottles are awkward for the bartender to use. What should you do?
5. Your hotel had many portable bars operating at a large reception. After the reception, there were several quart bottles of the same brand of whiskey open and there were just a few ounces left in each bottle. The total amount in all the bottles would be less than one full quart bottle. What would you do? Why?

26

Skulduggery

Objectives

This chapter contains many case histories of various ways employees and management have practiced dishonest tactics. After you have read this chapter you should:

1. Know various methods that have been used to steal from or to defraud a food and/or beverage establishment.
2. Know why it is recommended that you bond your employees.

"Skulduggery" is defined as: "Dishonorable proceedings; dishonesty or trickery."[1] That is what this chapter is about.

Any employee can engage in skulduggery—manager, cook, bartender, porter, service person—anyone. Many of the cases in this chapter concern bartenders. Theft is easiest at the bar, particularly if you do not have strong controls. Even if you do, the bar is still harder to control than other areas in a food and beverage operation.

In Chapter 2, Organization for Management, we talked about the ethics of the manager. If you, the manager, load your car with food and beverage items and take them home and you are not authorized by owners to do so, *you* are practicing skulduggery (a polite word for stealing). Your own ethics set an example for employees and the example has to be a good one. Your own personal example of honesty and your antitheft control systems are your only ways to stop theft.

Some of the activities described in this chapter—or other activities like them—could be going on in your establishment right now.

BAR SKULDUGGERY

A major problem in bar operation can be dishonest employees. Most bartenders are honest. But, unfortunately, there are some dishonest ones. If you do happen to have dishonest bartenders, they can cause you real trouble. Theft is common at the bar because of lack of controls. Theft occurs more frequently at the bar even *with* controls because the bartender is usually responsible for both preparing drinks and collecting money for them.

The following are examples of some of the types of tactics dishonest bartenders can use. These are not presented necessarily in order of importance —they're all important. Tactics like these can do a lot of damage to your bar operation and cost you money. The following techniques are a sampling of the kinds of things you have to know about and watch for. There are multitudes of ways (including those described in the following incidents) in which crooked bartenders can use. These are not necessarily presented in order of importance so you will really have to watch very sharply.

1. Failing to collect money for drinks.

You have probably heard this "old story": The bartender says to the owner, "What about that guy that just left! He gave me a dollar tip and forgot to pay for his drink." It's a very old bar joke, but there is truth in it. You have to make sure you collect for every drink. The money should be rung

---

[1] *Webster's New Twentieth Century Dictionary of the English Language,* unabridged, 2nd. ed. World Publishing Company. New York, 1969.

in the register as it is received. Bartenders should not be allowed to work with open cash registers.

2. Not ringing up each sale.

A bartender was not ringing up each sale as it occured. He was working with an open cash register. He was a very large man with a "bad back." He stood behind the bar with his hands tucked in back of him inside his belt when he wasn't busy—to "ease his back," he would say. Actually, he had a large pocket sewn inside the back of his pants. Every time he "eased his back" he was shoving money into this pocket.

3. Bringing in own bottle.

A bartender worked with an open cash register. He did not ring up every sale. And he brought his own bottle of whiskey to work each day. He drew a salary from the bar he worked for. His gimmick was that he was simultaneously in business for himself.

The whiskey he bought and brought to work with him cost him $5 a bottle. The bar operation paid $5 a bottle for *its* whiskey, too. He collected $15 for the drinks he sold from his own bottle. He collected $15 for the drinks he sold from a bottle of the bar's whiskey, too. And he put all the cash in the cash register, but he did not ring up the sales he made from his own bottle.

At the end of his shift, he would retrieve $15 from the cash register—$5 to pay for his bottle and $10 for his labor in selling his own bottle. The bar's cost of beverage was not affected. But he had sold his own bottle instead of a bottle of the bar's whiskey. The bar lost $10.

He was caught when the manager started a practice of marking every bottle with a special mark before it left the beverage storeroom. One day he took a surprise inventory at the bar and found a bottle of whiskey with no mark.

4. Shorting on shots.

Some bartenders deliberately underpour for a lot of guests until they get a few shots ahead. Then they pour these extra shots, collect for them, and pocket the money. This is one good reason why you should require your bartenders to use a uniform measure every time they pour.

The only time your bartenders might possibly be justified in pouring a smaller shot than standard is if they are pouring drinks for customers who are approaching the point where they have had too much to drink but insist on more. That is the *only* time bartenders might be justified in using their own judgment about shot size. This should be a rare occurrence and you should be told about it if it happens.

5. Free drinks.

Bartenders should not be permitted to decide on their own whether it is or is not permissible for them to give free drinks to guests at the bar. You make this decision, and you should have a clear, established policy about this. Once in a while guests still walk into bars, have two or three drinks, and then demand loudly, "When's the house going to buy?" Years ago it was a custom in many bars to have the house buy the guest a drink after the guest had bought several. But in those days it was also common to go into a grocery store, buy a week's supply of groceries, and have the grocer give you a free, friendly bag of candy. When is the last time your supermarket handed you a free, friendly bag of candy?

Generally, it is a good idea to keep the practice of giving free drinks to the barest minimum. You might decide to set a rule that your bartenders can give away three drinks a week (or none, or five, or ten, or whatever you think is appropriate and reasonable for your own operation). If you permit any free drinks, each time bartenders give a free drink to a guest, they should put a slip in the cash register and keep a written record of each drink they give away. In general, the fewer the better. If you have no definite policy established and no records kept, bartenders who give away drinks are lowering your beverage profit without your knowledge. Watch this. Dishonest bartenders can take advantage of a "free drink" policy. They can sell drinks, charge guests, pocket cash, and tell you the drinks were part of the "on-the-house" quota for free drinks.

6. Short-changing.

Some bartenders give guests less change than the guest should get (particularly if the guest is slightly inebriated) and pocket the rest. A variation of this is giving the guests a fast count on their change. "Fast count" means counting aloud more bills or coins than you actually hand out. Another variation of this is where one bill is folded in the middle, put between other bills, and both ends are counted so it looks like two bills.

7. Overcharging.

If bar prices are not posted (and in many bars they are not), bartenders can quote higher prices, overcharge guests, and pocket the extra money.

8. Drinking on the job.

Don't allow it. It can be a very serious problem and a difficult one to stop.

Many bartenders drink "cola" drinks throughout their shift. The "cola" drink can have vodka or something else in it, and it is virtually impossible to detect it. Unless, of course, the bartender gets obviously drunk.

Some beverage operations have a rule that bartenders can have a free drink at the bar after they punch out, but no drinking (no "cola," no anything) while they're on duty.

Then there is the story of a bartender who did not want to drink on the job but his boss forced him to. A student was hired as a bartender for a summer job. He quit after three weeks. Every time a guest wanted to buy him a drink as a tip, the owner would insist that the student-bartender had to drink the drink right then and there with the guest. The owner didn't want him to politely refuse a drink and accept a cash tip instead. He wanted the guest to buy the student a drink for a "tip" so the money went to the bar, not to the student. The student complained, "I've been drunk for the last three weeks and I can't take it." The owner's policy was shortsighted. If you have ever seen a drunk bartender overpour, you *know* how shortsighted the policy was.

9. Collusion.

A man bartender and wife or a woman bartender and husband working together can use dishonest tactics. The following is a case of collusion—conspiracy by two or more people to commit theft.

A bartender was in charge of a service bar and his wife was a cocktail waitress in the same operation. The manager suspected they were "knocking down" but did not know how they were doing it. They worked there six weeks. Then they left. Afterwards, records eventually disclosed that they had stolen over $1,000.

It is sensible for a manager to keep even closer antitheft controls in effect than usual when a husband and wife work together in a beverage operation. If they have dishonest intentions, they can usually work out a collusion plan to steal. Collusion is easier when individuals are related. They are more apt to trust each other.

Collusion can occur whenever *any* two individuals (or more) decide to work together to defraud the operation. Controls and checks and balances should be established to make it difficult for any collusion to succeed. If you have more than two employees working together in collusion, your problem can be very severe.

The above incidents describe just a few of the limitless kinds of beverage skulduggery that can go on. Most people who have worked in this industry could add stories and warnings of their own. There are some unscrupulous people working in the food and beverage industry, as in all industries, and the beverage operation can be very tempting to dishonest individuals. Some devise very sophisticated schemes to defraud the house. Then, too, there are others who are less sophisticated in their efforts to steal.

And some are downright funny. For example: the true case of the bartender who collected money from a guest and automatically shoved it right into his own pocket while the owner was standing in plain sight watching him!

How do you protect yourself from bartending skulduggery? How can you prevent things like these from happening in your own operation?

One very important thing you can do is to be very selective and careful when you hire employees. Check prospective bartenders' references extra closely.

Another thing you should do is pay bartenders good wages—at least average or slightly above average for your area. If you do not pay adequate wages, some bartenders may feel justified in stealing from you.

Establish clear-cut policies concerning what you expect from bartenders and what procedures they are to follow. And do not forget to treat bartenders (and all your employees) as fairly, thoughtfully, and nicely as you would like every one of them to treat you.

One final suggestion—feed your bartenders well. Some food and beverage operations make sure their bartenders eat all they want of whatever they want from the menu. They feel it is cheaper in the long run than trying to be strict about meals. It's probably a good idea. If you let your bartenders choose everything they want to eat from your menu, you will probably save the cost of the whiskey the bartenders might trade with the cook for steaks. You distinctly do not need a drunk cook to add to your burdens.

MANAGEMENT SKULDUGGERY

Management people can get involved in skulduggery, too. If they do, they may steal more than other employees. They usually have more opportunity and more access to funds.

An assistant manager who had been working very dependably for a year and a half would regularly close the bar and the establishment at night. When he did, he would always deposit the receipts in the night depository at the bank. One Saturday night, after a very busy weekend, the assistant manager was supposed to deposit the receipts in the night depository on his way home. When Monday came and he was due to report for work, he did not show up. He never did. The receipts never reached the night depository. Through the cash register tape, the beverage operation manager was able to reconstruct exactly how much cash the assistant manager had taken. But it did not do the manager any good. The assistant manager was not bonded.

Two individuals were in partnership in a bar establishment. Their records and controls were extremely poor. When one partner was on duty, he made it a regular practice to hit the "no-sale" key, take a handful of bills out of the cash register, and shove them into his own pocket. (His partner was totally unaware of what he was doing, which should tell you just how bad their records really were.) One day a customer saw him and went straight to the IRS and reported him. He was charged with income tax evasion for his practice of "skimming" (taking money off the top and not reporting it as income to the business).

SERVICE PERSONNEL SKULDUGGERY

Padding the check is a way of overcharging. This is when an employee tricks guests into believing that they consumed more than they really did. Service personnel (and maybe bartenders) may try this.

There is the case of a bar waiter who padded a check. A group of customers came in, sat down at a table together, and ordered cocktails. The first time around, everybody ordered a drink. The second time around, most re-ordered but a few did not. One guest (a suspicious fellow) tore a match from a matchbook for each drink to keep track of every drink received at the table. By the fourth round, some of the group had continued to order, some had not, but the pile of matches kept accurate tally. The observant waiter deliberately spilled a drink into the pile of matches, wiped them up, and padded the check.

Padding the check is not new. In taverns of old, bartenders or service people marked a drink tally—P for pint and Q for quart. If customers did not pay attention, they could be charged for pints and quarts they did not receive. This is the origin of the phrase, "Watch your P's and Q's."

CLEANING CREW SKULDUGGERY

Each night a bottle of whiskey disappeared from a bar. The bartender reported it to the manager. The bar was locked and an iron grill was drawn down in front of the bar each night. But the grill did not reach to the ceiling. Investigation showed that the night porter was using a lasso on the end of his mop to fish out a bottle every night.

A day porter was most conscientious about keeping the food and beverage establishment where he worked *clean*. Accumulations of trash really bothered him. He worked constantly emptying trash into wastebaskets and running out to dump them into the trash hoppers behind the establishment. His enthusiasm for his work brought him compliments and appreciation from the manager—until the night the manager saw him poking around in the trash hoppers behind the establishment after he had gone off duty. The porter rummaged in the hoppers and pulled out three cartons of cigarettes and a box of cigars. The manager fired him immediately but never did find out how long the porter had plied his own skulduggery gimmick. He did find out, however, that the hyperactive porter had emptied the wastebasket behind the cigar and cigarette counter often. As he did, he would brush a carton of cigarettes or a box of cigars into his basket and cover it with paper trash. Then he was off immediately on his appointed round to the big trash hoppers outdoors behind the establishment.

KITCHEN SKULDUGGERY

A cook regularly and very carefully wrapped chickens or hams or steaks in plastic and then newspapers, tied his bundles securely, put them in the trash barrel, and covered them with trash. Then he would thoughtfully help the porter carry the barrel outside and dump the trash into the outdoor hoppers. When he went off duty, he would go out to the outside trash hoppers, fish out his neat and sanitarily protected packages of chickens or hams or steaks, put them in his car, and go home.

A cook always came to work wearing flowing sports shirts. He was a portly individual and said that he felt his ample shirts made him look thinner. The assistant manager suspected that he was stealing but could not figure how he was doing it. The cook always took quite a bit of time in the employees' rest area at the end of the day and was always the last to leave. One night the suspicious assistant manager hid in a locker in the employees' rest area and saw the following: The cook took off his uniform. From his locker he took part of an inner tube. He carefully shoved two whole tenderloins inside the inner tube, tied the tube around his waist with a special elastic band, put on his flowing sport shirt, adjusted the inner tube so it was comfortable, inspected himself from all angles in the mirror to make sure he looked his normal rotund self, and sauntered out of the employees' rest area to go home. He was stopped at the front door by the assistant manager.

Then there was the cook who lacked *any* finesse or imagination. At the end of the day he took a lot of sliced ham, carefully wrapped it in wax paper, put it in his coat pocket, and started to walk out of the kitchen to go home. It is hard to say whether he was brazen, nearsighted, stupid—or all of these and then some—because the chef was standing right there in the kitchen watching his whole routine. The chef stared at him in disbelief and then yelled, "What are you doing?" The cook's reply was that he hadn't eaten his meal at the restaurant that day so he thought he would take it home.

WHAT DO YOU DO?

There is truth in every story in this chapter, and the stories could go on and on.

One thing you can do is bond all employees who handle cash or have any access to cash. Bonding companies will pay you for whatever was stolen, provided you have records to prove which individual took what. When you put in a claim to a bonding company, you have to be able to prove the bonded individual or individuals stole and exactly what they stole.

Obviously you should have the tightest control systems you can possibly put together. Divide responsibility in every way you can so that no one employee has complete control over an entire process involving money or merchandise. Very tight control systems should certainly discourage dishonesty.

"Talk amongst yourselves" with other managers in your community —tell each other tricks employees have tried. The more you know about skulduggery the more easily you can spot it. And keep looking for it always. Skulduggery is not there often, but when it is it can cost you money—a little or a lot. It can also hurt your operation's reputation in a community if your employees pull dishonest tricks on customers, who are good at spotting skulduggery if it affects *them*!

REVIEW AND DISCUSSION QUESTIONS

1. How does each method of skulduggery described in this chapter hurt a food and beverage operation?

2. Why should your bottles be marked or stamped before they leave your beverage storeroom? Should you ever change the special mark or stamp you use?

3. Why should bartenders be required to record each sale on the cash register as it occurs?

4. Why is collusion apt to be worse than theft by a lone employee?

5. Can you think of any other types of skulduggery (besides those described in this chapter) that could be tried in a beverage operation?

6. If you worked for a bonding company, what type of proof would you want before you paid a food and beverage operation's claim for employee stealing?

7. You see a bartender pick up a dollar from the bar and put it in her pocket. You rush over and fire her for stealing. She denies stealing and says it was a tip. What do you do?

8. What controls discussed in this book would detect or prevent which types of skulduggery described in this chapter?

27

A Final Word

Throughout this book we have said "managers should do this" and "managers should do that." Obviously managers do not personally perform all the work this book says needs to be done. Managers should understand all the work, however, and direct it. The emphasis is on managers because it is managers' responsibility to oversee total operation. President Harry Truman said, "The buck stops here." When you are the manager of a food and beverage operation, the buck does stop with you. The overall responsibility *is* yours. If things do not go right, it is your job to see that corrections and improvements are made.

One of your main responsibilities is to train, encourage, and supervise all your employees so they work as a cooperative team to create a profitable food and beverage operation. It is your job to attract good employees and help them develop good working skills. It is your job, too, to develop good managerial skills in yourself.

Devise a total management system. It is up to you to analyze, understand, and constantly try to improve your entire operation. You are the only one in a position to do it. Keep good accounting records and *really* use them. Pay attention to the overall general status of your operation and also to detail. Neither does you much good if you ignore the other. Think of both.

Try constantly to add to the skills and knowledge of your employees and yourself. You and your employees need "continuing education." Continuing education is more than just formal classroom lectures or reading on your own or learning from special trade seminars. Get to know the people in other food and beverage service operations. See what they are doing. You will find that you will motivate each other to learn more and do better. Find out how they are upgrading facilities and changing their methods of food preparation or presentation or marketing. Many a successful restaurateur got that way by copying ideas used by successful restaurateurs.

Successful food and beverage operators generally tend to participate in their local trade associations. They join as members and participate as actively as they can. Trade associations work to improve the whole food and beverage service industry and they help individual members. It has been the author's observation that more successful operators are the ones who participate most strongly in continuing education *and* in trade association activities. They are the ones who probably *need* it least but they do participate the most. There is a moral there. Join them.

There is more to the world than food and beverage service operation. Be aware of what is happening. Your own community is a starting point. A food service operation is part of the community in which it exists. You owe some help to, interest in, and active participation in your own community.

You also must be able to adapt to change. The *only* thing we know for sure is that change will occur. Tremendous change has taken place in the food service industry since the end of World War II. We have electronic cooking, pre-cut portion-controlled meats readily available, convenience foods of countless assortments, and on and on. We do not know what the future will bring except that it will bring change.

Maybe there will be less meat available. Maybe we will use more vegetable products. Perhaps the food service operations of the future will serve *nothing* but convenience foods. Maybe there will not be any cooking at all on the premises, maybe just final assembling. Maybe just unwrapping.

Methods of service could change. Self-service could become more popular or less popular. Use of machines and mechanized procedures may decline or may increase enormously. Perhaps customers will tell a computer what they want and the machines will do it *all*. Food service operations of the future may just provide drinking water and flavored pills—turkey pills, wine pills, highly concentrated nutrition pills, and so on.

It's interesting to think about the possibilities.

In the meantime, use every food and beverage control you can get your hands on.

Glossary

Ā la Carte Menu. Each item is individually priced.

Accelerated Depreciation. A method of depreciation. Faster than straight line depreciation because a larger proportion of the cost of the asset is charged to depreciation expense during the early years of the asset's useful life.

As Purchased (AP). Food items you have received and have not done any work on. They are still just the way you got them.

Asset. Anything of value owned by a business.

Balance Sheet. Statement that shows the financial condition of a business at a given instant in time. It contains asset, liability, and equity accounts.

Bar Whiskey (gin, scotch, and such). Brand (usually comparatively inexpensive) served by bar when no particular brand is specified.

Beverage Cost Formulas. A series of steps designed to show the cost of beverage sold on a daily or weekly basis or to show the amount of income that should be received.

Beverage Cost Percent (sometimes called Beverage Cost per Dollar Sale). How much you spent for liquor out of each $1 sale you got. To find it you divide cost of beverage sold by beverage sales. Multiply the answer by 100 to convert to a percentage. The percent you get is "beverage cost percent per dollar sale."

Beverage Inventory Turnover. The number of times the dollar value of your beverage inventory turned over. Can be monthly or yearly figure. To get monthly or yearly figure, you divide monthly or yearly cost of beverage used by average beverage inventory.

Bin Card. Form you use to keep constant perpetual inventory on every brand of beverage in your beverage storeroom.

Blind Receiving. No invoice accompanies an order, so your receiving clerks have to count, weigh, and record each item individually. Their list is checked with your purveyor's list in your accounting office.

Breakeven Point. You have no profit and no loss. Your income *exactly* equals your expenses.

Call Whiskey (gin, scotch, and such). Brand specifically requested by specific brand name.

Capital Expense (same as Non-Controllable Expense). Included in overhead expense. Manager cannot control it. Owner may or may not be able to exert some degree of control. The five expenses in this category are: interest, real estate taxes, general insurance, depreciation or rent, and income tax.

Cash Flow. Cash flow is income minus expenses paid in cash. It is the amount of cash you have available for increasing assets (buying new equipment), decreasing liabilities (paying what you owe), decreasing equity (paying dividends).

Cashier's Bank (also called Imprest Funds). Money cashier has for making change for guests. There are two kinds of cashier's banks—individual and revolving.

Combination Menu. Menu pricing that combines table d'hôte menu and à la carte menu pricing techniques. Some items are grouped together for a set price (like table d'hôte) and other items are priced individually (like à la carte).

Control. Restraint and direction (including the use of safeguards and procedures) management exercises to assure the profitability of a food and beverage operation.

Controllable Overhead Expense. "Overhead expense" means every expense that is not food expense, labor expense, or profit expense. "Controllable" means the manager can exert some influence and can act to lower the expense.

Convenience Food. Any type of food on which work has already been done so it is easier to handle or use. The term also applies to pre-prepared entrees.

Cost Control. Anything and everything you do to control expenses.

Cost Factor. A number. You get it by computing the cost of a product after you have done work on it. You relate this figure to the price you paid for the item. You use a cost factor to tell you what an item is costing you as the price you pay for the item goes up or down.

Cost of Beverage Sold (also called Beverage Cost). What you pay for all ingredients you use in drinks available for sale. Includes overproduction, waste, theft, and so on.

Cost of Beverage Used. All beverage items in the beverage production area which were available for sale.

Cost of Food Sold (also called Food Cost). What you paid for all food items used in food available for sale. Includes overproduction, waste, theft, and so on.

Cost of Food Used. All food items in the food production area which were available for sale.

Cyclical Menu. A series of menus for a period of time—7, 14, 28, 35 days. Cycles are normally based on the number 7. Usually there are several cycles in the course of a year.

Declining Balance Depreciation. A method of accelerated depreciation. Currently 150 percent declining balance depreciation is permitted (but laws on this can change). A 150 percent declining balance depreciation means that you could charge to depreciation 150 percent of what you would charge if you used straight line depreciation.

Demand. Economic term meaning the relationship between the price of an item or service and the number of people who want it. Usually higher price equals less demand, lower price equals more demand.

Demand Curve. Plotted on a graph. The relationship between the price of an item or service and the number of people who want it. Usually higher price means less demand, lower price means more demand.

Depreciation. Method of recovering the cost of an asset over its useful life. Can be straight line or accelerated.

Differentiated Product. Similar items available for sale. Advertised and presented as having unique qualities.

Direct Purchases (also called Direct Issues). Items you receive and put directly into your production area (kitchen or bar). These never go through your storeroom, so there are no requisitions for them.

Duplicate Check. Carbon copy or similar listing of guest check. A control measure. Original guest check is compared against duplicate check to make sure all items are accounted for and properly priced.

Edible Portion (EP). Food that can be consumed. All waste has been trimmed.

Elastic Demand Curve. A demand curve showing that when you lower a price, more items will be sold and total revenue will increase. Or if you raise a price, fewer items will be sold, but the percentage decline in number of items sold will not be offset by percentage increase in price. Total revenue will decrease.

Employee Turnover. Number of employees who leave your establishment. To calculate your rate of employee turnover, divide number of employees who leave by number of employee positions.

Estimated Costs. Costs you expect to occur. Calculated guess about what you expect expenses will be.

Estimated Sales. Sales you expect to occur. Calculated guess about what you expect sales will be.

Equity (also called Net Worth). Owner's original investment in a business plus retained earnings. (Retained earnings means profit put back into the business.) Equity is assets minus liabilities.

Extension. Price multiplied by quantity.

Fixed Cost. A constant cost, not affected by volume. Some items called "fixed" may actually be fixed only for a specific anticipated level of sales.

Food Checker. Someone who inspects food leaving kitchen or cafeteria line to make sure all items are correctly priced and accounted for.

Food Cost Control. Everything you do to maintain your predetermined standards while you buy, prepare, and sell food.

Food Cost Formulas. Series of formulas designed to show cost of food sold on a daily or weekly basis.

Food Cost Percent (sometimes called Food Cost per Dollar Sale). How much you spent for food out of each $1 sale you got. To find it you divide cost of food sold by food sales. Multiply the answer by 100 to convert to a percentage. The percent you get is "food cost percent per dollar sale."

Food Inventory Turnover. Number of times dollar value of your food inventory has turned over. Can be monthly or yearly figure. To get monthly or yearly figure, you divide monthly or yearly cost of food used by average food inventory.

Forecast. A calculated guess (estimate) of dollar sales and/or customer count.

Guest Check. Form used by service person to write down food and/or beverage items guests order and the prices of the items.

Individual Cashier's Bank. Cashier's bank is money cashier has for making change for guests. "Individual" means each cashier has a separate bank and is responsible for it and for seeing that it contains the proper amount for change-making purposes. Only one cashier has access to one individual bank.

Inelastic Demand Curve. A demand curve showing that when you lower a price, more items will be sold, but not enough more to offset the decline in price. Total revenue will decrease. Or if you raise a price, fewer items will be sold, but the percentage decline in the number of items sold will be offset by the percentage increase in price. Total revenue will increase.

Inventory. The number of items on hand available for sale.

Inventory Valuation. Methods of computing dollar worth of inventory on hand.

Issuing. Removing goods from storage area and taking them to another area. Issued items should leave storage only via requisitions.

Labor Cost. The cost of payroll for employees.

Liabilities. What a business owes.

Loss Leaders. Items sold for less than they cost. Not a good idea in the food and beverage industry.

Management Action. Management measures, evaluates, and then takes positive action (decides to do something) or passive action (decides to do nothing).

Market. Potential number of guests who could come to your establishment. The group you want to attract.

Master Menu Index. A very complete written list of all food items you sell or contemplate selling. A tool to help you write menus.

Menu Format. Arrangement and grouping on menu of number of items and categories of items offered for sale.

Missing Check. A guest check that has been issued to a service person but cannot be found or accounted for.

Monopolistic Competition. Economic term meaning that businesses compete by means other than price competition. They compete by selling a similar but differentiated product.

Net Profit. The amount of money left over after all expenses have been deducted from all income.

Net Worth (same as Equity). Owner's original investment in a business plus retained earnings. (Retained earnings means profit put back into the business.) Assets minus liabilities.

Non-Controllable Overhead Expense (same as Capital Expense). Manager cannot control it. Owner may or may not be able to exert some degree of control. The five expenses in this category are: interest, real estate taxes, general insurance, depreciation or rent, and income tax.

Oligopoly. Economic term meaning a few similar businesses compete with each other. They have some degree of control over their market and over each other.

One-Stop Shopping. A term that implies one purveyor can supply everything you need. From a food and beverage operation manager's viewpoint, a better term would be "fewer-purveyor purchasing." You use fewer purveyors and buy more from each, or just one purveyor who supplies you with everything you purchase.

Original Investment. Just the money an owner *originally* invests in a business. Not the same as "total investment" or "equity," which mean original investment plus retained earnings (profits put back into the business).

Overhead Costs. Overhead costs are all costs that are not food cost or labor cost or profit cost. Everything besides these three costs is lumped together and called overhead.

Par Stock. A predetermined quantity. Usually refers to storeroom control. You decide on a maximum and a minimum quantity for items. You do not want to have more than your maximum or less than your minimum.

Payroll Cost (same as Labor Cost). Cost of payroll for employees.

Percent. A figure obtained by dividing one number by another number and multiplying by 100.

Percentage Analysis (also called Common Size Analysis). A way to evaluate dollar figures by converting them to percentages. Can be an expense in dollars divided by sales in dollars, or an expense in dollars divided by total expense in dollars. Answer is multiplied by 100 to convert to a percentage. It is easier to compare the change in percentage as dollar amounts fluctuate than it is to try to compare the changes in absolute dollar amounts.

Percentage Index. A tool to forecast the number of individual items to prepare. It is a percent based on the number of menu items sold the last time the same menu was used in relation to total number of guests. Number of individual items sold divided by total number of guests.

Perpetual Inventory. A method of keeping track of dollar amount and/or number of individual items on a constant, continuing basis.

Physical Inventory. Counting the number of items on hand. To find the *value* of inventory, multiply quantity by price.

Portion Control. Work done to make sure the wanted number of servings is obtained from food and/or beverage items.

Potential Cost. Food cost or beverage cost obtained under ideal conditions. Norm or standard against which you compare actual food and/or beverage costs.

Pre-control. Everything that can be done ahead of time *is* done ahead of time. A major factor in the success of a business.

Pre-costing. Determining the cost of an item before you put it on the menu or sell it.

Predetermined Standards. Standards or norms for comparison figured out ahead of time, not left to chance.

Pre-portioned Foods. Food items divided into portions before they are served. Food service operations can do their own pre-portioning or buy many items already pre-portioned.

Pre-prepared. Implies that work has been done on food items ahead of time. Can be done by you or before you get the items.

Pre-set Register. The keys of the cash register are printed with names of food items. When a key is hit, the price you have pre-set for that item is recorded.

Product Mix. Grouping of individual items you offer for sale.

Profit. Money left after you have deducted all expenses from sales.

Profit and Loss Statement. Formal financial statement. Shows the results of income minus expenses for a period of time.

Rate of Return on Investment. Rate of return is dollar amount of profit divided by total investment.

Ready-to-Cook (RTC). Food item on which all pre-prep work prior to cooking has been done. It may have been done by the processor, purveyor, or food service operation.

Ready-to-Eat (RTE). Food item ready to be consumed. It may arrive at the food service operation already in this form, or the food service operation may do the necessary work.

Relatively Elastic Demand Curve. See *Elastic Demand Curve.* Called "relative" to refer to demand curve that falls in area between a perfectly elastic demand curve and a unit elastic demand curve.

Relatively Inelastic Demand Curve. See *Inelastic Demand Curve.* Called "relative" to refer to demand curve that falls in area between a perfectly inelastic demand curve and a unit elastic demand curve.

Requisition. Written form used to record items, quantities, and prices as items are moved out of storeroom into other departments. Also used in transferring items between departments.

Retained Earnings (also called Retained Income and Earned Surplus). Profit put back into a business.

Return on Investment. Profit returned to the owner for having invested in a business.

Revolving Cashier's Bank. Money cashier has for making change for guests. Same dollar amount of bank is given from cashier going off duty to cashier coming on duty. There is just one bank and it goes from one cashier to the next.

Rotate Stock. Method of arranging and rearranging goods in a storeroom so oldest goods are always used first.

Spanner Shift. A means of scheduling employees so they do not all arrive or depart with regular shift times. A spanner shift usually starts before or after a regular shift and ends before or after a regular shift.

Specification. Writen instructions specifically describing the characteristics and qualities you want in goods you are buying. Used as a guide in purchasing to make sure you will get product you want. Also used in receiving to make sure you *got* what you wanted.

Standard. Norm against which you make comparisons.

Standard Drink List. List of alcoholic beverages ordered most often in establishment.

Standardized Menu. Lists the same items for sale for same meal period day after day. Unchanging.

Standardized Recipe. Recipe you have tested and converted to produce the quality and yield you want consistently.

Storeroom Purchases. Items you receive and put into storeroom. All storeroom purchases items leave storage area only by requisition.

Straight Line Depreciation. Method of recovering the cost of an asset over the time period of its useful life. Cost of the asset divided by the number of years of its useful life.

Depreciation expense for the item does not change; it is the same amount every year with straight line.

Supply. Economic term meaning availability of different products at different prices.

Supply Curve. Plotted on a graph. Shows relationships between prices charged for an item and numbers of that item that will be supplied at varying prices. Usually higher price means more items will be supplied and lower price means fewer items will be supplied.

Surrounding Dish Cost. Cost of all items that accompany an entree. Or cost of items that go with a main ingredient (garnish with whiskey, or garnish with shrimp cocktail, for example).

Table d'Hôte Menu. Price of the entree is total price of the complete meal.

Transfers to Bar. Food items requisitioned from the kitchen by the bar and used at the bar in preparing drinks. Charged to bar cost.

Transfers to Kitchen. Beverage items requisitioned from the bar by the kitchen and used in the kitchen in preparing food. Charged to food cost.

Unit Elasticity Demand Curve. Economic term, plots the relationships between price of item and quantity sold. If price is lowered, quantity demanded will exactly offset the decrease in price. Total revenue will remain constant. If price is raised, the decline in quantity demanded will exactly offset the increase in price. Total revenue will remain constant.

Variable Cost. Expense (or group of expenses) that varies in relation to sales.

Weighted Cost. Cost of item multiplied (weighted) by a constant number.

Weighted Percent. To get weighted percent, divide weighted costs by weighted sales. Multiply by 100 to convert to percentage. Costs and sales are both multiplied (weighted) by the same constant number.

Weighted Sales. Selling price of item multiplied (weighted) by a constant number.

Yield. Number of portions obtained from preparation of quantity recipe.

Yield Tests. A study and examination conducted to find out the number of portions produced from a recipe or produced from items you bought.

Bibliography-Author

American Hotel and Motel Association. *Uniform System of Accounts and Expense Dictionary for Motels—Motor Hotels, Small Hotels.* American Hotel and Motel Association. New York. 1963.

Brodner, Joseph, Howard M. Carlson and Henry T. Maschal. *Profitable Food and Beverage Operation.* Ahrens Publishing Company, Inc. New York. 1962.

Club Managers Association of America. *Uniform System of Accounts for Clubs.* 2nd Revised Edition. Club Managers Association of America. Washington, D.C. 1967.

Coffman, C. DeWitt. *Marketing For a Full House.* School of Hotel Administration. Cornell University. Ithaca, New York. 1972.

Dukas, Peter. *How To Plan and Operate a Restaurant.* 2nd Edition. Hayden Book Company, Inc. Rochelle Park, New Jersey. 1973.

Folsom, LeRoi A. (edited by). *The Professional Chef.* 4th Edition. Institutions/Volume Feeding Management. Chicago. 1971.

Grossman, Harold. *Grossman's Guide to Wines, Spirits, and Beers.* Revised Edition. Charles Scribner's Sons. New York. 1955.

Grossman, Harold. *Practical Bar Management.* Ahrens Publishing Company, Inc. New York. 1962.

Haszonics, Joseph J. *Wine Merchandising.* Ahrens Publishing Company, Inc. New York. 1963.

Hoke, Ann. *Restaurant Menu Planning.* Hotel Monthly Press. Evanston, Illinois. 1954.

Hotel Association of New York City, Inc. *Uniform System of Accounts For Hotels.* 6th Revised Edition. Hotel Association of New York City, Inc. New York. 1963.

J. Walter Thompson Consumer Panel. *Consumer Panel Report on Dining Out Habits and Attitudes.* Standard Brands, Inc. and The National Restaurant Association. 1958.

Johnson, Hugh. *The World Atlas of Wine.* Simon and Schuster. New York. 1971.

Keiser, James and Elmer Kallio. *Controlling and Analyzing Costs in Food Service Operations.* John H. Wiley and Sons, Inc. New York. 1974.

Keister, Douglas C. and Ralph D. Wilson (compiled and edited by). *Selected Readings For an Introduction To Hotel and Restaurant Management.* McCutchan Publishing Corporation. Berkeley, California. 1971.

Keister, Douglas C. *How To Increase Profits With Portion Control.* National Restaurant Association. Chicago. 1966.

Keister, Douglas C. *How To Use the Uniform System of Accounts For Hotels and Restaurants.* National Restaurant Association. Chicago. 1971.

Kotschevar, Lendal H. *Quantity Food Production.* 3rd Edition. Cahners Publishing Company, Inc. Boston. 1974.

Kotschevar, Lendal H. *Quantity Food Purchasing.* 2nd Edition. John H. Wiley and Sons, Inc. New York. 1975.

Levings, Pat. *Profit From Foodservice.* Cahners Publishing Company, Inc. Boston. 1974.

Lundberg, Donald E. and James P. Armatas. *The Management of People in Hotels, Restaurants and Clubs.* 3rd Edition. William C. Brown, Inc. Dubuque, Iowa. 1974.

Maizel, Bruno. *Food and Beverage Cost Controls.* I.T.T. Educational Services, Inc. New York. 1971.

Miller, Edmund. *Profitable Cafeteria Operation.* Ahrens Publishing Company, Inc. New York. 1966.

Morgan, Jr., William J. *Supervision in Management of Quantity Food Preparation.* McCutchan Publishing Corporation. Berkeley, California. 1974.

National Association of Meat Purveyors. *Meat Buyer's Guide To Portion Control Meat Cuts.* Chicago. 1967.

National Association of Meat Purveyors. *Meat Buyer's Guide To Standardized Meat Cuts.* Chicago. 1966.

National Institute for the Foodservice Industry. *Applied Foodservice Sanitation.* Chicago. 1974.

National Restaurant Association. *NRA Washington Report—Weekly Newsletter.* (Information about changes taking place in the restaurant industry.) National Restaurant Association. Chicago.

National Restaurant Association. *Uniform System of Accounts For Restaurants.* 4th Revised Edition. National Restaurant Association. Chicago. 1968.

National Restaurant Association Educational Materials Center. *NRA Yearly Catalog.* (List of books, bulletins, films, pamphlets, etc.) National Restaurant Association. Chicago.

Peddersen, Raymond B. *Increasing Productivity in Foodservice.* Cahners Publishing Company, Inc. Boston. 1973.

School of Hotel Administration. Cornell University. *The Essentials of Good Table Service.* Revised Edition. Cornell University. Ithaca, New York. 1966.

Stein, Bob. *Marketing in Action For Hotels, Motels, Restaurants.* Ahrens Publishing Company, Inc. New York. 1971.

Vallen, Jerome. *The Art and Science of Modern Innkeeping.* Ahrens Publishing Company, Inc. New York. 1968.

Bibliography — Title

Applied Foodservice Sanitation. National Institute for the Foodservice Industry. Chicago. 1974.

Consumer Panel Report on Dining Out Habits and Attitudes. J. Walter Thompson Consumer Panel. Standard Brands, Inc. and The National Restaurant Association. 1958.

Controlling and Analyzing Costs in Food Service Operations. James Keiser and Elmer Kallio. John H. Wiley and Sons, Inc. New York. 1974.

Food and Beverage Cost Controls. Bruno Maizel. I.T.T. Educational Services, Inc. New York. 1971.

Grossman's Guide To Wines, Spirits, and Beers. Revised Edition. Harold Grossman. Charles Scribner's Sons. New York. 1955.

How To Increase Profits With Portion Control. Douglas C. Keister. National Restaurant Association. Chicago. 1966.

How To Plan and Operate a Restaurant. 2nd Edition. Peter Dukas. Hayden Book Company, Inc. Rochelle Park, New Jersey. 1973.

How To Use the Uniform System of Accounts For Hotels and Restaurants. Douglas C. Keister. National Restaurant Association. Chicago. 1971.

Increasing Productivity in Foodservice. Raymond B. Peddersen. Cahners Publishing Company, Inc. Boston. 1973.

Marketing For a Full House. C. DeWitt Coffman. School of Hotel Administration. Cornell University. Ithaca, New York. 1972.

Marketing in Action For Hotels, Motels, Restaurants. Bob Stein. Ahrens Publishing Company, Inc. New York. 1971.

Meat Buyer's Guide to Portion Control Meat Cuts. National Association of Meat Purveyors. Chicago. 1967.

Meat Buyer's Guide To Standardized Meat Cuts. National Association of Meat Purveyors. Chicago. 1966.

NRA Washington Report—Weekly Newsletter. (Information about changes taking place in the restaurant industry.) National Restaurant Association. Chicago.

NRA Yearly Catalog. (List of books, bulletins, films, pamphlets, etc.) National Restaurant Association Educational Materials Center. Chicago.

Practical Bar Management. Harold Grossman. Ahrens Publishing Company, Inc. New York. 1962.

Profit From Foodservice. Pat Levings. Cahners Publishing Company, Inc. Boston. 1974.

Profitable Cafeteria Operation. Edmund Miller. Ahrens Publishing Company, Inc. New York. 1966.

Profitable Food and Beverage Operation. Joseph Brodner, Howard M. Carlson and Henry T. Maschal. Ahrens Publishing Company, Inc. New York. 1962.

Quantity Food Production. 3rd Edition. Lendal H. Kotschevar. Cahners Publishing Company, Inc. Boston. 1974.

Quantity Food Purchasing. 2nd Edition. Lendal H. Kotschevar. John H. Wiley and Sons, Inc. New York. 1975.

Restaurant Menu Planning. Ann Hoke. Hotel Monthly Press. Evanston, Illinois. 1954.

Selected Readings For an Introduction To Hotel and Restaurant Management. Compiled and edited by Douglas C. Keister and Ralph D. Wilson. McCutchan Publishing Corporation. Berkeley, California. 1971.

Supervision in Management of Quantity Food Preparation. William J. Morgan, Jr. McCutchan Publishing Corporation. Berkeley, California. 1974.

The Art and Science of Modern Innkeeping. Jerome Vallen. Ahrens Publishing Company, Inc. New York. 1968.

The Essentials of Good Table Service. Revised Edition. School of Hotel Administration. Cornell University. Ithaca, New York. 1966.

The Management of People in Hotels, Restaurants and Clubs. 3rd Edition. Donald E. Lundberg and James P. Armatas. William C. Brown, Inc. Dubuque, Iowa. 1974.

The Professional Chef. 4th Edition. Edited by LeRoi A. Folsom. Institutions/Volume Feeding Management. Chicago. 1971.

The World Atlas of Wine. Hugh Johnson. Simon and Schuster. New York. 1971.

Uniform System of Accounts and Expense Dictionary For Motels—Motor Hotels, Small Hotels. American Hotel and Motel Association. New York. 1963.

Uniform System of Accounts For Clubs. 2nd Revised Edition. Club Managers Association of America. Washington, D.C. 1967.

Uniform System of Accounts For Hotels. 6th Revised Edition. Hotel Association of New York City, Inc. New York. 1963.

Uniform System of Accounts For Restaurants. 4th Revised Edition. National Restaurant Association. Chicago. 1968.

Wine Merchandising. Joseph J. Haszonics. Ahrens Publishing Company, Inc. New York. 1963.

Other Sources of Information

1. American Hotel-Motel Association
   888 Seventh Avenue
   New York, New York 10019

   777 Fourteenth Street, N.W.
   Washington, D.C. 20005

2. Club Managers Association of America
   5530 Wisconsin Avenue, N.W.
   Washington, D.C. 20015

3. Council on Hotel, Restaurant and Institutional Education
   Suite 534
   1522 K Street, N.W.
   Washington, D.C. 20005

4. Educational Institute of the American Hotel and Motel Association
   Stephen S. Nisbet Building
   1407 South Harrison Road
   Michigan State University
   East Lansing, Michigan 48823

5. National Institute for the Foodservice Industry
   120 South Riverside Plaza
   Chicago, Illinois 60606

6. National Restaurant Association
   Suite 2600
   One IBM Plaza
   Chicago, Illinois 60611

7. Schools, colleges and universities in your area that offer course work in hotel and restaurant management.

8. Outside U.S.A.: Contact national or local government bureau or department of education for schools and organizations.

   Inquire at major hotel, restaurant, catering organization, trade schools concerning information and industry associations.

Index

405